1989

PRINCETON STUDIES IN INTERNATIONAL HISTORY AND POLITICS

G. John Ikenberry and Marc Trachtenberg, series editors

RECENT TITLES

1989

THE STRUGGLE TO CREATE POST-COLD WAR EUROPE

MARY ELISE SAROTTE

PRINCETON UNIVERSITY PRESS
PRINCETON AND OXFORD

Requests for permission to reproduce material from this work should be sent to
Permissions, Princeton University Press

Published by Princeton University Press, 41 William Street, Princeton,
New Jersey 08540

In the United Kingdom: Princeton University Press, 6 Oxford Street, Woodstock,
Oxfordshire OX20 1TW

Library of Congress Cataloging-in-Publication Data

Sarotte, M. E.
1989 : the struggle to create post–Cold War Europe / Mary Elise Sarotte.
p.   cm. — (Princeton studies in international history and politics)
Includes bibliographical references and index.
ISBN 978-0-691-14306-4 (hardcover : alk. paper)   1. Europe—History—1989–
2. Europe—Politics and government—1989–   3. World politics—1989–   4. Post
communism—Europe.   5. Germany—History—Unification, 1990.   6. North Atlantic
Treaty Organization—Europe, Eastern.   7. North Atlantic Treaty Organization—
Membership.   8. Europe—Foreign relations—United States.   9. United States—
Foreign relations—Europe.   10. Russia (Federation)—Foreign relations—
Europe.   11. Europe—Foreign relations—Russia (Federation)   I. Title.
D860.S2694 2009
940.55′8—dc22   2009023740

British Library Cataloging-in-Publication Data is available
This book has been composed in Times and DIN 1451

Printed on acid-free paper. ∞

press.princeton.edu

Printed in the United States of America

5 7 9 10 8 6 4

FOR MJS

CONTENTS

CONTENTS

ILLUSTRATIONS

MAPS

FIGURES

PREFACE

A BRIEF NOTE ON SCHOLARSHIP AND SOURCES

Before beginning, I must acknowledge my scholarly debts to a number of previous authors and the places that provided the sources used in writing this book.

I am fortunate in that I have a rich body of literature to draw on, because many analysts have already devoted considerable time to 1989. A majority of them have seen that year as a moment of closure, most famously Francis Fukuyama, who called it the end of history even while it was unfolding. He and others have produced impressive studies tracing the Cold War's trajectory toward its ultimate collapse and dissolution. Particularly worthwhile examples have come from the writers Michael Beschloss and Strobe Talbott, James Mann, and Don Oberdorfer, and the scholars Frédéric Bozo, Stephen Brooks and William Wohlforth, Archie Brown, Robert English, John Lewis Gaddis, Timothy Garton Ash, Richard Herrmann and Richard Ned Lebow, Hans-Hermann Hertle, Robert Hutchings, Konrad Jarausch, Mark Kramer, Melvyn Leffler, Charles Maier, Gerhard Ritter, Andreas Rödder, Angela Stent, Bernd Stöver, and Stephen Szabo.[1]

As will become clear in the pages to follow, I see 1989 not as an end, but as a beginning. It created the international order that persists until today. The need to understand this nonviolent transition from the Cold War to the present is enormous, because we greatly prefer nonviolence to the alternative. As Gaddis has observed, the goal of historical scholarship "is not so much to predict the future as to prepare for it." The process of studying history expands our range "of experience, both directly and vicariously, so that we can increase our skills, our stamina—and if all goes well, our wisdom. The principle is much the same whether one is working out in a gym, flying a 747 simulator," or reading a historical study.[2] Trying to understand the transition of 1989–90 is a singularly useful exercise, since it established durable new democracies. We therefore need to look closely at this transition as it represents a quintessential example of what political scientist G. John Ikenberry has rightly called a reordering moment.[3]

I have chosen to investigate this particular reordering moment by looking at evidence from all key actors. Obviously, this means examining the role of the United States and the Soviet Union; but as Ellen Schrecker has complained in a book lamenting U.S.-centric Cold War studies, the fact that East Europeans "might have also had a hand in the process" does not figure often enough in the story.[4] The same could be said of West Europeans as well. As a result, this book will try to do justice to a number of significant parties on both sides of the East-West divide, not just the United States and the Soviet Union. It offers an international study of 1989 and 1990 based on research in archives, private papers, and sound and video recordings from—going roughly East to West—Moscow, Warsaw, Dresden, Berlin, Leipzig, Hamburg, Koblenz, Bonn, Paris, London, Cambridge, Princeton, Washington, College Station, and Simi Valley. On top of this, it draws on the published documents available from those locations, and from Beijing, Budapest, Prague, and other places as well.

The historical evidence for this time period is unusually, indeed astonishingly, rich for one so recent. Why is so much material available so soon after events? There appear to be three reasons for this. First, the overthrow of the established Cold War order took place both from above and below. My sources consequently consist of a number of items that have never been classified: broadcasts, manifestos, peace prayers, protest signs, and transcripts of meetings of round table and opposition groups, to name a few. Because of this, the research for this volume went beyond the usual sites of "high politics," and included work in media archives as well as the memorabilia, letters, and notes of individual church members, dissidents, and protesters.[5]

Second, a substantial amount of material emerged from now-defunct political entities—namely, the former member states of the Warsaw Pact, and even the Warsaw Pact itself—which either gave up or lost the ability to keep their materials hidden away from public view for the usual closure period. Particularly useful were the Russian materials from the Gorbachev Foundation, the volume of documents on divided Germany published by former Secretary General Mikhail Gorbachev and his adviser Anatoly Chernyaev, and the so-called Fond 89 assembled later by Russian leader Boris Yeltsin.[6] The East German party and secret police archives were essential sources as well, as were documents from other Warsaw Pact member states.

Although former Soviet Bloc materials are obviously useful to scholars, they can also lure historians into engaging in a kind of "victor's justice"—namely, the process of writing history from the point of view of the still-existing states based on the sources of the disappeared. To counter this problem, I scrutinized not just the records of defunct regimes but also of some of the most powerful entities in the world today. I was able to do so by reading published documents where available, and filing Freedom of Information Act (FOIA) requests or their equivalents where they were not; in the end, four countries released materials to me. I also piggybacked on FOIAs filed by others.

The surprising and extensive willingness of various gatekeepers to let me (and others) see such documents before the end of the usual classification period seems to be a result of the notion that success has many fathers. In other words, the end of the Cold War, from the Western leaders' point of view, was a triumph. They hoped to get credit for it, of course; but they also wanted to get information about the peaceful transition of 1989–90 into the public domain, in the hopes that its lessons could be learned. As a result, many of the politicians involved, most notably former German Chancellor Helmut Kohl, declassified and even published thousands of pages of documents. The appearance of Kohl's chancellery papers, documenting his past successes as a leader, occurred at the same time as a particularly close election, one that he eventually lost. These papers represent an extraordinarily useful resource. And thanks to the German Federal Archive's decision to allow me early access to some of the state documents that are not yet open to the public, I was able to read these published sources in the context of the original collections.[7]

Similarly, the George H. W. Bush Presidential Library in College Station, Texas, has approved FOIA requests for thousands of pages related to 1989–90. While many parts remain closed or redacted, the open portions nonetheless provide insight into top-level U.S. foreign policymaking, especially when read in conjunction with the detailed study written by U.S. participants Condoleezza Rice and Philip Zelikow.[8] I was able to read these Bush documents together with the extensive personal papers of the former secretary of state, James A. Baker III, thanks to his decision to grant me access to them. The Bush and Baker papers gave insight into the two critical components of U.S. foreign policymaking in this period—namely, the White House and National Security Council on the one hand, and the State Department on the other.[9]

West European leaders besides Kohl have been somewhat reticent, but the relatively recent British FOIA means that this study can draw on some of the first materials released from Number 10 Downing Street under Prime Minister Margaret Thatcher as well as the Foreign and Commonwealth Office under Douglas Hurd; the two did not see eye to eye in this period, so it is useful to look at both. Four years of petitions and appeals in the United Kingdom (UK) succeeded just in time for inclusion of both sides in this publication.[10] France does not have such legislation officially, but my individual petition for early archival access was approved as well. There is also a limited selection of primary documents published by François Mitterrand.[11] In addition, some top-level materials are available from Beijing.[12]

On top of all of these sources, two remarkable U.S. groups have done a great service to scholars by collecting, assembling, and in many cases translating documents from these and other locations around the world. The Cold War International History Project and the National Security Archive make these items available to scholars and often distribute them in the form of "briefing books" at major conferences. I have relied on these for their fascinating materials from, among other places, Czechoslovakia, Hungary, Poland, and Asian states.[13] In quoting these documents, any emphasis is present in the original unless otherwise stated in the note.

The usual disadvantage of work on contemporary history is the dearth of high-quality primary sources, but as explained above, that is not the case here. The advantage of work on a recent time period is the availability of interview partners. A number of participants in events were willing to let me speak with them, including Baker, Hans-Dietrich Genscher, Hurd, Charles Powell, Brent Scowcroft, Horst Teltschik, Zelikow, and Robert Zoellick; a complete list may be found in the bibliography. Their insights have helped significantly in the analysis of the original source materials listed above, and some of them were even willing to read drafts of sections of this work.[14] Moreover, a rich memoir literature and extensive collections of published documents from international institutions such as the Warsaw Pact, the North Atlantic Treaty Organization (NATO), and the European Community (EC, later the European Union, or EU) have helped as well.

In using these materials, I tried to choose crucial events and investigate the evidence from them as deeply and thoughtfully as possible. My research took place in three steps. The first stage involved years of locating, petitioning for, and examining sources and interviewing participants. Then, in the second step, I condensed these sources into a digital database of the thousand most important broadcasts, documents, interview comments, and television images. The third step involved constructing a detailed analytic chronology of the events, which became the eventual basis for the narrative chapters below.[15]

The methodological framework for this book comes roughly from Alexander George's concept of setting up structured, focused comparisons between suitable events.[16] To cite Theda Skocpol, comparative historical analysis "is, in fact, the mode of multivariate analysis to which one resorts when there are too many variables and not enough cases."[17] Variants on such a method have characterized many of the best histories of international relations to appear in the last few decades, such as Gaddis's *Strategies of Containment* (1982), Paul Kennedy's *The Rise and Fall of the Great Powers* (1987), and Odd Arne Westad's *The Global Cold War* (2005).[18] These studies employed a similar, and similarly successful, method. They all chose one complex issue (respectively, containment, imperial growth, and wars of intervention) and compared how crucial actors attempted to master the challenges involved. Gaddis compared their strategies of containment; Kennedy compared their strategies for imperial extension, which resulted in overstretch and decline; and Westad compared strategies of intervention.

Starting with the introduction, this book will attempt the daunting task of trying to follow where they have led. It will compare strategies for re-creating order after it has broken down—an enduring problem in history. A generation of leaders faced this challenge in 1989; they saw chaos, and sought to devise and implement plans to control it as quickly as possible. I explore who succeeded and why. Obviously my time frame is different than the studies mentioned above—months instead of decades or centuries—but the method remains valid. I will leave it to the reader to determine whether or not I have used it successfully.

ABBREVIATIONS

ATTU	Atlantic-to-Urals (military zone)
CDU	Christian Democratic Union (German)
CFE	Conventional Forces in Europe (Treaty)
CIA	Central Intelligence Agency (United States)
CSCE	Conference on Security and Cooperation in Europe
DM	Deutsche Mark, the currency of West Germany in 1989
EC	European Community
EU	European Union
FDP	Free Democratic Party (German), also known as the Liberals
FRG	Federal Republic of Germany, or West Germany
GDR	German Democratic Republic, or East Germany
IFM	Initiative for Peace and Human Rights, German initials for (East German)
INF	Intermediate-Range Nuclear Forces
KGB	Committee for State Security, Russian initials for (Soviet Union)
NATO	North Atlantic Treaty Organization
NSC	National Security Council (United States)
PDS	Party of Democratic Socialism (German)
PLA	People's Liberation Army (Chinese)
SED	Socialist Unity Party, German initials for (East German)
SNF	Short-Range Nuclear Forces
SPD	Social Democratic Party of Germany, German initials for
UK	United Kingdom of Great Britain and Northern Ireland
USSR	Union of Soviet Socialist Republics

1989

INTRODUCTION

CREATING POST–COLD WAR EUROPE:
1989 AND THE ARCHITECTURE OF ORDER

A whole generation emerged in the disappearing.
—East German Jana Hensel, age thirteen in 1989

This city, of all cities, knows the dream of freedom.
—Barack Obama, in Berlin, 2008[1]

On November 9, 1989, the Berlin Wall opened and the world changed. Memory of that iconic instant has, unsurprisingly, retained its power despite the passage of time. Evidence of its enduring strength was apparent in the decision by a later icon of change—Barack Obama—to harness it in his own successful pursuit of one of history's most elusive prizes, the U.S. presidency. While a candidate in 2008, he decided that the fall of the wall still represented such a striking symbol that it was worth valuable time away from American voters in a campaign summer to attach himself to it.

He also knew that lasting images had resulted from the Cold War visits of Presidents John F. Kennedy and Ronald Reagan to divided Berlin, and hoped to produce some of his own on a trip to the united city. In particular, Obama wanted to use the Brandenburg Gate, formerly a prominent site of the wall, as the backdrop for his first speech abroad as the clear Democratic nominee in summer 2008. However, the politics of the memory involved were still so vital that the right-of-center leader of Germany, Chancellor Angela Merkel—herself a former East German—decided to prevent Obama from appropriating them. She informed him that he did not have her permission to speak at the gate. It might be too evocative and look like an attempt by the German government to influence the U.S. election. Supporters of Obama's opponent, Senator John McCain, welcomed Merkel's decision; they derided the Berlin visit as an act of hubris that revealed a candidate playing statesman before his time. Undeterred, Obama chose instead to deliver his address as near as possible, at the Victory Column just down the street. The less emotional venue still drew two hundred thousand people to share the experience. "This city, of all cities, knows the dream of freedom," he told the cheering crowd.

1

Fig. I.1. Barack Obama in Berlin, July 24, 2008. Courtesy of Getty Images.

"When you, the German people, tore down that wall—a wall that divided East and West; freedom and tyranny; fear and hope—walls came tumbling down around the world. From Kiev to Cape Town, prison camps were closed, and the doors of democracy were opened."[2] The speech and the campaign succeeded brilliantly. Later in 2008, on the night that would turn Obama into the first African American president, he even returned in spirit to Berlin. In his victory speech in Chicago, he intoned a list of great changes. After remembering the dawn of voting rights for all and the steps of the first men on the moon, he added simply, "a wall came down in Berlin."[3]

Although Obama could celebrate the collapse of the wall as an example of peaceful change, no one knew whether or not that would be the case in 1989. Its opening had yielded not only joy but also some extremely frightening questions. Would Germans demand rapid unification in a massive nationalistic surge that would revive old animosities? Would Soviet troops in East Germany stay in their barracks? Would Gorbachev stay in power or would hard-liners oust him for watching the wall fall while failing to get anything in return? Would Communist countries in the rest of Central Europe subsequently expire violently and leave bloody scars? Would centrally planned economies immediately implode and impoverish millions of Europeans?[4] Would West European social welfare systems and market economies be able to absorb these new crowds, or be swamped by them? Would millions of young East Europeans like the thirteen-year-old Jana Hensel, who would later write the best-selling *After the Wall* about the shock of the transformation, be able to master the personal and psychological challenges of such a massive transition?[5] Would international institutions survive the challenges to come or descend into disabling disagreements about the future?

There was little doubt, in short, that history had reached a turning point; but the way forward was not obvious. With hindsight we know that the transition stayed peaceful, but why is less clear—through design, dumb luck, or both? Put another way, how can we best understand what happened in 1989 and its aftermath?

A generation of analysts has interpreted this year as a period of closure.[6] I see it differently: as a time not of ending, but of beginning. The Cold War order had long been under siege and its collapse was nearly inevitable by 1989. Yet there was nothing at all inevitable about what followed. This book seeks to explain not the end of the Cold War but the struggle to create post–Cold War Europe. It attempts to solve the following puzzles: Why were protesters on the ground able to force dramatic events to a climax in 1989? Why did the wall open on November 9? Why did the race to recast Europe afterward yield the present arrangement and not any of the numerous alternatives? Why did the "new" world order in fact look very much like the old, despite the momentous changes that had transpired?

To answer these questions, I examined the actors, ideas, images, material factors, and politics involved. Remarkable human stories emerged at every turn— from a dissident who smuggled himself back into East Germany after being thrown out, to the television journalists who opened the Berlin Wall without knowing they were doing so, to the pleading of Gorbachev's wife with a Western diplomat to protect her husband from himself, to the way that Vladimir Putin personally experienced 1989 in Dresden as a Soviet spy.

I will describe my findings in detail in the pages to come, but a few of them merit highlighting here. This book will challenge common but mistaken assumptions that the opening of the wall was planned, that the United States continuously dominated events afterward, and that the era of German reunification is now a closed chapter, without continuing consequences for the transatlantic alliance. I will show how, if there were any one individual to emerge as the single most important leader in the construction of post–Cold War Europe, it would have to be Kohl rather than Bush, Gorbachev, or Reagan; how Mitterrand was an uneasy but crucial facilitator of German unity, not its foe; and how Russia got left on the periphery as Germany united and the EC and NATO expanded, generating fateful

Fig. I.2. Vladimir Putin, future leader of Russia, poses with his parents in 1985 just before departing for his KGB posting to Dresden, East Germany. Courtesy of Getty Images.

resentments that shape geopolitics to this day. More broadly, I will question the enduring belief of U.S. policymakers that "even two decades later, it is hard to see how the process of German unification could have been handled any better." From a purely American point of view, this belief is understandable; but it is not universally shared. The international perspective in these pages will yield a more critical interpretation of 1989–90. To cite just one example, the former British Foreign Minister Hurd does indeed think that better alternatives were conceivable. In 1989–90 there was a theoretical opportunity "which won't come again, which Obama does not have, to remake the world, because America was absolutely at the pinnacle of its influence and success." Put another way, "you could argue that if they had been geniuses, George Bush and Jim Baker would have sat down in 1990 and said the whole game is coming into our hands." They would have concluded that "we've got now an opportunity, which may not recur, to remake the world, update everything, the UN, everything. And maybe if they had been Churchill and Roosevelt, you know, they might have done that." But Hurd finds that "they weren't that kind of person, neither of them. George Bush had famously said he didn't do the vision thing." In short, "they weren't visionaries, and nor were we."[7] Hurd remembers that they played it safe, which was sensible and indeed his preference, but that they may have let a big opportunity go by.

4

In exploring these questions, this book will focus on the contentious international politics of German unification that were at the heart of the creation of post–Cold War Europe. Many nations contributed to the demise of the old order over a series of decades in the past, but it was the contest over the terms of German unity that decided the future.[8] The dramatic months of transition between November 1989 and the end of 1990—the focus of this book—produced decisions about political order that have shaped international relations in the decades since.

This transition was swift, but its brevity does not negate its importance.[9] Changes do not need to be slow moving to be significant. Astronomers believe that the entire universe arose from a single instantaneous Big Bang, the consequences of which still determine life today. There is obviously an interplay between long-term and proximate causes; but the emphasis here will be very much on the events immediately surrounding the collapse of the wall and on the ways in which the new order emerged.

The argument of the book is as follows. For roughly a year following the collapse of the old order in November 1989, various groups of actors—some leaders of nation-states, and some not—competed and struggled vigorously to re-create order in a way most advantageous to themselves. The longer-term goal, of course, was to dominate that order in the post–Cold War world. Ultimately, Bonn and Washington, working together, would win this competition, but that was not a foregone conclusion. The legacy of their victory still has profound consequences for international relations today.

To explain how they won, I contend that we should follow the lead of the main participants in events by adopting their own metaphoric understanding of what was happening. Again and again, in multiple languages, key actors in 1989–90 employed the terminology of architecture to describe what they wanted: to start building anew, to construct a European roof or a common European home, to create a new transatlantic architecture, and so on. Leaders consciously proposed a number of competing blueprints for the future and described them as such. This metaphoric understanding, on top of its grounding in historical evidence, is an apt one for a study centered on Berlin, where so much real architecture went up after the wall came down. As a result, I will use this metaphor as the organizing strategy for the pages to follow; it will, I hope, make sense of a story playing out on many levels and in many locales simultaneously.[10] This book thus conceives of the competition of 1989–90 as an architectural one, where various models of future order—some more promising than others—competed against one another.

I must acknowledge that the use of phrases evocative of building—such as "constructed" and "fabricated"—has become a common scholarly method of questioning whether an objective reality exists. That is not the sense in which such phrases will be employed here, however. Rather, the metaphor is a more simple-minded one. It is the adoption of terminology from a field that has a similar goal to politics; in other words, politicians and architects want the same thing. They are both seeking permission to fabricate the future. Moreover, the idea of an architectural contest is helpful because it creates an awareness of ongoing episodes of competition. In such a contest, winning the selection round by no means guarantees that the victor will actually get to erect anything. It is one thing to wow the clients with a model, but quite another to get it actually built. Like politicians, architects must continue to cater to their supporters as they remove old detritus, prepare the site, and secure the necessary building permits. They rarely have the luxury of beginning work on a green field—the architectural equivalent of a blank slate. But there are consolations; one is that the process is path dependent. Put another way, once the foundation is laid according to the new blueprints, it is hard to remove. The normative power of the factual, a favorite concept of German theorists, comes into play; facts on the ground are difficult to change.[11] The legacy of both architectural and political decisions will last for decades, centuries, and even millennia, once the concrete is poured. It is therefore crucial to be the first to lay that foundation.[12]

The competition of 1989–90 centered on a specific future building site—that is, the center of divided Europe. Despite the fact that the Cold War conflict took place across the globe over a number of decades, it originated in Europe, and this book shows that the endgame was European as well.[13] Europe was the site of the culminating round not only of a contest of geopolitical power but also of modernities. Put another way, the Cold War was not just a military standoff but also a conflict between two completely different visions of modernity: a Western versus a Soviet one.[14] Ensuring victory for the Western model would, participants in events believed, signify not just a material but also an ideological triumph in the contest to define what was modern. Indeed, years later, both the Reagan and Bush presidential libraries would choose to display portions of the former Berlin Wall as trophies on their grounds; each wanted to lay claim to the success. In short, 1989–90 was the final round in a competition that was long-running, multi-layered, and profoundly significant.

During this final round, what specific models for the future did the key actors propose? This book will describe them in detail, after an introductory summary (in chapter 1) of why November 1989 became the moment that the models were launched. Chapters 2 through 4 will then focus on the four major variants, listed here in the chronological order in which they appeared.

(1) To begin with, in late 1989, there was the Soviet *restoration model*. The Union of Soviet Socialist Republics (USSR) hoped to use its weight as a victor in the Second World War to restore the old quadripartite mechanism of four-power control exactly as it used to be in 1945, before subsequent layers of Cold War modifications created room for German contributions. Moscow wanted to strip away those layers and revert to the legal status it had enjoyed at the start of the occupation. This model, which called for the reuse of the old Allied Control Commission to dominate all further proceedings in divided Germany, represented a realist vision of politics run by powerful states, each retaining their own sociopolitical order, whether liberal democratic or socialist, and pursuing their own interests.

(2) Next and almost contemporaneously, there was Kohl's *revivalist model*. This variant represented the revival, or adaptive reuse, of a confederation of German states. Such a Germanic confederation had not actually existed since the nineteenth century (Nazi expansion notwithstanding). It had endured rhetorically, however, into the period of détente—"two states in one German nation" was a common phrase—and it was now to be revived in reality for two twenty-first-century Germanies. This latter-day "confederationism" blurred the lines of state sovereignty. Each of the Germanies would maintain its own political and social order, but the two would share a confederative, national roof. There were echoes of this idea on a large scale; Mitterrand speculated about creating a Europe of confederations, yet neither Kohl's version nor the French idea was ever fully developed. Originally intended as serious options, they (like Gorbachev's initial restoration model) would be overtaken by events more quickly than anyone imagined.[15]

(3) Next, in early 1990, there was Gorbachev's challenge to his own original plan: a *heroic model* of multinationalism. Gorbachev dropped the restoration concept entirely and instead proposed to build a vast new edifice from the Atlantic to the Urals: the fulfillment of his desire to create a common European home of many rooms.[16] States under this model would retain their own political orders, but cooperate via international economic and military institutions. This model was heroic in the architectural sense of the word, which is much more ambivalent than the popular usage; indeed, "heroism" is a term that has fallen into disrepute among architects. The era of heroic modernism in the twentieth century produced a number of utopian design exercises, sometimes explicitly in the service of political regimes, that proved to be illusory or misguided. Gorbachev's vision fit into this pattern: it was sweeping in intent, but it was also fatally uncompromising. Ironically, former East German dissident movements, having done so much

to unsettle Soviet control, proposed a similar model. They wanted new construction as well, though of a more limited expanse. Their goal was the construction of an improved socialism in East Germany, with a curiously prescient kind of "property pluralism" that would allow both private property and state intervention in times of economic crisis.[17]

(4) Finally, the Western allies, and Kohl in particular, responded in 1990 with the fourth and winning proposal: the *prefab model*. In other words, the United States and West Germany convincingly made the case for taking the West's prefabricated institutions, both for domestic order and international economic and military cooperation, and simply extending them eastward. This institutional-transfer model had the advantage of being quick, and dealing in known and successful commodities, such as the West German Basic Law, the West German currency (or DM), and the Article 5 mutual defense guarantee of NATO, to name a few. Indeed, the fact that both the EC and NATO were structurally capable of expansion (and had already been enlarged from their original footprints) provided useful precedents. The prefab model was the one model that proposed to harmonize both domestic and international institutions in Eastern Europe to preset Western standards. Moreover, it helped Kohl to justify his drive for rapid unity to skeptical West Europeans. When faced with the question of how to reconcile his neighbors to a process that might well threaten the delicate balance of strength within the EC, Kohl, already one of the more pro-European leaders of his generation, could argue that German unity was an extension of European integration.[18] Just as West and East would unify within existing German structures, so too would West and East join under the existing EC institutions.

There was a large disadvantage to the prefab model, though. This disadvantage was not that prefab represented inferior goods; quite to the contrary, Western institutions had proven themselves to be durable and successful. Rather, it was the issue of perpetuating structures fabricated for a divided world into an undivided one, thus raising the issue of whether such a construct would in fact be suitable for the new site. Even as borders were dissolving, in other words, political institutions created and shaped by the decades-long Cold War *division* of international politics would exert and extend themselves eastward over a *unified* world. This was a necessary decision, born of the need to move quickly, with fateful consequences. Extending Cold War structures was a quick fix. But these structures, conceived in hostility, could not easily be recast to accommodate the great enemy—the Slavic other—because their original function was to resist that enemy. As the former secretary of state, Baker, later observed in his memoirs about this era, "almost every achievement contains within its success the seeds of a future problem." He was right; the problem in this case was that no clear place was carved out for Russia, while a window of potential cooperation between Russia and the West was open. Before long, it closed, and the opportunity was lost.[19]

In addition, designers of all four models had to deal with an overarching contradiction in 1989–90. The competition among their models of order unfolded in an extremely disorderly way. It commenced unexpectedly, with East European states and the Soviet Union itself all on the verge of collapse, and took place between a number of competitors of unequal size and resources. The struggle to create a new order oscillated between, on the one hand, the highly public events dominated by the crowds or electorates, and on the other, the behind-the-scenes maneuverings of political elites, who could make agreements in secret, but ultimately would have to face the public again.

If these were the four most prominent models, who got to choose among them? Initially, by dint of the timing of their first free election since the Weimar era, it fell de facto to the voters of East Germany to choose from candidates representing these models. The electorate had a clear choice among parties supporting each of the four options (as well as other, less likely ones). The fate of any given model depended partly on its merits and partly on the ability of its designers to convince the public that they were more competent than their competitors.[20]

In the eyes of the East Germans, the contest ultimately came down to a choice between Gorbachev's heroic attempt to build a mansion of many rooms, preserving some part of the old socialist order, and the wholesale adoption of the prefabricated institutions of the West. The latter won definitively. While there was some sympathy for expansive new multinational construction, the majority of these new voters felt that the safest option was proven structures to be put in place by proven politicians. As a result, the Western model under the leadership of Kohl would win, but not without some gloves-off power politics—particularly with regard to Poland and NATO—and not without problems in implementation.

If the East Germans got the initial say (and the timing of their input was significant), it was ultimately Germany's neighbors, East and West, who had to agree with what was proposed. Most importantly, the Soviet Union had the ability to cause enormous problems for Kohl. Even though the USSR was on the verge of ruin, it held legal rights emanating from World War II and maintained roughly four hundred thousand troops in East Germany; these facts gave Gorbachev leverage regardless of his situation at home. As a result, even after the prefab model emerged as the winner, Kohl still had to secure building permits to start work, and that process is the subject of chapter 5.

Fig. I.3. The Berlin Wall in front of the Brandenburg Gate, November 1989. Courtesy of Gerard Marlie/AFP/Getty Images.

Finally, this book's conclusion will look at the legacy of the contest of 1989 and 1990. It will discuss how, as in many architectural competitions, the model that won was not the most visionary one. Given all of the constraints involved, it was the most workable in the time frame available. It demonstrated the authority of competence crucial to all successful architecture and politics, and that proved decisive in the end. But workable is not the same as ideal, so it is necessary to be clear about the seeds of future problems that were sown by its victory.

In short, if Berlin is indeed the phoenix-like city that slowly rose from the ashes of Nazism and the Cold War division to realize "the dream of freedom," then we need to understand how that happened, and at what cost it was achieved. Historians have already put a great deal of effort into analyzing the earlier decades of the division of Europe. Now it is time to think about the struggle of 1989 and what it bequeathed to the post–Cold War world.

CHAPTER 1

WHAT CHANGES IN SUMMER AND AUTUMN 1989?

Had they deceived us
Or deceived themselves, the quiet-voiced elders
Bequeathing us merely a receipt for deceit?
—T. S. Eliot, 1943[1]

It is 1981. In the United States, Reagan is president. In the Soviet Union, Irina Scherbakova's seven-year-old daughter has just come home from school. Scherbakova asks her what she did that day. Her daughter replies that her class was given an assignment. The students were told to write an essay called "The Person I Hate the Most." Surprised and not pleased by the teacher's choice of assignment, her mother asks, who was your person?

Adolf Hitler, her daughter replies. But I was the only one. All of the other students chose Reagan.[2]

It is 1983. Superpower rivalry has reached a new intensity as the Soviet invasion of Afghanistan drags on, Reagan calls for his country to stand up to the evil empire, and short-range U.S. Cruise and Pershing II missiles are readied for installation in West Germany. In this overheated atmosphere, one of the members of the East German peace group Swords into Ploughshares, Roland Jahn, becomes a special target of the East German state security force, or the Stasi. Jahn has particular reason to hate the secret police: they took away a friend of his in April 1981, and the friend was dead two days later. Jahn has been a thorn in the Stasi's side ever since. The secret police decide that the most aggressive action is now necessary. They take him prisoner in June 1983, not for the first time; but this time they bind him inside a train.

Then, the Stasi agents watch as the train pulls out for the West, taking the unwilling border crosser with it.[3]

It is 1989. East Europeans can scarcely believe all of the miraculous things that are happening. Soviet troops are withdrawing from Afghanistan. The ruling Polish authorities have agreed to "round table" negotiations with the once-illegal Solidarity trade union. Hungary has legalized independent political parties. Gorbymania has swept the West, causing huge, adoring crowds to coalesce wherever

11

Gorbachev appears. In East Berlin, young East Germans hear that restrictions on crossing the Berlin Wall have changed. Two of them decide to test whether this is true or not, and try to cross the wall.

The border guards shoot one in the foot and the other, Chris Gueffroy, in the heart. Gueffroy dies within a few minutes. His friend survives, to be hauled away in the freezing cold of a February night and sentenced to three years in jail.[4]

These are only three tiny snapshots, from 1981, 1983, and 1989, but they capture the prominent features on the landscape of the Cold War's final years. A sense of conflict and stalemate persisted well into the 1980s, which made the dramatic events in the second half of 1989 all the more surprising. Indeed, the 1980s were some of the most anxious years of the Cold War, characterized by new tensions after the Soviet invasion of Afghanistan, the election of Reagan to the presidency and anti-Reagan campaigns in the Soviet Union, and the launch of the controversial "Star Wars" missile defense program in 1983. Within the USSR, the opposition movement began to lose hope of ever seeing a better future. A leading historian of the Soviet Union finds that in the 1980s, "the dissident movement seemed at its lowest ebb since its emergence in the 1960s. Most leading dissidents were in labor camps or exile. Those who remained at liberty were under constant KGB (the Soviet Committee for State Security) surveillance. Samizdat literature was reduced to a trickle."[5]

As Scherbakova's memory suggests, fear and hatred were constant components of that stalemated situation. Ordinary people living both in the East and the West worried about the destructive power afforded to world leaders by thermonuclear weapons—both rulers on the other side and their own. Such weapons cast a long shadow over everyday life. Instructing schoolchildren about the evils of the other side was only one manifestation of this.[6] The apocalyptic television film *The Day After* in 1983 was another. The film depicted the gruesome destruction of U.S. cities in a nuclear exchange with the Soviet Union and, as the title indicates, the horrific consequences of radiation poisoning for those who survived the initial attack. A poll about the film and its pacifist message, conducted by the *Washington Post* the next day, found that a staggering 83 percent of Americans wanted a freeze in the construction of any further thermonuclear weapons.[7]

Europeans had similar worries. They knew that thanks to the short-range nuclear missiles installed in the late 1970s and early 1980s by both military alliances, they would be near-instantaneous victims of a superpower shooting war. On one day alone in October 1983, a million West Germans turned out to protest the installation of such weapons. The following year, the pop singer Herbert

Grönemeyer made himself a wealthy man with a hit called "Amerika." The album containing this song, which suggested that Yanks and Russians should fight each other not in Europe but rather on some uninhabited place like the moon, spent eighty weeks at the top of the charts in West Germany. The lack of freedom of assembly, speech, and commerce on the other side of the iron curtain meant that there were not similar protests, pop hits, or sales, but the opposition movement made disarmament by both sides one of its credos; hence the name of Jahn's group, Swords into Ploughshares.[8]

Such fears have a larger conceptual significance. Some scholars now ask whether the Cold War was simply a deceit or fiction, an artificial notion, and a threadbare and risible one even while ostensibly still in place. Their argument is that when viewed with the advantage of scholarly hindsight, the continuities overshadow the changes. The so-called Cold War in fact represented the processes of empire and colonization continuing under new names. As a result, this school of thought holds that scholars "ought to remove the Cold War lens" and "transcend their own imaginary categories" that artificially distort the past.[9]

To some extent the concept of a Cold War completely divorced from what came before and after is indeed misleading, as there were certainly continuities with a number of preceding eras. The practice of projecting force beyond national borders clearly had imperial ancestry. But the population on the ground—most notably in Eastern Europe and the Soviet Union, but also in Afghanistan, Vietnam, and a number of other locations around the globe—had to pay for this particular fiction in unique ways, and kept paying for it until the end. Residents of the Soviet Bloc had to endure life in garrison states primed for nuclear conflict both internally and externally, with countless consequences for everyday existence. Extraordinary percentages of the gross domestic product of the USSR went to military procurement and deployment; contemporary major nations generally spend around 1 to 4 percent, but Gorbachev learned when he became general secretary that the Soviet Union was spending 20 to 30 percent. Militaristic schooling led to mandatory service. Even though East Germany had just sixteen million inhabitants, half a million of them had to carry weapons at the behest of the state, either as part of the military or the Stasi. Moreover, the need for security served as a justification for constant policing of the population to ensure good behavior. At its height, the East German secret police had 1 employee for every 180 East Germans. The technology of both weapons and surveillance, in short, created a unique era.[10]

It is, as a result, an oversimplification to consider the Cold War to be merely a coda to colonialism. The era may not have been unique, but it was hardly fictional.

Fears of thermonuclear destruction, and their consequences for societal order and generational beliefs and experiences, were new features both in the West and the East, and defined the age.

A second feature of the Cold War landscape in Eastern Europe emerges from the snapshot of Jahn. It is important to remember that hopes for a better future were not always synonymous with hopes of escaping to the West or importing a Western lifestyle. Getting shipped off to West Berlin was indeed a punishment for Jahn, as the Stasi intended it to be. He wanted to create a new German Democratic Republic (GDR), not put his feet up in a comfortable, capitalist country. In a daring move in 1985, Jahn smuggled himself back into East Germany. He flew to East Berlin's Schönefeld Airport, pretending that he would transit directly from there into West Berlin, but instead slipped away from the airport controls and sought refuge with old friends in his hometown of Jena. He also met with prominent members of the East Berlin opposition scene. To his dismay, they told him he had to stay in the West, because he could be of much more help to their cause there. With their aid, Jahn got himself back to West Berlin, where he would serve a critical role in 1989, to be described below.[11]

Relevant here is the point that many East German dissidents believed socialism—and not just the watered down variant of Western-style social democracy—still had a chance, if the corrupt leadership of the Warsaw Pact could be removed. In some ways this belief separated the East Germans from other East European protesters, who were more skeptical about socialism's chances. Once Gorbachev took power, such East German views ironically put the GDR dissident movement on the side of the Soviet leader; Gorbachev's "new thinking" was also aimed at producing a better socialism, not an imitation of social democracy. He knew that the Soviet Union was on the verge of ruin in 1989, but felt strongly that such new thinking was the answer, rather than the wholesale adoption of the democratic, market-economy example. In other words, his idea was to create something different from either the Soviet past or the West European present. This notion echoed visions of *la terza via* (the third way) and Eurocommunism popularized by the Italian Communist Party. Such notions served as powerful touchstones for reformists throughout Eastern Europe and Gorbachev, and could potentially have opened up avenues to the future.[12]

Finally, a third feature of the Cold War landscape emerges from the death of Gueffroy in February 1989; that year, pushing limits was still risky and indeed deadly. Just as there was a threat of nuclear violence on the international level, there was also an ongoing threat of violence at the individual level right until the

end. Gueffroy's case was an extreme example, but the violence used against protesters from Beijing to Berlin well into October 1989 shows what any challenger
to the status quo had to face. In hindsight we know that little blood was shed in
Europe, but the situation at the time was fraught with risk. The peaceful ending
in Central Europe was not an obvious outcome, particularly with the shoot-to-kill
practice still in place on the inner-German border in 1989, and hundreds of thousands of foreign troops still stationed there. Attempts to challenge the status quo
remained dangerous and costly at the ground level.

They were dangerous at the top level as well. In 1988, when Reagan met Gorbachev for the last time as president, the American repeated a favorite joke he had
gotten from Lyndon Johnson. Johnson had complained that if, while in office, he
had gone to the Potomac River and "walked out on top of the water," then the
press would have reported "that the President could not swim."[13] Gorbachev
laughed, and then pointed out less than politely that Reagan had told him the joke
before; but apparently the apt message (whether intended or unintended) did not
sink in either time. No matter how many miracles Gorbachev worked, it would
never be enough to impress his critics. Even though he and Reagan had done a
great deal with their arms control agreements to chip away at world fear of a
thermonuclear exchange, the public would want more.

Gorbachev's new thinking had indeed started to raise expectations among the
broader population that he could not fulfill. His reforms, creating new institutions
outside the party in 1989, gave his opponents a chance to air their views. His pri-
oritization of the Soviet Union's massive domestic economic problems—by 1990,
shortages were as intense as during wartime—contributed to a hands-off approach to Eastern Europe.[14] Meanwhile, the rulers in Poland and Hungary opened
new doors to the opposition. But if Gorbachev had been largely sympathetic to
the goals of reformist Communists and negotiation-friendly dissident leaders,
there were limits. He maintained that the events of 1968 in Prague were in fact a
disreputable counterrevolution; in other words, a dramatic overthrow of the Communist order was out of bounds.[15] Gorbachev, the great reformer, was thus not at
all happy at the dramatic change in divided Germany.

To sum up: if the characteristics of the Cold War landscape in the 1980s were
an ongoing mixture of threats on both the international and individual level, combined with hopes for a new kind of future, what changed in 1989 to yield the sudden opening of the Berlin Wall? Answering this question is crucial, because—as
subsequent chapters will describe—the nature and timing of the wall's disappearance produced an unexpected contest to define what kind of political and social
order would follow.

Obviously, in 1989 there were long-term developments coming to fruition, most notably the economic disintegration of the Soviet Union. Nothing described below is meant to deny the importance of such developments. Yet all of those developments had been going on for years. The goal here is not to recapitulate them, nor to describe every significant event of the late 1980s; rather, the question is a narrower one. What changed during summer and autumn 1989? Why did it become the year that the wall opened? Previously, gradual opening, cooperation, and slow reform served as the order of the day in Poland, Hungary, and even the Soviet Union itself, where semi-free elections took place in March 1989. But an entirely different process began after the wall unexpectedly crumbled.

Close analysis of five selected events from 1989 helps to provide an answer. The causal chain that ends with East Berliners drinking champagne in West Berlin on November 9 includes the following five significant developments: (1) the Beijing example fails to transfer to Europe and the consensus for nonviolence solidifies, thereby diminishing the sense of threat that had defined the Cold War until its final year; (2) the Americans choose to step back, forcing Gorbachev to do the same, and making it clear to people on the ground in Eastern Europe that change must come at their initiative; (3) East Germans, long the laggards in protest movements, take the lead in challenging the status quo; (4) their self-confidence increases as they do so; and (5) television transforms reality at a crucial moment.

TIANANMEN FAILS TO TRANSFER

In 1989, several significant anniversaries reminded the world of how changeable political order could be.[16] Forty years previously, a Communist China, two German states, and a new military alliance—NATO—had all emerged from the lingering chaos of World War II. Fifty years earlier, Hitler had destroyed the global order by starting that war. And during a fateful July two hundred years earlier, the French Revolution had rocked the monarchical establishment.

Protesters in Beijing were hoping that the fortieth anniversary of the People's Republic of China would be remembered for major changes as well, but they were to be disappointed. The opposing outcomes in the cities of Beijing and Leipzig showed that while violence against individuals remained a viable and successful option for Communist leaders in 1989, it would no longer be used in the European context. This was a critical and essential condition for everything that followed, which ensured that Europe would lead the changes in 1989 and

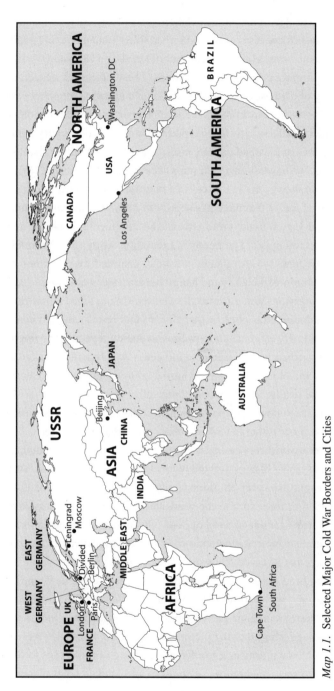

Map 1.1. Selected Major Cold War Borders and Cities

China would not. What happened in Beijing, and how was it different from Leipzig? Why did the Tiananmen example fail to transfer?

In late May 1989, masses of protesters had filled Tiananmen Square at the heart of China's capital city. They had been emboldened by a Gorbachev visit intended, ironically, to improve Sino-Soviet relations. These protesters openly challenged the authority of Chinese leader Deng Xiaoping and built a rough facsimile of the Statue of Liberty right in front of an enormous portrait of Mao Zedong at the entrance to the Forbidden City. Deng reportedly declared to his party's ruling Politburo members that they had only themselves to blame: "Our biggest mistake was in education. We haven't educated our kids and students enough." With forceful enough action, however, "it's possible a bad thing could turn into a good one." Presumably he meant that the tanks shortly to roll into Tiananmen Square would provide an education to the protesters, a kind of remedial lesson to make up for previous shortcomings.[17] The People's Liberation Army (PLA) forcibly cleared the square on June 3–4. An image of a lone, unarmed man standing bravely in front of a column of tanks immediately became the worldwide visual icon of Chinese suppression. When it was all over, the Chinese Red Cross carried out a canvas of major area hospitals in an effort to find how many had been hurt; the organization finally estimated that twenty-six hundred people had died and a further seven thousand were wounded. Gorbachev was reportedly taken aback and dismayed by the bloodshed, and it contributed to his desire to pursue a different course. These deaths had happened, after all, even as the election that would bring Solidarity to power in cooperation with the previous rulers was under way in Poland—a process that the Soviet leader preferred to violence.[18]

The Western world condemned the use of force, but the large number of European leaders voicing disapproval did not include any in East Berlin. The leader of the GDR, seventy-six-year-old Erich Honecker, was in failing health. Like Deng, he was searching for a cure to the headaches that Gorbachev was causing him, and saw China's example as a ray of hope. Given that both the People's Republic and East Germany were celebrating their fortieth anniversaries that year, Honecker decided that he could learn something from China.

He had the head of the Stasi order special protection for the Chinese embassy in the wake of "counterrevolutionary unrest" after the Tiananmen violence.[19] Next, Honecker directed the party-controlled television news program to broadcast reports suggesting that the pictures of wounded were fake.[20] Finally, Honecker sent his crown prince, Egon Krenz, on a high-profile visit to the Chinese fortieth-anniversary celebrations at the start of October 1989. Krenz met with Deng, along with Li Peng, Li Zemin, and others. Afterward, Krenz filed a report

Fig. 1.1. A lone demonstrator blocks a column of tanks at the entrance to Tiananmen
Square in Beijing, June 5, 1989. Photo by CNN via Getty Images.

that eerily echoed Deng's June comments word for word.[21] The Chinese Communist Party returned the favor by sending a delegation headed by Yao Yilin, vice premier and Politburo member, to appear in celebrations on the East German anniversary.[22]

East German dissidents did not miss the point; Honecker wanted to march in lockstep with his colleagues in Beijing. His efforts were clearly meant to intimidate protesters in places like Dresden, where the future Russian president Putin was serving as one of the many KGB officers assigned to spy on NATO. Soon, Putin would have to start burning documents so furiously that he would break the KGB's furnace, but that was in the future. In October 1989, it was not at all clear whether he would be burning or fighting; Putin felt strongly that he and his colleague had a right to defend Soviet interests by all means.[23] Other East Europeans were worried as well; the Czech dissident Václav Havel in particular was concerned that a second Tiananmen could occur in Prague.[24]

Evidence suggests strongly that Honecker did indeed hope to instigate a "German Tiananmen" on the night of Monday, October 9, in Leipzig. He chose that day because, by then, massive protest marches were occurring every Monday night in Leipzig. They followed the weekly peace prayers held at a major church.

That particular Monday was auspicious in his eyes because it was the first suitable day for unseemly bloodshed after the forced jollity of the GDR's own fortieth-anniversary birthday party, two days earlier.[25]

In preparation for that night, and acting on Honecker's orders, Stasi chief Erich Mielke ordered every authorized Stasi agent to start carrying a weapon at all times. Leipzig authorities fielded a force of eight thousand, consisting of not only police officers but also Stasi and National People's Army troops as well as others.[26] According to one of the local church leaders, Pastor Christian Führer, Leipzig doctors specializing in the treatment of gunshot wounds called him to say that they had been ordered to report for duty. Hospitals were told to have surge capacity beds and blood reserves available.[27] Foreign journalists, who had experienced rough handling when they tried to film the anniversary protests in Berlin, were banned from Leipzig altogether. Their reports about the violent attacks on peaceful protesters—sometimes using dogs—had displeased Honecker, and he wanted to avoid a repeat.[28]

Amazingly, despite the deployment for a German Tiananmen, the protest march of October 9 remained entirely peaceful. The guns stayed silent and hospital blood supplies went unused. A combination of Soviet unwillingness to interfere, public appeals for nonviolence by prominent Leipzigers, and personal ambition—Krenz seeing his moment for parricidal action—caused the East German Politburo to step back from the brink.[29] After all, Gorbachev had been warmly welcomed by East German crowds chanting "Gorby" during a visit to the GDR's fortieth-anniversary celebrations. The Soviet leader had made his displeasure with Honecker clear—even calling him an "asshole," although not to his face—so Krenz clearly had a mandate from Moscow. Gorbachev seems to have believed that sweeping but peaceful change would prevent more serious crises later and make the use of violence obsolete. The main victim of Honecker's lust to restore order with Chinese methods was, as a result, Honecker himself. Krenz formally replaced Honecker on October 18, thereby revealing the Politburo's inner divisions and fearfulness to the world.[30]

The Stasi's old foe Jahn succeeded in playing a role in the October upheaval from afar. Honecker's expulsion of foreign journalists from Leipzig prevented the broadcasting of live footage. The West German evening news program *Tagesschau* instead could show only a picture of its moderator talking on the phone to a Leipzig church leader.[31] But a camera that Jahn had gotten smuggled into East Germany made it to the hands of the stealth photography team Aram Radomski and Siegbert Schefke. Filling the void left by the absence of the Western journalists, they climbed a church tower and illicitly used Jahn's camera to film the mas-

Fig. 1.2. Protest in Leipzig, East Germany, October 1989. Photo by Chris Niedenthal/
Time Life Pictures/Getty Images.

sive crowds.[32] Their video from the night of October 9 in Leipzig appeared
on Western airwaves the next day. "For the first time, we have reporting about
GDR protests with some degree of accuracy," announced the news program
Tagesthemen, without identifying the actual source.[33] Former East German dissident Tom Sello recalls this footage, the first uncensored film of Leipzig protests
made by East Germans to be broadcast in the West, as a huge victory for the opposition. As Sello put it, for images to have an impact, there needed to be someone in East Germany to take them, someone to smuggle them to, and someone to
make sure they got shown, and thanks to Jahn, Radomski, and Schefke, all of that
came together in fall 1989.[34] Suddenly, Western television could broadcast the
immense size of the protest and the utter lack of any real response to it. The most
important audience for these pictures were East Europeans, viewing them (or
hearing descriptions of them) illicitly on Western channels that could be received
in the East.

The significance of Leipzig in October is that it negated the Tiananmen model
in the European context. The actions of the Chinese Politburo could have set the
agenda for violent suppression of protesters elsewhere, but they did not.[35] Instead, one of the many surprising aspects of 1989–90 is that the People's Republic of China played a minor role after June 1989. As one historian put it, "China,

having served as one of the catalysts in shaping a different international system, abruptly retreated, fearing an uncharted future."[36] Its leaders decided to turn inward, focus on economic changes, and insulate China as much as possible from the consequences of Gorbachev's initiatives.[37] The inability of a Communist ruling regime in Europe to implement what the Stasi called a "Chinese solution" served as a signal that the Asian model would not readily transfer.[38] With only a small exception for Romania later, it was clear after Leipzig in October 1989 that nonviolence had become the order of the day in Europe. The importance of this development cannot be overstated. It contributed greatly to the increasing self-confidence of protesters in Europe.

THE AMERICANS STEP BACK

This leads to another surprise in the second half of 1989: like China, neither the United States nor the Soviet Union served as leaders for the events that unfolded.[39] For that brief but important time, events on the ground in Europe mattered more than superpower action. Western countries and international institutions, such as the EC, NATO, and the United Nations, were basically spectators to the dramatic upheaval at the end of that year.[40]

For the United States in particular, this was a conscious choice. At the beginning of 1989, the newly installed President Bush intentionally instituted a pause in the rapid dismantling of Cold War weapons and attitudes. This desire for a slowdown became apparent as soon as the Bush staffers took the reins. It was clear immediately that they were going to pull hard in another direction, partly to steer clear of Reagan's shadow, and partly to get off of what they saw as the wrong track. As Robert Hutchings, a National Security Council (NSC) member under Bush, put it, an "entirely new team came in, representing foreign policy approaches fundamentally at odds with those of the Reagan administration." In essence, there was "no such thing as a 'Reagan-Bush' foreign policy. Before 1989 there was Reagan; afterwards there was Bush."[41]

Scholars still use the Reagan-Bush transition as an example of how vicious an intraparty White House handover can be. As one transition expert noted, "George H. W. Bush fired everybody."[42] There was a sense that Reaganite wild-eyed idealism about relations with Russia and nuclear disarmament had started to outstrip practical realities, and now the time for sober policymaking had returned. Robert Gates, the deputy national security adviser in 1989–91, and later the head of the Central Intelligence Agency (CIA) and the defense secretary, found that Reagan and Secretary of State George Shultz "had sped past both the U.S. military's analysis of the strategic implications and the ability of U.S. intelligence" in their bid for glory before the clock ran out in 1988.[43]

Now that it was their watch, Bush and Baker wondered whether there was any reason that the United States should continue to support the Soviet desire to change to the status quo. As Baker wrote in a summary of U.S.-Soviet relations in early 1989, the Russians "have to make hard choices. *We do Gorbachev no favors when we make it easier to avoid choices.*" Baker believed that necessity had definitely been the mother of virtue in Gorbachev's case. "He made a choice in Afghanistan because he saw the *need* for it. He made a choice in arms control because there was a need for it." Baker kept these thoughts private, but Secretary of Defense Dick Cheney told CNN bluntly that Gorbachev would "'ultimately fail.'" Eduard Shevardnadze would later respond to Cheney's comments by calling them unsurprising; "'I know that the Secretary of Defense needs money. How would he finance his defense programs if there were no Soviet threat?'"[44]

A clash between Baker and the former secretary of state, Henry Kissinger, was revealing. Bush had sent Kissinger as his envoy to Gorbachev in January 1989, even as the new president was just taking office.[45] When Kissinger met with Politburo member Alexander Yakovlev and then Gorbachev himself in Moscow on January 16 and 17, the American suggested that the USSR did not need to rush out of Afghanistan. "With regard to Afghanistan, we want you to withdraw, but we do not want you to have a security problem [as a result]." On the subject of Germany, Kissinger pointed out that the United States and the Soviet Union shared a common interest in preventing the rise of nationalists. Close U.S.-USSR contact— using himself as the go-between of course—was essential in preventing any kind of political explosions happening in Germany and the rest of Europe. There was a need for guarantees against the "recklessness of Europeans themselves."[46]

Kissinger faxed a summary of his meetings to Washington on January 21: "In my view Gorbachev is treading water with perestroika. He is looking to foreign policy as a way out. He will pay a reasonable price to that end."[47] But Baker was not convinced that Kissinger's understanding approach to Soviet positions was the best path forward and definitively quashed the nascent back channel. Baker's actions left Kissinger scrambling to control the damage to his own reputation with the new Bush team. In happier days past, Baker had sought Kissinger's advice about leading the State Department and dealing with its career bureaucrats. Kissinger had jokingly responded that Baker should watch out for the long-term civil servants, because they were "'very ingenious. They give you three choices: nuclear war, unconditional surrender, and their preferred course of action.'" Now, however, Kissinger had to engage in what Baker called Washington's "time-honored ritual" of reaching out to the offended party and groveling.[48] He wrote a private note to Baker: "The newspapers have been having so much fun describing how I will be influencing policy via surrogates that I think a note is appropriate." Kissinger promised that he would resist future meddling: "I have a firm policy never to volunteer policy advice to already overburdened senior officials."[49] He did not specify at what point in his life he had implemented that policy.

Contemporaries soon sensed the differences between Reagan and Bush. In a one-on-one meeting in June 1989, Kohl and Gorbachev compared the two presidents, to the benefit of the latter. Kohl recalled meeting Reagan when the former actor was still a presidential candidate in 1979. Helmut Schmidt, the West German chancellor at the time, had refused to meet the American because he considered it a waste of an hour. Kohl, however, made time to see Reagan, and was deeply disappointed by the experience. Reagan, he was shocked to discover, "knew practically nothing about Europe." Kohl asked himself at the time "what consequences that would have." The situation with Bush was "completely different," fortunately. "To a great extent, Bush sees many problems with European eyes . . . he understands more about Europe than Reagan."[50] Mitterrand had a different opinion, though, which he also expressed to Gorbachev just a couple of weeks later over a private dinner at his apartment in Paris. Despite Bush's efforts to improve U.S.-French relations by inviting Mitterrand to Kennebunkport, Maine, in May, the French leader still thought that "Bush, as a President, has a very big drawback—he lacks original thinking altogether." With both Kohl and Mitterrand, Gorbachev kept his own thoughts about the Reagan-Bush comparison to himself.[51]

The differences between the Reagan and Bush approaches became even more obvious on February 15, 1989. On that date, Bush announced publicly that he was calling for a large interagency study on U.S. foreign policy, known as National Security Review 3.[52] This announcement brilliantly managed expectations, which was presumably its goal, because it bought the new administration a few months of time during which both domestic and foreign audiences knew they should not expect anything. It sent out a clear message that the Bush administration was not nearly as determined a foe of the status quo as Reagan had been.

In policy terms it produced little. Gates admitted later that "there was never much expectation that the policy reviews would result in a dramatic departure." Scowcroft, the national security adviser, found the whole exercise to be a big disappointment. He began working on a replacement study immediately thereafter.[53] And Baker, who agreed that the result of the review was useless "mush," assigned the blame for its failure to the fact that it "was run by Reagan holdovers . . . these officials found themselves incapable of truly thinking things anew."[54] Yet Gates defended this much-criticized exercise on one account: precisely because of its failure to produce any new initiatives or approaches, the top-level officials in the Bush administration knew that they would have to come up with them personally. As a result, policy would come solely from "Bush, Baker, Scowcroft, and their respective inner circles working in harness together."[55]

Bush administration reserve about the Soviet Union extended to its allies in Eastern Europe as well. The Hungarians would complain repeatedly to the West Germans about the difficulty of getting aid out of the United States.[56] And President Bush came in for criticism both at home and abroad for being reticent with regard to Poland. Bush explained his thinking to Kohl in a confidential phone call on June 15 before his own July trip to Warsaw. The president knew that emotions were running high in Poland, but while he shared such sentiments, he also "felt it important to act carefully and to avoid pouring money down a rat-hole."[57] Bush came to this conclusion despite the strong ties between Poland and U.S. voters. As his ambassador in Warsaw, John Davis, advised him on the eve of the July visit, the "United States occupies such an exaggerated place of honor in the minds of most Poles that it goes beyond rational description. One opposition leader described it aptly as 'blind love.'"[58] None of this swayed the president. In his address to the Polish parliament on July 10, 1989, Bush focused on debt rescheduling and World Bank help for the country rather than direct U.S. aid, but did promise to ask Congress for funding.[59] Later in 1989, Congress would eventually authorize $938 million in aid over three years, but given that Poland was $39 billion in debt and had been unable to make payments on time, it needed more.[60] Bush also expressed unequivocal support for the candidacy of General Wojciech Jaruzelski for president. Following Bush's lead, Ambassador Davis urged Solidarity to ignore the fact that the general was the very person who had once implemented martial law against them. This support may have helped Jaruzelski in winning a narrow victory.[61]

In summary, despite travel to Germany and Poland, the Bush administration had intentionally stepped back. A sense that Reagan had gone too far, too fast, prevailed. This cautious attitude put the United States on the back foot during the drama of fall 1989.

THE STATUS QUO CEASES TO CONVINCE

For his part, Gorbachev could not make rapid headway without a like-minded U.S. president across the negotiating table, so he was stalled as well. His adviser

Andrei Grachev remembers that Gorbachev was enormously disappointed by the change in U.S. attitudes. After years of work on improving relations, he retained his zeal for changing the status quo and could not understand why the new team suddenly seemed to want a moratorium on doing so.[62]

Gorbachev was not alone in his desire to keep producing change, particularly in the field of arms control. Reagan and Gorbachev had signed the Intermediate-Range Nuclear Forces (INF) Treaty in 1987, but the Bush administration was not as interested in such cuts. At NATO's fortieth-anniversary summit in May 1989, the United States insisted on maintaining up-to-date short-range nuclear forces (SNF) stationed in West Germany. This conflict highlighted the importance of the existing NATO status quo to the Bush administration, and the centrality of the Federal Republic of Germany (FRG) to its strategy.

The practical impact of that status quo on divided Germany in 1989 was the presence of hundreds of thousands of foreign troops on its soil. Originally they had arrived as conquering armies, but they stayed on as alliance partners (in the case of East Germany, without democratic legitimization). As Kohl pointedly remarked to Bush in May 1989, even though the FRG was only as wide as Long Island was long, "900,000 soldiers are stationed and carry out exercises" within its borders.[63] On top of this, West Germany contained the largest concentration of nuclear weapons per square mile of any territory in the world, and all of them were controlled by foreigners. The much smaller East Germany held about 400,000 further troops, which added up to a total of 600,000 Soviet citizens along with their dependents.[64] Some unclear portion of the four power rights originating from the unconditional surrender in World War II were still in force 1989, if with various curtailments. Although Kohl was always careful to point out that Western forces were invited to be there and therefore not analogous to Soviet troops, both the Western and Soviet troops had at least two features in common. They had both arrived in wartime (when they most definitely had not been invited), and, despite the thaw in the late 1980s, had no intention of leaving; they did have the intention of reducing head count, but not withdrawing.

Worries that the West Germans might seek their own form of peace dividend in 1989, by asking to delay or cancel an update of U.S. missiles on its soil, gravely concerned Baker. The United States and the British wanted in particular to modernize the eighty-eight Lance missiles in West Germany. Such missiles were designed, with a range of about five hundred kilometers, to even out the conventional superiority of the Warsaw Pact, and were due for some kind of modernization or follow-on replacement.[65] But West Germans from all points on the political spectrum opposed any updating whatsoever. Left-wing peace protesters received support not only from the foreign minister, Liberal Party leader Hans-Dietrich Genscher. (Genscher both opposed the updating and wanted the U.S. to negotiate with Moscow about a reduction in the number of such weapons.) They also got it from more unlikely quarters—namely, the leader of the right-of-center members of parliament, Alfred Dregger. Dregger pointed out publicly that the most terrifying aspect of the missiles was that they could *not* fly very far; in other words, they would land on the other side of divided Germany. "The shorter the range, the 'deader' the Germans," he famously remarked.[66] Baker put the topic on an agenda for a meeting with Bush, noting that "Genscher is getting more extreme [in his opposition to modernization], and is likely to pull Kohl more in his direction. We must start the high-level discussion with Germans on SNF immediately before Genscher moves too far."[67]

Baker also spoke personally in April 1989 with both Genscher and the West German defense minister, Gerhard Stoltenberg, to tell them where the United States stood. "Let me be frank," read Baker's notes on what he planned to discuss at the meeting, "in stating my concern on where this will lead unless we're prudent. I think we're *slipping down a path of denuclearization* of *our defense*, with a big risk to *nuclear coupling*." He told them that if they were to "denuclearize the Alliance defense before there's a major change in the conventional force posture," they would be "unravelling the forward defense strategy, too." To these typed remarks, he added by hand the importance of the issue: it allowed the "Pres. of U.S. to *maintain* U.S. *forces in Europe*. We need those wpn's [weapons] to defend our own troops."[68]

Despite these forceful words, however, the issue remained unresolved even by the time of the formal dinner for the May 1989 NATO summit. Working past midnight, NATO foreign ministers essentially agreed to disagree, concluding that the Lance modernization question should be delayed to a later date.[69] The divergence over the desirability of the status quo—desired by the Americans but not the West Germans—was simply too great to overcome.

A fondness for the status quo was not limited to the United States. Thatcher felt it as well. The British memory of the first half of the twentieth century was a painful one; the second half looked much better in comparison, so she was understandably loath to make any changes. Since she had a good working relationship with Gorbachev, she decided during one conversation in September 1989 to make these sentiments clear to him.[70] According to notes taken by Gorbachev's close aide, Chernyaev, she explained to Gorbachev that he should pay no attention to any polite public comments made by NATO leaders calling for a united Germany. "Britain and Western Europe are not interested in the unification of Germany.

The words written in the NATO communiqué may sound different, but disregard them. We do not want the unification of Germany." The reason was that "it would lead to changes in the post-war borders, and we cannot allow that because such a development would undermine the stability of the entire international situation." She assured him that the United States shared this view; "I can tell you that this is also the position of the US President."[71]

The Polish head of state, Jaruzelski, heard much the same from the British prime minister. As Jaruzelski informed his East German counterparts, Thatcher had told him in a one-on-one conversation what she really thought but could not say publicly—"that unification was absolutely unacceptable. One could not allow this 'Anschluss,' otherwise West Germany would swallow up Austria too, and then there would be a real danger of war."[72] Gorbachev even told Willy Brandt, the former West German chancellor, that Thatcher was worried (and added that Mitterrand was as well). Gorbachev himself added that he was not happy with the nationalistic and irredentist tone of discussions within Kohl's party, the Christian Democratic Union (CDU).

To summarize, the United States was showing great interest in the status quo, which was new after all of the dramatic announcements of the Reagan era. It was not alone in doing so; Thatcher evinced much the same attitude. Yet the momentum for change that Reagan and Gorbachev had produced remained strong despite U.S. desires to slow it down. West Germans of all political parties disliked SNF. And the notion of an end to dramatic changes was particularly unacceptable to East Europeans. With the threat of violent repression definitively gone, the status quo had ceased to convince them of its own necessity. They realized that they would have to make change happen by themselves, and increasingly gained the confidence to do so.

EAST GERMAN SELF-CONFIDENCE RISES

The fourth development was a new self-confidence on the part of East Europeans and an unwillingness to accept previously tolerated strictures. In 1989, this unwillingness was particularly pronounced among East Germans, who had seemed quiescent in contrast with Solidarity in Poland and reformers in Hungary. The rise of East German assertiveness would be extremely important; the Berlin Wall would not just be opened, it would be breached.[73]

Several factors contributed to give East Germans the courage they needed to change their future. The rulers of the GDR had long exhibited uncompromising rigidity in all matters, with little tolerance for large-scale protest; but the regime's loss of nerve in Leipzig on October 9 revealed fatal weaknesses. Gorbachev's numerous hints to East German leaders and citizens that nonviolent reform was the order of the day removed the fear that the Soviets would act where the East German leadership had not.[74] Economic grievances contributed as well: enough was enough, ran the general sentiment. The sixteen-year wait for a car and the twenty-five-year wait for a telephone were no longer tolerable. Although the deprivation was not as bad as that experienced in Poland and Romania, it was still painful. In 1986–87, roughly a hundred thousand people living in thirty-five thousand houses had no heat in the depths of winter. In 1988 and 1989, consumers discovered that it was increasingly difficult to find meat (except on the black market). The comparison with the success of West Germany's economy exacerbated the resentment.[75] And repeated missteps by the ruling Socialist Unity Party (SED) intensified anxieties.[76]

East Germans decided that in order to improve their lives, they must either leave the country, confront their ruling regime, or accept what would come. In other words, they faced a choice between exiting, voicing their discontent, or staying quiet.[77] At first, Hungary's September 1989 announcement that it would allow East Germans to travel through Hungary to Austria made the exit option the most attractive.

This announcement was the result of Hungarian Minister President Miklós Németh's decision to change sides at the end of the Cold War. In spring 1989, he and Gorbachev had seemed to be like-minded souls, agreeing in a March conversation that there was "no difference between pluralism in a single-party system and in a multi-party system."[78] Political liberalization in Hungary over the summer, however, had an unexpected consequence. Not only Hungarians but also East Germans sought to take advantage of the May 1989 cutting of the fence on the Hungarian border to Austria. Due to treaty obligations, Hungary was not supposed to let East Germans utilize this new gap in the iron curtain; but East Germans came and camped at the border anyway.[79] At first a holiday atmosphere prevailed, but the crowds grew restless as conditions became wet and swampy in the waning days of a Central European summer.[80] Nervous Hungarian border guards even shot one East German after an altercation on August 21.[81] It was clear that something had to give.

In a hastily arranged secret meeting on August 25, 1989, outside of Bonn, Németh and his foreign minister, Gyula Horn, informed Kohl and Genscher that they would no longer prevent East Germans from crossing the "green border" into Austria and then going onward to the FRG. The Hungarian leaders were wisely seeking to make a virtue out of the necessity of resolving the unstable situation.

29

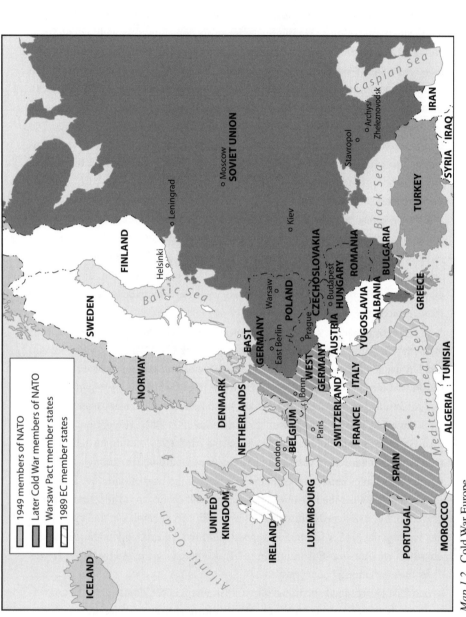

Map 1.2. Cold War Europe

Németh promised Kohl and Genscher that as long as no "military or political force from outside compels us to act differently, we will keep the border open for East Germans." The statement brought tears to Kohl's eyes. He asked Németh what the West Germans could do in response. Németh, at first protesting that Hungary did not want to exchange the border opening for money, went on to achieve exactly that. The chancellor agreed to encourage both the Deutsche and Dresdner Banks to consider requests from Hungary positively. A substantial amount of credit resulted.[82]

Németh kept his word and opened the border to East Germans in September. Dramatic scenes filled television screens worldwide as a mass exodus ensued. By the end of the month, roughly forty thousand had exited—far more than the Hungarian leadership or indeed anyone else had anticipated.[83] This opening was one of the single most important events leading to the breakdown of the old Cold War order. Genscher would later award Horn the Stresemann Medal for it, saying "everything that followed was a consequence of this decision."[84]

In response, the furious East German Politburo choked off travel to Hungary. But that only relocated the problem to Warsaw and particularly Prague. East Germans began filling the West German embassies there in the hopes of emigrating. Prague was especially hard hit because, as the Czech Interior Ministry noted in a report on events in fall 1989, Czechoslovakia had already emerged as a "transit stop" for East Germans heading to Hungary and subsequently crossing the border.[85] When denied the opportunity to go to Hungary, East Germans simply stayed there rather than go home.

Kohl and Genscher hoped they could solve this crisis by negotiating a special one-time release of East Germans from the Prague and Warsaw embassies. The East Berlin Politburo agreed, but there was a catch. The Politburo insisted that refugees had to travel on sealed trains that would cross back through the GDR before delivering their human cargo in West Germany. The risk of running through the GDR cast a pall over the agreement, since it meant that the Politburo had countless ways to stop the trains, and the image of sealed trains in Germany had frightening historical connotations. Still, there did not seem to be a better alternative. In a dramatic gesture, Genscher personally went to Prague to tell the crowd in the embassy of the deal. He was received with a mixture of joy and fear, as the East Germans scrambled to prepare for immediate departure.[86]

Sleep-deprived embassy officials in Prague and Warsaw rushed to get the refugees under way, to accomplish their transit to West Germany before the terms of the deal could change. In Prague, this meant jamming an estimated four to six thousand people on to six trains.[87] Pulling out in haste, hours later than

expected in the middle of the night, massively outnumbered West German official escorts did their best to control the train passengers. The escorts also had to
manage various state security teams that insisted on inspections of the trains at
numerous stops. The atmosphere would grow tense whenever special police officers would demand that passengers show their ID cards. Some refugees threw
their cards at the feet of the agents in response. The embassy officials were not
sure what they could do if the confrontation turned violent, had no means of
communication with the West whatsoever, and had no idea how it would all
end.[88]

One of the West German escorts out of Prague, Frank Elbe, recalled the experience as follows: "Our train rolls out after one in the morning." He remembered
that the mood was "anxious and fearful." The nighttime journeys were made even
more surreal when families with children appeared by the tracks. The trains were
only supposed to carry the original crowd; but others, among them East Germans
who had arrived in Czechoslovakia too late to make it to the embassy, figured out
where the trains would have to slow or stop for technical reasons. They rushed to
the tracks with whatever they could carry, in the hopes of boarding. Richard
Kiessler, a West German journalist on another of the Prague trains, remembered
that few succeeded.[89]

Confrontation loomed yet again when Elbe's train reached the final station in
Czechoslovakia. As it rolled to a stop, passengers saw a line of police on the platform. A handful of forlorn East German families faced the security forces. The
sound of a loudspeaker ordering them not to board echoed through the station.
No one knew how long the train would be stopped or what would happen.

Suddenly, Elbe remembered, "a family finds the heart to begin walking, carrying its suitcases, toward the train." It was a moment to make the heart stop: parents, clutching children and belongings, moving into a row of armed guards. They
had no idea what would result, only the belief that whatever it was, it could not be
worse than staying behind the iron curtain one day longer. The sight of the lone
family advancing in the predawn light inspired other waiting families; they began
to follow. From inside the train, Elbe recalled that "hands that want to help stretch
out to them, and pull them in." The Czech police chose to do nothing. The train
moved on, slightly fuller than before.

Such success helped the confidence of the passengers to grow with every mile
they moved closer to the West. At their final stop in the GDR, a teenager threw all
of his East German currency out the window. Hesitatingly at first, but then en
masse, the rest of the train followed suit, divulging itself of the essentials of an

everyday life that had ended: cash, ID cards, and apartment keys.[90] A train station employee reacted to the shower of coins and keys by tipping his hat to the jubilant passengers. And the next stop was the West. Elbe remembered that moment as a time when "a joy that you cannot imagine breaks out."

When Elbe and others reported to their superiors that more passengers had gotten on to the ostensibly sealed trains under way, Bonn decided to provide cover to such people. Instructions went out saying "the fact that further people got on the train during the transit should not be explicitly acknowledged" if questions arose.[91] On the whole, Elbe found the entire experience to be a sign that more than just a refugee issue was unfolding. West Germany had taken in fleeing easterners before, but this was different. He began wondering if East Germany itself could survive. (Later, he would become one of the key diplomats in the unification process, working closely with Zoellick in the U.S. State Department.)[92] Like Elbe, the Politburo of East Germany clearly saw the flow to Prague as a potentially fatal threat, because it tried to stave off further such scenes through the act of closing the GDR's borders to Czechoslovakia on October 3. It thereby hermetically sealed its own country into an island of discontent, but not before media accounts and images of the refugees leaving Hungary, Poland, and Czechoslovakia had flooded television screens worldwide.[93]

Chernyaev confided to his diary that the Prague trains in particular had produced "awful scenes" that West German television had filmed "and is broadcasting everywhere in the GDR. All of the Western media is full of articles about German reunification."[94] He tried to put a positive spin on events, saying it was fortunate that Gorbachev had set this process in motion.[95] Kohl felt compelled to call Gorbachev and reassure him that the FRG was not trying to destabilize East Germany.[96]

Such coverage influenced the lives of the so-called "stay-at-homes" in the GDR and pushed them toward the option of voicing their unhappiness. "You're still here?" quickly replaced "good day" as a greeting. During daylight hours, the stay-at-homes saw how many people were missing from the workplace. During the evening, West German television brought pictures of their cheering, exuberant neighbors now in the FRG back into their living rooms.[97] As a result, a new pressure added itself to the already-extensive frustration: now an easterner had to justify staying as opposed to leaving. This pressure increased the willingness of GDR citizens to use confrontation with the government as the needed justification for staying home, which greatly benefited hitherto small opposition groups and sympathetic churches.[98] Artist and dissident Bärbel Bohley, who had also

Fig. 1.3. Bärbel Bohley, former East German dissident leader, in 2004. Courtesy of Michael Urban/AFP/Getty Images.

been expelled to the West but returned, spoke for many in October 1989 when she defended this tactic. "Confrontation arises naturally today when the truth is spoken. A person who wants to avoid this confrontation is a person who wants to avoid the truth."[99]

Previously, the staff of the West German permanent mission in the GDR had been dismissive about local dissidents. Franz Bertele, the senior West German figure in the mission, had reported throughout the summer and fall that the East German opposition was too hapless to seize the opportunity. "The reports in our press about an 'opposition' are exaggerated," he concluded. "Bärbel Bohley . . . makes an amateurish impression and has real problems . . . carrying out her goals." The followers of dissident groups were only "intellectuals, with no political talent whatsoever visible among them."[100]

Whatever organizational shortcoming Bohley and other prominent dissidents may have had previously, in fall 1989 she and others overcame them and served as important catalysts, and that was what mattered. Participation in protest events organized by opposition groups and churches grew by orders of magnitude throughout October and November 1989, and climaxed in the half-million-strong marches of November 4 in Berlin and November 6 in Leipzig.[101] Every march or protest that took place successfully inspired more people to join the next one as self-confidence began to snowball. Even loyal party members wrote to Krenz demanding change.[102] Dissent, expressed throughout most of the summer and fall in the form of mass exit, had been forced by the border sealing into voicing itself in mass demonstrations. These two forms of expression—equally devastating to the workers' and peasants' state—had an important qualitative difference. While the two groups were not entirely mutually exclusive, by and large the emigrants wanted to escape the GDR while the demonstrators wanted to change it. The main chant of earlier demonstrations had been "we want out!" Now the chants became "we are the people" and "we're staying here!"

The SED tried new travel and emigration regulations to appease the crowds, but they were too similar to existing rules. Local party offices were flooded with complaints. In numerous demonstrations, GDR protesters let the SED know what they really wanted.[103] Signs carried at an East Berlin protest illustrated sentiments felt across the country: "Here's for putting graffiti on both sides of the wall," "All the way to Hawaii without any visa," and "Passports for everyone—marching orders for the SED," they proclaimed.[104]

The consequences of failing to meet those expectations were not hard to guess: even more flight to the West and increased domestic instability.[105] The country could hardly take more of either. Belatedly, East German leaders had realized that their month-old sealing of all GDR borders had caused an intolerable escalation of tension and frustration within the country, as shown in the increasing number of participants in street demonstrations.[106] The Politburo hoped that a new safety valve to Czechoslovakia might defuse the anger and thus allowed travel there to resume. Czech leaders, fearful of the spectacle of East Germans again roaming Prague's streets, immediately announced that GDR citizens would be permitted to exit from Czechoslovakia directly into the West. Between November 1 and 7, over thirty-seven thousand East Germans left by this route; the rate sometimes reached three hundred per hour.[107] And despite this new escape route, the protests in the GDR continued to increase in number.

The beginning of the end came when the SED decided to issue further "new" travel regulations, but ones that still included extensive fine print of the kind that had always prevented foreign travel. Notionally, East Germans had the right to leave the GDR, since their country's constitution said as much. Yet "national security" exceptions—still in place in the regulations—had always stopped the exercise of that right.

The "new" travel regulations with their fine print received approval from the distracted party leaders on November 9.[108] The top leadership was busy processing

35

other problems, such as learning that it was bankrupt. On becoming head of the SED, Krenz had asked for an honest assessment of the GDR's economic health (as opposed to the rosy reports that had been given to Honecker). He discovered that the GDR was "dependent to the greatest possible extent on capitalistic credit."[109] Gorbachev was horrified when he was informed of this, since East Germany was the Soviet Union's largest trading partner.[110] He had assumed that East Germany was much healthier than that, and he was not alone. As late as 1987 the CIA, making a significant mistake, stated in its *Factbook* that the East German gross domestic product per capita was $100 *higher* than that of West Germany.[111]

The bad economic news distracted party leaders from the travel regulations—including, importantly, from the fact that the wording of the most recent alterations was getting confusing as it passed through the hands of various authors. These alterations were not meant to end all restrictions, although they were beginning to sound that way. Yet the point that no one, at any stage in the alteration process, discussed such seemingly fundamental issues as consulting the Soviets about opening the border, or assigning extra border guards to duty to handle the increased traffic, or even telling border guards anything at all, showed that free travel was not the planned outcome. Gorbachev would later be amazed that the East Germans had opened the wall without consulting him; the deputy Soviet ambassador in East Berlin thought that the entire GDR leadership had gone mad; in reality, no one told the Soviets it would happen because they did not know themselves.[112] Nor did anyone comment on the wisdom of opening the wall without getting compensation from the West for it, or doing so on the anniversary of Kristallnacht, a Nazi attack on Jews and synagogues. In short, there were no signs that anyone realized that the new regulations were going to detonate under the wall on the evening of November 9.[113]

That evening at 6:00 p.m., a member of the East German Politburo who also served as its media spokesman, Günter Schabowski, was scheduled to hold a press conference. Shortly before the press conference began, he received a piece of paper with an update on the latest travel law alterations and the suggestion that he mention them publicly. Schabowski had not been present at any of the discussions about these "new" regulations and did not have time to read them. He decided to remark on them in passing toward the end.

Schabowski got around to the regulations only in the fifty-fifth minute of an otherwise uninteresting hour-long press conference. It was so uninteresting that U.S. anchorman Tom Brokaw, who was present at the conference, remembered that he was "bored" by it. Then, just as it was about to end, a journalist's question about travel seemed to spur Schabowski's memory. He tried to summarize the new regulations in a wordy and confused fashion in response. A number of incomplete sentences trailed off incoherently. Sprinkled among his long-winded phrases, however—"Anyway, today, as far as I know, a decision has been made, it is a recommendation of the Politburo that has been taken up, that one should from the draft of a travel law, take out a passage"—were unclear but exciting snippets like "leaving the GDR," "possible for every citizen," and "exit via border crossings."

Schabowski was surprised to see that every journalist in the room suddenly wanted to ask questions. "When does that go into force?" shouted one. "Excuse me?" Schabowski replied, puzzled. "Immediately?" shouted another. The press spokesman, irritated, started flipping through the papers in front of him in search of an answer. The question was insistently repeated: "When does that go into force?" Visibly rattled, and mumbling to himself for a while as he tried to concentrate on the papers on his desk, Schabowski uttered the phrase "immediately, right away."

Brokaw remembered that it almost felt as if "a signal had come from outer space and electrified the room." The commotion intensified. Some journalists rushed out to file reports, not waiting for Schabowski to finish. A number of questions were called out all at once, among them, "What will happen to the Berlin Wall now?" Alarmed about what was unfolding, Schabowski answered with obvious relief: "It is 7:00 p.m. This is the last question." Evasively, he concluded the press conference by responding to the wall question as follows: "The question of travel, of the permeability therefore of the wall from our side, does not yet answer, exclusively, the question of the meaning, of this, let me say it this way, fortified border of the GDR." After this vague reply, he tried another approach. "We have always said that in that case, there are many other factors that must be taken into consideration." Furthermore, "the debate over these questions could be positively influenced if the Federal Republic and if NATO would commit themselves to and carry out disarmament."[114]

As it was doubtful that NATO would disarm itself by breakfast, it is clear that Schabowski did not expect much to happen that night. His attempt to pour cold water on the speculation about the wall came too late, though, because a number of journalists had already left the room to spread the news they thought they had heard. And Schabowski himself left matters hanging when, true to his word, he ended the press conference fifty-four seconds after 7:00 p.m. He did not allow even a full minute of clarification. Little did he know that he had just lit the fuse on an explosive.[115]

Map 1.3. Divided Germany

TELEVISION TRANSFORMS REALITY

If the rising self-confidence of the East German population was the fourth major development in summer and fall 1989, the intersection of this confidence with the impact of mass media was the crucial fifth and final one.[116] Television in particular played a special role. Of course, television broadcasters had had an enormous impact on international politics throughout much of the Cold War. In 1989, however, they were clearly causal factors in bringing down the wall, a new height of significance.

The zenith of their influence was November 9. Schabowski's mumbled comments suggested that travel rules had been liberalized. But the wall was not yet open; that would only emerge as a result of a combustible mixture—namely, overly optimistic reporting combined with the willingness and desire of the newly self-confident East German population to believe in it and risk a trip to the border on the basis of it. If I can see it on television, it must be true, or at least true enough, ran the mantra of the evening. With no more than that belief as their defense, hopeful East Germans braved the armed border. How did media reports turn into reality on November 9?

Journalists, hating to miss the scoop of a lifetime, had rushed out of Schabowski's press conference at 7:00 p.m. and reported the most favorable possible interpretation: the Berlin Wall was open. The wire agencies, on which news organizations around the world relied for their own reporting, sent out this message loud and clear. Reuters was first, at 7:03 p.m., followed by the Deutsche Presse Agentur one minute later. Even as these messages were going out, Brokaw was conducting a prearranged interview with Schabowski. The two had agreed to speak right after the press conference, and now the American, believing that the Berlin Wall had just been opened, was determined to get an unequivocal statement to that effect out of the East German. Working through a translator, Brokaw tried to pin Schabowski down. Attempting to put words in the East German's mouth, Brokaw said, "It is possible for them [East Germans] to go through the wall." Schabowski, running on little sleep and unnerved by the fuss that the final minutes of his press conference seemed to be causing, cut the American off with a more cautious statement: "It is possible for them to go through the border." Since the laws of East Germany had always permitted its citizens the possibility of going across the border—though hardly anyone received permission to realize that possibility, of course—Schabowski was safe in putting it this way. But he would not be drawn into making a clear statement about the wall. However, when Brokaw subsequently uttered the phrase "freedom to travel," the translator said in English that Schabowski replied "yes, of course, it is no question of tourism. It is a permission of leaving the GDR."

Brokaw and his team decided they had enough, despite the strangely incomprehensible reply. Shortly thereafter, he and his crew headed to the lifeless and empty Brandenburg Gate, and broadcast a live bulletin back to the United States.

The anchor reported that East Germans "could now cross the wall." A local television team filmed Brokaw making this broadcast, so Germans on both sides of the border could see it as well.[117]

Because of the time difference to the United States, Brokaw's staff had hours to mull over the wire reports and the Schabowski interview footage before the "hit time," or start of broadcast, of the full *NBC Nightly News* program. The West German television channels did not have that luxury. One of them, ARD, had to decide what to broadcast from the 7:03 p.m. wire reports on its evening news show at 8:00 p.m. At first, the channel staff decided to take a relatively cautious approach, guessing that the wall "should become permeable." A long report on Kohl's arrival in Poland for a state visit, originally intended to be the lead story before the Schabowski press conference, dominated the program.

For the 10:30 p.m. news broadcast, though, the ARD staff decided to go big. The moderator, a man named Hanns Friedrichs who enjoyed the status that Walter Cronkite had in the United States, solemnly intoned at the opening of the show, "One has to be careful with superlatives . . . but this evening, we may risk using one." Then, forgetting the superlative altogether in his excitement, he proclaimed, "This ninth of November is a historic day. The GDR has announced that, starting immediately, its borders are open to everyone." Declaring that "the gates in the wall are wide open," the show cut live to Berlin. Breathless television viewers did not know what to expect.

They got some confused footage, and then one lonely and uncomfortable-looking correspondent, Robin Lautenbach, standing in front of the still-lifeless Brandenburg Gate and Berlin Wall. Although it had been three and a half hours since the end of the Schabowski press conference, the wall was devoid of crossers or celebrants. Lautenbach looked painfully aware that Friedrichs had just tossed him a hot potato. Berlin reality was failing to live up to media-fueled expectations. Lautenbach and the show did their best to fill time. The program cut to a prerecorded report about the wall. Then Lautenbach tried interviewing West Berliners who said they had heard that East Germans had gotten out. Next the show repeated footage of the press conference and finally even gave the sports report. After trying one last time to get some exciting news out of Berlin, the program essentially had to admit defeat, informing viewers that the big surge of people "has perhaps not yet happened."[118]

The journalists had gotten out ahead of reality. But reality was making a determined effort to catch up. An enormous number of East Germans had the ability to watch shows like this one and listen to radio reports, despite the fact that doing so was theoretically forbidden. Chernyaev remembers Kohl estimating that about

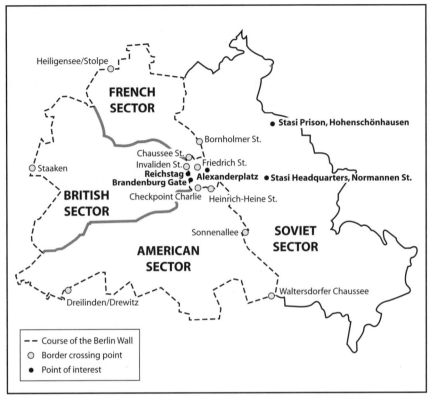

Map 1.4. West Berlin (American, British, and French Sectors) and East Berlin (Soviet Sector)

90 percent of East Germans watched West German television.[119] Western analysts speculated that the GDR regime tolerated this massive illegal viewing because it quieted protest against travel restrictions. East Germans could partake in a virtual "nightly emigration" to the West via their television sets every evening instead of actually trying to leave.[120]

Now, however, in the context of 1989, television was not a placating but rather a motivating factor. Viewing television coverage in the early evening and then seeing increasingly more confident announcements like that of Friedrichs later, East Germans became convinced that they could in fact cross the border. Some even rushed out while in pajamas or with children asleep in another room, since they only wanted to look at the West while it was possible, not leave for good.

The decades-long Cold War division of Germany ended shortly after 10:30 p.m. on the night of November 9 at the Bornholmer Street border crossing in East

Berlin. No prominent East or West German politicians were there. No representatives of the four occupying powers were present. Why did it happen there? Divided Berlin contained a number of crossing stations, but a constellation of factors made Bornholmer Street the hot spot. The buildings around the Heinrich-Heine Street crossing, for example, included a number of desirable new residences that had been given to members of the police or army. They would hardly storm the wall, and their neighbors would be more afraid to do so. The crossing at Friedrich Street train station catered to foreigners. But Bornholmer Street was not only in a central and accessible location, it was in a central location for the opposition. The percentage of those who failed to vote in the surrounding neighborhood (a sin in the eyes of the SED, which sought electoral participation as close to 100 percent as possible for its rigged elections) was higher there than elsewhere—a clear sign of rejection of the ruling regime.

Bornholmer Street border guard Harald Jäger had been on the job since 1964, and had never dreamed that what was about to happen was even possible. He was inside the station that night as usual, eating some dinner on the job and watching Schabowski's press conference on television, when what he heard just before 7:00 p.m. made him choke on his food. He was dumbfounded by Schabowski's remarks, and he was not alone.[121] After telling his fellow guards that Schabowski's words were "deranged bullshit," Jäger started calling around to find out if anyone knew what was going on. His superiors assured him that travel remained blocked as always. But by 7:30 p.m., Jäger and his team were busy trying to wave back would-be crossers, telling them that the border was not open. The guards received reinforcement when a police van with a loudspeaker pulled up and started announcing the same message, but the crowds kept growing. Jäger and his colleagues were armed and in theory could use deadly force. He and others had received an oral order not to shoot, however, presumably after the public condemnation of the shooting of Gueffroy. It seems that Gueffroy's unknowing legacy, the result of his death at age twenty, was the unwillingness of the East German border guards to use the deadly force available to them on November 9.[122]

An enormous crowd built up, and the situation grew increasingly ugly. The border guards were massively outnumbered, and police efforts to dispel them had failed utterly. This situation was repeating itself at other checkpoints as well; the guards at the Invaliden Street crossing called up armed reinforcements in the form of forty-five men armed with machine guns. But it was at Bornholmer Street that events came to a head soonest. After more phone calls, Jäger and his team started to let a trickle of people through, a few at a time, in the hopes of easing the pressure. They would check each person out individually, take names, and then penalize the rowdiest by refusing them reentry later. At about 9:00 p.m., his team started this process, putting stamps on the faces of the photos of those to be kept out. They managed to do this for an hour and a half, by which time the truly massive crowd was ominously chanting "open the gate, open the gate!"

By the time that the television anchorman Friedrichs was going on air at 10:30 p.m., the border guards at Bornholmer Street were realizing that their attempts to reduce the pressure by processing a few individuals at a time were simply not working. After debating among themselves, Jäger decided that the only course of action (other than mass violence) was to open the barriers, and he told his men to do so. A massive surge ensued. Later, Jäger's team would estimate that several thousand people pushed their way out within just thirty minutes. The division of Germany was over.

Had Lautenbach been standing in front of Bornholmer Street at that time rather than the Brandenburg Gate—which was admittedly photogenic, but lacked a border crossing—he would not have wanted for amazing pictures. Luck was instead with reporter Georg Mascolo and his cameraman Rainer März of Spiegel-TV, who took the pictures of a lifetime at the Bornholmer crossing. Their video footage would later appear around the world and feature prominently in documentaries such as the CNN history of the Cold War.[123]

Other crossings in Berlin and between East and West Germany proper opened in the course of the night in much the same way: individual guards, fearing crowds and unable to get clear instructions, decided to raise the traffic barriers.[124] And every opening meant more people flooding into the West in front of cameras, which meant more images beamed back to the East, which in turn sent more people out on to the streets to see for themselves; it became a self-reinforcing feedback loop. Stasi headquarters, in a rushed report prepared the next day, estimated that 68,000 East Germans crossed from East Berlin to West Berlin on foot, and another 9,700 cars had driven over. Of those, some 45,000 people and 5,200 vehicles had returned home by 4:00 a.m. on November 10.

By far the biggest single site of crossing was Bornholmer Street. Jäger and his colleagues estimated that 20,000 people had exited there. Optimistically, they also reported that all 20,000 had returned. The idea of keeping some out proved to be unworkable; those who had left children at home broke down in tears when told that they could not return. Jäger let them back in on his own authority. No questions were ever asked of him afterward.[125]

The scenes in East Berlin repeated themselves elsewhere in the country. A further 5,404 people and 2,192 vehicles crossed into the West from places elsewhere in the GDR; of those, only 1,099 people and 335 vehicles had returned by 4:00 a.m.

Fig. 1.4. The Bornholmer Street border crossing from East to West Berlin, in the early
hours of November 10, 1989. Courtesy of Bundesarchiv, Bild 183-1989-1110-
016. Photo by Jan Bauer.

The Stasi report found that the reason for the massive emigration was clear: the
impact of the mass media. As the report stated, it "was obvious that the decision
to travel can be traced back to the reports in Western media."[126] The Stasi had
often blamed behavior that it found objectionable on the instigation of the Western media; but the comments of those who came to the border that night suggest
that in this case it was accurate, if unintended.

In an enormous stroke of good luck for those crossing, nearly every person senior enough to make strategic decisions was locked in crisis meetings. The main
one was the East German Central Committee session, which was running well
over schedule, debating until 8:45 p.m. instead of its scheduled 6:00 p.m. ending.
In an era before cell phones and texting, this meant that the participants were cut
off from the news, and underlings on the outside were too timid to walk in and
interrupt. As a result, those who might have contemplated ordering bloody repri-
sals were uninformed and unaware.

On top of this, the senior military leadership had called for its own meeting to
start at 7:00 p.m., following on the expected 6:00 p.m. ending of the Central
Committee meeting, since senior officers had to attend that first. This scheduling
had the unintended consequence that military leaders who were too junior to be

members of the Central Committee assembled punctually in their own appointed conference room just before 7:00 p.m., missing the crucial final minutes of the press conference and sitting in ignorance for nearly three hours until their superiors finally broke free from the Central Committee and rushed to join them after 9:30 p.m., amazingly enough without getting any substantive updates en route. Presumably no one wanted to be the bearer of extremely bad news to the big bosses.[127]

The deputy minister for national defense, Manfred Grätz, would later recall sadly that "at this crucial time, we sat around a lot, we talked a lot, sometimes we talked uselessly, and the time slipped away." Although a few people were finally called to the phone during the late night military meeting, only after its midnight ending did most of the military leadership—those most capable of using massive, organized force to prevent a border opening—find out what was going on.[128]

Within the next three days, approximately 3 million GDR citizens visited West Berlin and West Germany. In a rearguard action, the ruling party at first tried to insist that would-be travelers procure visas. So strong were old habits in East Germany that despite the scenes of visaless travel on the night of November 9, over 5.2 million East Germans still sought and received such visas. Offices responsible for their distribution were overrun and could not distribute them fast enough.[129] Nor could the East German state supply what travelers really needed: Western currency. The "welcome money" that West Germany gave to all East Germans who made it over was hardly enough for an extended trip.[130] And not until November 12 was the practice of shooting persons trying to cross the border without visas—which had killed Gueffroy just nine months earlier—officially and fully repealed.[131]

CONCLUSION

By the night of November 9, these five developments had permanently altered the Cold War and produced a causal chain that resulted in the unintentional opening of the Berlin Wall. The first was the failure of Tiananmen to transfer into the European context; this failure revealed that a consensus for nonviolence had fully established itself in Europe.[132] The protests in China in spring and summer 1989, and the response of the Chinese party leaders, are still useful as a contrast, because they show that violence remained a real option for Communist leaders in 1989. Numerous signs suggested that the East German leader Honecker approved of this method and hoped to implement it. A combination of factors—the nonviolent behavior of the Leipzig protesters, the feeling among other Politburo members that they should follow Gorbachev's rather than Honecker's lead, and general chaos—meant that Honecker could not implement his bloody dream. But despite all the problems that the GDR had, it still could have used force in October 1989, and the consequences would have been unpredictable. Once it did not, once it was clear that there was a consensus for nonviolence among both rulers and ruled, the fall revolutions cemented their uniquely peaceful character.

Second, even as that consensus emerged, an older one was in question. The Cold War consensus on Europe—that it would remain divided but peaceful—no longer looked so settled in 1989.[133] East Europeans made it clear in the 1980s that they were no longer willing to live with this arrangement. And because of the conscious decision of the United States to step back and refrain from big initiatives in 1989, Gorbachev could make little headway. Thus, the initiative for change now came from the streets, particularly those in Hungary, Poland, and East Germany.

Third, even as East Europeans ceased to be willing to tolerate the status quo, the renewed U.S. preference for components of that status quo became plain. Leading NATO countries were aware of how hard fought the compromises involved in coalition diplomacy and action had been, and did not want to alter them lightly. Reagan's initiatives had had a number of detractors in NATO and his own vice president's office, and now Bush was in charge. This interest in slowing down the pace of change and sticking to what had been decided, most notably the maintenance of short-range nuclear weapons, clashed with the desires of European protesters both in the East and the West.

The fourth significant development was the rise in the self-confidence of East European protesters, and it was extremely steep in East Germany, which had previously had no counterpart of equal weight to Solidarity or even reform-minded Hungarian party leaders. Dissident leaders gained massive popular support over the course of 1989, and rulers saw their support fade as soon as they were subjected to popular assessment (whether via the ballot box, as in Poland, or the streets). The gap in living standards with the West along with the incompetent leadership that had produced that result had long been apparent, but in 1989 protesters decided to voice their anger.

When they did so, radio broadcasters and more importantly television cameras were there to record—and, remarkably, to shape—the powerful scenes that resulted. Throughout the fall, images televised in the West, but also received in the East, had their own impact on events. This mechanism was most apparent on the night of November 9, when East Germans demanded to cross the wall because they had heard on radio and television that they could.

The nature of this causal chain suggests that theorists of power and theorists of ideas need to pay attention to each other to understand what happened. On the one hand, some developments were based on old-fashioned realist calculations. The Bush administration chose to institute a pause in negotiating with the Soviet Union because it felt it could take advantage of declining Soviet power without making more concessions, despite the fact that the Soviet Union retained an edge in conventional forces and a vast nuclear arsenal.

On the other hand, some developments were ones of attitude rather than capability, of ideas rather than material abilities. The East German regime had the capability to suppress street protests with the use of military weaponry, just as the Chinese had done. Indeed, preparations were made to do just that in Leipzig in October. But like Gorbachev, Krenz and his followers were willing to believe that their long-term survival would be better ensured by a peaceful approach to protest. Similarly, the rising self-confidence of the protesters in Eastern Europe did not emerge after Soviet troops had left their countries; it emerged while they were still there. The Soviet Union retained the military ability to end protests in 1989, as it had done in 1953, 1956, and 1968. But East Europeans now knew that the USSR was unwilling to pay the bloody cost necessary to crush them, which represented a change of perception rather than of actual force structure. And in a clear example of the power of words, television and radio broadcasts may fairly be given credit for finally opening the Berlin Wall.

In short, in the course of 1989, half of Europe had come to the conclusion that it need not continue to live under nondemocratic regimes in the interest of maintaining the stability of the whole. Put differently, that half decided that it was not stuck with the receipt for deceit in perpetuity. Western Europe might have had a good Cold War, but Eastern Europeans most definitely had not, and they wanted fundamentally different life choices, now that the threat of violent repression was gone.[134] Change to the existing order, as in 1789, 1939, and 1949, was once again possible in 1989. The division of Germany had ended. Would peace or conflict follow? What new model of political and social order would emerge to replace one that had failed so comprehensively?

CHAPTER 2

RESTORING FOUR-POWER RIGHTS, REVIVING A CONFEDERATION IN 1989

At midday the Germans brought basins of turnip soup or loaves of bread and left you to shift for yourself for the day. First it was the reign of the knife . . . after all the knife is the knife, a simple principle of established order. However, that did not last three months . . . new delegates, designated who knows how, cut black bread in six slices to the nearest millimeter, under the penetrating stare of universal suffrage. A rare and instructive sight. I was witness to the birth of the social contract.
—François Mitterrand, reflecting on his wartime experience in a German prison camp

Freedom and chance are a question of the middle distance, a matter of how far away you are. Do you understand?
—from the bestselling German novel *Measuring the World,* 2005[1]

The East German street—meaning protesters old and new—had brought down the wall, with the help of the media. Most of the rest of the world had simply sat in front of a television set and watched in amazement. It was a good show; the contest between the power of the party and the power of the people played out on a grand scale. The end of the spectacle was the realization that the party and its Soviet backers were not willing to shed blood to maintain the Cold War order.[2] Clearly new models for order were needed, and five key actors would soon propose them. They would become the crucial players in the international politics of the unification of Germany.

Before looking in detail at these five and what they did after the wall opened, it is worth taking a moment to define the notion of "key actor."[3] This definition rests not so much on rank as on capability. At a time of revolutionary change, when norms and institutions were all called into question, the capacity for successful action became more important than any particular title, collective designation, or structural niche. At times the expected, traditional figures—heads of government and state, plus their aides—were more significant; but at other times the masses on the street dominated. What mattered most was the ability to achieve change in a desired direction, or put another way, to emerge as a leader in the struggle to define a new order. Moreover, there was a dynamic component as well; the same individuals were not always able, throughout the transition between November 1989 and October 1990, to maintain their leading roles, so the "mantle" of key actor passed often from one group to another.[4]

Chronologically, the five emerged in the following order: (1) The first was Kohl, together with his closest aides, but as distinct from the government of West Germany; distinct, because the chancellor often formulated policy in secret from the liberal Free Democratic Party (FDP), ostensibly his governing coalition partner. This practice was risky. Without the Liberals' support, and that of their leader, Foreign Minister Genscher, Kohl's government would fall; so the chancellor had to be careful not to push them past the breaking point. He understood this dynamic well, because it was how he had become chancellor in the first place. In 1982, Genscher and his party had deserted the previous left-of-center chancellor, Schmidt. They had shifted their support to Kohl. Despite knowing all of this, the chancellor would often daringly keep Genscher in the dark. It would be, however, too simplistic to say that Genscher was not a key actor. It was when he and Kohl worked together (as in July 1990) that they would accomplish the most. They did not always cooperate, though, and so it is best to maintain an awareness of Kohl as separate from the full coalition.

(2) The second key actor was a kind of twentieth-century constitutional convention, formed at the end of 1989. Leaders of the East German protest movement decided to create this new "round table" with the very forces that had repressed them in the past, in a bid to bridge old divides and act in a unified fashion to create an autonomous East Germany. Such a round table in Poland had helped bring Solidarity into a workable coalition government with the ruling regime, and the East German version initially commanded a great deal of attention, as it seemed like it might duplicate that success.

(3) The Americans realized that after intentionally disengaging for much of 1989, they needed to step forward. Bush, Baker, Scowcroft, and their aides, in close consultation with Manfred Wörner, the secretary general of NATO and a West German himself, began working closely with Kohl. A small dinner in December 1989 between Bush and Kohl personally, overshadowed at the time by the Malta Summit and the U.S. invasion of Panama, was crucial in starting this process. Cooperation between Washington and Bonn switched into high gear at the start of 1990.

(4) Next, Mitterrand, together with a few senior EC leaders, would come to play a critical role. He first had to consider alternatives and make his peace with the prospect of rapid German unity. However, this would happen in the early months of 1990.

(5) Finally, both Gorbachev and his inner circle, but also their high-level opponents in the party and military, were central to all developments. Although the Soviet Union was in a state of economic collapse, the already-mentioned fact that it maintained troops on the ground in East Germany meant that nothing could be finalized without its agreement. Such agreement emerged fitfully between February and September 1990.[5]

What immediate impact did the news about the opening of the wall have on each of these five actors?

ON THE NIGHT OF NOVEMBER 9

Kohl was getting the feeling that he was in the wrong place at the wrong time, and he did not like it. He had arrived in Warsaw earlier that day with an enormous delegation, including nearly all of his top aides, to great pomp and fanfare. They were there for what, by any standard, was a necessary event: an extended visit to Poland on the fiftieth anniversary of the Nazi attack in autumn 1939. Kohl's goal was to improve West German–Polish relations, now that members of the independent trade union Solidarity were out of prison and in government. But questions about East Germany kept coming up from the minute he landed, including in a conversation with the world-famous Solidarity leader Lech Wałęsa. Kohl and Wałęsa had started talking at 6:05 p.m., even as the 6:00 p.m. Schabowski press conference in East Berlin was just beginning. Wałęsa had surprised Kohl by asking what it would mean for Poland if the wall opened. Kohl had dismissed the idea outright, saying that the East German crowds were simply not that radical.[6] Wałęsa's instincts, though, were better than Kohl's; even as the chancellor took leave of Wałęsa and made his way to the opening banquet, he began getting word that Schabowski might have announced something big.

Now, at the elegant dinner, the head of Kohl's press office, Johnny Klein, was doing the unthinkable. Klein was coming to the chancellor at the banquet table and interrupting Kohl's conversation with the Polish prime minister, former Solidarity activist Tadeusz Mazowiecki. The excuse was that earlier reports of some kind of sensation at the Schabowski press conference seemed to be true. Around 9:00 p.m., Kohl excused himself from the table and called one of the few trusted aides left back in Bonn, his head of public relations, Eduard Ackermann, to ask what was going on. "Mr. Chancellor, as we speak the wall is falling!" his aide replied enthusiastically. "Ackermann, are you sure?" the chancellor demanded. The aide responded "yes," he was sure, because there were already crowds assembled on the eastern sides of border crossings, hoping to exit. Indeed, if he was rightly informed, a few had already made it out; presumably Ackermann was referring to the trickle out of Bornholmer Street that would soon turn into a wave. Kohl had to take Ackermann's word for it. Even in the West German embassy in Warsaw, it was not possible to get FRG television channels. Sitting inside Warsaw Pact territory, the chancellor had limited ability to send or receive sensitive communications. In other words, he was now certain that he was in the wrong place at the wrong time, and would have to do something about it.[7]

Kohl, born to a Catholic family in 1930 as the youngest of three children, had grown up admiring another Catholic politician: the first chancellor of West Germany, Konrad Adenauer. The younger man admired Adenauer's attempts to revive democracy after the disaster of the war, in which Kohl's older brother Walter had died at age nineteen. The young Helmut decided to become active in politics as early as possible, by joining the youth organization of the CDU and studying political history in college. He would eventually earn a PhD in history at the University of Heidelberg, with a dissertation on the formation of West German political parties after 1945. Kohl's studies in no way interfered with his political career; a shooting star within the CDU, Kohl was already governor of the state (or "Land") of Rheinland-Palatinate by 1969, before turning forty. Later, his talent for local and party politics proved to be a success on the national level as well. Kohl became chancellor of all of West Germany in 1982, after winning the support of the Liberals (as described above). He would eventually hold the position for sixteen years.[8]

In 1989, however, he was on the verge of what could potentially be the biggest crisis of his chancellorship. As a student of history, he was not about to make the same mistake that Adenauer had made. On the advice of the Western allies, Adenauer had not gone to Berlin in 1961 in the midst of his own major crisis, when the wall went up. The old man had been soundly criticized for staying away from the scene of the action, and Kohl did not want to face the same criticism. Tracking events as best he could after the formal banquet ended that night and into the wee hours of Friday, November 10, Kohl decided that he had to go back—not to divided Berlin, but rather to his seat of power in the West: Bonn.[9]

First, he had to find a way to extract himself from Poland without insulting his hosts. After a morning that retraced the footsteps of Brandt, the former chancellor who had fallen to his knees at the memorial to the Warsaw Ghetto victims on his own visit to the city, Kohl got more unsettling news. The mayor of West Berlin, Walter Momper, a member of Brandt's opposing Social Democratic Party of Germany (SPD), had organized the first major press event for 4:30 p.m. that very afternoon. It would be held at the Schöneberg Town Hall, or Rathaus, the location where President Kennedy had made his own pilgrimage to Berlin. Missing it would make Kohl and his party seem out of control. Kohl's close aide Teltschik, his most trusted adviser on foreign and security policy, thought that was precisely the point.

The chancellor called President Jaruzelski at noon and got his agreement to reschedule their talk, originally set for that afternoon. Kohl made similar arrangements with the rest of the Polish leadership, who were less than happy about it. The chancellor then had to deal with the fact that under still-binding occupation air traffic rules, a West German plane was not allowed to fly to West Berlin. To get there by air from Warsaw, a trip of 320 miles, the chancellor did what Cold War realities required. He asked the United States for help.[10] The U.S. Air Force agreed to have an American aircraft meet Kohl's in Hamburg and take his party to West Berlin. With a 2:30 p.m. departure from Poland, Kohl and his advisers just made it to the site of the event at 4:30 p.m.—only to find that the starting time had been pushed back.

For their efforts, they were greeted by boos from the hostile West Berlin crowd and worse news from the home team. The local branch of Kohl's party, the CDU, had organized yet another event for the same night. Kohl would obviously have to speak there as well afterward; the chance of getting back to Bonn any time soon, where he had access to support staff and secure communications with other world leaders, was dwindling. It was too much for the man who was supposed to be in charge, and instead had been scurrying from Warsaw to Hamburg to West Berlin on little notice. The chancellor exploded with rage and declared every member of his party in West Berlin to be incompetent.[11]

Going on stage, he in turn had to face another explosion of anger, this time from the audience. West Berlin was known for its vocal and active left-wing political organizations as well as its regional pride. Even if it had been a less dramatic moment, a left-wing West Berlin rally would not have been an event at which a conservative Catholic politician from the Rhineland—that is, Kohl—would be welcome. Now, with emotions running high, the crowd had no patience for him whatsoever. Having just applauded a hero of the Left—"Berlin will live and the wall will fall," the elderly Brandt had told the crowd, to great effect—the spectators wanted to show their opposition to the CDU by drowning out Kohl and driving him off the stage.

Ignoring their deafening catcalls, Kohl focused on the millions who would be watching on television, particularly in the East. "I would like to call out to everyone in the GDR: You are not alone! We stand at your side! We are and will remain one nation, and we belong together!"[12] It had been a long time since a leader of West Germany had spoken that way. Momper subsequently called Kohl's appearance an embarrassment. "He is stuck in yesterday's thinking," the mayor proclaimed. He had "apparently failed to comprehend that the people of the GDR are not interested in reunification, but rather in a free Europe with open borders."[13]

Indeed, there was some question as to whether the people of the FRG were interested in reunification. Pollsters in 1987 had found large majorities who said simultaneously that they favored unification in theory but had no particular expectation that it would ever happen. A West German identity, committed more to a multinational European vision than to the nationalistic and problematic German past, had established itself with younger generations. Momper and many others in his party, the SPD, were guessing that Kohl was falling afoul of that identity. Europe should matter more than the nation-state at the end of the twentieth century, they felt.[14]

They were not the only ones unhappy about Kohl's expressions of nationalism. While the rally was going on, Teltschik was called to the phone to take an ominous message from Gorbachev. Its gist, which was repeated to other Western leaders the same night, was that the events of that evening "could create a chaotic situation with unpredictable consequences."[15] Such a message did not bode well, and capped a deeply unsettled couple of days. In short, the experience of November 9–10 for Kohl was one fraught with disruption, uncertainty, and risk.

The hostility directed at Kohl contrasted with the joy experienced by the crowds that succeeded in crossing the border. Thousands poured into West Berlin and West Germany, to be met with hugs, kisses, tears, and champagne offered by complete strangers. Throughout, the mood remained peaceful and joyous. Yet not everyone on the streets of East Germany was pleased to hear about the opening of the wall. For a long time, the GDR protest movement had been a kind of bedraggled elite: a small group that would often lose members to the West when they were expelled. The numbers of protesters had swollen massively with the advent of new reinforcements in fall 1989.[16] But the opening of the wall exposed a fatal gap between the old and the new. Rather than fighting for a better socialism, would new protesters simply prefer to move West?

Claudia Rusch, eighteen years old when the wall opened, expressed this fear in a memoir that she wrote as an adult. Rusch was the daughter of outspoken dissidents. For her entire childhood, she thought that the word "cockroaches" meant the men who spied on her parents regularly. She was no fan of the East German ruling regime, even though she had not consciously chosen to be a dissident. "I didn't make the decision with my parents to go into opposition; I was born into it." But she was grateful for it. "I know exactly what kind of country I grew up in. No one can tell me that I don't know what I'm talking about."

She knew what she believed in: an independent East Germany. The opening of the wall signified the dwindling of that dream. "That was the end. . . . The wall was open and the path to Aldi [a West German discount store] was open. It was too early, it meant reunification."[17] Although she was only a child at the time that it happened, her sentiments echoed those of adult members of the dissident movement as well. They would soon begin to organize the round table in an effort to exert control over the future course of their own country.

As East Germans tried to understand what November 9 meant for their lives and their country, leaders in capitals around the world tried to understand what it meant for them as well. Not long before Kohl's press speaker interrupted his dinner in Warsaw, on the other side of the globe another aide—this time J. Stapleton Roy of the U.S. State Department—interrupted another meal, this time a luncheon. His boss, Baker, was hosting Philippine president Corazon Aquino. Roy slipped him a note. Baker read it aloud, raising his glass in tribute: "The East German Government has just announced that it is fully opening its borders to the West. The implication from the announcement is full freedom of travel via current East German/West German links between borders."[18]

Soon thereafter Baker began receiving pages of press reports from around the world. He wrote on top of them in thick black pen: "Something we've wanted for 40 yrs * Eur that's whole + free." This phrase—"A Europe whole and free"—had been the theme of a major address by Bush given in Mainz in May 1989.[19] His administration would repeat it often in the wake of the opening of the Berlin Wall, considering it a better idea than a "common European home" in which the Americans had no room.

In the following days Baker would speak multiple times with the U.S. ambassador in Bonn, Vernon Walters, who would continually assure him that the situation remained peaceful. The secretary also dealt with and approved a West German request to use U.S. military facilities to provide temporary housing to refugees, who were arriving at the rate of ten thousand per day. As all of this was going on, Baker made time to appear on a number of television shows, partly to counteract what commentators were calling a lackluster response from the president himself.[20] Lesley Stahl, interviewing President Bush on the *CBS Evening*

Fig. 2.1. President George Herbert Walker Bush, third from left, with his main advisers; from left to right, Chief of Staff John Sununu, Secretary of State James Baker, National Security Adviser Brent Scowcroft, Vice President Dan Quayle, Secretary of Defense Dick Cheney, Deputy NSC Adviser Robert Gates, Chairman of the Joint Chiefs of Staff Colin Powell, and Office of Management and Budget Director Richard Darman. Courtesy of Time and Life Pictures/Getty Images.

News on November 9, had been puzzled by his lack of jubilation. "You don't seem elated and I'm wondering if you're thinking of the problems," she asked. Bush responded, "I'm not an emotional guy, but I'm very pleased." He admitted that developments had caught him by surprise and said that he was determined not to create some kind of a backlash by acting in a triumphalist manner.[21] As Zelikow and Rice, both NSC staffers at the time, would explain in their own joint memoir later, this behavior was "characteristic of Bush . . . often well reasoned on substance but inattentive to the ceremonial dimension of the presidency."[22]

That same evening, Baker tried to be clearer, with mixed success. Speaking with Chris Wallace of ABC's *Primetime Live*, he pointed out "that it has been the policy of the NATO Alliance and it has been the policy of the United States of America to support reunification for over forty years." Wallace, unimpressed, responded: "That sounds like boilerplate." Baker countered: "That is our policy."

Wallace missed a key hint: Baker had spoken of NATO in his comment, and the organization would loom large in the coming months. For Washington, it would be at the heart of all that was to come. Soon, extending NATO over a unified

Germany would establish itself as the highest priority for Bonn and Washington, and finding the right way to react to this strategy would similarly become the most pressing item on the French and Soviet agendas.[23]

In light of the importance of NATO at this crucial time, President Bush was particularly pleased that its head was Wörner, a man with whom he enjoyed a warm friendship. In fact, Bush would later be one of the last people to speak to Wörner, only four days before the German's early death of cancer in 1994.[24] This personal connection meant that Bush was open to suggestions from and cooperation with Wörner—something that would prove critical in the process of reconciling NATO and German unification. It was also helpful that Wörner was a member of Kohl's party, the CDU, and therefore was trusted in Bonn.

Besides NATO, the other important international organization in Europe in 1989—the EC—had a rotating presidency, which was held by France in the second half of 1989, the two hundredth anniversary of its own revolution. Mitterrand therefore spoke not only as the president of France but also as the leader of the EC that November. And both he and Kohl were powerful presences within the EC regardless of whether their countries held the presidency or not.

On November 9, Mitterrand was as shocked as the rest of the world by what happened. He had (at Kohl's urging) expressly stated that he was not afraid of German unification at a press conference just six days earlier, but without knowing that it would become a real possibility so soon.[25] The French president was slow to develop his response to the opening of the wall, yet the unification process could not go forward without his response. Simply put, for German unification to be acceptable to its European neighbors, it had to take place in a way that was agreeable to both France and the EC. Mitterrand had long emphasized the essential nature of a European framework for any theoretical future German unification in his public remarks. He maintained that view even as unity became a lot more likely, but there still were many possible ways to construct such a framework. Forceful action by either France itself or the EC under its leadership could potentially slow the process of unifying Germany.

Indeed, if events developed in such a way that either France or the EC, or both, felt threatened, Mitterrand could potentially align a powerful constellation of European actors to block unification. No-holds-barred comments by senior European leaders to the effect that rapid unification was ruining the EC, circulated in an election year among a West German population that believed strongly in European unity and worried about paying for the needs of the East German population, could have made life difficult for Kohl.[26] As it was, Thatcher turned out to be the only one willing to make such take-no-prisoners comments in public, and her interest in the EC was limited. Others would confine themselves to private expressions, which did not have the same impact. Indeed, years later Scowcroft was still puzzled that the British, French, and Soviets did not manage to find any agreed strategy at the outset to slow the process down.[27] For all of these reasons, the role of France is crucial in understanding the events of 1989–90.[28]

One of the factors that complicated the response of France and many of Germany's other European neighbors, such as the Dutch, was the painful memory of the Second World War. The key Americans involved—Bush and Baker—had little in the way of personal experience with the Nazis. Bush, born in 1924, had served as a naval aviator in the Pacific theater during World War II. Baker, born in Houston in the same year as Kohl, 1930, had served in the Marines in 1952–54. Thatcher and Mitterrand, in contrast, had experienced the German onslaught throughout their youth and young adulthood. Thatcher, born in 1925, had vivid childhood and teenage memories of the war; Mitterrand's involvement with German aggression went much further.

Born in a provincial town in 1916 during World War I and in the armed services himself by 1938, he (unlike Thatcher) saw his home country become the subject of Nazi occupation. Even worse, Mitterrand became a German prisoner of war in 1940. Held captive in Kassel and Weimar, he learned hard lessons about "the reign of the knife" before succeeding, on his third attempt, in escape. Yet despite these experiences, he would return home and collaborate with the German-sponsored Vichy regime in southern France. In fact, Mitterrand would remain friendly throughout his life with Vichyites like Jean-Paul Martin and the infamous René Bousquet, who was facing trial for crimes against humanity when he was murdered in 1993.[29] Mitterrand would eventually come to oppose Vichy and work to aid other prisoner of war escapees, coordinating with General Charles de Gaulle by means of clandestine trips to London, and taking part in the parade celebrating de Gaulle's return to Paris on August 25, 1944. Later in life, Mitterrand would relive the more savory aspects of this wartime history with regular visits to sites associated with his escape; but an exposé about his Vichy connections put the unsavory elements back into the public view and caused a sensation in 1994. Even after his death in 1996, controversies would still rage over Mitterrand, and his personal history and achievements. There was no doubt, however, that Franco-German relations were a matter of great significance to him. During his presidency, reconciliation between France and West Germany was clearly his primary European concern. After leaving office, he went to his grave trying to finish writing a book titled *Of Germany and of France*.[30]

Fig. 2.2. President François Mitterrand of France and Prime Minister Margaret Thatcher of the United Kingdom, circa 1986. Courtesy of Getty Images.

This personal and emotional experience with Nazism was an attribute that Mitterrand shared with the Soviet leadership. The Soviet foreign minister, Shevardnadze, born in 1928, had lost his brother Akaky in the early days of the war. One statistic encapsulates the suffering inflicted on his generation: of the seven hundred thousand men called up from his home region of Georgia, only half would ever return. As Shevardnadze would write in his memoirs about 1989, "Even when we were forced to face facts by the pace of events, none of us dared to ignore the inborn wariness of our people about German unity." It grew out of "the memory of the two world wars unleashed by Germany, especially the last war, which cost our country 27 million lives." On some level, Shevardnadze found "it was useless to appeal to forgiveness. . . . The victors had become losers. When the heart is in such pain political rationality has little chance."[31] Dealing with Shevardnadze in 1990, Teltschik had the impression that it was harder for him than for Gorbachev to take a conciliatory line with the Germans, and that Shevardnadze's advisers (often holdovers from his predecessor, Andrei Gromyko) made matters worse.[32]

Gorbachev himself, born in the village of Privolnoye in the Stavropol region of southern Russia in 1931, had been too young to serve, but his hometown was occupied when he was a child. His village, it was rumored in January 1943, was scheduled to be the next target of mass executions that had been carried out elsewhere; but before that could happen, Soviet troops retook the city. "The battle front passed once more through our area, this time moving westwards," Gorbachev remembered later. Everything had been destroyed; "no machines were left, no cattle, no seeds. Spring came. We ploughed the land by hitching cows from our individual households. The picture is still fresh in my memory, the women crying and the sad eyes of the cows."[33]

As a result, in their conversations in the days and weeks immediately following November 9, Gorbachev, Mitterrand, and Shevardnadze would resort to Nazi metaphors to describe what was happening, as will be described below. These elements of their personal experience and background seem to have militated against the rapid formulation of policy in the early days, and meant that both were slow off the mark. While Mitterrand would eventually recover and get up to speed with Kohl, Gorbachev would never really do so.[34]

The problem was, of course, bigger than simply getting over bad memories. The Soviet leader had tolerated and encouraged reformers within Communist and Socialist parties, but the complete breakdown of order in divided Germany had not been part of his vision. It further endangered the existence of the Warsaw Pact and made the economic weakness of socialist states, including his own, undeniably plain. Gorbachev had an additional reason for anguish: as the leader of the Warsaw Pact, he reasonably expected to be informed of major decisions affecting it, such as the decision to open an armed border to an enemy state. Given that there was no decision to open the Berlin Wall, in hindsight it is clear why there was no information about it available to the Russian; but that was not apparent at the time. Moscow was thus upset that in its eyes, the party had only received updates on how the new travel regulations were progressing and not word of the headline news that the border would open.[35]

From the night of November 9 onward, Gorbachev and other Soviet leaders increasingly found themselves reacting to events rather than shaping them—an uncomfortable role. Chernyaev confided his thoughts to his diary: "The Berlin Wall has collapsed. . . . Only our best friends Castro, Ceaucescu, Kim Il Sung are still around—people who hate our guts," he wrote. On a more positive note, he concluded: "This is what Gorbachev has done. And he has indeed turned out to be a great leader. He has sensed the pace of history and helped history to find a natural channel."[36] Gorbachev would later admit in his memoirs: "I should be less than sincere if I said that I had foreseen the course of events and the problems the German question would eventually create for Soviet foreign policy."[37]

Mitterrand and Gorbachev, as shocked as they may have been about the wall opening, at least had some leverage over the process and would belong to the group of key actors shaping events in the future. The experience of November 9 was even more frustrating for those who would largely remain spectators, such as the governments of Poland and Great Britain. In summer 1989, Solidarity was ascendant. Its indispensable ally, Polish-born Pope John Paul II, continued to dominate the Vatican, and Mazowiecki was in charge at home. Bronislaw Geremek, a Warsaw Ghetto survivor, Solidarity supporter, and future foreign minister, put the feeling into words: "The winds of history have normally blown against us Poles. Finally they are blowing in our direction." Solidarity's success seemed likely to earn an extraordinary amount of West German economic and financial aid for Poland. It had caused Kohl to agree to the five-day state visit that started on November 9. Nor was the trip meant to be an empty show; in conversations with Bush around the time, Kohl repeatedly stressed the need for the West to help Poland. Even when the two leaders spoke on November 10, the day after the wall opened, Kohl talked so much about Warsaw that Bush finally had to say pointedly that he had no further questions about Poland and wanted to talk about Berlin instead.[38]

Kohl's interest in helping reforms in Warsaw was partly to incentivize the same in the GDR. But when the border was suddenly open and the easterners in need of aid were now Germans, Polish leaders realized immediately that they had lost priority. Even as Kohl was preoccupied with how to get back to West Berlin in time for the public rally, Mazowiecki and his finance minister tried to get as much of the chancellor's attention as they could, and presented a long list of requests for aid from Germany. They expressed their hope that this aid would come in the form of a gift.[39] With the begging bowl clearly out, they had little leverage and enormous worries that the eastern border of a united Germany might creep closer to Warsaw. Some West German legal scholars felt that despite all the various accords that had been signed since World War II, the border status remained an open question in juridical terms.[40]

In short, the Poles had a weak hand, but would play it well, focusing on one strong card: world sympathy for Poland. Mazowiecki and others would use press conferences, public forums, their contacts in the United States, and every possible venue to make it clear that they viewed the 1989–90 period as a time when West Germany's status as a trustworthy democratic state needed proving. "I am of the opinion that [in] this historic hour . . . the value of all kinds of words and declarations about the readiness to reconciliation will be tested," Mazowiecki would remark publicly.[41]

Similarly, Thatcher was in an awkward position. In her case it was partly by default and partly by her own choice. With British forces based inside West Germany, she had no choice but to be involved. With British memories of two twentieth-century wars with Germany, and (as already mentioned) her own personal childhood memories of World War II, Thatcher had no choice but to be concerned. But perpetually at odds with the EC, in deepening political trouble at home (she would have to turn over Number 10 Downing Street to John Major before the end of 1990) and soon to be at odds with both Washington and NATO leadership, she had trouble finding like-minded souls who agreed with her strong desire to resist rapid change in divided Germany. She could no longer rely on her relationship with Reagan as a means of influencing foreign policy, since he was out of office and her connection to Bush was not nearly as strong.[42] Mitterrand would have been her most likely possible coconspirator; over the years she had found a rapport with him, despite their party differences. Indeed, Mitterrand had once approvingly commented that he liked Thatcher because she had the eyes of Caligula and the mouth of Marilyn Monroe.[43] The Frenchman's habit of auditioning several different strategies before deciding on one often gave various conversation partners the sense that he agreed with them, and Thatcher thought that he might. Her foreign secretary apparently tried to caution her that this might not be the case, but to no avail.[44]

Another potential ally for Thatcher was the man who was still nominally NATO's main enemy: Gorbachev. Already in September 1989 (as described in the previous chapter) Thatcher had tried to stiffen his spine with regard to divided Germany by telling him, off the record, that no one in NATO wanted unification. In the months to come, she would continue to appeal to Mitterrand and Gorbachev, and world opinion, in her hopes of slowing down the process.

WHAT NEXT?

As these key actors and the rest of the world experienced the night of November 9 and tried to comprehend the new reality, the biggest question was obviously, what next? It was clear that the Cold War order was crumbling, and that piece-meal changes would no longer be enough. As the financial newspaper *Handels-blatt* put it, "The politics of taking small steps . . . is over."[45] The Cold War order was in rubble. But what new political and social order would follow?

The first two answers to this question to emerge were short-lived, but highly significant: the Soviet idea of restoring four-power control and the West German concept of reviving a confederation. Both of these were backward-looking solutions, yet with a difference. Restoration meant reinstating quadripartite control exactly as it had been in 1945, with subsequent alterations stripped away; accordingly, the issues of 1945—reparations and borders—would become major ones. Revivalism, on the other hand, was the more feasible process of adapting and modernizing an older structure to make it suitable for use once again. Both the restoration and revival models would become public, garner adherents, and dominate headlines—and then suddenly become obsolete, when events and second thoughts overtook them.

None of this was immediately apparent late on the night of November 10, when Kohl finally returned to his office in Bonn after the West Berlin rallies. Although he had only that night and the morning of November 11, a Saturday, it was enough to get an overview of the situation from his staff before heading back to Poland. He attempted to reach all of the four powers, and managed to speak to Thatcher and Bush in the final hours of November 10.[46] Both conversations included lengthy discussions of Polish needs in addition to talk about the wall. Kohl also spoke to Mitterrand (whom he somewhat less than believably assured that "the process is evolutionary, not revolutionary"), Krenz, and Gorbachev. To the latter, Kohl emphasized the need to speak to each other "without dramatic accents" in their dialogue. Presumably this was to signal that the phone message of the night before had gone too far in that direction for Kohl's taste.[47]

Crucially, he got an assessment of the situation from experts whom he trusted, whether in person, on the phone, or through quickly prepared reports and telegrams. He assembled his closest aides for a Saturday morning meeting: Ackermann, Klein, and Teltschik, of course, but also his trusted personal assistant Juliane Weber, who had been with him for twenty-five years, along with the head of the chancellery, Rudolf Seiters, and a few others.[48]

Kohl also received even more surprising information, if that were possible, from East Berlin. Bertele informed the chancellor that the most significant event in divided Germany since the war had been a mistake. Border guards had been clueless and had no instructions. Sources within the East German government suggested that it might still try to reverse what had happened. Western media reports that the borders were open had been exaggerations. Bertele was right; the border was still, in the eyes of the SED, theoretically a deadly no-go zone. Starting at 3:00 a.m. on November 10, East German border guards forcibly cleared the area between the wall and the Brandenburg Gate. They continued using water cannons as late as November 11 to drive people off the wall itself. Guards at Invaliden Street, where armed support had been called up on the night of the ninth, successfully reinstated border controls by dawn on the tenth. More ominously, a motorized division with air support, trained in urban warfare, had been placed on alert for deployment in East Berlin following the opening of the wall, although in the end it had not left its base. The incompetence at the top would become increasingly apparent in the days to follow. Reports to Bonn indicated a growing sense that no one was in charge and the emergence of a "save yourself if you can" mentality. And Kohl's finance minister, Theo Waigel, gave the chancellor a quick estimate of how much this was all costing. Bonn was already subsidizing East Berlin, but now it had the added burden of supporting the large number of refugees in the West.[49]

As a result, while traveling back to Poland later on that Saturday, Kohl could mull over two salient facets of the recent developments. The first was that they were not planned, and therefore even more chaotic than they already seemed; and the second was that West Germany was going to spend a lot of money on the problem, one way or another. An out-of-control, expensive problem is particularly unwelcome in an election year, and Kohl, who had often been mischaracterized as slow-witted, was a savvy politician who understood this.

He knew that the focus of attention would turn from West German–Polish relations to events in divided Germany, and that he needed to wrap up matters in Poland in a way that would satisfy a variety of audiences. In an effort to do so, Kohl visited Auschwitz, but also insisted (despite the shortened schedule and adverse weather conditions) on traveling by bus on Sunday, November 12, to Silesia, a past source of much conflict between Poles and Germans. There, he and Mazowiecki jointly took part in a Catholic mass held on land that once belonged to Helmuth James Graf Moltke, who had been convicted of attempting to assassinate Hitler on July 20, 1944, and was executed in 1945.[50]

Kohl insisted on this visit because he wanted to strike the right balance between acknowledging the past while keeping open freedom to maneuver in the present.

He knew that irredentist issues would surely emerge and wanted to have leverage with such groups; taking the time to visit their old homeland would help him. Kohl also had to be alert not only to those West German voters (or their families) who had been expelled from their homes in now-Polish territory in the wake of the Nazi defeat, however, but also the sizable number of voters who were far more concerned about good relations with all European neighbors, East and West, than any lost territory.

The chancellor also wanted to forestall fresh talk about a peace treaty for World War II, which would raise the unhappy issue of reparations. It was a tricky situation for an elected politician, and yielded some benefits for the Poles. The Polish trip culminated with a joint statement on November 14, in which West Germany agreed to forgive extensive Polish debts dating back to 1975, along with other measures.[51] But as the coming weeks would show, it would not be enough to assuage Polish anxieties, especially after Kohl subsequently failed to convince Bush to provide $250 million in credit to Warsaw.[52]

Kohl had to assuage anxieties on his Western borders as well. Mitterrand called for a short-notice dinner in Paris on Saturday, November 18. Sitting around the table would be just the leaders of the twelve EC member states. The aides would be at a separate dinner, presided over by Mitterrand's foreign policy adviser Jacques Attali. Clearly, the "grown-ups" were going to speak their minds plainly in advance of the end-of-year EC summit.[53]

Dinner proceeded without serious incident, but according to both Kohl and Attali (presumably informed by Mitterrand afterward), Thatcher made her move over dessert. As a summary written the next day by her private secretary Charles Powell noted, the prime minister made it clear that there could be "no question of changing Europe's borders, which had been confirmed in the Helsinki Final Act. Any attempt to raise this or the issue of reunification would risk undermining Mr. Gorbachev's position . . . [and] open a Pandora's box of border claims right through Central Europe." Kohl replied by pointing out that NATO had in fact endorsed German reunification at a summit in 1970. Thatcher, according to Kohl, snapped that this endorsement happened then because nobody believed it would ever take place; Kohl responded that be that as it may, the NATO decision still stood. His reply angered Thatcher so much, he remembered, that she started stamping her feet in fury. Kohl was on some level grateful to know where he stood: "The Iron Lady wanted to keep the status quo." He also observed that Mitterrand seemed to approve of Thatcher's remarks.[54] The EC—or at least its most powerful members—were going to demand something in return for tolerating Kohl's talk of a united German nation.

Kohl realized that he would have to prove his commitment to European integration even more than he had already done. His first foray in doing so, at a special meeting of the European Parliament on November 22, became a kind of test. Kohl knew that it was crucial, after the tempestuous dinner in Paris, that the Franco-German motor appear to be running smoothly. He asked Mitterrand to appear jointly with him before the special session. As late as the day before, Mitterrand avoided agreeing. But when the time came, Mitterrand decided to stand with Kohl, and the event proved to be a success from the German point of view. The parliament, after hearing Kohl speak, passed a resolution saying that the East Germans had the right "to be part of a united Germany."[55] For his part, Mitterrand justified the need for the special November 18 dinner, and asked for the EC to pay attention to the needs of those farther to the east than Berlin. "Has the Community answered the expectations of those who have faith in it? Has it really answered Mr. Mazowiecki's anguished appeal asking us not . . . to perpetuate the Europe of the poor and the Europe of the rich?"[56]

THE FOUR (OCCUPYING?) POWERS

Even as Kohl tried to assess the situation, the four countries with troops in divided Germany—Britain, France, the United States, and the Soviet Union—tried to do the same. In 1945 they had collectively become the highest ruling authorities in defeated Nazi Germany, which had surrendered unconditionally, and had begun occupying the country. Yet modifications to quadripartite rule had emerged in the following decades. Western occupation zones merged and formed the FRG in 1949, while the Soviet zone became the GDR in the same year. The three Western powers, seeking a united front against the Soviet threat, subsequently acknowledged de jure what had already happened de facto—namely, that Bonn had regained some ruling authority in the West. In particular, an October 1954 treaty allowed West Germany to become a member of NATO in May 1955, thereby making it much more a partner and much less an occupied subordinate. Still, important limitations remained, especially with regard to West Berlin. The four allies retained a large military and political presence there in particular, controlling among other things all air routes into the city; as mentioned, this prevented Kohl from flying nonstop on November 10. Meanwhile, East Germany and the Soviet Union also technically became allies in the Warsaw Pact, but the GDR remained subordinate to the USSR.[57]

In summary, the original four-power rights still existed in 1989, albeit in modified form. A shared quadripartite interest in preventing nationalist developments in Germany from threatening international stability and security survived as well. But it had been quite a while since there had been any "quadripartitism"—that is, occupiers exercising those rights over the heads of the Germans. The fact that the occupied had regained some authority (much more so in the West than in the East) and that new military alliances had appeared (a much more voluntary one in the West than in the East) had added layers of complexity to the situation.

In the wake of events calling the post–World War II reality into question, Moscow's initial instinct was to strip away those layers and revert back to the legal situation as it existed on day one of the occupation. Gorbachev and his advisers wanted to restore quadripartitism. This goal of restoration would culminate in an old-fashioned, four-power-only meeting on December 11, in the very same building used in the 1940s.[58] The West Germans would be aghast to discover that despite all the various treaties and declarations of the 1950s, 1960s, and 1970s, the three Western powers were still willing in 1989 to sit down with just Moscow. Making sure that the USSR did not duplicate the feat rapidly became one of Kohl's highest priorities.[59]

How, in detail, did the Soviet restoration model emerge? Gorbachev had proposed it as early as November 10. He contacted London, Paris, and Washington, saying that he had already informed his ambassador in divided Berlin to make the necessary initial preparations.[60] It was obvious to the first U.S. recipients of the message, Gates and Rice, that Gorbachev wanted a four-power meeting at an even higher level, and they let their boss, Scowcroft, know. But Bonn was able to fight off Gorbachev's November 10 initiative. After hearing from Gates and Rice, Scowcroft immediately called Teltschik in Bonn. Teltschik made it clear that the West Germans would have no patience with exhuming the moldy specter of four-power-only decision making.[61] The idea came to nothing in the short term as a result.[62]

But despite this stab in the heart, the specter refused to die. The four powers were in frequent contact in late November, so they were well aware of each other's concerns about the collapse of the wall. Bush was the most relaxed; the potential unification of Germany was not a sensitive issue for him. As he told *New York Times* journalist R. W. Apple, Jr., in October 1989 (acting on a request by Kohl that he make some public comment), the possibility of German unification did not worry him.[63] "I must confess I did not feel that strongly about whether we should push the matter," he commented in his memoirs later. Remarkably, he even said that if "the NSC or State Department had argued it was a bad idea, I certainly would have been receptive." Yet because "I was not afraid of reunification, I probably set a different tone for the Administration on the issue than it might otherwise have had." Bush did, indeed, set the tone, through a series of steps that indicated that he would let Kohl take the initiative. As Scowcroft recalls, "President Bush was the first in the administration to back reunification unequivocally." The key event was a dinner in Laeken, Belgium, in December 1990, as will be described below.[64]

In contrast to Bush, Thatcher had a firm opinion from the outset. Already upset by arms control initiatives begun under Reagan, she was not about to let the status quo dissolve further if she could do anything about it, and worked hard at getting this message out. CBS News aired footage of the British prime minister on November 10 saying "I think they're going much too fast, much too fast." On November 11, she and Baker, according to his notes, agreed "that immediate contacts among Four Powers in Berlin are approp[riate] + should be held w/out delay."[65] In a speech in London's Guildhall on November 13, scrutinized by the U.S. National Security Council, she painted a dramatic picture of the dangers of change: "We must remember that times of great change are times of great uncertainty and even danger."[66] The Iron Lady also had a private message sent to Gorbachev, saying "I agree with you that the speed with which these changes are taking place carries its own risks of instability."[67] And she took full advantage of an invitation to vent her feelings to Bush face-to-face at Camp David on November 24. The president said that he "was looking forward to the two of them putting their feet up at Camp David for a really good talk," and that was what he got.[68] Thatcher informed Bush that "there had been a consensus at the meeting of EC Heads of Government in Paris on 18 November that the issue of borders should not be raised." Instead, the "first and overriding objective should be to see genuine democracy established throughout Eastern Europe and eventually the Soviet Union." The implicit imperative was that unification would only take place *after* democratic regimes had emerged east of the iron curtain. She added that "reunification was not just a matter of self-determination: the Four Powers had certain responsibilities." Thatcher emphasized the risks of rash action; should "Gorbachev be toppled" then "our larger vision of democracy in Eastern Europe [would] vanish."[69]

In Washington, Baker had lunch on Sunday, November 12, with the Soviet ambassador to the United States, even though it was a holiday weekend. The ambassador emphasized the concerns that Gorbachev had already expressed. Baker noted his reply in his file for that date: "We said we understand [the] imp[ortance] of keeping order."[70] At the top level, Bush and Gorbachev had already agreed to their first meeting, albeit a low-key one, in Malta at the start of December. Corresponding with Bush in advance, Gorbachev expressed his happiness at the timing of their meeting. "In the current critical period some particularly sensitive problems have arisen in the world which require that big powers such as the Soviet Union and the United States give them special attention and show extraordinary caution," he wrote.[71]

Meanwhile, on the ground in divided Germany, the chief of staff for the Western Group of Forces of the Soviet Union contacted his peers in the U.S., British, and French forces to ask for their help in maintaining order.[72] On top of this, Gorbachev and Mitterrand spoke on the phone on November 14; according to Chernyaev, during the call Gorbachev expressed his satisfaction to Mitterrand that the Soviet Union and France had "a mutual understanding on this really cardinal issue." Mitterrand said that "the French position is as follows: We would like to avoid any kind of disruption. . . . I do not think that the issue of changing borders can realistically be raised now—at least up until a certain time."[73] As a result of these contacts and concerns, the notion of four-power collaboration refused to go away. It would reemerge after events on the ground and actions by Kohl meant that the United States could no longer resist the desire of its allies for such a meeting.

CANDY, FRUIT, AND SEX

Even as the head offices in capitals around the world buzzed with debate over what to do, the European streets continued to buzz with people. In the East, Czechoslovakia's Velvet Revolution began unfolding in late November, and unrest grew in Romania. In the GDR itself, the size of protest marches actually increased after the wall opened; the Monday marches in Leipzig went from tens of thousands to a quarter million strong.[74]

On the border to the West, people continued to flow over in a tidal wave. One million people crossed in the first few days alone. The mayor of West Berlin estimated that at any given time the population of his city was swollen by 200,000 or 300,000, stretching the capacity of the subways and infrastructure to its limits.[75] Nine million people, representing a majority of the GDR's population, crossed the borders in the first week. In the month of November, 130,000 decided to move to West Germany permanently.[76] The locations that distributed the previously mentioned "welcome money"—a practice of handing out a hundred DM gratis to each East German, with more for families, instituted when the number that made it over was orders of magnitude smaller—were overwhelmed.

Stores were swamped as well. A trend immediately became apparent that would continue to have an impact on unification: the lure of consumer goods.

Earlier in the century, after wars had ravaged all of Europe, deprived consumers had hungered for U.S. wares.[77] The iron curtain had largely cut the East off from high-quality American and Western goods. Now the East Germans, while not experiencing a war in the last decades, suddenly had their own opportunity to make up for that lack.

Shops overflowed and West Germany's normally strict closing hours were impossible to maintain. Candy and fruit proved to be especially popular—as did erotica, particularly that sold by sex shop entrepreneur Beate Uhse. She had long shown a flair for the dramatic, so she found the circumstances of 1989 congenial. Born in 1919 to a medical practitioner, Uhse had overcome all gender and other obstacles to her life's goal: learning how to fly. She married her instructor and followed him into military aviation after he was called up in 1939. Rising to the level of captain in the Luftwaffe, she at one point personally flew their young son out of danger. Uhse survived the war, but her husband did not. Afterward, as a young widow, she faced a different kind of fire. She endured numerous lawsuits charging her with promoting fornication because she sold birth control to women who wanted to avoid pregnancy in the terrible conditions after the defeat.[78] When better days dawned in the 1960s, Uhse branched out by launching a successful eponymous chain of adult stores.

After the wall came down, Uhse had a stroke of genius: her sex shops began giving away her glossy catalog for free. This proved to be a savvy move. Long lines formed outside her stores as a result, and she gained hordes of loyal new fans. An obituary published on September 10, 2001, estimated that she had attracted two million customers in former East Germany.[79]

Unlike Uhse, the West German stock market did not know how to react to the tidal wave of new consumers. At first, fueled by the promise of profits from all of those new buyers, it rose sharply. But it quickly gave up its gains because of increasing fears about what was to come.[80] It was becoming clear to Western leaders that the GDR economy could not survive in its present state.[81] What would happen when one of the most highly developed states in the world suddenly had to provide not only for new consumers but also for new infrastructure? How would East Germans survive their sudden exposure to market conditions? What would happen to the entitlements they had come to expect under socialism?[82] What would it cost the prosperous West? Was an avalanche of expenses about to overwhelm Western taxpayers?

Worry was not limited to the West. The ruling regime in East Germany watched in horror as people and power flowed away from it. Continuous upheaval in the leadership ranks ensured that no one effectively headed the party during its biggest crisis. Eventually a reform-minded party leader from Dresden, Hans Modrow, emerged as the standard-bearer. He broke with decades of practice by emphasizing his government titles rather than his party ones. In other words, rather than being known as a party secretary, he preferred to go by the title of minister president, a government rank, thus confirming the erosion in value of the SED.[83]

Meanwhile, the leaders of dissident and opposition groups bravely launched an attempt to fill the growing leadership void in the GDR. The most significant groups, working together with church leaders, decided that it was time to form a parallel body to the existing party and state structures. They sent out an invitation on November 24, 1989, calling for a Polish-style round table to begin—in other words, an ongoing meeting of both established and oppositional forces, as an interim means of ruling.[84]

THE PORTUGALOV PUSH

The ruling regime in East Berlin had fallen apart. The East German economy was melting down, and the end of the country's ability to pay its debts was in sight. Spontaneous alternatives to state authority were emerging. There was discord among fellow EC and NATO members over what it all meant. There was disagreement even within West Germany over whether Bonn should push for unification or not. Spontaneous joy at the border opening was giving way to second thoughts. The FRG's most prominent author, future Nobel laureate Günter Grass, raised the question of whether unity was morally permissible given the damage that the last iteration of a united Germany had inflicted on the world. West German philosopher Jürgen Habermas was also publicizing critiques of unification.[85] In short, there was no obvious way forward.

In the midst of these conditions, a catalyst appeared and produced the first clear West German model for order after the wall. Specifically, this catalyst walked into Teltschik's office on Tuesday, November 21, in the person of chain-smoking Nikolai Portugalov, a not particularly high-ranking adviser to the Central Committee of the Soviet Communist Party. Portugalov's sense of irony—he would excuse his habitual note taking by saying, "I must report precisely and correctly to my superiors at all times," while simultaneously rolling his eyes—appealed to Teltschik. Finding him to be a rather savvy character and appreciating his ability to speak German, Teltschik would seek out conversation with him on occasion as a source of information about Moscow. Given the dichotomous nature of Soviet leadership—there was a government, but it was the party hierarchy that really mattered—such party emissaries were an essential counterpoint to formal diplomatic contacts. And since government representatives would meet with their formal peers from the West German foreign ministry, headed by Teltschik's archival Genscher, meetings with Portugalov provided him with an independent means of gaining news from abroad.

Portugalov said that he had a message for Kohl and handed Teltschik some handwritten pages, apologizing for the haste with which they had been translated. Teltschik did not care about the wording or poor penmanship, because he was "electrified" by what he read on them. One of the papers insisted that the hour had come to free both "West and East Germany from the relicts of the past." It asked a "purely theoretical" leading question: Was West Germany preparing to talk about reunification or some kind of new unified entity? If so, then it was also time to talk about the procedures for exiting both NATO and the EC.

For its part, "the Soviet Union was already thinking about all possible alternatives with regard to the German question, even the unthinkable." The Soviet Union also wanted to know what West Germany would do about the need for a peace treaty. It might be willing to approve some kind of "German confederation" as long as Germans agreed that they would never again have foreign nuclear weapons on their soil.

Presumably to provide deniability, this sensational message carried the title "Unofficial Position." It was, however, accompanied by an "Official Position," which Portugalov assured Teltschik had the approval of both Chernyaev and Valentin Falin, the leading German expert within the party.[86] While not as breathtakingly blunt as the unofficial version, the official one nonetheless called for the construction of a new "all-European order of peace."[87]

Teltschik was astonished. If senior Soviet leaders were already, less than two weeks after the wall opened, thinking about the long-term consequences of German confederation or even unification, including an exit from NATO and the EC, then it was high time that Bonn started doing the same. Portugalov had given an enormous push to Teltschik and by extension Kohl.

What remains in dispute is the extent to which Portugalov's messages reflected the actual thinking in Moscow at the time. Portugalov did not explicitly claim that he had Gorbachev's approval, only that of Chernyaev and Falin. Both Chernyaev and Falin distanced themselves from Portugalov later; Chernyaev said that Portugalov presented himself and his messages as more important than they actually were.[88] There may also have been an unintentional misunderstanding due to the rushed translation. Zelikow and Rice think that this might have been a case of Teltschik hearing "selectively" what he wanted. Teltschik, though, maintains that he understood Portugalov perfectly well: the highest level in Moscow was coming up with potential models for order in Europe. The race was on to define the future. It was clear that Teltschik could present these messages to the chancellor as a catalyst for change as soon as the meeting ended.[89]

Teltschik could only catch Kohl briefly after Portugalov left, but Kohl agreed that decisive action was needed because "the unbelievable was starting to happen." Portugalov's memo seemed to fit well with a message that Bonn had received from Shevardnadze, suggesting that peaceful change was welcome. Kohl felt that he should try to talk to Gorbachev in person as soon as possible, and that in the meantime, Bonn needed to develop its own concept for the future.

By Thursday, November 23, just two days later, Kohl and Teltschik had agreed that the chancellor should announce a model for achieving German unity to the Bundestag as soon as possible. A small team set to work on drawing up blueprints for one. By Saturday afternoon, a "Ten-Point-Program" was ready; a driver took it to Kohl at his home in Ludwigshafen, where he discussed it with trusted hometown friends and his wife. Kohl decided that he would present it to the world that Tuesday, November 28, as part of the Bundestag's scheduled budget debate, which seemed like the earliest suitable opportunity.[90]

Like Gorbachev's initiative, Kohl's model reflected older political formations, but the goal of the latter model was to adapt, not restore. Kohl advocated revivalism, already defined as the adaptive reuse of a previous style—that is, taking an out-of-date model, but altering and updating it for modern conditions, thereby building something new with older roots.[91] The model he and his team chose to adapt (although they did not acknowledge it explicitly in public since references to the German past were always fraught with difficulty) was the concept of Germany as a national space with multiple states within it—in other words, a confederation. This idea had never disappeared from German political life. Brandt and his advisers had often talked of two states in one nation during their time in office in the 1960s and 1970s.[92] And viewed historically, the German-speaking peoples had existed as a loose national grouping of individually governed political units for a number of centuries. In the nineteenth century, particularly powerful regions—most notably Prussia—were much stronger than the loose grouping of the whole. Indeed, the existence of one unified German nation-state was actually a bit of an anomaly, a recent invention achieved by the wars and skills of Prussian Chancellor Otto von Bismarck in 1871. His success turned the King of Prussia into Emperor, or Kaiser, Wilhelm I. But Bismarck's empire, meant to last for the ages, would be disassembled just seventy-four years later at the end of Hitler's war, and Germany would return to a fractured state.[93]

To be sure, there would be differences between what Kohl wanted to do and what had come before. Instead of hundreds of principalities as in previous centuries, there would only be two, West and East Germany. Instead of using confederation as a rhetorical strategy, as Brandt had done, Kohl wanted to use it as a practical goal that would guide the construction of both tangible and intangible new confederative structures. Instead of seeing the confederative state as permanent, the ultimate goal would be unity. But the basic idea was the same: beneath an overarching sense of shared Germanic culture, identity, language, and nationality, there would be for some length of time discrete political entities with their own governments.

Kohl and his advisers envisioned this situation as lasting for quite a while, since at this point they thought that too rapid of a unification process would overwhelm West Germany. While the necessary confederative structures were under construction, the Ten-Point-Program would provide immediate aid to shore up the East German economy and stop the tide of refugees. All of this would take place in a manner consistent with the principles of the EC and the Conference on Security and Cooperation in Europe (CSCE), a convention signed by both superpowers and nearly all of Europe. "The future architecture of Germany must fit in the future pan-European architecture," stated the Ten-Point-Program clearly.

According to Teltschik, he and Kohl agreed that only an enormous streak of luck would make it possible to achieve these goals within a decade; they estimated that it would probably take much longer. Few observers at the time dared to disagree with them, although one particularly prescient U.S. State Department memo of December 14 concluded that events were pointing toward "rapid reunification" and that any kind of truly free government in the GDR "must have reunification as its first agenda item."[94] For Kohl and his aides, confederation was a serious proposal; they had no idea how quickly they themselves would choose to drop it.

Once the substance was set, Kohl and his chancellery advisers faced another important decision: whether or not to release information about the proposal in advance. Daringly, the chancellor decided to tell almost no one about it before inserting it in the Bundestag session, and then use the time-honored strategy of asking for forgiveness rather than permission. Other than Bush, no one—not his friend Mitterrand, and not even his coalition partner Genscher—would receive word before it happened.

According to Teltschik, this decision was the start of a pattern. He and Kohl agreed that they could and should make necessary decisions on their own, but one person always had to be informed: Bush. As a result, Washington was the only place to receive information before the Bundestag session (and Kohl also spoke

Fig. 2.3. Former West German security adviser Horst Teltschik in 2006. Courtesy of Joerg Koch.

to Bush for half an hour on the day after).[95] Writing in English, Kohl said that in 1989, just as in 1776, the highest goal was to ensure "life, liberty and the pursuit of happiness!"[96] It was a wise rhetorical choice, associating himself implicitly with a previous generation that had sought to create a new political order and succeeded.

Kohl's message arrived in Washington too close to the start of his speech for the English translation to be completed before he began speaking. In assessing his words afterward, Walters, the U.S. ambassador in Bonn, pointed out "the fact that he [Kohl] felt confident about springing this approach without prior consultation is further evidence of the greater political self-assurance of an FRG which is already widely recognized as a weighty economic power."[97] Nonetheless, Teltschik recalls, Bush and Scowcroft valued knowing how high they stood in Kohl's priorities. Kohl and his close aides would also soon be dealing more openly with their U.S. peers in the White House than with their colleagues in their own Foreign Ministry.[98]

The strategy of asking for forgiveness rather than permission reflected Kohl's need—indeed, the need of all heads of government facing crises beyond their borders—to balance between domestic and foreign politics. In light of what he thought he knew about Moscow's intentions, he felt that he had to put forth his own plans for Germany. He believed that he sensed what East Germans wanted to hear, and that he could sell it in a way that would be acceptable to West Germans. But the allies and his neighbors were not going to like it, so he decided to present them with a fait accompli in light of the ongoing chaos in East Germany.[99] And he was right. They were not happy.

In fact, Kohl did not even get through the announcement of the plan to the Bundestag without contest. When he explained that his offer of confederative structures was dependent on East Germany releasing all political prisoners, a member of the Green Party yelled sarcastically, "you're not so petty when you're dealing with Turkey!"[100] Moscow had other terms for Kohl's behavior besides petty. Speaking with the leader of Italy, Prime Minister Giulio Andreotti (who was himself not jubilant about the ten points), Gorbachev complained the next day that Kohl was "playing the vengeful note for the forthcoming elections."[101] His press spokesman, Gennady Gerasimov, told Western reporters that if Kohl had included an eleventh point—namely, a clear statement that Germany would not seek to restore its 1937 borders—then they would have thought more kindly of the program.[102]

And when Genscher visited Moscow a week later, even though—as Gorbachev was well aware—the foreign minister had had nothing to do with the

75

Ten-Point-Program, the general secretary and Shevardnadze aimed their frustration at him nonetheless. According to Chernyaev, who attended the meeting, Gorbachev called Kohl's actions "crude" and a violation of the sovereignty of East Germany. Shevardnadze suggested that Kohl was worse than a Nazi leader, saying that "even Hitler did not allow himself anything like that." Gorbachev concluded that Bonn had "prepared a funeral for the European processes" and that Kohl was now marching to music in his own head.[103] Genscher remembered this as the "unhappiest meeting" that he ever had with Gorbachev; the Soviet leader was so upset that it was, for the time being, simply not possible to discuss any important issues seriously.[104]

Teltschik prepared a summary report for his boss of world responses to the Ten-Point-Program. Mitterrand, understandably, was shocked to have been left in the dark. He had appeared with Kohl at the European Parliament, and the two had corresponded just one day before Kohl's Ten-Point-Program speech.[105] The French president had expressed support publicly, but added that the European peoples did not want to be confronted with decisions made in secret.

Teltschik personally defended Kohl on December 1 to *Le Monde*'s Bonn correspondent, Luc Rosenzweig. The West German pointed out to Rosenzweig, somewhat disingenuously, that Mitterrand would never ask Bonn for permission before making decisions on French national issues, so West Germany could hardly be expected to do so. But trying to make up for the affront, Teltschik spelled out what he really meant clearly. "The government of West Germany would now have to agree to practically any French initiative for Europe. If I were French, I would take advantage of that."[106] Unification would mean that France would get more or less whatever it wanted in the arena of European integration. In other words, the doors to rapid European integration opened in December 1989, allowing a clear view of Maastricht on the horizon. Such a view held little charm for Thatcher, who did not share the French goal of expanding EC authority and competencies. Rather, Teltschik reported to Kohl that the current status quo gave Britain "a guarantee of stability on the continent," and as a result any changes to it were frightening to the Brits.[107]

SPECTERS REVIVE

Bonn, or at least the chancellery, had now decided on a plan and a course of action. Kohl set about scheduling talks in East Germany to begin the construction of confederative structures. He agreed to meet the person now in charge of the GDR, Modrow, in Dresden in December. Given that Mitterrand still wanted to carry out a December 21, 1989, visit to East Germany that had been initiated years before, Kohl decided to travel east first, so the date of December 19 was booked.

But London, Moscow, Paris, and Washington were still struggling with their own models for the future. As Zelikow and Rice recount, within the Western alliance there was enormous tension over the various options. By late November, "the U.S. government and its key allies were avoiding an open clash over Germany only because they could all agree that they shared a short-term national interest in seeing political reform continue in the GDR."[108]

Bush and Gorbachev, meeting on ships in the exceptionally stormy seas around Malta on the weekend of December 2 and 3, made little headway on what to do about Germany. Bush went to Malta in a cautious frame of mind. He had received private advice from former President Richard Nixon that he found worthwhile and shared with Baker, Scowcroft, and others. Nixon argued that it had been "a mistake for Reagan to put his arm around Gorbachev physically and rhetorically in Red Square." The former president strongly advised Bush against doing the same in the Mediterranean. "For you to leave a similar impression after your meetings in Malta," cautioned Nixon, "would only add credence to the mistaken idea so emotionally being propounded by the prestigious Beltway media that because the wall is coming down, we have no differences with Gorbachev that can't be settled by a few friendly meetings and warm handshakes." Nixon maintained that Gorbachev's real goal was denuclearization, and "the withdrawal of all foreign troops from Western and Eastern Europe. This is, of course, simply the son of Reykjavik, when [sic] he got Reagan to agree to the elimination of all nuclear weapons within ten years." Nixon also thought that Bush should take a hard line and update the Monroe Doctrine, telling Gorbachev that "any sale of arms to a government in the Western Hemisphere which is unfriendly to the United States is simply unacceptable." Nixon's conclusion was as follows: "I would strongly urge that you indicate that you are *not* going to negotiate German reunification or the future of NATO with Gorbachev." Bush asked his advisers to discuss this "interesting thinking" with him as part of the preparation for Malta.[109]

Baker had received advice as well, in his case in-house from the man he had chosen to be his counselor at the State Department, Zoellick. Preparing Baker not only for Malta but also for the NATO summit that would immediately follow it, Zoellick wrote that the secretary's overall theme should be the need for a "New Atlanticism and a New Europe that reaches farther East." Yet the "architecture of the New Atlanticism and New Europe should not try to develop one overarching structure. Instead, it will *rely on a number of complementary institutions* that will be mutually reinforcing," including NATO, the CSCE, the WEU [West European Union], and the Council of Europe.[110]

According to both Baker's and Chernyaev's notes from the actual summit, their bosses neither made decisions on Germany nor talked much about it.[111] This was due in part to the cancellation of a number of events because of the extremely rough weather. It would eventually become too dangerous to move between the U.S. and Soviet ships in the rough seas, and crew members would end up enjoying lavish rations when VIP meals were canceled.

It was not just the weather that dampened events, though. There was also reluctance on the part of the Bush delegation to make big changes. In his opening statement, Bush echoed Nixon's letter, saying, "I do not propose that we negotiate here." Rather, according to Baker, the president suggested that they hear each other's opinions and then move forward "over a longer time-frame."[112] The focus was on troop reductions and arms control measures in both the nuclear and conventional realms. Gorbachev told Bush that under "no circumstances" would the Soviet Union "begin a war." Bush assured Gorbachev that the United States would avoid provocative actions with regard to questions of German unification. Both hoped that the Vienna talks, which would eventually yield the Conventional Forces in Europe (CFE) Treaty, would succeed. When Germany did come up, Bush said "we can't be asked to disapprove of reunification." Gorbachev did not push the matter.[113]

More important than the Malta summit was a meeting that took place immediately after, on the night of Sunday, December 3, 1989, in Laeken outside of Brussels. Bush went directly from Malta to Brussels for the NATO session starting there the next day. Kohl arrived early as well. The two met for dinner; it was their first face-to-face meeting since the wall had come down.[114] Bush would have been well within his rights to be displeased with Kohl. The West German had launched a major surprise initiative, with no consultation, just days before Bush had to meet not only the Soviet leader but all the heads of NATO. He thereby put Bush in the position of going to a number of meetings with major world leaders, all of whom would want to know Bush's opinion of Kohl's plan, without giving the U.S. president any chance to have input into it. Being required to discuss an unfamiliar proposal on short notice—one that he knew nothing about before it appeared, and had no role in creating—might be common tasking for a Washington subordinate, but not for a president. It clearly showed that the initiative came from Bonn, not Washington. And Bush had just endured a tiring summit meeting on ships in a storm. Kohl came to Laeken prepared to justify himself.[115]

Remarkably, far from being Kohl's comeuppance, the Laeken dinner became, in Scowcroft's words, a major "turning point." It was where Bush decided to give the strongest possible support to the chancellor's plans. Scowcroft, who was there, remembers watching it happen. Kohl's plans and vision deeply impressed the president, and after hearing them, Bush made remarks along the lines of, I'm with you, go for it. Scowcroft recalls his jaw dropping open as he saw the future of U.S. foreign policy take shape. Bush remarked afterward that he realized he trusted Kohl "not to lead the Germans down a special, separate path." Zelikow recalls that Bush was, at heart, a deeply emotional man who trusted his instincts. In Laeken, those instincts were telling him that Kohl was right.[116]

How did the chancellor win the U.S. president over? By giving him a convincing description of the problems on the ground and the solutions he wanted to apply. Bush listened sympathetically as Kohl explained that East Germany was in meltdown. "Can I tell you about what happened today in the GDR? Everyone has resigned." The extent of corruption among the leadership was just becoming known, and it was clear that a dangerous backlash was mounting. Scowcroft, hearing how fragile East Germany really was, would later wonder how the West had gotten it so wrong and been so worried about the Warsaw Pact.[117] Kohl continued, saying that "we cannot afford to pay 100 DM for each visitor anymore. It already amounts to 1.8 billion."

Then the chancellor began talking about the Ten-Point-Program and made sure to say "thank you for your calm reception of my ideas." The chancellor promised not to do anything "reckless." Bush asked about attitudes to the ten points in both East and West Germany. Kohl said that East Germans needed more time to figure out what they wanted; but in West Germany, his political opponents were already denouncing the plan simply because it was his. And they were not alone; Thatcher was "rather reticent." Bush interjected, "that is the understatement of the year." Kohl, agreeing, said he didn't understand why Thatcher was opposing unity instead of trying to get out in front of it. She should follow France's example. "Mitterrand is wise," Kohl continued, pointing out that the Frenchman knew how to find advantages in the process for his homeland. The two then discussed Gorbachev, and Kohl wanted to know if he had asked Bush for financial help. The president replied that no, Gorbachev was too proud to do so. In summary, their two-hour dinner conversation was wide-ranging and open. The effect that it had on Bush was apparent the next day, when his public comments at the NATO summit showed that he was strongly supportive of Kohl. Rather than echoing calls for caution, he said that it was time "to provide the architecture for continued change."[118]

Kohl's Ten-Point-Program had a polarizing effect. Even as it caused Bush to respect Kohl as a strong leader, the other three powers became more worried because of the way in which he had blindsided everyone with it, including members of his own government. By December 8, Gorbachev was confident enough of British and French anger about it to threaten to hold a quadripartite meeting once again. He had Shevardnadze send a message "to propose to the three powers' administration in West Berlin arranging [it] within the shortest possible time."[119] He also delivered a speech to his Central Committee the next day that was highly critical of Kohl; Bonn assumed that West Germans, and not the people in the room, were the intended audience. Gorbachev was right in his assessment of British and French views. On that same day, December 8, Mitterrand and Thatcher spoke privately. According to the British record of the conversation, Mitterrand explained that he was "very worried about Germany" and that "the time had come for action. He and the Prime Minister needed to consider what role might be played by the Four Powers." Thatcher agreed readily that the "Four Powers ought to meet soon" otherwise there "could be a total collapse of the system with increasing demands for reunification." If that were to happen, "all the fixed points in Europe would collapse: the NATO front-line: the structure of NATO and the Warsaw Pact: Mr. Gorbachev's hopes for reform." She found that "we must have a structure to stop this happening and the only one available was the Four Power arrangement." Mitterrand agreed, saying that he was particularly worried about Soviet troops in East Germany; if some kind of violence against them were to occur, "they would not doubt open fire." Given all of the dangers, he concurred in her view that a four-power meeting was necessary.[120]

Either unable or unwilling to prevent the resurrection of this idea of restoring quadripartitism, and fearing a rift with London and Paris, Washington finally went along. Baker conducted a number of conversations on December 9, trying at least to make sure that the scope of action would be limited. He got agreement that the meeting would discuss only Berlin. "Hurd + Genscher said OK to go ahead. . . . U.K. wants to do at Amb[assadorial] level to push FRG down a bit. . . . Have Ministers in Berlin meet + discuss only Berlin," read his handwritten notes from that day.[121]

The meeting took place in the very same Allied Control Commission building that had been used at the end of the war. Even the kind of language employed at the December 11 quadripartite meeting was extraordinary; the year could easily have been 1945. "Since we have emerged as the victors of the war, we have taken on the responsibility of providing for . . . a peaceful future," intoned the Soviet ambassador to East Germany, Vyacheslav Kochemasov. He then tried to open a long conversation about "the way in which the four powers" would address the present issues—that is, not including the Germanies. Kochemasov also called for the institution of regular ambassadorial meetings.[122] The U.S. participants (who had sent their proposed discussion topics to Bonn in advance, which was a break with previous four-power practice and an attempt to appease Kohl's chagrin about being excluded) tried to keep the content of the discussions focused on Berlin. But the significance of the meeting was that it happened at all, not its content.

THE RESTORATION AND REVIVAL MODELS FALL APART

Even as American representatives took part, they knew that this was the way back, not the way forward. U.S. Ambassador Walters was embarrassed. He called photos of the attendees gathering in front of the old Allied headquarters the worst of the year.[123] Added insult came from the fact that Baker himself carried out a trip to divided Berlin the day of the meeting and then gave a highly publicized press conference the next day, December 12. The combination of the four-power session, Baker's presence in the city at the same time, a surprise meeting with East German leaders, his remarks at the press conference, and the fact that Kohl had to come to West Berlin to breakfast with Baker (rather than receiving him in Bonn) all looked like Kohl receiving a reprimand. It is no surprise that, as Baker notes in his memoirs, Kohl was "irritated." The secretary's public comments had been meant to convey the need for "a new architecture for a new era," and a "New Europe and New Atlanticism." But what hit the headlines were his remarks that the United States was interested in a "stable" process and "that is the political signal that we want to give with our presence here today." Dan Rather, covering the event for CBS, called it "an unscheduled rescue mission for [the GDR's] Communist prime minister." Baker was the highest-ranking U.S. official ever to visit East Germany, and the timing of the visit looked like a clear signal. Press reports concluded that Baker had intended the trip as a slap in the face to Kohl's plans for change.[124]

The event was such a fiasco that Baker had to apologize in writing to Kohl: "Dear Helmut, I regret very much that comments I made during a press conference caused problems for you. I wanted to achieve exactly the opposite." He assured Kohl that "the furthest thing from my mind was to be critical. I hope that you know how much importance I assign to German-American relations, and particularly relations with you. With greatest respect and warm personal greetings, Jim."[125] After this disaster, it was clear to both Bonn and Washington that there should be no further quadripartite meetings; but some kind of mechanism needed to be devised that would at least pacify Gorbachev.

One would eventually emerge, but at this point only decisive, concerted action by the British, French, and Soviets could have preserved the restoration model. Such action was not unthinkable; old divisions were fading, and new bonds could have been forged at this point. The key player here, as at so many other junctures, was actually Mitterrand. Gorbachev and potentially Thatcher would have been willing to continue down the path of restoration. And the French president's state visit to the East German regime at the end of December showed that he was hardly averse to dealing with relics of the past.[126]

Mitterrand, who liked to speak in terms of what France wanted or needed, showed his choice of policy through his actions rather than words. That is, he liked to have several conceptual irons in the fire for a while before choosing one. Although he complained to Gorbachev on December 6 that Kohl was moving ahead too quickly, the French president was increasingly realizing that the smart move would be to accept Kohl's plan and see what percentage there was in it for France and the EC.[127] Already in October, Kohl had told the EC Commission President Jacques Delors that helping Mitterrand was one of his main priorities (presumably hoping Delors would pass it on).[128] And as Teltschik had told *Le Monde*, if Paris let Bonn take the initiative on *national* unification, then Bonn would agree to practically anything that France wanted in *European* integration.

This dynamic had already become apparent at the final major meeting of the French EC presidency, the European Council session in Strasbourg on December 8 and 9.[129] Kohl once again endured heavy attacks from Thatcher and other anxious European leaders. "I will never forget Thatcher's furious remarks," he wrote in his memoirs. "'Twice we've beaten the Germans! And now here they are again!' she said." Kohl estimated that of all of the EC leaders, only the Spaniard Felipe González and Irishman Charles Haughey (about to take over the EC presidency) had no reservations about his plans.[130]

But the chancellor sealed an important deal nonetheless. In exchange for a Council declaration that endorsed the desire of the German people to "regain its unity through free self-determination," and a tasking to the EC commission to prepare an EC strategy for unification, Kohl fulfilled Mitterrand's desire to make substantive progress on economic and monetary union within a year.[131] The basic decision for this union had already been made, but Kohl had wished to delay further specific plans for implementation until after he had survived West Germany's federal elections—which according to its electoral law, had to be held by January 1991—fearing that the idea of giving up the DM would inhibit his ability to get votes.

Now the need for French approval of his plans for Germany, however, was expediting the schedule. In advance of the Strasbourg meeting, Mitterrand had sent Kohl a letter making it clear that an intergovernmental conference had to happen in the second half of 1990—that is, before the next West German elections. Kohl's position had been that the date for such a conference should be set in 1990, not that it should actually take place, but it was not enough for the French president. Moreover, Mitterrand pointedly ignored Kohl's desire to have a discussion about expanded rights for the European Parliament before such a conference.

Analyzing this letter, the French expert on Kohl's chancellery staff, Joachim Bitterlich, concluded that Mitterrand saw Bonn's concern for the parliament as a mere diversionary tactic, meant to delay monetary union. It was of little interest to Mitterrand, not least because the French wanted to give the parliament only "symbolic powers." Bitterlich further concluded that Mitterrand was trying to send a personal message to Kohl: the chancellor's present level of engagement with and commitment to a realistic calendar for the implementation of monetary union "was not enough for him [Mitterrand]." Getting the project of economic and monetary union well under way was "*the* ultimate goal" for Mitterrand in his remaining time in office, concluded Bitterlich, and so he was pushing Kohl to make sure it happened.[132] In the end, Kohl agreed to call for the necessary intergovernmental congress before the end of 1990. On top of this, the French leader also succeeded in getting agreement to launch a "European Bank for Reconstruction and Development" and a "Stabilization Fund" for Poland.[133] Ultimately, however, these were not enormous concessions on the part of the West German chancellor. He would have preferred to postpone the conference longer, but fundamentally believed in monetary union, and now he was seeing a way that his preexisting commitment to European unity could help advance the cause of German unity. It might even help to win over skeptics within the FRG if they thought that European integration was the price of national unity.

Mitterrand, as a result, had within three days in December 1989 previewed his two main alternatives for dealing with the prospect of German unity: using either the quadripartite route, or the EC, in conjunction with a like-minded commission president, Delors.[134] The French president's subsequent actions show that he viewed the latter as the greater opportunity. By working within both the EC and the Franco-German bilateral relationship, Mitterrand could help to ensure stability and watch out for French interests during the transitions that were to come.[135] There was also a subtext to the project of monetary union—namely, whether West Germany would agree to it because of or despite its own economic self-interest.[136]

Fig. 2.4. West German Chancellor Helmut Kohl in Dresden, with East German Minister President Hans Modrow (foreground), December 19, 1989. Courtesy of Patrick Hertzog/AFP/Getty Images.

In comments kept secret even from members of his own government, Kohl told Baker that his support for rapid economic and monetary union was self-sacrificing. The chancellor had conceded on timing in Strasbourg even though it was "against German interests" and the president of the West German Federal Bank, or Bundesbank, was particularly opposed. But "the step had been important politically, because Germany needs friends." Simply put: "There cannot be any mistrust of us in Europe." He didn't mind if France got all the credit, but without his giving in, it would never have happened.[137] Kohl was presumably exaggerating for effect, but his past efforts to postpone specific steps toward monetary union before the next West German election showed the extent of his worry about whether voters would find it in their interest or not. Mitterrand was presumably not unaware of this subtext. Regardless of whether Kohl's remarks were exaggerated or not, French support for unification was now effective leverage for guaranteeing that Kohl would move forward on monetary union quickly. Realizing all of this caused Mitterrand to lose interest in the restoration model, and since it could not succeed without him, it began to fade.[138]

The exact same fate befell revivalism as well. Even as he traveled to Dresden on December 19 to begin implementing his own confederative ideas, Kohl realized that he could do better. Amazingly enough, the trip was Kohl's first extended immersion in the powerful, street-level reality of the East German revolution. Other than brief stops in West Berlin, he had been working at some distance from the GDR since the opening of the wall, spending time traveling to Paris, Poland, and even three days in Hungary (to thank the leadership for opening the border), but not in the other half of Germany.[139]

Kohl, Teltschik, Seiters, and a few others flew in a small Challenger aircraft directly to Dresden. As they rolled to a stop on the runway, they could see hundreds of people waving at them from the airfield as well as the roof and windows of the airport. Kohl remembers that sight, and the experience of getting off the plane to that roaring welcome, as the single most important moment for him personally in fall 1989. Standing on the tarmac, he knew instantly that he had a mandate to unify Germany as fast as possible. He turned to Seiters and muttered a colloquial phrase meaning roughly "it's a done deal." Nonetheless, he went through the motions of negotiating with soon-to-be impotent East German government officials.[140] He also met with dissident leaders, who would in time become impotent as well; but unlike the SED, they still enjoyed enormous legitimacy and authority at this point.[141] Much more significant than any of the talks was a speech that he gave.[142] Looking at the tens of thousands who had gathered on a dark December afternoon in front of the ruins of a church destroyed in World War II, Kohl heard them chanting "unity, unity, unity." He announced that there would be free elections in the spring and that confederative structures would follow. But he made clear what he really wanted, to an enormous cheer: "My goal—if this historical hour will allow it—is the unity of our country." He pushed on, choking up with emotion, to close by saying that "Christmas is the festival of the family and friends. Particularly now, in these days, we are beginning to see ourselves again as a German family."[143]

Yet the joy of the Dresden crowd had a less happy echo. The sight of throngs of Germans cheering a strong leader revived fears of an older specter than four-power control—one that Kohl would have to address and overcome if he wanted to reunify the country. Just before Kohl's departure for the city, the Israeli prime minister, Yitzhak Shamir, warned the chancellor in a letter that "we cannot forget the pictures of cheering masses in the 1930s and what resulted."[144] Shamir was hardly alone in worrying about what it all meant for the future. Right there in Dresden, the local KGB office—which included Putin—watched with anxiety. It is not clear whether Putin was in the crowd while Kohl was speaking, but it is certainly possible and even likely, given that he would melt into crowds at other points in 1989. And Putin's wife, Lyudmila, who had accompanied him to his KGB posting in Dresden with their two small daughters, remembered that they both had a "horrible feeling" at the end of 1989 about what might come next.[145]

CONCLUSION

After the Dresden visit in December 1989, the slow boat to confederation was already sunk in Kohl's mind. In other words, the actions of the population of East Germany convinced him, and would convince others, that there would be no time for the new confederative structures that he had just promised. It was not the first or last time that the actions of the East German street would be decisive. The four-power idea was not viable either. Both the restoration and revivalist visions were dead on arrival; new ideas were needed.

Now Kohl, sitting at a middle distance from the revolution—neither immersed in its calls for freedom, nor as remote from it as Moscow or Washington—would be the one to realize fully the chance that it presented. Until his Dresden visit, he had worked on the assumption that unity would be a slow process, and formulated his models for the future accordingly. After his firsthand contact with the three critical components of East German society—party leaders, dissidents, and the broader public—he realized that the former two were ignoring the third. The crowds wanted neither the continuation of their old regime in a confederation nor a revamped East Germany, which were the goals of the first two groups. They wanted unity, but they did not yet understand that questions involving countries far beyond their borders would need settling for that to happen.

Rather than trying to slow down the process, Kohl realized that there was opportunity in the midst of crisis. He could use the desires of the East German crowds as a justification to his foreign partners for dramatic action. Whether he could have slowed the process down (as Gorbachev and Thatcher fervently wished) became a moot point after Dresden, because he was no longer interested in doing so. Whether his own slow process of creating confederative structures might have been a financially more astute strategy for merging with East Germany also became moot.

Kohl was a politician facing a West German election sometime before January 1991 and he was sensing a winning strategy. There was a multilevel competition under way for the creation of some durable political order in all of Germany, which in turn had an impact on the future shape of Europe and its alliances in the world. Kohl realized that his ability to connect with average East Germans as well as potentially pull along West German voters toward a future they did not yet completely desire might allow him to shape events. But there would be many others who wanted to shape events too.

CHAPTER 3

HEROIC ASPIRATIONS IN 1990

... whatever may be our situation, whether firmly united under one national government, or split into a number of confederacies, certain it is that foreign nations will know ... and they will act towards us accordingly.
—*The Federalist Papers,* no. IV, 1787

I am not one of those who left the land
to the mercy of its enemies.
Their flattery leaves me cold,
my songs are not for them to praise.
—Anna Akhmatova, 1922

I said to the guard who was standing at the door: "When I was condemned to death in the Nazi era, my parents were allowed to be present in court. They also received permission to speak to me for half an hour after the reading of the verdict." I do not know if the socialist Cerberus understood me properly, because he gave a disarming reply: "Well, now you see, we don't live in the Nazi era any more."
—Robert Havemann, trying to attend the trial of his sons in East Germany in 1968[1]

Robert Havemann had carried out an unusual comparative study for a chemistry professor. He had—involuntarily—investigated the best methods for surviving both Nazi and Stasi interrogations. When he was interrogated in 1943 in the infamous cells of the Gestapo on Prinz Albrecht Street, he willed himself to believe that the blows of his captors did not hurt. Havemann drew pleasure from their obvious fury at his refusal to confess to helping Jews in hiding. His tactic for the Stasi in 1966, this time on Magdalenen Street, was different: confuse them with his extensive knowledge of the legal rights available to a suspect. The result in both cases was the same: short-term defeat, resulting in a death sentence in the Nazi era, and the loss of his job and freedom in the Stasi era; but long-term triumph.

Havemann lived to see his own victory over the Nazis. Friends convinced the Gestapo that Havemann was worth more alive, thanks to his chemistry training. His jailers agreed to postpone his death sentence month by month if he developed poison gas in a lab set up for him in a Brandenburg prison. As if he were not in enough danger already, Havemann used the reprieve, which lasted twenty months, to organize resistance in the jail. He built his own radio and circulated a "newspaper" to other inmates—every day—with reports from the outside world. He kept this secret long enough to be freed by the Red Army in May 1945. For his actions during the war, he would become one of Yad Vashem's "Righteous among Nations."[2]

Havemann felt (not unreasonably) that he owed his life to the Russians who released him. Such gratitude, and the fact that Havemann had been a member of the Communist Party of Germany since 1932, helped him to become the recipient of a shower of honors in the state of East Germany, including a professorship at the Humboldt University in Berlin. But when Joseph Stalin's successor, Nikita Khrushchev, revealed the depth of Stalin era crimes in a secret speech in 1956, Havemann came to realize that he had been deceived. The professor began once again to question and to challenge the authorities. His critical attitude resulted in interrogation by the Stasi, expulsion from his profession, the persecution of his family (particularly his children), and years of house arrest.[3] Havemann could probably have arranged exile in the West, where he had numerous admirers who would have helped him, but he wanted to remain in the GDR even under those conditions. He hoped for peaceful change and better days, both for Germany and for socialism, but died in April 1982 without seeing either.[4]

In life and death, he served as a powerful example to the dissidents who would come to prominence in 1989. The group New Forum, an overarching protest movement organized by Bohley and Rolf Henrich together with Havemann's widow, Katja, was founded in the Havemanns' living room in September 1989; for this, Bohley was called the "mother of the revolution" in Western media. And the slightly older group Initiative for Peace and Human Rights (IFM in German) bore the imprint of his thinking as well. In recognition of his importance, Havemann would be rehabilitated posthumously in 1990 and his works reprinted. And when the day came, a foundation and archive dedicated to the protest movement would be called the Robert Havemann Society.[5]

Three components of Havemann's legacy were particularly crucial in early 1990, after the initial jubilation at the fall of the wall. The first was a firm belief in socialism, if not in existing socialist regimes. As he wrote in 1970, "I believe,

Fig. 3.1. Robert Havemann, East German dissident, in 1979. © dpa/Corbis.

now as ever, that the socialist states, including the GDR, have not yet definitively missed their connection to the future." He therefore represented an ambivalent hero to the West, because he condemned Western countries as fascist and milita-ristic in no uncertain terms. He deplored what he called the imperialistic U.S. ac-tions in Vietnam, the racist treatment of African Americans, and the unjust power of West German business. In 1982, together with the Protestant minister Rainer Eppelmann, he authored the "Berlin Appeal," which called for *both* the Warsaw Pact and NATO to remove their forces from East and West Germany. A corresponding second component was his commitment to staying put in a socialist state, rather than becoming one of those unfortunate souls—so devastatingly denounced by poet Anna Akhmatova in an earlier era—who left their land to the mercy of enemies, both internal and external. One had to stay and fight at home. The third and final component was his bravery and refusal to be cowed by the agents of repression, whether they were Nazi or Stasi. These three beliefs would inform the dissidents of 1989 as they sought to formulate their visions for the future. They now had the chance that he was denied—namely, to remake East Germany—and the question was how to live up to his legacy of heroism.

As admirable as it was, that heroic legacy carried within it its own problems. Obviously, "heroism" means having courage, vision, and bravery. But, as mentioned in the introduction, there are less favorable connotations as well. A heroic skyscraper, an awesome feat of engineering, inspires little love from the people evicted from their homes in well-established older neighborhoods to make room for it. The effort of reaching for the sky can be awe-inspiring, but also foolhardy.

Both the positive and negative connotations of heroism would define two models proposed in 1990. The first was an extremely detailed version, in the form of a new constitution, drafted largely by former East German dissidents as part of the round table. The second was an extremely vague version, sketched by Gorbachev and his aides after their realization that the restoration model would not work. Both would begin with great hopes yet ultimately fail to gain sufficient support for their models.

The authors of the first—the East German dissident movement—would in fact lose their popularity with the broad mass of East Germans precisely because of their quixotic quest to create an autonomous East Germany with its own constitution. Dissident leaders and huge popular crowds had joined together in fall 1989, despite the fact that the long-term protest movement was led by intellectuals hoping to reform socialism, while the newer wave of protest in 1989 looked toward a capitalist future.[6] As a result, there was always a certain amount of disconnect between the long-term dissidents and the newer adherents. In 1990, the heroic ambitions of the dissidents and a brush with internal violence would lead to a final split between the two. Meanwhile, the authors of the second plan—Gorbachev and his advisers—would face challenges from both external and internal opponents. Unlike the East Germans, they would never think their ideas through fully, and their plans would remain vague until the end.

THE ROUND TABLE

As indicated already, leading protest organizations and East German church elders had called for a round table in the GDR. The "contact group" that issued this call consisted of the movement founded in Havemann's living room—namely, the New Forum—as well as IFM, Democracy Now, the SPD of East Germany (newly refounded by the pastor Markus Meckel), and the Democratic Awakening group including Eppelmann and a new political activist, the physicist and future chancellor, Merkel.[7] Originally the contact group worked in secret, but events moved so quickly that it was possible to issue invitations to the first meeting publicly. By December 7, dissidents and religious leaders were sitting down across a table from the leaders of the ruling regime.[8]

It was a surreal scenario for protesters like Gerd and Ulrike Poppe, who had undergone years of persecution at the hands of the Stasi. Both great admirers of Havemann, they had irritated the SED for years in every possible way. As a result, Gerd, a trained physicist, had been barred from work in that field and instead given manual labor; Ulrike also faced restrictions. Such measures proved to be unwise, as the couple channeled their extensive energies into protest instead. They organized clandestine meetings in their apartment with everyone from censored authors to West German politicians. They opened a day care center meant to counter the indoctrination of their own and other children by the state; the authorities closed it in 1983. Ulrike also challenged mandatory military training for children in school and was arrested for it. They formed the protest group IFM in winter 1985–86 with their fellow enemy of the state Bohley. They published the provocatively named samizdat newspaper *Grenzfall*; one meaning of its name was "border collapse."[9] They worked across state lines; Ulrike was one of the people whom Jahn met when he smuggled himself back into the GDR, and Gerd maintained strong contacts to Czechoslovakian and Hungarian dissidents.[10] In short, the idea that they would now sit at a table together with the SED and the members of the CDU and the liberals in the East, who had long since been turned into cheerleaders for the SED, was simply remarkable.[11]

The round table's first pressing task was to define itself and its role. Much discussion was devoted to this at the first meeting.[12] Their most basic function, the members decided, was to serve as a source of proposals for remaking the GDR, to be voted on in free elections. The existing government had been "elected" by blatantly fraudulent proceedings, and no real vote was yet scheduled. The round

Fig. 3.2. Ulrike Poppe, East German dissident, in October 1989. © Alain Nogues/
Corbis Sygma.

table called for a free national election in May 1990 (to ensure that it was not too
close to West German elections due by January 1991).[13] In the meantime, the
round table would serve as a kind of check on arbitrary acts by the government;
it would dissolve once the elections occurred.[14]

And as a further check on the power of the ruling regime, it called for the dis-
solution of the Stasi.[15] If anything was going to cause the peaceful 1989 revolu-
tion to enter a stage of terror, the continued existence of the Stasi would be it.
Rather than moving decisively to dismantle the secret police, as many had hoped,
Modrow had instead appointed a new director and misguidedly renamed it the
Office for National Security. This yielded the unfortunate German acronym of
Nasi and the more unfortunate result that the Stasi continued to exist.[16]

By the day of the first round table meeting, there had been scattered attacks on
Stasi/Nasi buildings around the country. Some agents had been held captive in
their own office blocks for extended periods. In Dresden, KGB agent Putin took
advantage of such events to carry out reconnaissance. By this point he had already started straining the office furnace by burning documents, and thinking
even further ahead, he wanted to plan for a possible attack. During one sack of a
Stasi/Nasi branch, he melted into the masses, "stood in the crowd and watched it
happen," so that he would know what to expect for himself and his colleagues

in the future. He was determined not to let a mob enter the KGB offices. "We were prepared to defend ourselves against the crowd, and we would have been within our rights to do so," he remembered later. Crowds did indeed show up at the doorstep of the KGB in Dresden. "We were forced to demonstrate our readiness to defend our building. And that determination certainly made an impression on them," Putin recollected, until the Soviet troops they had called arrived and the crowds backed down.[17]

Because of her fears about such events, the mother of the revolution, Bohley, contacted the head of the West German mission in East Berlin, Bertele, on the day of the first round table meeting. She told him of her "enormous fear that individual acts of violence could lead to an explosion that would consume the entire GDR." Bohley asked him to pass a message to Bonn, which he did: Please appeal for calm, and do not exacerbate the situation by suggesting that reunification (and presumably absolution from violent crimes against the old GDR regime) will be coming soon.[18] Internal Stasi/Nasi reports show that it shared Bohley's worries. One local branch feared that agents would be punished as scapegoats, when in fact they had just been "carrying out orders."[19] Word that dissident leaders, of all people, were helping to protect Stasi employees from physical harm leaked out to the press. The newsmagazine *Der Spiegel* pointed out how ironic it was that the secret police, "in its hour of need," sought help from those whom it had long persecuted.[20]

In the meantime, the round table took far-reaching steps of its own. Its members, divided into the so-called old forces (mainly the SED) and new forces (mainly dissidents), agreed on a core principle. They shared a mutual worry about the "independence and long-term development" of their country, as stated in a unanimously adopted resolution at the first meeting.[21] A West German observer invited to all of the sessions, Uwe Thaysen, remembered this phrase in hindsight as a major mistake. Thaysen was not at all sure that the broader population of the GDR was interested in the "independence and long-term development" of East Germany, unlike Havemann's heirs and the SED. This statement seemed to Thaysen to be a fundamental decision, and one that would have been better left to an elected parliament.

The round table also decided on a further role for itself: that of a constitutional convention. Like a more famous convention in the United States in 1787, the table assigned to itself the task of writing the basic law of the land.[22] Kohl had already announced his Ten-Point-Program and confederative structures. The round table members decided that they had to come up with an indigenous East German model of their own (despite Gerd Poppe's accurate objection that they did not have the "democratic legitimation from the population" necessary to do so). They felt that if they did not, other states would do it for them; the authors of the U.S. Constitution had worried about precisely the same phenomenon.[23]

The SED representatives agreed with the dream of a new constitution for the GDR, since they had no desire to merge with West Germany either.[24] The party unfortunately had lost its best bargaining chip, the Berlin Wall, for nothing; had it retained control over the situation, it could have earned quite a profit from West Germany in exchange for opening it.[25] Now the SED had to make do with the dissidents at the round table and its representative there, Gregor Gysi, knew that.

COUNTERREVOLUTION?

A fissure between the long-term dissidents and the large number of new 1989 demonstrators, who had made common cause despite differences over the desirability of unification, quickly became apparent after the wall opened.[26] This split worsened as a result of events around the turn of the year. The first was Kohl's visit to Dresden on December 19, following hard on the heels of the second round table meeting. At that session, former dissidents had expressed their intense dismay at Kohl's impending appearance. They had warned Kohl not to regard the GDR as "the land of low salaries" for West German business.[27] The massive Dresden crowds that assembled to hear him, however, did not seem to share the round table's dismay. Instead, they sent a clear signal that they were hungry for immediate change.

Kohl had realized that his confederation concept would not work, but had not yet moved on to a new model. He sensed the need for speed, but if he were going to move a lot more quickly, then he would have to make sure that he had covered his back. In January and February he would thus travel to the three countries that mattered most: France, Russia, and the United States.

The first visit took place on January 4, when Mitterrand received Kohl at his private house in Latché. The two talked for hours. Mitterrand had recently spoken in his public New Year's address about the need for Europe to be less dependent on the superpowers, that is, to "come home" to its own history and geography, and was plainly searching for a Eurocentric vision of the future. Both he and Kohl felt that Gorbachev had provided them with a rare opportunity; if Gorbachev fell, hard-liners would follow and matters would become more difficult. Mitterrand told Kohl that "Gorbachev's fate depends more on you" than on the hard-liners. Kohl agreed and said "Gorbachev knows this too." The conversation was an extremely open and far-ranging one. It seems to have done a great deal to incline Mitterrand toward the belief that the best way forward was with Kohl and the EC, suppressing the inevitable discomfort that the specter of a unified Germany created.[28]

The most significant event in shaping the plans of both Kohl and the round table, however, was Modrow's decision not just to tolerate the continued existence of the Stasi/Nasi but also to relaunch and revitalize it.[29] This ill-starred idea became public after vandals defaced the Soviet war memorials in Treptow, on the outskirts of Berlin, by painting neo-Nazi slogans on them.[30] It is likely that Stasi agents themselves were responsible for this, because it gave the SED and Modrow precisely the justification they needed.[31] The January 3 issue of the party newspaper *Neues Deutschland* denounced the vandalism, and called it a sign that right-wing West Germans were planning "to enter the GDR by the thousands and establish operations here."[32]

Five days later, the round table learned about planning for a coup. The Gera branch of the Stasi/Nasi had issued an appeal that had just come to light. Addressed to "Comrades, Citizens, and Patriots of the Invisible Front, Both at Home and Abroad," it called on them to rise up and "restore the rule of law." In a thinly veiled threat to the round table, the appeal sneered that "whoever plays with power can also have it taken away from them, especially during a revolution."[33]

The opposition groups demanded to know if this call to carry out a coup had in fact been sent to its intended recipients. Angered by the Gera "invisible front," the round table denounced the unwillingness of the Modrow government to answer the questions about the Stasi that it had been posing since its first meeting: Where are its weapons? When will it be dissolved? Even the SED, now having changed its own name to the Party of Democratic Socialism (PDS), agreed that the government response had been inadequate. The groups that had come up with the idea for the round table in the first place issued an ultimatum to the Modrow government: Answer all of our questions in a week, by January 15, or else.[34]

What was the "or else"? What leverage did the round table have over the government? The answer was the same as in November 1989: public opinion. At first, Modrow foolishly tried to ignore the round table. He told Nikolai Ryzhkov, the Soviet prime minister, that the vandalism would be his excuse for transforming the old Stasi into "a stabilizing force in society." Modrow's hope was to "prevent the sell-out of the GDR's economy to West Germany."[35] The next day, at a parliamentary session, he unveiled his plan: a beefed-up Stasi/Nasi, renamed yet again as the Office for the Protection of the Constitution. As Modrow omi-nously proclaimed, "surveillance and disruption of plans to disturb the peace . . . will remain an important goal and task." This announcement sounded like a counterrevolution from above, a response to the revolution from below. The re-action was immediate: massive strikes and protests on the same night and the next day.[36]

In response, the New Forum called for a demonstration at the Stasi/Nasi head-quarters on Normannen Street in Berlin on January 15. Unbelievably, more than two months into the revolution, the main office remained intact and open, scaring off those who would challenge it.[37] Like Putin in Dresden, those inside were using the time to destroy documents. Now, posters and leaflets called on East Germans to face their fear, and advertised the showdown in big block letters: "NORMANNEN ST., Monday, Jan. 15, 5:00 p.m." A New Forum leaflet pro-claimed its demands: "Immediate closure of all Stasi offices. . . . The start of trials against the Stasi. . . . No special privileges and payments to former Stasi agents. . . . No creation of new secret services."[38] To make sure that the Stasi got the point, the leaflet said, "We are going to shut the doors of the Stasi! Bring stones and mortar for constructing a wall!" The last point was not rhetorical. It was a signal to attend and to build a wall—a powerful symbol in East Germany.

More anxious observers wondered if this was the beginning of a stage of terror in Central Europe. A U.S. State Department memo from December had specu-lated that if the public sought violent revenge, Stasi agents might seek the protec-tion of Soviet troops, thereby enmeshing them in the conflict and requiring action by Moscow. The author of the document, Policy Planning adviser Harvey Sicher-man, concluded that if Moscow authorized the use of force, "I have no doubt the Russians will obey an order to fire upon the Germans." On top of this, it was not entirely clear whether Soviet troops would obey the opposite order—to stay in their barracks—if one came from Gorbachev.[39]

Because of the potential for disaster, January 15 represents one of the most sig-nificant single days in the competition to shape the future after 1989. Too late to stop the Normannen Street protest, Modrow backed down, announcing that he would put off any discussion of an Office for Constitutional Protection until after the elections. He turned up in person at the round table meeting that day to grovel and invited members of the round table to join him in representing the GDR on an upcoming visit to Bonn to see Kohl. It was the first in a series of steps that would lead to the creation of an interim "Government of National Responsibil-ity" that would include former dissidents.

Even as he was doing so, word began arriving that things were going badly wrong at Normannen Street. Instead of the peaceful protest out front, the crowds had gotten inside and started destroying the building. Police officers burst into the round table meeting and pleaded with dissident leaders to come with them to the Stasi headquarters in the hopes that they could restore order. In a season of surreal events, this one must have been the most bizarre: a convoy of police cars driving through the dark streets, carrying protesters to the very building where some of them had been persecuted for the purpose of protecting it.[40]

When they got there they found chaos and tried to figure out what had happened. There seemed to have been roughly a hundred thousand people outside the headquarters by 5:30 p.m.[41] Protesting workers were building a wall, as promised, and demonstrators were chanting slogans like "open the door," when (as one participant put it) "to everyone's amazement, it actually opened." Later, the party would accuse the protesters of breaking in; for its part, dissidents would claim that the door had opened from inside and there had been Stasi agents planted in the crowd to turn the event into a violent one. Regardless of the cause, the consequences of the door's opening were immediate. The crowd rushed in. People screamed when they saw portraits of Honecker still hanging on the walls, even though he had been ousted three months earlier. Someone also found a portrait of the détente era Soviet leader Leonid Brezhnev. According to one eyewitness, "what happened next must be condemned and not called good. Doors were broken down and what we saw took our breath away." Stockpiles of silver and crystal, canned goods and alcohol, and meat lockers filled with vast quantities of delicacies horrified the crowd. Two hours of vandalism, pilfering, and theft from what was essentially the high temple of repression followed. Yet even as some protesters broke windows and spray-painted walls, others tried to preserve the peaceful nature of the East German revolution by yelling "no violence!" Only after Modrow and the dissident leaders arrived, and appealed for calm, did protesters eventually leave the building.[42]

Within forty-eight hours, the round table's "Working Group: Security" announced that it had secured the files at the Stasi headquarters and henceforth none would leave. The meeting of the round table on January 22 concluded that the building was still functional and could have been used to reactivate the secret police. By March 31, most of the employees of Normannen Street were out of a job. Nevertheless, portions of the Stasi would continue to operate and destroy documents; as late as September 1990, Bohley and Havemann's widow would find it necessary to occupy a main Stasi archive building, to force access to the files even as the two Germanies finalized unification.[43]

THE CONSEQUENCES OF THE BRUSH WITH A STAGE OF TERROR

This brush with mass violence had three significant consequences. First, it eliminated any remaining authority held by Modrow and indeed all members of the old guard. Throughout fall 1989, the GDR public had been increasingly horrified to learn of the luxuries that their party leaders hoarded while ordinary people had to do without heat or meat; now they had further confirmation of corruption behind Stasi office doors and were fed up. The former leadership of the country would soon be charged with high treason. Modrow saw a danger (as he told Seiters) "that things would go completely out of control."[44] He also looked to Gorbachev for help, complaining that strikes and continued mass emigration were crippling the country, and the necessities of daily life were becoming scarce.[45] Ominously, Modrow also pointed out that animosity toward the Soviet troops stationed there was growing.

Second, even though the January 15 protest showed the dissident leadership and the crowds as a united entity, it would be the last time. As a result of the chaos of mid-January, members of the round table would join the government in the hopes of steadying the ship of state. They forced Modrow to accept an earlier date of March 18, 1990, for the East German elections, thereby making both his tenure and that of the round table even shorter.[46] And they intensified efforts to produce a new constitution in time for the March election. In other words, they accelerated their heroic efforts to create a new model for East Germany's future, precisely as all remaining popular interest in that version of the future evaporated. Convinced by the events of January that reform in the GDR was simply not possible, crowds would turn out en masse for election speeches by leaders of Western parties.

Third, the January upheaval confirmed Kohl's belief that establishing confederative structures with East Germany was not worth any time or effort. As the chancellor explained to the U.S. ambassador in West Germany, the January 15 affair was "catastrophic."[47] Although Kohl still had various conversations scheduled with Modrow, they would be empty exercises, and Modrow's pleas for fifteen billion DM in aid would simply go unanswered.[48] Kohl became convinced that the East Germans could not even maintain a functioning government and so he—and not the four powers or anyone else—had to provide one as soon as possible. This meant, among other things, preventing any further quadripartite activity without his involvement. As Kohl put it to Modrow, on one of their rare points of agreement, the four powers "are not allowed to regard us as a protectorate."[49]

One of Kohl's aides, Peter Hartmann, reported to him in January that the best option for Bonn would be to come up with some kind of process that included the four powers but also constrained them. The goal was to keep them busy, but not in a way that would "allow them to assume a role that we find undesirable." So if Bonn could successfully define a narrow realm of action for the big four, it could thereby assume responsibility for the rest. The main problem with regard to the four powers, Hartmann predicted, would be the issue of troop stationing. Put more precisely, how could Bonn get the Soviet troops to leave while the Western forces stayed? That was clearly a tall order. To make sure that he was on top of all of these issues, Kohl should, well before the East German elections on March 18, come up with his own new model of the path to unity.[50]

Kohl's resolve only hardened when he heard about an interview that Thatcher had given to the *Wall Street Journal* at the end of January 1990. Thatcher had decided to air her grievances publicly, and chose a U.S. newspaper to do so, meaning that Washington could not miss her point. She argued that "early German unity could create such enormous political problems for Gorbachev that he might lose power. That would be a disaster for everyone." The British prime minister called on Kohl to put a "longer view of Europe's needs" before his own "more narrow, nationalistic goals." She cautioned that "building democracy is much harder than tearing it down" and hasty actions would not work. Nor was the EC ready for German unity, given its democratic deficits: "The irony of West Europe going to more central, non-elected decisions at the same time as East Europe is crying out for democracy is too absurd for words."[51] This latter line was not one to warm the heart of Mitterrand, given his devotion to the cause of the EC. Speaking on Italian television the day after the Thatcher interview appeared, he dismissed the idea that there should be a "lapse of time" before Eastern Europe could join the EC.[52]

And of course, nothing in the article warmed hearts in Bonn, which was presumably the point. Teltschik's assessment of the article was that Thatcher was stuck in the nineteenth century and still felt that Britain had to watch over Europe.[53] Foreign Minister Hurd tried to undo some of the damage with a speech in Bonn, stating that "we had accepted, and indeed advocated, the right of self-determination by the German people for many years."[54] He would also meet with Kohl soon after it appeared. Usually a foreign minister and a head of government meeting would be a breach of protocol, but with communication between the chancellor and the prime minister "being virtually non-existent, each was willing to compensate by extending courtesies to the other's Foreign Minister." Nothing helped. The British Foreign Office estimated afterward that the *Wall Street Journal* interview had caused "enormously great pain" in the chancellor's office. No matter how much Hurd or others might try to be cooperative, "it is widely believed in Germany, in the press and at the very highest level there, that the Prime Minister has radically different views on the subject." As a result, "the views of the British Ministers other than the Prime Minister are of little significance in the present circumstances."[55]

In another sense the article was useful to Bonn, because it made it clear to the West Germans that Thatcher was on her own. The prime minister might wish to "dilute German influence in Europe," as she privately told Hurd that she wanted to do, but she was failing to build a coalition to achieve that goal. Washington was supportive of Kohl, and Mitterrand was not willing to be obstructive, so it was really Gorbachev that Kohl had to worry about. The approval of the United States and France might be necessary, but it was not sufficient. Ultimately it would be Moscow, with over half a million troops and dependents on German soil, that would decide whether unification could happen or not.[56]

Unfortunately, Gorbachev was stonewalling. Kohl had been trying to arrange a face-to-face meeting since the day that Portugalov had shocked Teltschik. But Gorbachev had simply not responded. Instead, he had let it be known that he was trying to reduce his foreign appointments in early 1990.[57] Partly this was due to the pressure of internal affairs, most notably the economic situation and rising secessionist pressures. In January, Gorbachev traveled personally to Lithuania in an attempt to halt its drive for independence, and the Red Army forcibly suppressed unrest in Azerbaijan.[58] Partly this was due, however, to a lack of clarity in Moscow as to how to proceed, and Gorbachev could hardly face Kohl until he had decided. In the meantime the Soviet leader had made another attempt to revive the restoration model, but it had failed.[59]

Gorbachev was in dire need of a new strategy. A serious assessment of the German situation was overdue. He, like everyone else, hardly wanted violence to consume a country where he had four hundred thousand troops stationed. Amazingly, though, from the November collapse of the wall until late January, there appear to have been no substantive evaluations of the German situation among party leaders in Moscow. The military seems to have been completely in the dark as to his thinking. And internal affairs remained pressing; as already mentioned, by 1990 shortages would become as severe as they had been during World War II. Gorbachev's penchant for indecision and procrastination on foreign policy was becoming harmful. As a result, Gorbachev finally assembled his advisers in his office at the end of January 1990 for what can only be called a brainstorming session.[60]

According to Chernyaev, Gorbachev opened the meeting by acknowledging that the authority of their allies in East Germany was collapsing. The real question now was where to place the bets: "Kohl or the SPD." To some extent this was a false question, since Moscow had recently increased its dependency on Kohl. At the beginning of January, Shevardnadze had admitted to Bonn that Moscow was facing a shortage of foodstuffs, particularly meat. Kohl responded by approving a government subsidy for the sale of 220 million DM worth of food to the USSR, and documents to this effect would be signed in February 1990.[61]

But despite this weakness, the Soviet Union was not entirely without leverage. Party leaders in Moscow had numerous contacts in the SPD, having worked closely with them in an earlier political generation to negotiate détente. Moreover, Soviet leaders knew that the Social Democrats were heavily favored to win the March elections in East Germany. The SPD might become the leading all-German party of the future, and those contacts could prove useful. On top of this, whoever won on March 18 would still have to deal with the Soviet troops there, which gave Moscow a role regardless of the outcome of the vote.

Vladimir Kryuchkov, the head of the KGB, felt that the SED's days were numbered, but argued for taking a closer look at the eastern socialists—that is, the SPD of East Germany. A Politburo member, Yakovlev, suggested that Modrow could be made to enter the SPD and propose unification, with Soviet backing. Objections came from Falin's deputy, Rafael Fedorov, who shared Falin's worries about a united Germany. He said that this could go badly wrong, and much of West Germany did not want reunification anyway. Chernyaev noted afterward that Fedorov and Falin were still very much attached to the SED, whereas he focused more on international relations than inner–German party politics. Chernyaev suggested that perhaps the "six"—meaning the four powers but this time with the two Germanies—should create a forum to decide matters. Bonn and Washington had already started thinking about such a forum as well.

The January brainstorming session did not yield a precise plan; rather, Gorbachev summed up the meeting by saying that the most important goals were winning time and prolonging the reunification process as much as possible. He suggested that Moscow should play on the fears of the West Europeans, including West Germans, about the cost of suddenly supporting sixteen million East Germans: "This is our strategy." In the meantime, Marshal Sergei Akhromeyev, the former chief of the general staff and now Gorbachev's military aide, should start thinking through the implications of Soviet troop withdrawal from East Germany.[62]

What specifics did emerge from this session concerned the scheduling of future bilateral meetings. Gorbachev would finally respond to Kohl's request for a personal meeting, but only agree to meet after talking to Modrow at the end of January and then Baker on February 7–9, 1990, to get the lay of the land.[63] As a result, the group agreed that Kohl could not be invited for a date any sooner than the last day of Baker's visit, but that he should arrive as soon as possible after that; Kohl, eager to move forward, would travel to Moscow on Saturday, February 10.[64]

EMERGING CONTROVERSY OVER REPARATIONS AND NATO

In the meantime, Kohl was becoming increasingly aware that in the run-up to the East German election, foreign and domestic politics were a combustible mixture. There were two major issues. The first problem was the extent of Polish unhappiness about events in divided Germany. Polish economic rejuvenation, which had been one of Kohl's main priorities earlier in the fall, was now less important to him in the face of an East German election in March. But the prospect of major changes in East Germany reopened questions about territory and reparations. The tenor of the contacts between Bonn and Warsaw, which had been respectful earlier in the fall, became increasingly fraught. A speech that Kohl had given in mid-January in Paris had failed to reassure Poles and others.[65] Mazowiecki pushed on January 30 for even more financial help than had been agreed in November.[66]

Soon, Mazowiecki and others would also begin pressing for fresh guarantees of the inviolability of the East German–Polish border. Back in 1945, the Potsdam Conference had left the final definition of that border open, pending a peace settlement. The subsequent West German–Polish Treaty of 1970 and the CSCE Final Act had, in contrast, recognized existing borders as inviolable. If the clock was turning back to 1945, when the unity of Germany had been an open question, then Poland wanted to be sure it had locked down its western border, particularly after having lost much land in the East to the Soviet Union.[67] Largely for domestic political reasons, Kohl would be slow to give such guarantees. Indeed, he would further anger his opponents by citing Stalin era accords to justify his actions. At the beginning of 1990 this nastiness was still in the future, but it would not be long in coming.

A second problem involved the mixture of two kinds of alliance politics—namely, West German domestic political alliances and NATO. Kohl's current partner, Genscher, was now becoming his competitor as well. Both of their parties, the CDU and the FDP, had affiliates in East Germany and would be competing with each other for votes. Genscher's fellow liberals in the East, along with Moscow, the media, and indeed most of the world, were expecting the SPD to become the dominant party in East Germany after March 18, so too much closeness to the CDU was not advisable. Kohl had decided in the meantime that the East German CDU should face the election in an alliance with other parties, but that the Liberals would not be one of them. Instead, the chancellor served as the guiding spirit behind the formation on February 5 of the Alliance for Germany, combining the East German CDU and minor parties. (Among other consequences, this alliance eventually created the national political career of the future chancellor, Merkel. She was originally a member of one of the smaller parties, Democratic Awakening, as indicated previously; but her party would eventually merge with the CDU.)

Not coincidentally, two days later Kohl also unveiled the alliance's most useful campaign tool: the promise to seek rapid monetary and economic union between the two Germanies. The immediate goal of this announcement was to persuade the masses of would-be refugees, still moving west in droves, to stay home. Protesters had been marching with signs reading, "If the DM doesn't come to us, we will go to it." Now they were being told that it might, in fact, come to them. The longer-term goal was to secure electoral advantages for the Alliance for Germany.[68]

As a result of the intensifying competition in January and February 1990, Genscher therefore had an incentive to raise his profile, and his actions blurred the line between domestic and foreign alliance politics. The foreign minister made his own views about the future plain in a speech at the Evangelical Academy in Tutzing on January 31. In this controversial address, Genscher called on NATO to state clearly that "whatever happens to the Warsaw Pact, an expansion of NATO territory to the East, in other words, closer to the borders of the Soviet Union, will not happen." Any attempt to put East German territory into NATO was undesirable because of the risk that it would block the rapprochement between the Germanies and cause a backlash in the Soviet Union.[69]

Genscher then traveled to Washington on Friday, February 2, to see whether his fellow secretary of state, Baker, agreed with him about this. In a friendly two-and-a-half-hour conversation in front of a roaring fire, Baker stressed the need for continued West German membership in NATO. The secretary in turn sought Genscher's thoughts on a new idea. Like Kohl's and Gorbachev's advisers, Baker and his State Department team were independently coming to the same conclusion: some kind of forum for the four powers plus the two Germanies was necessary. In other words, a "4 + 2" mechanism could supervise the external aspects of German unification. It would address such questions as how quadripartite powers would be relinquished, but not the technicalities of the inner-German merger.

Genscher said he would support the idea if it was clearly a "2 + 4" mechanism—that is, with the Germans clearly identified as the most important states at the table—and not 4 + 2. Baker concurred with this, and so the 2 + 4 concept was validated. Afterward, in a joint press conference at 7:45 p.m. on Friday, Genscher stated publicly that he and Baker had agreed that "there was no interest to extend NATO to the East."[70] Baker, aware that Genscher and Kohl did not always tell each other what they were planning, instructed his ambassador in Bonn to report personally to Teltschik about these events, so Baker could be sure that Kohl was informed about it.[71]

After the weekend, Baker would leave on Monday for an extended trip that would eventually take him to Moscow. He was therefore out of Washington as resistance to what he and Genscher had just agreed started building in the NSC.[72] Scowcroft and his team wondered how West Germany could stay in NATO, combine with the East, and yet not extend NATO to its new territory. It made no sense to the NSC from the point of view of German unification alone, to say nothing of military considerations.

Similarly, Genscher would soon face opposition in Bonn from Defense Minister Gerhard Stoltenberg, a member of the CDU, for much the same reason. The NSC and Stoltenberg had identical worries about their respective foreign ministers' plans: that an East Germany de facto excluded from NATO would be impossible to defend.[73] Indeed, the prospect of acquiring an indefensible territory might derail unity altogether. This was not the first time that Stoltenberg had disagreed with Baker. The two had clashed over interest rates when they had been finance minister and treasury secretary, respectively, contributing to the crash of October 1987.[74]

But Baker had headed to Moscow with the idea fixed in his head that the agreement with Genscher—no extension of NATO eastward—was the basis for his negotiations. This idea would have consequences far beyond the immediate time period of German unification. In Moscow, he would find a leader who, having realized the restoration model would not work, was now swinging toward the other extreme—namely, a heroic model, with new pan-European institutions replacing both the Warsaw Pact and NATO.

Such an idea was not entirely new. In May 1989, the Warsaw Pact had issued a statement indicating that the end of both alliances might be desirable. Shevardnadze repeated a similar idea in a speech to the Supreme Soviet in October 1989 and again three days later in Warsaw.[75] The new Czechoslovakian president, former dissident Havel, had shocked Washington by suggesting that *all* foreign troops should leave Europe, so Europe could set up a security commission and provide for its own defense. Even Falin, opposed to Gorbachev on so many issues, saw the end-of-both-alliances option as viable.[76] Now, Gorbachev's briefing papers from early February for his meeting with Baker show that he had decided to prioritize this concept. He wanted a pan-European structure, or a common European home, intended to make both alliances obsolete. It would contain a Germany that would be neutral for the time that the pan-European structures were under construction. Although he appears not to have known it, some of these ideas echoed the thinking of Thatcher. Her foreign minister, Hurd, had encouraged her to "come forward with some positive ideas" so that the UK did not "appear to be a brake on everything." She replied to him that British efforts should focus on "building a wider European association, embracing . . . the East European countries, and in the long term the Soviet Union." Such an association would in turn link to a strengthened CSCE. If Gorbachev knew of this idea, he did not make use of the overlap between it and his own; he similarly missed an opportunity to emphasize the commonalities between his ideas and those of many East European leaders.[77]

Gorbachev's heroic visions do not seem to have been the result of consensus in Moscow; rather, they represented the thinking of the Soviet leader and his closest allies. Gorbachev and Shevardnadze had, for a while, achieved something roughly similar to what Nixon and Kissinger had done in the détente era: they kept the real decision-making secret from their own colleagues. Falin would complain bitterly that Gorbachev and his closest aides excluded nearly every member of the party and government leadership from either taking part in conversations with foreign leaders or seeing transcripts of them afterward. By keeping old military and party hierarchies out of the real decision-making process, the two had created what one historian calls "virtually unlimited space for foreign policy innovations."[78] They could essentially launch trial balloons all by themselves.

But this came at a cost: having cut critics out of the loop at home, they were less prepared than they should have been for critics abroad. No domestic constituencies had forced them to make their visions specific. Gorbachev and his trusted aides thus lost time mulling over broad ideas, and were not prepared for the rapid pace of events. In addition, after they made top-level decisions, lower-level negotiators who disagreed with them would seek to have input belatedly, by undercutting their bosses in the details of implementation. Countries dealing with the Soviet Union would, as a result, continually face contradictions between what seemed to be agreed on at the top level and what would actually be offered in practical terms once experts got down to work. Gorbachev and his aides also seemed to miss the urgency of the timing of events; their own views would not ripen soon enough. A U.S. State Department assessment of the Soviets' ideas concluded that "beneath it all is an increasingly plaintive insistence that they must be given some new, enduring role."[79] Nonetheless, it was with this vague concept of pan-European unity that Gorbachev would greet Baker during his Moscow visit of February 7–9 and Kohl one day later.

"NATO'S JURISDICTION WOULD NOT SHIFT ONE INCH EASTWARD"

Baker's visit proved to be a fateful one, and later, the source of a conflict about NATO expansion.[80] What happened when Baker visited Moscow in February 1990? In order to understand the answer, it is worth taking a moment to survey the mental maps of those involved. Baker and Gorbachev brought different expectations and experiences to this meeting, even though on paper they seemed similar. Both had been born within a year of each other (Baker in 1930, and Gorbachev in 1931), gotten married in 1953, started families soon thereafter, and climbed to the highest political levels of their respective home superpowers. But Gorbachev had attained adulthood in a country devastated by two world wars, whereas Baker did the same in a country made rich and powerful by them.

Gorbachev's childhood memories of the 1930s included the disappearance of his grandfather, Pantelei Yefimovich Gopkalo, who was taken away in the middle of the night during Stalin's purges of 1937–38. His grandmother moved in with the Gorbachevs, and neighbors shunned them as a result, fearing guilt by association. Even relatives would only visit at night. Gopkalo was eventually released, but refused to say what had happened, and would die not long afterward. Later in life, Gorbachev would write about how he tracked down the records of his grandfather's interrogation and spoke to his cell mates. Gopkalo had refused to confess, which intensified the tortures. When beating did not work, both of his arms were broken. When that did not work, he was forced to sit on a burning stove. Gorbachev, when he met his future wife, Raisa, would find out that his family had been lucky; they had at least seen their grandfather again. Hers, arrested under similar circumstances, had been convicted and executed.[81]

In contrast, having the good fortune to grow up in a democratic and prosperous country, Baker had quite different memories of the 1930s and 1940s. Baker thought of the River Oaks Country Club in Houston, Texas, as his "second home" when he was a child, and forged a close bond with his tennis coach there, Andrew Jitkoff, whom he correspondingly viewed as a second father. A refugee, Jitkoff had been born in Russia at the turn of the century, but fled during the Bolshevik revolution. Jitkoff would reminisce about Russian history to Baker, who later, as a student at Princeton University, would choose to study the subject for himself.[82]

Even though both Gorbachev and Baker went on to attain success in their chosen fields—the former in party work, and the latter in the law—the discrepancy in the living standards between their two countries continued to shape the men's lives into adulthood. When newly married, even though he was the first secretary of the Stavropol city party organization, Gorbachev and Raisa lived in a small room. They had no running water; instead, they had to fetch it from a pump. The intervention of well-connected friends got the young couple moved to an apartment with both a kitchen and a toilet—but also roommates, including "a welder, a retired colonel, a mechanic working in a garment factory, and their families" along with "an alcoholic bachelor and his mother" in addition to "four single women."[83] The Soviet Union's chronic housing shortage meant such combinations were not uncommon. Gorbachev even felt lucky compared to the conditions in the countryside. Later in life he remembered a visit to the nearby Gorkaya River valley. "As far as the eye could see, scattered at random," there were groups of "low, smoke-belching huts, [and] blackened dilapidated fences." He could hardly believe that "in those miserable dwellings, people led some kind of life." The streets, which hardly deserved the name, "were deserted" as if "the plague had ravaged the entire village," and "no contacts or ties existed between these shanty-town microcosms, just the everlasting barking of dogs." He recalled that this sight, sad as it was, inspired him, because he wanted his country to be able to provide a better life for its residents.[84]

The material conditions of daily life in Houston in the 1950s and 1960s were vastly superior to those in Stavropol, especially for someone at the apex of the city's social ladder. Baker enjoyed the fruits of his hard work and success as a lawyer, including membership at the Houston Country Club, where he and his doubles partner, Bush, won repeated championships. Despite his wealth, however, Baker was not untouched by suffering: doctors were unable to save his wife from an early death of cancer, leaving him a single father in 1970. Bush's efforts to distract Baker from his sorrow afterward included getting him involved in politics, and the two began their ultimately successful rise to the White House and the State Department.

Baker only fully appreciated the discrepancy in living standards between the United States and the USSR when he finally visited the Soviet Union for the first time in May 1989. As his car drove into Moscow, he felt as if he "had been transported back in time. . . . Stalinesque buildings that seemed to have been built in the 1930s and 1940s looked as though they hadn't been repaired or painted since then. The few cars and trucks on the streets appeared to have come from the 1950s and 1960s." But he was also struck by Shevardnadze's hospitality. The Soviet foreign minister invited Baker and his second wife to a dinner at his private apartment. Baker was particularly pleased when Shevardnadze gave him a shotgun as a gift. The evening was the beginning of a "warm friendship."[85]

Now Baker was back in Moscow, but between his initial visit in May 1989 and the one in February 1990, the world had changed significantly. Back in May, Baker had been impressed by Gorbachev's positive outlook. The secretary remembered that the Soviet leader "exuded optimism, and in this regard, he reminded me time and again of Ronald Reagan. President Reagan filled the room with his upbeat outlook, buoying everyone in it." In February, though, Gorbachev and his advisers were in a tougher position. That week's Central Committee meeting had been overshadowed by an unprecedented protest of a quarter million people in Moscow, calling for greater democracy. Rising nationalism was intensifying throughout the Soviet Union, causing intense regional conflicts; the following week, ethnic rioting would erupt in Tajikistan, and problems with the Baltics would intensify soon thereafter. In contrast, the United States saw its star in the ascendant in the Cold War contest, given the clear desire of East European countries to separate from Moscow. The two men's backgrounds, and that of Shevardnadze as well, would all play a role in how they dealt with these issues.[86]

In addition to these problems, Gorbachev and Shevardnadze approached their talks with Baker with a further expectation that would prove to be a liability. They had both grown up in a system with decision-making authority concentrated at the top. A few men, or even one man, made far-reaching decisions—ones that sent grandfathers to interrogations or soldiers to the front. Those decisions overrode any written constitutional or legal guarantees. Soviet negotiators of all ranks might be sticklers for legalistic detail in their dealings with the West, but the elite level was another matter. Baker, in contrast, had made his professional living in the contentious field of the law. He understood the dynamic between speculation and agreement; that much could be said, contested, denied, or promoted in discussion, but that what was agreed in writing at the end was what mattered. In his memoirs, he wrote that he viewed international politics as "ongoing negotiation." Moreover, both he and Kohl understood that when an agreement was reached, it was advantageous to use publicity to solidify that agreement. As Gates remembered, "what he [Baker] didn't know about dealing with—and manipulating—the press was hardly worth knowing." At one point Baker would even advise Gorbachev on how to deal with the media, telling him that "you need to feed them to make them happy."[87]

Baker's meetings began on February 7. He spent two days in talks with Shevardnadze, and then saw Gorbachev at the end of the visit. As in the past, arms control was a large component of all meetings. It was an abiding passion of Gorbachev's. One study of Gorbachev describes him as follows: he "was admirable, as Reagan was, in his sincere belief in a nuclear-free world—a mirage that made it difficult for the two leaders to reach an agreement on more practical matters."[88] Bush did not share that dream, but he did believe—despite the objections of Baker and Cheney—that it was time for a reduction in conventional forces. As a result, in his January 1990 State of the Union address, President Bush had proposed the reduction of U.S. and Soviet troops in Central and Eastern Europe from roughly 300,000 and 600,000, respectively, to 195,000 each.[89] Yet he wanted to keep more U.S. troops in Europe outside the central zone, and the Russians were not happy about it. The issue was not resolved there, but later in the month Gorbachev would accept Bush's proposal.[90] Chemical weapons and the negotiations on conventional forces in Europe, ongoing since March 1989, were also discussed.[91]

The future of Germany also received attention from the foreign ministers.[92] The secretary's handwritten notes from their meetings indicate that they discussed the 2 + 4 framework as a better alternative to four-power meetings, which the "Germans won't buy." They also discussed the U.S. desire for Germany to remain in NATO. In the handwritten notes, Baker put stars and an exclamation point next to one of his key statements: "End result: Unified Ger. anchored in a *changed (polit.) NATO—*whose juris. would not move *eastward!"[93]

According to both Baker's and Gorbachev's records, Baker repeated this remark to the Soviet leader on February 9. Gorbachev followed up on this by emphasizing that any expansion of the "zone of NATO" was not acceptable.[94] Baker responded, according to Gorbachev, "we agree with that." This agreement was extremely significant to the Soviet leader. He later recalled it as the moment "that cleared the way for a compromise" on Germany.[95]

It also formed the nucleus of the controversy that remains unresolved to this day. Unwisely, Gorbachev let the meeting end without securing this agreement in any kind of written form. Emerging from a political culture in which the word of a leader overruled the law, hoping that he could still find a way to disband both military alliances entirely, and hesitating to agree to his end of the bargain (a unified Germany), Gorbachev did not try to resolve the matter there in writing. In the future, once NATO started expanding, he would therefore leave the Soviet Union's successors empty-handed when they protested against NATO enlargement. Later, Russian presidents would assert that this meeting had given them assurances that NATO would not expand. The United States would remember this meeting differently: as one in a number of conversations and negotiations limited solely to Germany, and until the final documents were signed, changeable.[96]

Moreover, the matter could hardly be decided without the West Germans, who were arriving the next day. Baker intentionally departed for Romania and Bulgaria even as Kohl was landing in Moscow on Saturday, February 10. The secretary and the chancellor wanted to avoid meeting. The goal, as Baker put it, was to prevent "the public impression in the Soviet Union that somehow the Americans and the Germans were conspiring against them." In reality, of course, "we were consulting continuously." Even while he was still at the negotiating table with the Russians, Baker had delegation member Dennis Ross, his trusted director of policy planning, begin drafting a secret letter summarizing the U.S.-Russian talks for Kohl's eyes. Baker later approved this letter and made sure it was given to the West German ambassador in Moscow, Klaus Blech, who arranged for Kohl to see it as soon as possible once he arrived in Moscow on February 10.[97]

"Dear Mr. Chancellor," Baker's note began. "In light of your meeting with President Gorbachev, the President wanted me to brief you on the talks I've had in Moscow." The secretary summarized Gorbachev and Shevardnadze's fears about German unification, and indicated that he had tried to assuage them by proposing the $2 + 4$ mechanism, in which they seemed interested. Baker said that he had also explained to Gorbachev that a united Germany would choose to stay in NATO. "And then I put the following question to him. Would you prefer to see a unified Germany outside of NATO, independent and with no US forces or would you prefer a unified Germany to be tied to NATO, with assurances that NATO's jurisdiction would not shift one inch eastward from its present position?" Baker quoted Gorbachev's response verbatim: "'Certainly any extension of the zone of NATO would be unacceptable.' (By implication, NATO in its current zone might be acceptable.)" In short, Baker thought that Gorbachev was "not locked-in" and he looked "forward to comparing notes with you after your meeting. Sincerely yours, Jim."[98]

Baker's cover note was the second major missive that Kohl had received from top U.S. leadership in the same number of days. He had gotten a letter from Bush the night before, as he was preparing to depart for Moscow, saying that the president wanted "to confirm again to you my view of the role of a unified Germany in the Western alliance." This presidential message, put together by the NSC out of its concern about Baker's formulations, sounded a different note from Baker. Instead of using general language about NATO's jurisdiction, the presidential letter used specific language about East Germany. Bush indicated (picking up a phrase originated by Wörner) that he would agree to a "special military status for what is now the territory of the GDR."[99] Zelikow remembers this extraordinary presidential missive as an attempt to make it clear to Kohl that the White House, concerned about the implications of Baker's wording, preferred a different approach. The idea was that a letter from the president would trump a letter from the secretary.[100]

As a result, by the time that he arrived in downtown Moscow, Kohl had received personal messages from both Bush and Baker with their preferred wordings—and they were not identical. The open question was which language he would use in his talks with Gorbachev. When the moment arrived, he would echo Baker. Whether Kohl would do so because he had missed the discrepancy between the two, or because he knew what the discrepancy meant but found Baker's approach more useful as a short-term negotiating tactic, is unclear. What is clear is that he and Teltschik were trying hard to soften up Gorbachev. They had already prepared the ground before their departure with a well-timed announcement that the sky was falling. In a briefing for journalists before the Moscow trip, Teltschik had strategically let slip that East Germany was on the brink of insolvency. It would be unable to pay debtors in a few days. This caused an enormous splash in the media, and so headlines about the dawn of economic doomsday in the GDR accompanied the chancellor to Moscow and strengthened his case that drastic measures were needed.[101]

The critical Soviet–West German bilateral meeting involved Gorbachev, Chernyaev, Kohl, Teltschik, and translators. The chancellor began by bemoaning Modrow's botched efforts to reinvigorate the Stasi. State authority had broken down completely as a result. Kohl was particularly worried about the safety of East Germany's nuclear power program and mentioned Chernobyl in passing. The chaos should worry Gorbachev as well, he argued, "given that 400,000 Soviet troops plus their dependents are stationed there." Increasingly, only the DM was accepted in exchange for goods.

For all of these reasons, Kohl wanted to institute economic and monetary union as quickly as possible. Five weeks earlier he had not thought this way, but now he did. He admitted that this decision had subjected him to attacks from the West Germans who would have to pay for it, but he could live with the criticism "and it did not disturb him unduly." The time to act was now. The question of unification had become unavoidable. He wanted to unify Germany and bring it into NATO. And Kohl assured Gorbachev that "naturally NATO could not expand its territory to the current territory of the GDR." Kohl also emphasized his agreement with Adenauer's saying that the German problem could only be solved under a European roof.

Gorbachev asked a number of questions in response. He wanted to know about the potential timeline and about border issues with Poland. He understood that Germany did not want to become a neutral state, but asked if it could perhaps be nonaligned, like India. According to Kohl, Gorbachev agreed, less than heartily, that the question of internal unity was one for the Germans themselves to decide. Sensing what the quid pro quo might be, Kohl made it clear that Gorbachev could count on him for help. The chancellor pointed out that the German economy was in a healthy state. Indeed, "the last eight years were the best since the war." It was therefore "natural" that West Germany and the Soviet Union "could do much together."[102]

Kohl knew that he had to lock in this somewhat uncertain agreement as soon as possible. He called for a press conference for 10:00 p.m. that same night. Like Baker, the chancellor understood the power of the press and wanted to use it right away. West German television viewers heard him proclaim by satellite that it was "a good day for Germany and a happy day for me personally." The Soviet leader had agreed that it was the "sole right of the German people" to make decisions about their future.[103] "Secretary General Gorbachev has promised me clearly that the Soviet Union will respect the decision of Germans to live in one state, and that it will be a matter for Germans themselves to decide the path to, and timing of, their unification." Teltschik, who had helped to draft this announcement, expected the assembled journalists to jump to their feet and applaud, but they did not. He thought that perhaps the reporters did not realize what had just happened: Moscow had agreed to let Germans begin the process of internally unifying their country. If the journalists missed the significance, Kohl did not. He was so moved by the event that he needed a long walk through Red Square with a few colleagues before he could calm down enough to go to sleep in the small hours. Only the next day, when the Soviet news agency TASS released a statement confirming what Kohl had announced, does Teltschik remember West German journalists starting to take sufficient interest.[104]

These two bilaterals were the origin of a later controversy. Moscow would claim that they represented a promise, or pledge, that NATO would remain in its 1989 borders, as indicated above. Because of this, it is worth reviewing these meetings in light of the Russian assertion.

Baker, according to the book by Zelikow and Rice, made clear to Kohl what he had discussed with Gorbachev: a unified Germany, tied to NATO "with assurances that NATO's jurisdiction would not shift one inch eastward from its present position." Baker and Zelikow said that the discussion with Gorbachev dealt solely with East Germany and no other states of the Warsaw Pact. During an interview in 2009, Baker recalled that this position was not a pledge, but a speculative proposition for the purpose of negotiations. Had Gorbachev agreed to it at the time, it might have become a deal. But the Soviet leader did not and it was superseded by later changes to the U.S. position, which were made public by the time of the Camp David meeting later that February. Baker remembered that Gorbachev did not object to this changed position at the time or later, when it was twice personally communicated it to the Soviet leader by both the secretary and President Bush, once in Moscow and once in Washington. Indeed, Gorbachev approved the Soviet Union's signing of a number of final agreements consistent with the changed position.[105]

More problematic are the events of the next day, February 10. Kohl arrived and reinforced Baker's proposition by echoing it in his own conversation with Gorbachev, despite at least suspecting that it was based on a U.S. position that was still evolving. Unlike the U.S.-USSR bilateral, however, the USSR–West German bilateral did not end in speculation. Instead, Gorbachev agreed to his component of the bargain: he said that Germany could unify. Kohl took this concession and publicized it within hours of receiving it. As such, in understanding the origin of Russian resentment about the events of February 1990 (to be discussed further in the conclusion to this book), it is essential to consider not just U.S.-Soviet contacts but also the role of the West Germans as well. Gorbachev did not act on Baker's speculation, but he did act on Kohl's. The way in which this happened was problematic in at least two ways: on the part of Gorbachev, and on the part of Kohl. Gorbachev did something unwise—namely, fulfilling at least some of his part of the bargain without getting written assurances that the other side would do the same—and Kohl got such a bargain on the basis of a U.S. position that was already in flux, as he knew from the Bush letter. If Gorbachev had been a more aggressive negotiator and had not had so many other distracting balls in the air, he might have pressed for written guarantees from either Baker or Kohl. But he did not, and by the end of February it would be apparent that he would never get them. Gorbachev seems not to have understood this sequence of events at the time, although by the end of the year he would angrily turn on Kohl. As for Kohl, in the course of the upcoming Camp David meeting at the end of February, he would come to agree with the Bush position: only full NATO membership for a united Germany would be acceptable, with a special status for East Germany. The chancellor agreed with the president despite the fact that this was not identical to the language he had used with Gorbachev on February 10.

At the time of these bilaterals, there is no evidence that the thinking about NATO's future went beyond East Germany, although such ideas would emerge within the year. In separate interviews, Baker, Zelikow, and Zoellick all indicated that there were musings at the State Department in the latter half of 1990 about the possibility of NATO expansion, although only in a speculative way. An internal State Department document, to be discussed below, hints at theoretical conversations as early as March 1990, but not at the time of these bilaterals. Regardless, the seeds of an enormous future controversy were sown. For the moment, however, Kohl felt that it was a "good day for Germany." [106]

PROPERTY PLURALISM

If February 10 was a good day for Kohl, it was not a good one for the round table of East Germany. Events were moving too quickly. The worst fears of its leaders were being realized. If they did not form a stable government, and soon, then foreign governments (which for them included Bonn) would do it for them. The round table therefore took steps to advance its own authority. Eight of its members became ministers in Modrow's government. Some of them, including Gerd Poppe, Wolfgang Ullmann of Democracy Now, and Eppelmann of Democratic Awakening, took part personally in a trip to Bonn on February 13, just days after Kohl got back from Moscow.

It was a visit, the records show, that they took seriously but Kohl and his aides did not.[107] The chancellor was fresh from his success with Gorbachev, had already decided that Modrow was hopeless, and was willing to bet that he could beat the would-be knights of the round table in the electoral duel next month.[108] Poppe, who had put himself into the contest as a candidate for the dissident party Alliance '90, tried to pin Kohl down on guarantees that "the social net would not rip." Ullmann complained that Kohl wanted an "Anschluss" with the GDR. Kohl, rejecting the application of the term Anschluss to the actions of democratic states, informed the East German delegation bluntly that "the details of the path to unity are not up for discussion." [109]

These diplomatic activities went far beyond the round table's original vision for itself, which was to serve as an entity separate from the government, but one that would challenge it when necessary (as it had done over the Stasi).[110] Now, in addition to projects like the closure of Stasi buildings, the round table also began taking stances on foreign policy. On February 19, it drew up a resolution opposing NATO entry for a future united Germany. "A NATO membership for the future Germany cannot be combined with the goal of German unity achieved in the context of a European peace-order and is therefore rejected." Rather, the two Germanies should first unite, hold a constitutional convention (as foreseen in Article 146 of the West German Basic Law), write a new all-German constitution, have elections on the basis of it, and only then let those elected decide on alliance membership.[111]

In addition, the round table was creating an entirely new model for the future of East Germany. By March 12, the working group charged with drafting the new constitution—coordinated by the energetic Gerd Poppe—could present a lengthy document to the sixteenth and final meeting of the round table. This draft intentionally diverged from both the existing East and West German constitutions. Echoing Gorbachev's own attempts to redefine the notion of property, it agreed neither with the notion that the private ownership of property was morally and ideologically wrong nor with the U.S. model that private ownership of property was essential. The controversial U.S. historian Charles Beard—a man whom the Poppes would have found sympathetic—had argued in 1913 that the U.S. Constitution was essentially an economic document—one that protected the rights of property from popular majorities. Beard meant this controversial claim as an indictment, in an era where alternate views for the economic organization of society competed for attention; it caused a furor at the time. Although it is unlikely that Poppe or any other round table members knew of Beard, they clearly shared his criticism of Western constitutions.

The draft was, in essence, an attempt to find the much-discussed third way in the contest between the visions of modernity offered either by Communism or capitalism. The goal was to balance social justice with individuality and property ownership.[112] One of the concepts behind it was the notion of "property pluralism." Instead of a Western-style constitution founded on the rights of private property, or an Eastern-style one founded on the socialist concept of "the people's property," New Forum member Klaus Wolfram suggested that the GDR Constitution have property pluralism. In other words, it should consider both kinds of property to be equal in the future society.[113] By that he seems to have meant that private property would be the default, but there would exist a number of agreed-on situations in which the state could intervene. In a crisis, it could take aggressive action, as suggested in Article 34 of the draft.

Moreover, there would also be a right to work enshrined in Article 31 of the "Basic Rights" section of the new constitution. Men and women would have to be treated equally. The citizens of the future GDR would additionally have the constitutional right to social security, health care and disability coverage, and unemployment support. Presumably the enforcement of these articles would justify state intervention. There was also an implication in Article 34 that such intervention might happen if property were to be used in a way that damaged the environment.[114]

The moved-up elections in March put an end to the round table, but its working group for constitutional drafting kept going until April 4. It sent a letter on that date to the newly elected East German delegates to the Volkskammer, or People's Chamber, with a copy of the unanimously approved final draft. It requested that "you engage yourself in getting the Volkskammer to put this Constitution into force."[115] The letter expressed the hope that its draft could not only provide a model for the future of East Germany but also influence a future unified Germany. If West Germany were to follow its own Basic Law's road map to unification— that is, calling a constitutional convention under Article 146—success in creating a GDR code of laws would give East Germans a sound basis for negotiating in that future convention. In other words, perhaps the East German vision for property pluralism and other social protections would become enshrined in the future all-German constitution.

The round table's expansion of its own authority caused many East Germans to put pen to paper and send in their opinions. The long time lag between the dates on the postmark and the dates of receipt in Berlin testified to the breakdown in basic postal services.[116] Some correspondents welcomed the efforts of the round table to establish an enduring order for the GDR. "Are we going to be sold for nothing and the citizens of our country betrayed?" asked a woman from Leipzig on February 8. "Every reasonable person sees the dangers awaiting us if we are steam-rolled into a monetary union with West Germany," read another letter. One correspondent was even more worried: East Germans "will become an army of slaves on Kohl's plantation."[117]

But a significant number thought that the arduous attempts of the round table to map out a third way were unnecessary. "Take the hand that West Germany is offering. . . . [T]he people are fed up. The revolution continues, but it is becoming less peaceful," suggested one letter writer. From Merseburg came the question of when the round table's members had last spent any time talking to people besides each other. When, the author asked, did you last visit real workers? Most of them "are clear about the fact that we will not be able to start over all by ourselves," and so the GDR should accept help from West Germany, not make demands of it.[118]

Other letters were even more blunt. When, asked one, will you finally say yes "to a speeded-up tempo for monetary union and reunification?"[119] Or another: "Quick monetary union is the only thing that can save us. Half of Leipzig is already working in the West." This author called on the round table to disband as well, because it could do nothing—a sentiment that an anonymous letter writer shared: "You idiots! Why are you still working? Your time is up."[120]

CONCLUSION

In the course of early 1990, both East Berlin and Moscow began offering their visions for the future. Socialist dissidents followed Havemann's example by producing a specific legal road map for the future of an independent East Germany, including property pluralism with mechanisms for the state to intervene in economic crises. Meanwhile, Gorbachev and his advisers marched to their own drummer and postulated grand but vague futures.[121]

These visions were heroic models in both the positive and the negative senses of the word. They reached for the sky, with laudable goals. With more time, they might have become more developed and feasible.[122] But they would require superhuman effort, and neither Gorbachev's opponents in the Soviet Union nor the East European population were willing to give them the time that they needed. By the end of the 1980s, in the words of one historian, public opinion had become an "effective solvent of power."[123]

The broader East German population had been willing to support the opposition "elite" in fall 1989 and early 1990, when both shared the goal of tearing down the SED regime. If they agreed on what needed to go, however, they did not agree on what the future should hold. After the brush with a stage of terror, the latter redoubled efforts to move on to reformed socialism in East Germany, while the former turned West. The shortcomings of daily life had left Eastern Europe with a profound distrust in grand socialist narratives and little tolerance for edited versions.

The beneficiaries of these conflicts were Bush and Kohl. Neither the president nor the chancellor wanted to indulge in creating vast new institutions, and neither was willing to sit back while others tried to produce a third way in everything from property rights to international security. As a saying making the rounds among West German businesses at the time put it, the third way would lead to the third world. In their view, that could not be allowed to happen in a united Germany.[124]

CHAPTER 4

PREFAB PREVAILS

What kinds of inner joy does politics have to offer . . . ? Well, first of all, it confers a feeling of power. The professional politician can have a sense of rising above everyday existence . . . from the knowledge that he holds in his hands some vital strand of historically important events. But the question facing such a person is which qualities will enable him to do justice to this power. . . .
—Max Weber, 1919

Prefabrication: Manufacture of parts or all of a building in a factory before they or it are brought to the site.
—*The Oxford Dictionary of Architecture*, 1999

So many people, with so many different views and so many different voices. And inside each of us so many more people still, all struggling to be heard. For a moment one voice rises above the others, and everyone picks up the tune. And then the cacophony resumes.
—Lines delivered by playwright Michael Frayn's version of Brandt, in *Democracy*, 2003[1]

On March 18, East Germans would have their first opportunity since the dawn of the Nazi era to cast their ballots freely. Roughly twelve million voters would choose among twenty-four parties. As their choices would highlight, these new voters were not persuaded by the dissidents and former dictators (who had become uneasy allies at the round table) that there was a future for an independent GDR. The idea of a revived East Germany, heroically blazing the trail for a new kind of socialism and property pluralism, seemed like too big of a risk. Kohl was confident that his party, the CDU, could offer the voters something that would appeal to them more: institutional transfer, or the chance to install preexisting Western institutions and laws on to East German territory as soon as possible.[2] Militarily, NATO would provide a sufficient security umbrella; politically, new East German states could simply import the West German Basic Law; and economically, the West German currency and market rules would do fine. Since all of these institutions and structures were prefabricated, and (in Kohl's view) ready for set up in the East without much subsequent alteration, unification could proceed rapidly indeed. The chancellor believed that the West German faith in corporatism—defined as the establishment and use of institutional mechanisms to resolve conflicts among different segments of society—was not misplaced, and would transfer well to the East.[3] Moreover, it would be to Kohl's advantage to proceed swiftly with his prefab plans, because it would ensure that the process took place while Gorbachev was still in power, and it would prevent critics from trying to suggest changes. In short, Kohl knew that the campaign in the GDR was a vital strand in historically important events, both domestically and internationally, and that he could potentially dominate it even though he was not officially on the ballot.

The German theorist Max Weber had argued in 1919 that what mattered was whether a politician had the qualities to do justice to such a historic opportunity. Kohl's opponents, ranging from the dissidents in East Berlin to the SPD in Bonn, felt that he did not, particularly when he began invoking the Stalinist era at a key moment. As will be described below, they campaigned hard against what they saw as a developing tragedy—namely, a CDU victory and the concomitant loss of a chance to create a third way. Kohl's opponents simply did not believe that he and his party colleagues in the East would be willing or able to live up to the opportunity to create a new Germany, and perhaps a new Europe.

These events mattered to more than just Germans because, in early 1990, international relations would become tied tightly to German domestic politics.[4] Kohl was betting that if he could win at home, then he could win abroad, and his friends and enemies had to wait and see whether he was right. A big victory on March 18 would provide his prefab model with so much domestic legitimacy that he would be difficult to challenge on the international level.

As a result, Kohl decided that he should do absolutely whatever it took to emerge victorious in East Germany, even if that meant offending other countries in the short term. The former U.S. secretary of state, Dean Acheson, used to say that 80 percent of the job of making foreign policy was managing one's domestic ability to have a policy at all.[5] For Kohl in March 1990, even though he was not officially on the ballot in the GDR, it became close to 100 percent of his job. And if he did win big, there would be an added bonus: he could claim to his international partners that the desires of East German voters, and not he himself, drove the process.

THE SECURITY SOLUTION: TWO PLUS FOUR EQUALS NATO

Kohl got off to a good start in his campaign, thanks to Gorbachev's agreement that German unity was a matter for Germans alone to decide. This success, secured over the weekend of February 10–11 in Moscow, was multiplied by events in the days immediately following. On the day that Kohl left Moscow, TASS released a Soviet government pledge to "secure the withdrawal of all foreign troops from other people's territories in Europe by 1995–96 and the elimination of all military bases on foreign territories by the year 2000."[6] Then, through their foreign ministers, he and Bush began to go on the offensive together at the Ottawa conference of February 11–13.

This conference, which brought together the foreign ministers of both NATO and the Warsaw Pact to discuss international aviation, could not have been better timed for the purpose of German unification. It meant that the foreign ministers of all significant states were in one place and allowed them to hold conversations at a tempo otherwise unimaginable. Baker, who was still on the continuous road trip that had started February 5, managed in just one day (February 13) to speak at least five times each to both Genscher and Shevardnadze, meet with Hurd and French Foreign Minister Roland Dumas, and hold a NATO ministerial caucus, all while carrying out the scheduled program on aviation.[7] In the course of one of these meetings, Shevardnadze finally accepted Bush's proposal for a mutual 195,000 limit on ground and air personnel in the central zone of Europe. The Soviet foreign minister, changing a previous position, did not demand that the United States give up the troops outside that zone as well.[8]

Even though neither Bush nor Kohl was in Ottawa, they were still directing events via phone calls to the conference and each other. Kohl called Bush on Tuesday, February 13, at 7:45 p.m. German time.[9] It was his first conversation with the U.S. president since his historic meeting with Gorbachev the previous Saturday. The lack of word from Kohl for three days afterward had made Scowcroft concerned. "We had done the most we could to encourage our preferred outcome," he remembered, including sending the presidential letter to Bonn on the night before Kohl's departure. But, Scowcroft added, despite this precaution, "we were more than a little nervous. We had great faith in Kohl, but Gorbachev might decide to push hard. We could not rule out the possibility that Gorbachev could tempt—or threaten—him."[10] Kohl's February 10 conversation with Gorbachev had reminded Scowcroft of what he already knew: that there was a version of the future that involved only Bonn and Moscow as the decision-making centers, not necessarily Washington.[11] Indeed, Falin advised Gorbachev around this time to offer "very attractive" proposals to both Germanies—calling for the establishment of a "neutral, democratic, and basically demilitarized Germany"— against which the three Western powers could do little. Falin also thought that the Soviet Union could win the support of Britain and France for such an idea.[12]

Scowcroft and Bush were reassured, however, by Kohl's February 13 call. The chancellor told Bush that "the neutralization of Germany is out of the question for me." Kohl was hopeful that he could avoid that issue and still attain unity. "I feel we will find a solution" to the outstanding problems, Kohl said, "but it will be hard work." "We must find a solution," Bush agreed.[13]

Bush subsequently spoke to Baker to find out how one possible solution, the 2 + 4 forum, was faring in his conversations in Ottawa. What he heard from Baker was not satisfying. Shevardnadze was insisting that 2 + 4 meetings begin even before the elections on March 18—something that Baker opposed. Genscher, using Baker's hotel room phone, called Kohl to see what he thought; Kohl agreed to the Soviet demand, and Genscher informed Baker.

Some interesting personal politics ensued. On hearing this, Bush and his White House team insisted on calling Kohl personally. They did not trust Genscher, whom they saw as willing to give anything to the Soviets for unity. Embarrassingly for Genscher, even though he had phoned Kohl in Baker's hotel suite with Baker there, he had to wait while Bush tested his veracity. In his memoirs, Genscher recalled that this was the only time this happened to him in his sixteen years as foreign minister to that date. Baker looked uncomfortable, but they both made the best of it, passing the time with small talk.[14] Genscher told a story that showed there was at least one place that trusted him: the town where he was born, now in East Germany. On Friday, he would attend a ceremony at which his old high school would be named after him.

In the Oval Office, Bush felt compelled to explain to Kohl why he was calling Bonn again at 9:01 p.m. German time when they had already spoken that day: "I don't want to get crosswise with you, and I am talking about Helmut Kohl as well as the FRG," explained the president. "I don't want to get caught up in internal matters." Kohl replied, "I understand that well." He assured Bush that, yes, he had spoken to Genscher and, yes, what Genscher had said was right. The importance of getting started with 2 + 4 outweighed all other concerns. "I want to be frank," Kohl said. "I worry if this question remains open." If it did, "others in the East and the West [will] want to join up with the Four. Then we will have a big problem." Although he did not mention it particularly, Kohl was worried about Poland. Bush saw the point; he found the idea of involving as many as thirty-five nations of the CSCE to be a "non-starter."[15] Kohl also pointed out that it would be May before an East German coalition government could form itself after the multiparty elections, so nothing would really happen until then anyway. He reassured Bush: "That gives the two of us enough time."[16] Time to do what was not specified, but presumably map out the plan for the future before others could do so. In other words, it did not matter when the $2 + 4$ meetings began, because $2 + 4$ did not really matter. Bush and Kohl would sort out the important decisions between themselves. Still, they needed to be seen publicly endorsing a forum in which the other countries could at least feel they were being heard. Such a forum was necessary not only for the Soviet Union. As Thatcher would explain to Genscher when he stopped in England on his way home from Ottawa, "Germany's allies . . . [are] feeling ignored or excluded."[17]

Bush, now having the express permission of the chancellor, said that he would authorize Baker to go ahead. He hung up at 3:10 p.m. Washington time and, according to Baker's memoirs, was ringing the phone in the Ottawa hotel room five minutes later, giving Baker the green light. Genscher had passed his humiliating test and decided to swallow his anger, realizing that the origin of the distrust lay not in Washington but in Bonn.[18]

Ironically, it seems that Baker may have received the same questioning himself around the same time. Baker's delegation member Ross remembered that the West Germans had worries of their own as to whether Baker was freelancing. If so, this may have been due to the discrepancies between the letters Kohl had received from Baker and Bush on February 9 and 10. Bonn appears to have double-checked whether or not Baker still enjoyed Bush's confidence and received a positive reply.[19]

Once everything was settled, Baker and Genscher sprang into action. "Having finally received a clear green light from our capitals, Genscher and I decided to go ahead and issue the Two-plus-Four statement. We didn't want to give anyone time for any more second thoughts." Using the method of locking in an agreement by publicizing it immediately, they got the British and French foreign ministers to agree to a short-notice press conference. Their written release announced that the two Germanies and four powers had agreed to meet "to discuss the external aspects of the establishment of German unity, including the issues of the security of the neighboring states." Events had moved so quickly that other NATO members present at the same conference did not even know that $2 + 4$ was final; Baker remembers that they were irritated to learn from journalists what had happened.[20]

Baker and Genscher were right to move quickly; back home in Moscow, Gorbachev's opponents were trying to shoot down the idea of $2 + 4$. Chernyaev remembers that Shevardnadze's willingness to agree to it was viewed in the Soviet Union as a sign of weakness and a capitulation.[21] Gorbachev's opponents thought that it should at the very least be named $4 + 2$, since the four powers had defeated Germany. A month later, Gorbachev would have to defend himself against the rumors that Baker's delegation members were going around proclaiming that in

Ottawa, as in the Cuban missile crisis, the Soviets blinked first. Gorbachev was so upset by this that Baker felt it necessary to write him a personal note saying that any such remarks were unauthorized.[22] This exchange altered nothing, however; the deal was done. Baker knew, as Kohl did, that once an agreement was in writing and released to the press, it was hard to undo. Publicized written agreements, not private gentleman's agreements, were the way of the world in 1990.

There was no rest for Baker and his delegation members when they finally returned to Washington after the eventful eight-day trip to Europe and Canada. Although they had succeeded in selling their ideas about NATO and 2 + 4 abroad, they still had to sell them back home. At a State Department background briefing after his trip, run by Margaret Tutwiler, a journalist asked if someone could "talk a little bit about how you see this shaking down. If both sides get to 195 [thousand troops in the central zone of Europe] do the 195 Soviet troops stay in an otherwise demilitarized East Germany that is part of a unified Germany that is part of NATO? That sounds a little surreal to most of us." The answer: "I know. But German unification used to sound surreal to a lot of people too."[23]

The notion of an East German region with Soviet troops but without NATO still sounded surreal to the NSC as well. Scowcroft in particular was worried about Baker's pledge that NATO's jurisdiction would not move one inch eastward, because it could interfere with German unification. Acquiring an indefensible territory would simply not be a viable solution for a united Germany, so Scowcroft and Teltschik discussed how to deal with Baker when they saw each other at the annual Munich international defense conference, called Wehrkunde, held every year in February. If the Soviet Union could in fact get guarantees that NATO would never expand, then it could stall or prevent unification. Trying to undo some of the damage that the NSC thought Baker had done, staff member Rice (who went to Moscow with the secretary and then faced a barrage of questions about why she had not stopped Baker when she got back) had a conversation with Vadim Zagladin. She emphasized to Zagladin, who worked in the Communist Party's own de facto foreign ministry, the International Department of the Central Committee, that membership of united Germany in NATO was extremely important to the United States.[24]

Meanwhile, similar concerns arose in both London and Bonn. Thatcher thought it essential that all of Germany have full membership of NATO. The only feasible concession would be for "NATO to forswear the deployment of non-German forces in the former GDR" which would, as will be described in the next chapter, eventually emerge as the answer. Her briefing papers on the topic indicate concern that the Russians would also demand "that no nuclear weapons be present on German soil" which could lead to the "de-nuclearisation of Europe." If the Soviets were to do so, "the bulk of German public opinion is likely to be sympathetic," particularly influential church leaders in East Germany who had "already taken a strong stand on the issue." As a result, Western leaders would have to handle this issue very carefully if they hoped to maintain their nuclear deterrent in a united Germany. At the same time, in West Germany, Defense Minister Stoltenberg and Bundeswehr General Klaus Naumann continued to share Scowcroft's doubts. They wondered how an East Germany outside of NATO could possibly be defended. At a meeting of a chancellery team assembled to plan for unity, Genscher pushed back against Stoltenberg. The foreign minister insisted that a way would have to be found to defend the GDR, because moving NATO to East Germany would meet with "opposition from all sides." The dispute spilled out into the open and Kohl had to intervene. In the short run, he supported Genscher's view, since it agreed with what he had told Gorbachev; but the issue of defending East Germany was clearly still unresolved.[25]

The outcome of the similar standoff in Washington was the opposite. Zelikow remembers that Baker had to "walk back from his February position" because it was simply untenable.[26] The secretary of state ceased using his line about NATO not moving eastward after February 1990. He also had to defend the 2 + 4 forum. This forum had become a reality much faster than anyone had expected and without serious NSC discussion of it. Scowcroft would later remark that it was his fault for not scheduling a discussion, "but I had thought that Baker was only taking soundings among the allies" and the NSC would have a chance to vet the idea later, once Baker got back from his trip.[27] Scowcroft and his staff were afraid that the 2 + 4 mechanism was both too weak and too strong. Too weak because, as Rice noted, Gorbachev could "dillute [sic] the 2 + 4 process" with his preference for "'all-Europeaness."[28] It might also be too strong, because it would give the Soviet Union another means of obstructing unity.

Zoellick reportedly defended Baker's belief in 2 + 4 by saying that "the presence of 380,000 Soviet troops in the GDR was means enough for obstruction."[29] The 2 + 4 would recognize and manage that obstructive power, not add to it. Besides, it was now a done deal. The public announcement had cut off not only other countries but also the NSC. The best they could do was to ensure that the 2 + 4 did not have real veto power.[30]

Baker addressed these concerns personally in a meeting at the White House on Friday, February 16. As part of his preparation for selling these ideas to the home team, he spoke with Wörner. Baker was therefore up-to-date on NATO thinking and ready to defend himself. To those who claimed that 2 + 4 might cause obstruction, he would reply that 2 + 4 was about "discussions, not decisions." His handwritten notes emphasize this point: "2 + 4 is not negotiation it's consultation. Soviets[,] Brits. + French will want more decision making auth[ority]." He was right. Thatcher would soon be arguing that "the Two plus Four negotiations *should* negotiate on wider issues."[31] In response to such pressures, Washington would simply "[k]eep saying 'it's a framework + mech[anism] for managing ext[ernal] aspects of German unif[ication].'" In his view, the 2 + 4 forum was not a worry but a success. Since neither the "2, 4, 16, or 35 would work"—meaning that the two Germanies, the four powers, the sixteen members of NATO, and the thirty-five CSCE states were all inappropriate groupings, and the "12," or the EC, apparently did not merit consideration—this was the least bad alternative. In fact, it "is probably the bare minimum process the Soviets will need to express their interests and justify the result at home." The implication was that it would prove to be the least costly way of getting a united Germany into the Western alliance; two plus four would equal NATO membership. The gist of Baker's argument was that the benefits of the 2 + 4 forum would be worth the exertions needed to ensure that its scope did not expand. Bush would make such exertions in April, when he met Thatcher in Bermuda and explicitly told her that 2 + 4 would not address the truly major issues, namely "Germany's membership in NATO; the status of Western nuclear and conventional forces stationed in the FRG; the size of German armed forces; or . . . new discriminatory limits to place on German sovereignty— a sure recipe for future instability." He also met Mitterrand and told him the same thing.[32]

In addition, Baker argued that the 2 + 4 forum had a major additional benefit— one that addressed Scowcroft's worry that Bonn and Moscow could shut out Washington. "*Frankly, it's in our interest as well* as it *prevents separate German-Soviet deals* that could be prejudicial to our interests." Any possible concerns could all be discussed with Kohl personally, as he had accepted an invitation to Camp David and would be arriving in a week. "Do we know whether Kohl intends to bring Genscher? Frankly, it's difficult to manage this on two tracks, and it would help us if we could urge the Germans to make it easier for us to discuss these items with the two of them together," Baker added.[33]

Kohl did not, in fact, bring Genscher when he arrived at Dulles Airport on Saturday, February 24. Instead, only Teltschik, aides Walter Neuer and Uwe Kaestner, and Kohl's wife, Hannelore, came along. In his memoirs, Kohl said that he left Genscher behind because "the American side" had announced Baker would not attend; but Baker was not only there, he had hoped Genscher would be too.[34] Either someone other than Baker on the U.S. side had quietly vetoed Genscher's participation, or more likely, Kohl had decided that he wanted to make important decisions without his difficult coalition partner.

The meeting was the first visit to Camp David by a West German chancellor—a particular honor that was not lost on the FRG delegation. Teltschik remembers a warm and friendly atmosphere developing as they sat in front of a fire.[35] Although the setting was informal, the meeting accomplished a great deal of business, both on the overall manner of proceeding and particular issues. The Americans wanted U.S.–West German consultations on all issues of significance, which would then form the basis for later consultations among the four powers and finally by the 2 + 4. The West Germans naturally found this agreeable.

There were notes of discord. The Poles, with the clear backing of Thatcher, had already asked for additional West German aid on top of that agreed on in the November 1989 visit. Repeating the old Polish cry of "*nic o nas bez nas*" (nothing about us without us), they also sought a seat at the new 2 + 4 table. The foreign minister, Krysztof Skubiszewski, was calling for a peace treaty to end World War II as well. Thatcher also found such a treaty to be essential. To her dismay, she had been advised by her Foreign Office that CSCE did not actually prevent the changing of borders in Europe. The consequences of this finding—"that any frontier can be changed easily & without reference to any other state" distressed her. To avoid such changes, "we *need* a *PEACE TREATY soon*" (as she wrote in the margin of the relevant briefing paper with multiple underlinings).[36] The concept of such a treaty also raised the question of reparations, as mentioned previously, which was something that the chancellor hoped fervently to avoid. He told Bush that reparations would be "unacceptable" for him. Not only had West Germany already paid a hundred billion DM in reparations, Kohl complained, but the large portion that had gone to Poland had been frittered away by a corrupt regime rather than forwarded to the intended recipients. A peace treaty would be equally unworkable, because at the end of hostilities in May 1945, Germany had technically been in a state of war with 110 countries. Presumably all of them would have a right to be involved in negotiations for such a treaty.[37] In light of the potentially limitless delay and financial exposure, Kohl wanted to avoid a peace treaty altogether.

Bush nonetheless urged Kohl to make some kind of concession to the Poles, who had strong allies in the U.S. Congress. The U.S. president was hardly the only one pushing Kohl in this direction; the West German press was also calling for some kind of border statement. Bush encouraged Kohl to endorse the inviolability of the future German-Polish border. Kohl felt that such a statement was superfluous since it already existed in the Warsaw Treaty of 1970, and he did not plan on repealing that accord.[38] Kohl repeated to Bush a comment that he had made to Mazowiecki—namely, that the issue was a "psychological problem" in West German domestic politics. Kohl wanted to avoid alienating the Germans (and their descendants) who had been expelled from now-Polish territory after the war.[39]

Although they could not find a common approach to Poland, the president and the chancellor reached an agreement on how to deal with Gorbachev. Moscow needed money badly and was in a weak position. (Indeed, the very next day massive protests in Moscow would further undermine Gorbachev.)[40] Bush felt that the Soviet Union could not make demands about the future: "To hell with that! We prevailed, they didn't. We can't let the Soviets clutch victory from the jaws of defeat."[41] He would not allow Russia to determine NATO's membership. It seems that Bush's tough talk persuaded Kohl to abandon an idea that he had been toying with—that is, some kind of so-called French solution. Under this concept, a united Germany might remain in NATO but leave its integrated military command. Yet it appears that in the course of the Camp David meeting, Kohl came to agree with Bush that he should push hard, and push fast, for full NATO membership for a united Germany. The Russians would eventually accept it, they were sure, but Kohl was also certain that "they will want to be paid for it." Since Bush and Baker had already affirmed that the United States would not be offering financial support to their longtime enemy, it was clear who would be paying. Bush pointed out that the chancellor had "deep pockets," but the hint was not necessary.[42]

Afterward, the Bushes, the Kohls, Baker, Scowcroft, and Teltschik sat down for a cozy dinner. Over a hearty meal of roast beef in the president's cabin, the evening became less a summit and more a Saturday night dinner party among friends. Kohl remembered this evening in particular as a happy one for his wife, Hannelore, who would later seclude herself from public life and ultimately commit suicide; but that night she and Barbara Bush seemed to enjoy themselves. There were a lot of long conversations and laughter all around. Bush even screened a movie afterward, but most of the jet-lagged Germans begged off and went to sleep.[43]

The next morning, after a church service attended not only by the participants but also numerous Bush grandchildren, the president and the chancellor had a final conversation.[44] They did not reach an agreement on Poland and the gap between their two positions became apparent at the final press conference immediately afterward. Bush stated that the United States recognized the current border, while Kohl would only say that the matter would be settled after unity.[45] Moreover, although the two leaders had accurately predicted that the central Soviet concern would be financial support, neither of them could figure out when it would come to a head. In February, Gorbachev was not yet ready to make big concessions.[46] Kohl guessed that Gorbachev would want to make the deal on the most important issue, Germany in NATO, with a peer state. It would probably happen at the U.S.-Soviet summit scheduled for Washington in June, the chancellor thought.[47] On this point, Kohl was wrong: the crucial final round would come down to just Gorbachev and himself in July 1990.

THE POLITICAL SOLUTION: ARTICLE 23

As a result of Camp David, the Western security solution was now clear. Washington and Bonn would insist that a united Germany—including former East German territories—would be part of NATO. The only concession that they would make was, in the words of Wörner, to give the Eastern territories a "special military status." Baker's notion that NATO would not expand its jurisdiction one inch eastward, seconded by Kohl, had turned out to be a limited-time offer, and now the time was up. Although Gorbachev did not realize it immediately, he would not be able to get that deal again. Instead, as consolation, he got the 2 + 4 process (which he preferred to call "the six," thereby trying to make it more palatable to his enemies by demoting the two Germanies). He hoped at the outset that 2 + 4 would serve as a brake on German unification and give him a veto. As would soon become apparent, however, and as Washington and Bonn intended, the important decisions would not be made at the 2 + 4 sessions.

One of those decisions concerned the legal means for carrying out political unification. The history of World War II and its aftermath played an enormous role in this decision. The FRG had, as mentioned, come into existence in 1949 after the three Western occupying powers, deciding that antagonism with the Soviet Union had reached such a level that four-power cooperation was no longer possible, decided instead to unite just their zones of occupation into a new country. They worked with the leaders, or minister presidents, of the various reconstituted German states in their zones to figure out how authority between occupier and occupied would be divided in the new entity. The three powers eventually suggested that the local minister presidents help produce some kind of constitution for the new country.

The Germans agreed, but insisted that the new country and government should clearly be temporary structures. In other words, they did not want to divide Germany permanently. The capital of the new country should not be a major city like Frankfurt but rather a small, sleepy university town like Bonn; and the new country should not have its own constitution but merely a Basic Law instead. Indeed, the drafters of this Basic Law even prepared explicitly for unification (to take place at some unknown point in the future) by including instructions in Article 146 as to how it should happen. According to this article, once the German people were again united in free self-determination, they would finally write a true constitution for all of Germany. The Basic Law would correspondingly "lose its validity on the day that a constitution, agreed upon by the German people in a free decision, comes into force." One expert described its effect as follows: the governance of the FRG was "explicitly designated as a provisional arrangement."[48]

That had been the vision in 1949, at the founding of West Germany; but the world had evolved a great deal in the subsequent forty years. The supposedly temporary Basic Law, the democratic institutions that it had created, and the coalition parliamentary governments that had resulted were all durable and successful. Politicians at home and abroad routinely referred to the Basic Law as the best constitution that the Germans had ever had, even though it was technically not a constitution at all. Under it, West Germany had risen from the rubble, literally, to become a respected democracy and one of the wealthiest states in the world. It was a reliable leader in the EC and a trusted member of NATO.

As a result, the notion that West Germany's de facto constitution would self-destruct in 1990—and thereby call into question all treaties—was breathtaking. Article 146 was clearly the official road to unity, but executing it would be risky in the extreme. In short, it did not fit in the least with the prefab model that Kohl was working so hard to develop.

This legal issue was clearly central to unification, so Kohl asked his interior minister, Wolfgang Schäuble, to look into the matter. At this point Kohl and Schäuble were extremely close; the latter was the heir apparent and a rising star in the CDU. Schäuble's own dreams of the chancellery would disappear into the dual tragedies of a brutal assassination attempt in October 1990—leaving him in a wheelchair—and a party finance scandal, but all that was in the future. At the start of 1990, he was on the way up, and about to become the point man for negotiating the treaties that would unify Germany legally. Since he hoped to inherit a united Germany as chancellor on his own one day, he had a strong incentive for making sure that it was unified in a way that he thought was right.[49]

In a lengthy report, Schäuble informed Kohl that it was impossible to estimate how long the Article 146 process laid out in the Basic Law would take. Merely deciding what to do first, in order to deconstruct one constitution while constructing another, would be enormously time-consuming. Actually carrying out those tasks would be an immense challenge. Moreover, during the transition from one constitution to another, all state institutions would be called into doubt. From a purely legal point of view, they would, of course, continue to enjoy the authority that the old Basic Law granted them until a new constitution came into force. Politically, however, they would become weak and open to attack. On top of that, it was not at all clear how the four powers would be involved. Most problematically, a case could be made that in the places where the 1949 Basic Law talked about Germans coming together in self-determination, it was referring to all those who had been living within Germany's 1937 borders. Many of these regions were now in Poland. "It will not be possible to realize the participation of the German population living beyond the Oder-Neisse border [that is, eastward of the GDR]," Schäuble stated plainly. He was thereby making a virtue out of a necessity; it was another argument against Article 146, which he did not like anyway. In fact, about the only positive remark that Schäuble had for Article 146 was that it would "raise the level of acceptance" of unification.[50]

There was another legal and political option, though, and one that fit well with the overall model of taking existing Western institutions and transferring them to the East. The drafters of the Basic Law of 1949 had hoped that even if Germany did not unify, it might at least be possible for West Germany to regain some of the territory that it had lost during the war by peaceful means. They had thus included the controversial Article 23, which de facto allowed former parts of Germany— presuming the affected regions were in favor and they could resolve any outstanding international issues—to choose to put themselves under the jurisdiction of the Basic Law. The militarization of West Germany's borders to the east ended any immediate hopes that Article 23 might be used for Eastern regions, but it turned out to be useful in the west. Thanks to it, the coal-rich Saar region joined West Germany more than a decade after the war ended. The area had spent the intervening period under an autonomous government set up under French occupation authority, but a popular vote in 1955 confirmed that it wished to join the FRG. On New Year's Day in 1957, under Article 23, it became Saarland, the tenth state of West Germany.[51]

Schäuble viewed this precedent as a useful one. In his view, Article 23 was the equal of Article 146; in other words, it was a second and fully legitimate way to achieve unity—and one with numerous advantages. First, the four powers had tolerated exercise of this article when the Saar region had invoked it.[52] That would make it harder for them to complain in 1990. Second, it meant that the Basic Law would go into effect immediately in East German regions, as soon as they organized themselves into states and indicated that they wished to come under its jurisdiction. There would be no waiting for a new constitutional consensus to emerge. Third, since the Basic Law would stay in effect, there would be no need to renegotiate all of West Germany's treaties. The united country would remain firmly anchored in the EC and NATO. Finally, existing institutions would not have their authority questioned during the transition period.[53] An added benefit that Schäuble did not mention was the fact that Genscher had already voiced support for Article 23; at least on this issue, the chancellor would not have to fight with his own coalition partner.[54]

There would be some challenges, but not insurmountable ones. For one, there would be a need to reconcile existing East German treaty obligations with the Basic Law, although that was a much less daunting task than designing a new constitutional order altogether. Then too, the population of West Germany would have no vote in the matter, but Schäuble felt that the results of past elections signaled that they would accept what Kohl did.

Finally, there would be the unavoidable appearance that another Anschluss was happening. A great deal of resistance to Article 23 would arise for this reason. Indeed, Shevardnadze used just this word when criticizing it, and closer to home, the left-of-center West German and East German political parties were already voicing their disagreement with it as well.[55] The Poles would be especially upset by it, since the spectacle of Eastern regions rejoining a united Germany would raise questions about parts of Polish territory. Nevertheless, Schäuble felt that reasonable arguments could counter that appearance, since it would be a voluntary merger of new East German states with West Germany. He had in fact already started defending Article 23 on a recent visit with Baker in Washington. Schäuble had assured Baker that after the article's final use to unify Germany, a way would be found to nullify it and prevent any future invocations of it. The new united Germany would do so because leaving such a controversial possibility open, Schäuble explained, would otherwise sour the foreign relations of the expanded country.[56]

THE ECONOMIC SOLUTION: MONETARY UNION

To prove that the use of Article 23 would be voluntary, Kohl had to get people to vote for his party, which decided to endorse it as the path to unity. With so much resting on the March 18 elections, Kohl decided that he could not simply leave campaigning to inexperienced East German CDU leaders, tainted by years of cooperation with the ruling regime. He mobilized numerous West German members of the CDU to go to the East to help with the elections, and was pleased when the effort brought new vigor to the Western party as well.[57]

More importantly, as mentioned already, he forged an East German election block called the Alliance for Germany. Kohl did so even though he was not personally on the ballot. Rather, he decided after some hesitation to cooperate with the East German CDU leader Lothar de Maizière, a relatively minor figure in GDR politics who had studied music before pursuing a career in politics. De Maizière had emerged as head of the eastern CDU in the chaos of November 1989, when the Eastern party ended its long practice of rubber-stamping all SED decisions. He came from a suitably symbolic family; originally of French origin, it had prominent branches in West Germany as well. His uncle Ulrich de Maizière had even served as the inspector general of the Bundeswehr, and Ulrich's son Thomas, already active in CDU politics in 1990, would eventually become the head of the chancellery for Merkel in a united Germany. As a result, Lothar seemed like an appropriate enough figurehead for the East German CDU, in spite of the fact that he had been a member when it had tainted itself by submission to the SED, because he had a background suggesting the possibility for cooperation across borders. De Maizière, as it would turn out, would come into conflict with Bonn on a number of crucial issues (and ultimately fall under suspicion of having worked too closely with the Stasi); but in the spring of that year, he seemed like a safe enough ally. The West German and East German branches of the SPD had entered into a cooperative agreement in mid-January, and several former dissident groups had also followed suit and formed their own electoral alliances, so Kohl clearly felt that he needed to set up what at least looked like East-West cooperation between the two halves of the CDU as well. Ultimately, two dozen parties and various alliances would compete for the votes of 12.2 million newly enfranchised East Germans.[58]

On February 6, also mentioned previously, Kohl launched the Alliance for Germany's not-so-secret weapon: he began promising to try to achieve an economic and monetary union between the two Germanies—a vow sure to appeal to voters. This was a political decision, made without consultation with central bankers and without an assessment of what it might do to other European currencies. By February 20, after receiving Gorbachev's permission, he simply instructed a commission of experts to figure out how to make such a union work.[59] The cornerstone of it would be the introduction of the DM as the legal currency of East Germany as soon as possible, even before any kind of political unification.

The election platform of the Alliance for Germany, once finalized, called for a transition to the DM at an exchange rate of one to one for at least some of the amount switched over. This exchange rate was significantly higher than the actual black market rate for changing East German marks into West German DM, and the source of opposition in the Bundesbank, but that did not matter politically. As mentioned, East German crowds had started chanting, "if the DM doesn't come to us, we will go to it." Kohl intended to prevent that from happening.[60]

Monetary union had an additional advantage for Kohl, although he would only describe it privately at first: he thought that it would be an indirect but effective way to get rid of Soviet troops. His aide Teltschik had already started looking into legal means to ask the Soviets to leave, and had been heartened to discover that the Soviet Union had signed a "temporary" agreement on troop stationing with the GDR in 1957. Though the de facto practice clearly diverged from the de jure agreement—thirty-three years later, the troops were still there—the legal documents nonetheless stated that their presence in East Germany was "temporary." A united Germany therefore would have a legal leg to stand on, if it were to call for the Soviet Union to bring the "temporary" stationing to a close.[61]

But such legal arguments might not be enough. Given this, Kohl felt that the introduction of the DM might help too. Soon, he reasoned, the economy in East Germany would blossom and provide an array of high-quality consumer goods. Kohl told Gorbachev that once the Soviet troops stationed in the GDR started to see such goods, which they could presumably not afford because they would still hold rubles, they would grow resentful, and cause problems both in Germany and for Moscow. Gorbachev would want to pull them out as a result, because their behavior might otherwise embarrass the Soviet Union.

Kohl's idea was not idle speculation; problems with black marketeering had already arisen elsewhere. The fifty thousand Soviet troops and three divisions in Hungary, and the seventy-five thousand troops and five army divisions in Czechoslovakia, scheduled to withdraw in 1991, were already causing trouble by selling their weapons and other equipment for hard currency.[62] As Kohl explained to Mitterrand over breakfast during one of their many meetings that spring, Moscow had agreed to pull them out of Eastern Europe so quickly because "discipline had dissolved." Soldiers had destroyed barracks, ripped out telephone lines, blown up ammunition, and created an environmental disaster by dumping oil and other noxious supplies. "They were selling weapons and equipment up to and including tanks." On top of this, "the number of deserters was enormous, especially once the borders opened." Kohl felt strongly that the impact of consumer goods on troops was enormous regardless of their nationality. He pointed out that even U.S. troops in West Germany had something of a "ghetto psychology" because of their insistence on clustering around base stores carrying familiar consumer goods priced in dollars, rather than interacting with the local economy.[63]

Kohl thought that Moscow had pulled out quickly elsewhere because of rampant black marketeering, and felt certain that it would do so in East Germany as well.[64] What the chancellor did not realize at this time was that the Soviet troops had an effective counter. Collectively, they had saved a large amount of East German marks in a so-called "field bank," and they would soon demand the ability to transfer those to DM as well. When he became aware of it, Kohl would find this demand costly, but hard to resist. In the short run, however, Kohl did not know about these troop savings, and he was certain of both the power of consumer goods, and that the proposal of rapid economic and monetary union would be a vote-getter. Although he was not a candidate, he chose to deliver this campaign message personally to East German voters nonetheless. There was a great deal that was unclear about how the elections should proceed—as late as February 20, there was not yet a new election law in the GDR—and the chancellor decided to take advantage of the uncertainty about the role of Western parties to jump into the fray.[65]

The East German round table tried to resist this decision by Kohl and others, passing a resolution against election speakers coming from the West to campaign in the East. The resolution had little effect, though, as the major Western parties simply ignored it. This display of impotence further undermined the authority of the round table. Letter writers wrote in to complain that their government was asking for fifteen billion DM in aid from Kohl at the same time it was telling him that he was not welcome to give so much as a speech. Some letter writers did support the round table, but many could not understand why it had passed the resolution. For its part, the West German newspaper *Bild* began to picture East Germans as ungrateful—a trend that would continue: "Here We Go Again: GDR Forbids Speeches by Brandt and Kohl," read one headline.[66]

THE ELECTION CAMPAIGN AND THE WAYS OF THE WARD HEELER

Kohl dove into the campaign on February 20 in Erfurt, with the first of what would eventually be six rallies in the East. As he explained on the phone to Canadian Prime Minister Brian Mulroney, he had never seen a turnout like the one in Erfurt. In a city with a total population of 200,000, an estimated 150,000 had found their way to the plaza in front of the cathedral by the 5:00 p.m. start of the event.[67] Kohl's speech emphasized the social welfare side of the West German market economy, assuring the crowd that even after having DM in their hands, they would still have a safety net. Teltschik remembered an enormous amount of applause at the end of the speech.[68]

The chancellor's next appearance, on March 2, was successful as well, but there was a cloud over the event. The crowds were still large and enthusiastic—200,000 people in Chemnitz—but Kohl's message was overshadowed by increasing international calls for some kind of new guarantee of the Polish border. Kohl was still unwilling to create one. Border recognition, he said in public, would only occur if linked to Polish renunciation of any further reparations and guarantees of the rights of ethnic Germans in Poland.[69] Moreover, it would happen only after unification, not before, as Warsaw wished. Kohl insisted it had to be after, because he felt that the current West German government could not speak for the future united Germany, and could not sign treaties in its name. Legal scholars questioned this assertion, saying that, under Article 23, East Germany would simply join the existing state of West Germany and leave all of the FRG's treaties intact anyway, including any that might be made with Poland.

Kohl's opinion remained firm, however; no treaty until after unification.[70] Teltschik recalled that Kohl wanted to make sure not only that he won the election, but that a clear majority in both the Bundestag and the Volkskammer would support the legal measures that would follow. It would be much harder to unify the country if a third of the Bundestag voted against it because of objections to accords with Poland.

Teltschik, who was researching the issue at Kohl's request at this time, unearthed some useful, if unfortunate, history. In two agreements from the 1950s, earlier Polish governments had agreed in writing to a cap on, and subsequently the elimination of, reparations from Germany. The chancellor decided to emphasize this information publicly, despite the fact that both agreements lacked any kind of democratic legitimization.[71] Kohl's willingness to rest his own arguments on Stalin era accords proved just how high the stakes were.

In a move that made the realities of 1990 plain, the chancellor had a controversial parliamentary resolution drafted. The resolution promised, on the one hand, a joint statement by the Bundestag and the soon-to-be elected East German Volkskammer to the effect that Polish borders would not be violated, in keeping with the terms of the Warsaw Treaty. On the other hand, the resolution underscored that there would be no further reparations, citing one of the two agreements from the 1950s specifically as the reason.[72]

The response was swift. The press was highly critical. Poland pushed back and said that the 1950s accords did not apply to individuals who had suffered under the Nazis, particularly in concentration camps; those victims retained the right to petition individually for redress.[73] Gorbachev, in an interview, expressed disapproval, and said categorically that German membership in NATO was "absolutely ruled out."[74] Genscher distanced himself from Kohl's remarks. Opponents could not believe that Kohl would talk about Stalin era treaties in the same breath as the FRG's own democratically ratified Warsaw Treaty.[75] Kohl had to defend himself to his allies in a Bundestag debate on the resolution. The criticism was so intense that Teltschik was surprised Kohl did not retreat. The chancellor was pulling out all the stops to win the election at home, regardless of the reaction abroad. It had presumably not escaped Kohl's notice that the first free elections in the Soviet Union, held the same day as the March 2 rally in Chemnitz, had given a large majority to the nationalists in Lithuania. Let outsiders complain that he was being too nationalistic; he had an election to win.

Kohl emerged victoriously from the parliamentary debate; the Bundestag adopted his resolution, including its point about reparations, by a large majority.[76] He also carried out a successful visit to Brussels, where he defended his actions to his NATO allies. Privately, he complained to Teltschik about how effective the Poles were in finding allies abroad to support their cause; they were "world champions in winning sympathy."[77]

Kohl had won that round, but he had made both his enemies and friends nervous. The leader of the SPD in East Germany, Ibrahim Böhme, reassured Shevardnadze that he would behave much more sensibly once the SPD was in charge there. Böhme agreed completely with Moscow's view that the process of unification should only happen once new European structures, especially a new security alliance, had been erected. Shevardnadze was pleased to hear that the East German SPD would resist rapid unification and immediate NATO membership. The Soviet foreign minister pointed out that in trying to block those events, the Soviet Union was not without leverage: it supplied East Germany with its gas and oil, after all.[78] Similarly, Gerd Poppe, now a candidate himself, traveled to Moscow to complain to Gorbachev about the election conduct of the West German parties. Their interference was leading to a "new destabilization." In an ironic twist of fate, the former dissident was now calling on the leader of the Soviet Union for help. Poppe argued that Gorbachev should press harder for his plan of new pan-European structures, which the Soviet leader did in a lengthy *Pravda* interview the next day.[79]

As for Kohl's allies, they were not entirely happy either. Mitterrand, whom the chancellor regarded as a close friend, was particularly upset by Kohl's election campaign. He disagreed vehemently with Kohl about Poland. Mitterrand was about to host Jaruzelski and Mazowiecki for a state visit; during it, the three of them would publicly belittle the Bundestag resolution. They criticized it as not clear enough, and argued that some kind of "international juridical act" was needed.[80] In a series of conversations with Kohl both before and after the Polish visit, Mitterrand tried to get the German chancellor to be more accommodating, pointing out that "France could not stay silent" on the border issue.[81] The French leader was also upset by what he viewed as disrespectful actions toward his troops stationed in West Germany.[82] In an effort to remind the public that France still had a say, Mitterrand ordered a military parade in West Berlin in late February 1990, but was subsequently horrified when Berliners pushed back and asked for the parade to be canceled.[83]

As a consequence of all of these issues, a massive argument erupted just a few days before the election between the chancellor and the president. Kohl was furious that Mitterrand would cast doubt on the sincerity of a resolution approved by the democratically elected West German parliament. The chancellor could not understand why the Poles were publicly demanding treaty negotiations with the West Germans before even officially contacting Bonn about it. Kohl pointedly told Mitterrand that he was trying to achieve *both* German and European unity, and was willing to make big strides on monetary union within the year as a result, but was getting very little credit for what he was doing. Mitterrand responded by insisting that the Poles needed to be heard at the $2+4$ talks. Kohl conceded somewhat, allowing the $2+4$ at least to invite the Poles to attend a session. Although it was rough going, in hindsight Kohl remembered this phone call as the storm that finally cleared the air between friends.[84] The chancellor had been trying to say to his alliance partners, in so many words, let me do whatever I need to win the election at home, and then we will sort everything out abroad. After the middle of March, Mitterrand decided to give him the space to do so.

Washington kept a close eye on the election as well. In the final week before voting, a member of Baker's policy planning staff, Sicherman, composed a synopsis of the East German election and its potential impact on U.S. policy. Since this summary contained prescient speculation about the future course of events in Europe, it is worth examining in detail. Sicherman delivered this memo on March 12 to both Ross and Zoellick, who in turn passed it on to the secretary; Baker saved it among his personal papers when he left office. In it, Sicherman expressed surprise at the "absence of German political unity over unification"; he found that "if the politicians are divided, thus far the GDR population is not." East Germans clearly wanted unification, even if the West Germans were ambivalent about it. "Kohl, who has the ambition to be a historic figure but the ways of a ward heeler has had his finger intermittently on this very pulse." By this, Sicherman meant that the chancellor's heart was in domestic affairs and the give-and-take between local political machines within his country. Kohl was trying to use those skills on a bigger stage, albeit awkwardly. Hence, "he had aligned himself, sometimes clumsily, to prove that he stood for a swift drawing together."

Moreover, the fact that Kohl and Genscher had finally agreed on something significant—the need to use Article 23 to reunify Germany—had not yet sufficiently registered in the West. While this was great news for the United States and NATO, since it meant that all current treaties and alliances would persist, it nonetheless created serious problems. Both the Poles and the Soviet Union would feel uncomfortable, to put it mildly, about a Germany that was suddenly reactivating a part of its constitution that allowed it to annex territory. They were already turning to each other for help as a result.[85] The State Department analyst noted the irony that Poland was cooperating with the Soviet Union to fend off an expansive Germany: "Stalin has had the last laugh. By locating the Polish border westward to incorporate German areas, he forced the Poles to look eastward for support against German complaints," giving "Uncle Joe's ghost . . . a good frolic as the Solidarity Poles rediscovered the virtue of Soviet troops." In Sicherman's view, the United States would "fail utterly if we cannot give Poland and the other nations a choice of more than a Russian domination or a German domination."

Fortunately, the $2 + 4$ process could manage this because it was really "the 'two by four'" process. In other words, the $2 + 4$ mechanism was "in fact a lever to insert a united Germany in NATO whether the Soviets like it or not, but which gives them a role that ought to keep them out of a desperate corner." The Soviets, whose power was "recoiling upon itself at . . . a frightening speed," were gradually realizing this. Having "agreed at a weak moment," they were now looking for ways to backtrack but were not finding any, even as the $2 + 4$ meetings started on March 14.[86] Although Sicherman did not say it, $2 + 4$ also had the advantage of making the British and French feel more involved in the process of unifying Germany. Hurd found that it was particularly helpful in calming Thatcher, at least at first. Only after its implementation would the British realize that for all the expertise they brought to these talks, they were still not involved in the most important U.S.–West German decisions.[87]

These $2 + 4$ meetings also had another advantage for the United States: they gave Washington "a handle on a German unification process that might otherwise be left to the tender mercies of the Germans and the Russians." As Scowcroft feared, Moscow could potentially make Bonn an offer it couldn't refuse, although Sicherman did not expect it.[88] Rather, looking to the future, he predicted that other East European countries would not only accept Germany in NATO, they would even seek the benefits of membership for themselves. In other words, the transatlantic alliance "is the best way out of the German-Russian security dilemma and, with the Czech exception, the Hungarians and the Poles already see it." He was right; they did see it that way. Already on February 20, 1990, Horn had suggested that his country, Hungary, should begin forging closer ties to NATO with a view to "'eventually being integrated'" in its political bodies. At the time this suggestion was speculative, and tentative Polish feelers in the same direction initially received a cool reply. In the years to come, however, both countries would succeed in pressing for membership themselves.[89]

The Sicherman memo of 1990 rightly came to the conclusion that the United States "offers these nations great opportunities on all these scores." But Washington had to be sure that "1) taking on the burden of 'organizing' this region is really a vital interest [and] 2) we have the means to do so. My answer tentatively is that we alone do not have the means but that NATO and the EC surely do." Ross remembers that this memo triggered his own realization that in the long-term, the East European states were not going to feel secure until they were in NATO. Membership for them would also be a way to institutionalize democratic civil-military relations in these countries.[90]

Sicherman had argued that the Soviets would have to accept a united Germany in NATO eventually—but only if the East German elections showed clear support for it. A great deal was hanging on the March 18 outcome. The secretary general of NATO once again, as he so often did at key moments, suggested an idea that might improve matters and make Germany in NATO more palatable to the Soviet Union. Wörner was in regular touch with his old CDU party colleague Kohl throughout March 1990. Presumably in agreement with him, Wörner made public remarks on March 13 to the effect that Soviet troops could stay in Germany after it was unified. They would just have to agree on a departure date in the future.[91]

With all eyes focused on East Germany in the final days before the election, polling still suggested that the SPD would emerge as the strongest party, and perhaps even win an absolute majority.[92] Ever since the opening of the wall, Brandt, the SPD's greatest statesman, had been making numerous personal appearances in the GDR—although he was seventy-six years old and only the honorary party chair. A former member of the resistance to Hitler and the first chancellor of the FRG from the Left, he had also become the first West German leader to visit the other half of divided Germany in 1970. Hundreds of East Germans had braved the Stasi to welcome him even then.[93] For his efforts to ease the inhumanities of the German division, Brandt had received the Nobel Peace Prize in 1971. His dramatic successes and failures—Brandt had to resign in 1974 as a result of sex and spying scandals—eventually became the subject of an award-winning play, *Democracy*.[94] In 1990, he was the most prominent member of the SPD to wel-

Fig. 4.1. Former West German Chancellor Willy Brandt at a campaign rally in East Germany, March 11, 1990. Courtesy of Getty Images.

come unity. With no Stasi threat, hundreds of thousands of people turned out to hear him speak in places like Gotha and Leipzig.

Brandt, who had never ceased to be a German patriot, spoke warmly of unification; but he was not entirely representative of the SPD in this attitude. His party was ambivalent about unity and officially endorsed Article 146, meaning that the SPD preferred the slower path to unification. Its soon-to-be candidate for the West German chancellorship, Oskar Lafontaine, spoke in very different tones about unity. But Brandt, who wanted to be, once again, the voice that rose above the cacophony to show the way forward, pressed on with his remarks and speeches nonetheless. The warm reception that he received from the crowds showed that he personally still had appeal, even if the rest of the party's hesitancy about rapid unification did not.

Despite Brandt's enormous popularity and doubts among even CDU supporters about their chances, Kohl pushed on with his own campaign speeches throughout March.[95] Given that the attendance was regularly in the hundreds of thousands, by the time of the last speech in front of three hundred thousand in Leipzig, he had personally addressed over a million people. He proudly told Bush this in a phone call on March 15. He also told Bush that the crowds had applauded loudly when he spoke about NATO and the alliance; "it is a pity you weren't there, George." The momentum carried his alliance through a crisis, when just days before the election Wolfgang Schnur, one of the CDU's alliance partners, had to resign after evidence of his collaboration with the Stasi became public. Kohl told Bush that he truly did not know if his efforts had succeeded or not, or how the election would turn out. The chancellor just hoped for "a reasonable coalition."[96] He was about to get a lot more than that.

THE RESULTS OF MARCH 18

To the astonishment of everyone, including the CDU itself, the Alliance for Germany won 48 percent of the popular vote. The fact that it almost reached an absolute majority in a pluralistic, multiparty election was quite an achievement. The CDU was particularly surprised by how well it had done in the regions of Thuringia and Saxony, which had had Socialist and Communist governments during the Weimar era (the last time they had been able to choose their leaders).[97] With an election participation rate of over 93 percent, it represented a clear mandate. Kohl's allies, headed by de Maizière, would dominate the future East German parliament. The SPD, with about 22 percent of the vote, would hold only eighty-eight seats out of the four-hundred-member Volkskammer in East Germany (Table 4.1)[98]

On the night of the election, the former dissident groups and the SPD were all in disbelief. Gerd Poppe personally won election to the Volkskammer, but his party, Alliance '90, had gained only about 3 percent of the vote. Brandt was crushed and clearly looked every one of his seventy-six years. Visibly shaken by the result, he refused to appear for a scheduled on-air interview on ZDF, one of the two main West German channels. The television moderator was upset about this abrupt rebuff, remarking sarcastically, "well, sorry, the fact that he wanted to give an interview was on the schedule!"[99]

Kohl, however, had sympathy for Brandt's anguish. The events of 1989 and their shared desire for Germany unity caused the superstars of the Left and Right to develop a friendship in the little time that Brandt had left to live after 1990. Kohl believed that Brandt, with his deep personal desire for unification, had become an uncomfortable exception within his own party, and was understandably frustrated by the SPD's failure to seize the chance to shape the future in 1990. The chancellor concluded that Brandt, who already on November 10 had called for the two Germanies to grow together, correctly sensed the East German mood when the rest of the party had not. Two years later, as Brandt neared death, Kohl was one of the last visitors he would receive, and the elder former chancellor asked the younger to organize his funeral.[100]

TABLE 4.1
Election Results in East Germany on March 18, 1990

Name of Party or Alliance	Percentage of Vote	Seats in Volkskammer
Alliance for Germany (CDU and smaller affiliates)	48.0%	192
SPD	21.9%	88
PDS (formerly SED)	16.4%	66
Numerous smaller parties, including Eastern liberals and groups organized by former dissidents	13.7%	54

Participation: 93.4% of eligible voters
Source: DESE

The election result represented more than the competition between the two ti-
tans of West German politics, though. East German voters had a clear choice between the various models for the future. If they liked the concept of restoration,
they could vote for the SED/PDS. If they liked the idea of moving slowly toward
unity under Article 146 and reviving confederative structures in the meantime,
they could vote for the SPD. If they liked heroic visions of the future, including
a revitalized socialism as well as pan-European political and security structures,
they could vote for the very dissidents who had headed the 1989 revolution and
drafted a new constitution. Or if they believed that the prefabricated structures of
the West German political and economic system should be installed in new Eastern states, they could vote for the CDU. On March 18, they chose in overwhelming numbers to do the latter. When the election results hit the news that evening,
it was apparent to the world that Kohl now had enormous leverage.

Kohl lost no time in moving forward and using it. Although the chancellor celebrated with friends and colleagues into the early hours of Monday over champagne at an Italian restaurant, by Tuesday he was fully back to business and strat-
egizing with Bush. The U.S. president congratulated the chancellor, telling him
that he was "a hell of a campaigner!" Kohl pointed out that Bonn now had an entirely new level of support and legitimization for getting a united Germany into
NATO. This legitimacy would help him both at home and abroad; now he had
more leverage to contradict Genscher's ongoing attempts to limit NATO expansion, which Kohl had still endorsed in February.[101]

His victory would also enable him to solve the conflict with Poland. Mazowiecki was about to visit Washington, and Kohl asked Bush to pass on a message
to the Polish leader. "Please tell him I want to help him be successful, but I also

have to be sure I am successful with my policies in my own country. I don't usually say that publicly, but the election results also have a bearing on these questions." Neither the chancellor nor the president agreed with a Polish request that the 2 + 4 talks should take place in Warsaw, but Kohl was ready to negotiate the wording of a future border agreement. "I am firmly determined to accept the Oder-Neisse border. I am not hiding anything . . . there is no secrecy." Now that he had won the election, he had more room to maneuver, and it was time to resolve the border issue.[102] On April 4, he would write to Mazowiecki directly, offering to begin negotiating a treaty. By the end of April, the Polish foreign minister had made it clear to Bonn that Warsaw was willing to compromise in the interests of signing such a treaty.[103] Although there would be ongoing tension over the details, the Polish border issue was on its way to being settled. An accord eventually signed on November 14, 1990, in Warsaw would declare the Oder-Neisse line to be the final German-Polish border.[104]

Speaking to Shevardnadze the same day that Bush talked to Kohl, Baker reported that the Soviet foreign minister "was more pensive than I have ever seen him before" about the German question. March had been a hard month for Gorbachev and his advisors. Nationalist problems had reached a new crisis point when Lithuania declared independence on March 11.[105] Warsaw Pact members had failed to agree on a unified line toward NATO.[106] Shevardnadze refused to discuss Europe with Baker, but did say that it "would be a big problem" if Germany were in NATO, and "we don't know the answer to this problem." The Soviet foreign minister was not so much worried about current German leaders as about what future German leaders might do with a powerful and united country. Baker concluded that both Shevardnadze and Gorbachev "seem to be genuinely wrestling with these problems, but have yet to fashion a coherent or confident response. They also have yet to shape their bottom lines."[107]

On the home front, within forty-eight hours of the election result, the process of institutional transfer got under way with a government declaration that economic and monetary union would take place by summer 1990; later, the day was set for July 1.[108] The debate was now over how, not whether, the economic systems would be merged. Kohl's minister of labor, Norbert Blüm, argued that anything other than the expected exchange rate of one to one would cause an intolerable level of social upheaval. The new East German leadership agreed with him. Yet the president of the Bundesbank, Karl-Otto Pöhl, felt certain that this would push costs to such an unbearable level for most East German firms that they would collapse.[109]

This process raised questions about other levels of economic integration. In other words, West Germany was going to extend its institutions to the East more or less as is; would the EC do the same? Now that Kohl had a mandate for quick reunification, the ways in which German and European integration were going to mesh had to be made clear. The chancellor was fortunate in that he had a strong personal rapport with Delors, the president of the European Commission. They shared a belief in the desirability of German unification, as did European Commission Vice President Martin Bangemann, even if they differed over details. Delors saw the changes in Europe as an opportunity to demonstrate the vitality and efficacy of the EC, and he did not want to let that chance slip away. He had said publicly in January that there was "a place for East Germany in the Community should it so wish," by which he meant that the EC would be willing to deal directly with East Berlin.[110] Delors organized a trade agreement between the EC and GDR, which was signed just in time for its own obsolescence, as it was superseded by German monetary and economic union. Kohl and Mitterrand, in contrast, disliked Delors's idea of having both Germanies in the EC. They thought that it would make much more sense simply to allow the existing German member of the EC—the Federal Republic—to grow by seventeen million citizens. Here, at last, Kohl's and Mitterrand's interests coincided: Kohl wanted to subsume East Germany and unify it with the West, not elevate it to the status of an EC member, and Mitterrand agreed: he could see "only one Germany" in the EC. This would be their joint (and ultimately successful) goal.[111]

REASSURING EUROPEAN NEIGHBORS

But even if the existing West German state would simply expand, there were still a number of unresolved issues. Some EC members worried that Kohl might focus so much on national unification, he would have no time whatsoever for European integration.[112] Poorer EC members were also beginning to wonder if they might lose their subsidies to the cause of East German reconstruction. The French foreign minister, Dumas, played on these worries by commenting publicly that while a united Germany might have a lot of "economic potential," the future was not "entirely rosy" because there was so much economic recovery work ahead.[113] And both Dumas and the British thought that there should be more attention paid to the Helsinki Final Act of the CSCE.[114]

As ever, Thatcher was particularly irritated by West Germany's plans. Hurd and his colleagues at the Foreign Office had been unsuccessful in their ongoing attempts to convince her that rather than oppose unification, she should work (as Mitterrand was doing) to tie a united Germany firmly into Europe.[115] Instead of taking this advice, Thatcher convened a group of advisers and academics at the prime minister's country residence, Chequers, on the weekend after the East German election to assess what it meant for Britain and Europe. A summary of the meeting written by her private secretary, Powell, recalled that the group asked "how a cultured and cultivated nation had allowed itself to be brain-washed into barbarism. If it had happened once, could it not happen again?" According to Powell's report—the accuracy of which was later disputed by participants—the group concluded that the "way in which the Germans currently . . . threw their weight around in the European Community suggested that a lot had still not changed." Phrases like this meant that Powell's summary was too controversial to remain secret—a subsequent investigation into illicit copying of the half-dozen originals of the report stopped when it found over a hundred copies—and it caused a scandal when it was eventually leaked and published in the national press over the summer.[116] Even Washington was wondering how EC expansion would interact with its favored international institution, NATO. Baker worried that the "French want our military presence, without recognizing our political presence"; closer political unity in the EC might exacerbate that.[117]

Kohl used his newfound leverage, garnered in the election, to address these worries in late March and early April. In a meeting with the European Commission five days after the March 18 election (which Delors had helped him to arrange), he argued that German unity would actually promote, not slow down, European integration. Saying that a united Germany would be neither the "Fourth Reich" nor the elephant in the china shop, he assured his European partners that he was committed to moving European integration forward in a way that would not be costly to the EC.[118]

The chancellor also went to England at the end of March and met with Thatcher alone for the first and only time between the fall of the wall and unification.[119] It was not a particularly successful meeting; their face-to-face encounters never were. Kohl remarked on this phenomenon in his memoirs, saying that although in the abstract they both had sympathy for each other's goals, they were no good in the same room together; she thought he improvised too much, and he found her "grim obsession with details" to be "burdensome."[120] For her part, Thatcher was rumored to have been deeply insulted by a long-ago meeting in Salzburg when they were both in the opposition. Kohl had reportedly ended a scheduled meeting with her early since he was bored by it, claiming that he had pressing business; but Thatcher later caught a glimpse of him enjoying cream cakes at a café right afterward. Whether it actually happened or not, it became widely known in London as the "cream cake incident."

But despite their personal incompatibility, at least in March 1990 they were speaking again. By April 11, the U.S. ambassador in London, Henry Catto, could report to the State Department that Thatcher, who was preparing to meet Bush in Bermuda, was honestly trying "to patch things up with her European partners, particularly Germany and France."[121] Baker noted after the Bermuda meeting that the United States and United Kingdom were "genuinely in sync" while the British summary expressed the sentiment in London that "it had been a much better meeting . . . than Camp David."[122]

All of these steps were precursors to a special session of the European Council called for April 28 in Dublin, with the intent of accelerating integration. Kohl's meeting with Thatcher and others had allowed "the Germans to continue to propel themselves as 'good Europeans,' willing to accelerate the process of integration and surrender [of] sovereignty to EC institutions," reported the U.S. ambassador in Bonn. The trip to Britain was just "the latest in a series of steps aimed at reassuring other EC partners" in advance of the Irish meeting. Kohl's hope was that the "payoff for all these efforts will be a strong endorsement of German unification at the April 28 EC summit in Dublin."[123]

To prepare for the Dublin meeting, Teltschik began coordinating closely with key Mitterrand advisers Attali, Elisabeth Guigou, and Hubert Védrine on April 4.[124] Despite some conflicts, this cooperation resulted in a joint Kohl-Mitterrand "initiative," a statement forwarded to the current president of the EC, Irish Prime Minister Haughey, in the middle of April. In it, Kohl and Mitterrand jointly called for a conference in Italy before the end of 1990 (which had long been Mitterrand's goal) to advance European economic and monetary integration, thereby hitting the accelerator on creating a single market.[125] The initiative also called for preparatory work for political union to begin as well. Kohl's motive in joining France was not stated explicitly, but it was plain. He wanted the blessing of his European allies for rapid unification, and in exchange would aggressively promote European integration. He also, over the course of the summer, made it clear to the poorer member states that they would not lose funds to the cause of East Germany. West Germans would pay instead.

The initiative worked. Both Mitterrand and Kohl got what they wanted. The French president, who had auditioned a number of possible strategies with Gorbachev, Thatcher, and the Poles, had made up his mind to work with Kohl. Now, in Dublin, he felt vindicated and validated in his choice. A sequence of events that would eventually lead to the Maastricht Treaty and the common currency had been set in motion.[126] In June, a second Dublin summit called for another intergovernmental conference to transform the EC into a political union with a common foreign and security policy. Mitterrand's biographer concluded that the French president saw the Dublin events as the "Franco-German relaunch of the EC" and a "quantum leap in the history of European integration."[127] The U.S. ambassador in Paris, Walter Curley, reported to Washington that "the lovers' spat between Paris and Bonn is over and the two countries will be going hand in hand towards . . . greater bilateral cooperation across the board."[128]

As for Kohl, he was pleased that the April 28 meeting approved a three-phase plan for the Eastern German territories that would allow them to join as part of the FRG. Delors agreed that there was, as a consequence, no need for East Germany as a separate state to go through the lengthy negotiations usually imposed on potential new members. It would slot into the preexisting membership of the FRG.

Teltschik concluded that the Dublin summit was the moment when, finally, all of the other eleven members of the EC made their peace with German unification.[129] The chancellor would return home from it and announce to the Bundestag that "our partners in the EC unanimously and without reservation supported German unity." He set the date for the start of the single market for December 31, 1992, and pointed out that German unity would not happen "at the expense of others in the EC."[130] Kohl could celebrate his sixtieth birthday in April 1990 knowing that he had accomplished a great deal.

CONCLUSION

Kohl's model—copying existing structures on East German territory—had clearly beat out other visions of the future. His plan was that in all ways, East Germany would become part of the West: militarily in NATO, economically in the EC, and politically under the Basic Law. He had agreed on this approach with the Americans; in doing so, his close relations with Bush, so evident at Camp David, had helped a great deal. He had then sold the concept to the East German population via his campaign speeches; in doing so, his ability to promise quick monetary union at a favorable exchange rate had helped a great deal. Voters opted partly for the model and partly for the architect; they clearly trusted Kohl more than the others to deliver on his plans. He had used his executive authority skillfully both at home and abroad.

Finally, the leverage that he gained as a result of his electoral victory allowed him to sell his model to the EC as well. He decisively lured Mitterrand away from Gorbachev and Thatcher. The French president felt that his best chance for securing a post–Cold War order dominated by the EC was to work with Kohl. German unity did not initiate European monetary union but it was certainly effective in catalyzing it. Previously Kohl had wanted to wait until after the next West German elections, due at the latest in January 1991, to make serious progress. Bonn was also interested in achieving parallel progress toward political union, which would clearly take time. Now, Mitterrand had made a deal: Kohl got quick German unity, and Mitterrand got quick monetary unity that would significantly outpace political unity.

For his part, the chancellor was willing to bet that his own constituency, the voters of West Germany, would accept rapid unity now that East Germans and the EC had endorsed it. His strategy was consistent, in other words, and up to this point consistently successful: achieve a fait accompli with one audience to convince another to accept your plans.[131] But he still had to convince one more audience. The final phase of Kohl's attempt to restore order in divided Germany would be dedicated to winning over Gorbachev.

CHAPTER 5

SECURING BUILDING PERMITS

Men's indignation, it seems, is more excited by legal wrong than by violent wrong; the first looks like being cheated by an equal, the second like being compelled by a superior.
—Thucydides, fifth century BC

"Utopia" has been, since the early nineteenth century, a controversial concept, used by everyone against everyone else. At first this reproach was hauled out on to the field of battle against the abstract thinking of the Enlightenment and its liberal descendents. Then it was aimed at Socialists and Communists, but also against Ultra-Conservatives—against the former, because they were loyal to an abstract future; against the latter, because they were loyal to an abstract past. Because everyone was infected with utopian thinking, no one wanted to be a utopian.
—Jürgen Habermas, 1985[1]

By May 1990, it was apparent that the prefab model for the future had eclipsed all others. In architecture as in politics, however, winning does not automatically ensure that the victorious model will get built. To start work, both architects and politicians have to fight against backlash from the losers, secure building permits to start anew, and clear the site of detritus. Kohl was now in that position. He had achieved a critical mass of consensus. He had gotten the nod from the East Germans to construct their future. His party's victory in their first free election enabled him to secure the approval of his fellow members of the EC. He already had the strong support of Washington. But there were still resentful, major holdouts to his persuasive powers, and they were all east of the Oder-Neisse line. Gorbachev in particular was still hoping that if not a pan-European utopia, then at least some more ideal solution than simply extending Western structures eastward could be found.

The chancellor knew that he would have to convince Gorbachev otherwise, because Kohl needed some form of permission from not only Moscow but also Warsaw to proceed with his plans for East Germany. Most importantly, Gorbachev would have to agree to remove Soviet troops from the GDR; Kohl would spend the rest of 1990 dedicated to convincing the Soviet leader of this. And while doing so, he would seek to keep both East German and West German voters happy, provide the economic upswing at home that he had promised them, and see his own party was safely through the West German elections. The story of the second half of 1990 is about his balancing act in front of all these audiences.

While he pursued Soviet agreement, the chancellor was aware that he had to balance between being careful and being quick. Kohl suspected that Gorbachev's tenure in office was uncertain, given the extent of the USSR's economic difficulties and the number of people opposed to the Soviet leader's handling of them. If the chancellor pursued his goals too aggressively, it might weaken Gorbachev to the point where he would no longer be in a position to grant East Germany permission to become NATO territory. On the other hand, if Kohl moved too slowly, then the Soviet leader might fall, and the opportunity would be lost.

Thus, Bonn and Washington, working together, decided to use an approach of carrots and sticks to win Gorbachev over. Neither of them needed to invent sticks, since a big one already existed: the deteriorating economic condition of the Soviet Union. The carrots they decided on were large sums of money and the reform of NATO. The former carrot was Kohl's, because he was the leader of a wealthy state and could afford it; indeed, Bush had repeatedly indicated that Bonn would bankroll Gorbachev, not Washington. Because it was clear that Moscow could not master its domestic problems without foreign aid and credit, and because Bonn and West German banks susceptible to Kohl's influence were about the only places willing to give Gorbachev money anymore, Kohl had unique leverage. As such, the real question was not whether to offer Gorbachev aid but rather when and how; it had to be done in a face-saving manner. One U.S. analyst insultingly put it as follows: such funding could not look like "'an Ethiopian relief program.'"[2]

Kohl did not have control of the second carrot, NATO reform. It required the approval of the United States and other NATO member states. Fortunately for Kohl, the Bush administration agreed with this approach. Close cooperation between the Kohl and Bush teams ensued—which involved the chancellor and his aides making repeated trips to the States in spring and summer 1990, often just weeks apart—with the mission of finding ways to convince their NATO allies to make reform a reality in time to sway Gorbachev. As Gates explained, it was obvious to both Bonn and Washington that they shared the same goal: "to bribe the Soviets out of Germany."[3]

THE FIRST CARROT: MONEY

Although Kohl's party had won the East German election of March 18, he could not just immediately begin doing what he pleased. For starters, it was still technically a separate country, now with its first freely elected democratic leadership under de Maizière, not himself. On top of this, since the Alliance for Germany had not achieved an absolute majority in the end, the East German leader would have to produce some kind of coalition in the Volkskammer in order to govern. De Maizière opted for a large one, including both the SPD and liberals.[4] One of the parliament's first acts, just after the government formed on April 12, was to issue a parliamentary denunciation of the Holocaust. The official rhetoric of East Germany during the Cold War had long blamed the fascist West for the Nazi era, but the newly elected members of the Volkskammer wanted to assume their share of German responsibility.[5]

Soon, statements by de Maizière himself and his new ministers began to worry Bonn. Chancellery staffers in Bonn noted with particular dismay that the declaration announcing the formation of the new government in East Berlin had thanked many people and groups for their help, but not NATO. This omission was not a mistake. At the end of April, on his first visit to Moscow as prime minister, de Maizière informed Gorbachev that East Germany did not think it was necessary to enter the Western military alliance. The kind of all-European structures that Gorbachev himself advocated were preferable. Gorbachev agreed heartily with the new East German leader, even if he disagreed with de Maizière's support for using Article 23 to unify Germany. And in June de Maizière personally told Thatcher that the GDR "did not want unification to look like the victory of West Germany over East Germany: it should be a victory for the ideals of freedom and democracy." Thatcher responded that she "sympathised" with what he was saying; she herself "quite often had to stand up to Chancellor Kohl and stop him trying to bulldoze his point of view through. He had done a great deal for West Germany, but subtlety was not his most obvious characteristic."[6]

De Maizière was hardly the only leader in East Berlin thinking this way; the dissident and SPD leader Meckel, now the GDR's foreign minister, also hoped to realize heroic visions of a pan-European structure with a neutral zone at its core.[7] Meckel, a pacifist and devout Christian who had daringly refused to perform mandatory military service in the GDR when a teenager, had an important forum at which he could express his views: he now represented the GDR at the 2 + 4 talks. Yet it became clear to both de Maizière and Meckel from the beginning of

2 + 4 that despite an initially warm welcome, none of the other five states involved (including West Germany) expected or wanted East Germany to be an equal sixth member. De Maizière would later refer to himself as a cuckolded husband, always the last to know what was really transpiring, either in Bonn or at the 2 + 4 table. And Meckel felt like he was fighting a two-front war. Publicly, the bearded former pastor was surrounded by five experienced foreign ministers, unwilling to take his idealistic proposals for demilitarization in Central Europe seriously; back in his office at the Foreign Ministry, he was surrounded by the old bureaucracy of SED apparatchiks, unwilling to take a shaggy-haired dissident seriously; and both sets of critics felt that the theologian was hopelessly out of his depth in the swift-moving currents of international relations. Conflicts with Meckel's own ministry quickly grew to be so serious that he preferred to use West German cars for his chauffeur service, because he suspected that the East German Foreign Ministry cars were bugged. Conflicts with the other foreign ministers and Bonn would eventually grow to be so serious that Meckel would be forced out of office in August 1990.

Despite all of this, Meckel did his best in the time that he had between April and August 1990 to advance a vision of the end of the Cold War as the end of both military alliances, even though that vision did not accord with Bonn or Washington's wishes. British negotiators in the 2 + 4 talks were amazed at the degree of divergence between the delegation from Bonn and the idealistic theologian from East Berlin. One British report concluded that the East German delegation represented a "loose cannon and on a number of issues departed from the FRG line." They were particularly amazed when Meckel proposed at the June 22 meeting of the 2 + 4 that all of Germany be denuclearized. Bush had told Kohl that spring, "no nukes, no troops," so the Americans wanted to avoid a 2 + 4 debate on the subject. Similarly the new East German defense minister, Eppelmann, was also a Protestant minister with pacifist leanings who had refused to perform military service. As mentioned earlier, he had co-authored a 1982 appeal with Havemann calling on both NATO and Warsaw Pact troops to leave German territory. Shortly after taking over the Defense Ministry in April 1990, Eppelman told his Soviet counterparts that, as a compromise, "the Western Group of Soviet forces should remain on GDR territory as long as NATO troops are stationed in the Federal Republic." He thereby not only established precisely the linkage that Bonn and Washington were fighting to avoid but also hinted that there might be an end to the presence of NATO. Despite the fact that Eppelmann had allied himself with Kohl and the CDU in the recent elections, the defense minister clearly differed from Bonn's view of the future. Eppelmann felt strongly that the new united

Germany was "supposed to, and will, assume a bridge function between NATO and the Warsaw Treaty." In response, Soviet military leaders repeatedly told Eppelman and other Warsaw Pact Defense Ministers that they found German membership in NATO to be unacceptable under any circumstances.[8]

On top of this dispute, the economic situation in East Germany continued to deteriorate. As the West German representative Bertele reported from East Berlin, the problem was that the March election campaign had raised expectations significantly, but real economic reform was still some time away. Given that hardly anyone accepted the East German mark as payment anymore, currency union had essentially already happened de facto—but without a concomitant social safety net. Hence, there was a great deal of "anger and disappointment" at rising costs and growing unemployment numbers. This disappointment, Bertele predicted, would turn into fury at Bonn, if it failed to deliver improvements soon.[9]

Worry about this possibility caused Bonn to open the money spigot. By the beginning of May 1990, the West German government had decided that it would merge the two currencies at an exchange rate of two to one Eastern to Western marks for many purposes, but individuals would enjoy a one-to-one rate for some of their savings, and importantly, their salaries and pensions.[10] This rate was much higher than the actual exchange on the streets, and leading bankers and economists, including the president of the Bundesbank, warned that it could destroy East German firms that would have to trade on the basis of it. But while economically questionable, this exchange rate was politically useful because it would serve to blunt complaints. Kohl suspected that financial generosity would help matters with the Soviet Union as well, and this view would soon receive abundant confirmation.

For the time being, Gorbachev was sticking to his opposition to NATO membership for a united Germany. The country could unify, as he had agreed in February 1990, but it had to find a new solution to its security needs, and the Soviet leader continued to advocate vague but sweeping plans for some kind of pan-European alliance as the solution. Gorbachev had a vision for a European Germany, but by that he meant something quite different than Kohl, who saw it as linked to the EC and NATO.

A number of remarks made in spring 1990 showed that Gorbachev still hoped that Germany could become the core, rather than the Eastern fringe, of European economic and military institutions. First, he discussed his vision with Hurd, the UK foreign secretary, in mid-April 1990. In a wide-ranging conversation of an hour and a half, Gorbachev told the British foreign minister that he still wanted a new European security structure, stretching from the Atlantic to the Urals.

Although Gorbachev remarked at the end of the conversation on how frank it had been (according to Hurd, Gorbachev said that it had been a "long time since he had spoken so freely to a Western visitor"), it seems that he left unspoken the fact that such a structure would exclude the Americans.[11] The Soviet leader then subsequently speculated with the Polish president, Jaruzelski, on April 13 as to whether the Warsaw Pact should *increase* its presence in East Germany until such a pan-European structure came about. Jaruzelski agreed, and thought that because there were not only U.S. but also British and French troops in West Germany, it would make sense for Polish and Czechoslovakian troops to be based in East Germany as well. Gorbachev was pleased to hear this, saying that he found this idea to be a serious and important suggestion.[12] As the State Department analyst Sicherman had suspected, Stalin's ghost was indeed being treated to the spectacle of Polish leaders seeing the value of Soviet troops. Finally, the U.S. ambassador in Moscow, Matlock, reported home on May 1 that Gorbachev was contemplating a quick fix: create a pan-European security pact instantaneously by putting a united Germany into both NATO and the Warsaw Pact simultaneously. Matlock summarized Gorbachev's logic as follows: if "Germany can participate without difficulty in the G-7, the EC-12, the NATO-16 and the CSCE-35, why couldn't it also accept participation in all or part of the Warsaw Pact political framework—an Eastern E-7, so to speak?"[13]

Nevertheless, with his own position continuing to weaken and Kohl's confirmed by the March 18 election, Gorbachev was facing an uphill battle, both at home and abroad. The crisis caused by the Lithuanian desire for independence from the Soviet Union was sapping energy and support; Moscow decided to cut supplies of fuel and other goods to the region in an effort to force an end to the crisis.[14] Matlock found that Gorbachev was starting to look "less like a man in control and more [like] an embattled leader." Moreover, the "signs of crisis are legion: Sharply rising crime rates, proliferating anti-regime demonstrations, burgeoning separatist movements, deteriorating economic performance . . . and a slow, uncertain transfer of power from party to state and from the center to the periphery."[15] Thatcher, who spoke to Gorbachev on the phone around this time, remarked to Powell that the Soviet leader sounded like a man who had just lost his father.[16]

Matlock also noted that Gorbachev was having increasing difficulties with factions within his own party. The more likely a speedy German reunification became (and it became a lot more likely after the March 18 election result), the more upset Soviet military leaders and old-style foreign policy experts such as Falin became. One U.S. policymaker heard from his contacts in the Red Army around this time that senior military leaders were wishing they had shot Gorbachev on the tarmac when he flew back from his December 1988 visit to the United States. During that visit, he had announced unilateral force reductions in a speech to the United Nations without consulting his military leaders.[17]

Now, in spring 1990, far more than just troop reductions were under way. On April 17, a draft of the treaty that would eventually produce economic and monetary union was leaked to, and published in, a West German newspaper.[18] This leak caused fresh consternation in Moscow among Gorbachev's opponents, because the draft seemed devoid of awareness about the potential impact on the USSR. A Soviet diplomatic protest to Bonn resulted. Moscow complained that the needs of GDR-USSR trade were not sufficiently considered in the draft. Given that something on the order of 35 percent of the East German workforce (about five hundred thousand people) was engaged in enterprises that exported to the Soviet Union, and that such exports represented 40 percent of the GDR's total, it was not a small issue. What would be the exchange rate between an East Germany that would have a convertible currency and a Soviet Union that did not? How would the two countries introduce real prices for commodities, particularly oil and gas, into the existing trade agreements between East Germany and the Soviet Union?[19] And finally and perhaps most importantly, how could Gorbachev prevent what Kohl believed would happen—namely, the rise of resentment among Soviet troops in East Germany as their salaries became worth less (or even worthless) locally?[20]

Falin wrote to Gorbachev on April 18—the day that Schäuble began working with his East Berlin counterparts to produce the internal legal documents for political unity—to complain that German reunification had become a fiasco. The Soviet Union had "spoiled Washington" by conceding too much; "now we need to be strong." It was becoming apparent that the 2 + 4 forum was, in Falin's view, simply a venue for the United States and West Germany to present the USSR with decisions they had already made. As a result, Russia would have to find other ways to assert itself. Politically, Moscow should emphasize the "rights and responsibilities that it took on at Yalta and Potsdam." Militarily, a united Germany should be allowed in NATO at most only as a transitional step on the way to something more to the liking of the Soviet Union. Finally, in economic terms, Falin thought that Gorbachev should press Kohl for specifics on how he would help the USSR. The chancellor's habit of avoiding clear promises, saying only that "all will be well," was not enough. In his complaints, Falin had support from military leaders, who for their part would soon begin finding ways to classify the short-range SS-23 missiles in Eastern Europe in such a way that they did not fall under the already-signed INF treaty. Military analysts would also try to find loopholes in the conventional forces treaty currently under negotiation in Vienna.[21]

Falin seems to have taken matters into his own hands when he did not get a satisfactory reply from Gorbachev. The Soviet ambassador in East Berlin, Kochemasov, reportedly acting on instructions from Falin, ordered de Maizière to come to see him.[22] This demand represented protocol turned upside down. An ambassador should attend on a head of government and not the other way around. The ingrained habits of obedience to the Soviet Union were so strong, however, that de Maizière still came when called. Teltschik, who was advising de Maizière and his government in secret to avoid the impression that Bonn was remotely controlling them, told the East German that he should not have accepted; but the damage was done.[23] The irony was heavy, of course; the West German was advising de Maizière not to jump when the Soviets demanded it, but Bonn certainly expected East Berlin to follow its lead. Kohl and Teltschik were just more careful about keeping the process private.

When de Maizière showed up for the meeting, Kochemasov informed him that Moscow was deeply worried about the rush to unify Germany under Article 23. The Soviet Union expected East Germany to maintain all of its trade agreements with the USSR after monetary union, regardless of how or when unity happened.[24] To this end, there should be talks between the GDR and Moscow to clarify how such treaties would be respected. The implicit "or else" was a blockage of the 2 + 4 talks. As a result, USSR-GDR meetings commenced at the end of April 1990. The fact that Kochemasov, and by extension Falin, ordered this of de Maizière and not of Kohl shows their hopes of bullying the politically inexperienced East German leader.[25]

Moscow could not bypass Bonn entirely, though, since ultimately it would be the heir to East Germany's trade relationships. Kohl summoned the Soviet ambassador in Bonn, Yuli Kvizinski, to his office on April 23, in the midst of his preparations for the EC meeting in Dublin. The chancellor complained about what Moscow had done. He assured Kvizinski that he would take the Soviet Union's needs into account as the German economies merged. In return, the Soviet ambassador made his leverage clear; unless Bonn was forthcoming, Soviet troops would insist on staying in Germany as long as NATO troops were there.[26] Kohl decided that the issue required top-level attention. He immediately sent a letter directly to Gorbachev, suggesting that a united Germany would be willing to sign a new treaty of economic cooperation with Moscow to make sure that its interests were addressed.[27]

This contretemps had its uses: it confirmed Kohl's belief, already voiced at Camp David in February, that the bottom line with Moscow would be a question of money. In other words, Kohl felt certain that the Soviets were more worried about securing lucrative future economic relations with united Germany than they were about preventing its NATO membership (although they were obviously not happy about the latter).[28] If he could reassure both Gorbachev and his foes that West Germany would be a reliable source of support, then he would empower Gorbachev to give permission for a united Germany to enter NATO.

Indeed, Kohl even ran interference on Gorbachev's behalf in the Baltic crisis. In a meeting on May 11, he bluntly told the prime minister of Lithuania, Kazimiera Prunskiene, to backtrack from her demands on independence because she was endangering Gorbachev's position. Kohl explained to her in no uncertain terms that all significant Western leaders were on the side of Gorbachev. As the chancellor put it, "with him, we know where we stand; what comes afterward, we have no idea." He explicitly assured her that Bush, Mitterrand, Thatcher, and indeed all reasonable leaders in the West felt the same way.[29] Left unspoken was Kohl's interest in the matter—namely, keeping Gorbachev in office until he got Germany unified. The irony, of course, was that he was telling Prunskiene to suppress her national goals in order to achieve his own.

Kohl was right in his intuition about Moscow's priorities. Around this time, Chernyaev confidentially advised Gorbachev that it was probably no longer possible to prevent full German membership in the Western military alliance. Chernyaev thought that to a certain extent it did not even matter. The balance of forces that counted was the nuclear one, and that would not change even if a united Germany joined NATO, since it had no homegrown nuclear weapons.[30] The real problem—which Shevardnadze also would emphasize in the 2 + 4 talks—was not the balance of power but rather the balance of opinion. Getting Gorbachev's domestic enemies, and in fact the broad mass of people in the Soviet Union, to accept Germany in NATO would be an enormous political challenge. Once again, domestic politics cast a long shadow over international relations. Shevardnadze tried to stall in the 2 + 4 talks, suggesting that the internal and external processes of unification should happen at different times.[31] Seeing Shevardnadze do this, Baker advised President Bush that "the Soviets don't know how to square the circle" of getting over their psychological difficulty with a united Germany.[32]

As part of an effort to prevent such stalling, a series of bilateral FRG-USSR meetings began, parallel to the GDR-USSR talks that Falin had produced with his bullying. In the course of all these bilaterals, Moscow's expectations became increasingly clear—and pricey. Kohl was right to think that he could buy Soviet approval (even though he would not publicly use that phrase), but the price was going to be high.[33] Kohl, as mentioned above, had recently been telling anyone who would listen that the Russian troops in East Germany would want to leave because their relative economic status would decline once the locals were holding hard Western DM. At the beginning of May, however, he finally heard from Teltschik about the Soviet troop savings in a "field bank." By Teltschik's estimate, the savings were an enormous sum, on the order of several hundreds of millions of East German marks. The soldiers of the Red Army felt that they should be able to exchange their now-meaningless savings into DM at the same rate as the locals.[34] Since this issue involved hundreds of thousands of armed soldiers, their desires could not be neglected.

On top of this, Moscow was seeking twenty to twenty-five billion DM in credit.[35] Shevardnadze let Teltschik know that the Soviet Union was ceasing to be able to secure loans on its own on the international credit market—a problem that Teltschik confirmed with Hilmar Kopper of Deutsche Bank and Wolfgang Röller of Dresdner Bank.[36] Kohl was convinced, however, that there remained a case for lending to Moscow. Whatever came after Gorbachev would, Kohl thought, be worse, so it would be in the self-interest of the West to keep him afloat as long as possible. Kohl was able to convince Kopper and Röller of this belief. On short notice and in secret, they flew with Teltschik to Moscow on May 13. The pilots of their Challenger aircraft did not even receive the names of the passengers whom they had on board, although they recognized Teltschik's face.[37]

Teltschik's mission had to be kept quiet from the West German Foreign Ministry, because by speaking directly with Gorbachev, Teltschik was almost acting like a foreign minister himself. In an interview in 2008, he remembered that his main task on this secret trip was indeed momentous: to make it clear that he would secure credit for Gorbachev in exchange for agreement with full German NATO membership, but Teltschik was not supposed to put it that bluntly.[38] Instead, there was a lot of beating around the bush.

Presumably in an effort to save face, Gorbachev grandly announced to Teltschik that the Soviet Union would not be dependent on any other country. Rather, it was seeking an investment in its future, which it would repay once it had gotten over some rough spots. "We need oxygen in order to survive two or three years," he explained. Unfortunately, direct hints to the United States that this kind of help would be appreciated had fallen and would continue to fall on deaf ears. Teltschik voiced sympathy and understanding; he hoped that his short-notice visit convinced Gorbachev that Bonn was serious about helping. Although Teltschik did not then add "and in return we want to join NATO as a united country," he did express Kohl's strong desire to meet again personally with the Soviet leader, where NATO would presumably be the main topic. Gorbachev agreed to a July 1990 summit between himself and Kohl. Yet he then went on to repeat his desire for a dissolution of both military alliances. Clearly, Gorbachev was either missing or ignoring the implicit quid pro quo.[39]

Teltschik flew back to Bonn just in time to help finalize several key plans for unification. He scrutinized the final version of the treaty that would create economic and monetary union, which was completed on May 18.[40] Kohl had also decided that the next West German election (which, as previously mentioned, under its electoral law did not have a fixed date but had to happen before January 13, 1991) should in fact take place at the start of December 1990. This would allow Kohl to get the West German election over, just, before the opening of the Italian conference that would begin the risky process of replacing the DM with a European common currency, as agreed in Dublin.

But there were complications. The chancellor also hoped to turn this West German election into the first all-German election since the 1930s, now that he knew that the CDU had such strong support in the East. He wanted the GDR's population to become part of the electorate in time for the voting, but that meant unity even before December 1990, a tall order. Easterners were strong advocates of Kohl's push for rapid unity, but West Germans were developing mixed opinions. A major poll in the FRG in April and May 1990 showed that the number of West Germans seeing unification as a "cause for joy" and a "cause for concern" were roughly equal. Worryingly, a majority of West Germans felt that the FRG was already doing too much to help East Germans who moved to the West.[41]

If the election really was going to be an all-German one, Kohl needed Soviet acquiescence to the various open issues soon. He decided to use his leverage to get his friends in banking to loan Gorbachev money in the hopes of speeding events up.[42] His leverage was clearly strong, because the end result of its application was that Kopper and Röller informed Moscow it could borrow up to five billion DM, with the West German government as its backer.[43] Gorbachev reacted "euphorically," Teltschik remembers, on hearing this news.[44] He would later call this credit a "chess move" made at the right moment; it meant a great deal to him.[45] The July summit between Kohl and Gorbachev, arranged by Teltschik on his secret mission in May, was shaping up to be a promising one.

THE WASHINGTON SUMMIT

Kohl now had proffered the first carrot. Preparing the second, the reform of NATO, became even more urgent. Bush and Kohl agreed that making NATO more palatable to the Soviets would ultimately enable Gorbachev to accept unified Germany as part of it. To this end, Bush called for a NATO summit in summer 1990 as a means of publicizing NATO's willingness to present a different face to the Soviet Union in the future.[46] Kohl agreed that such a summit would be useful, but also risky; he told Baker that it should not take place until after Gorbachev survived the upcoming Communist Party Congress of July 2–14. The Soviet leader had recently restructured governance in Moscow and become "president," a state title that he now used instead of his party one of "general secretary," so he would clearly have to defend this downgrading of the party at the July congress. Separatist uprisings and Red Army alarm at the concessions being contemplated in the CFE talks would be tricky items as well. In short, the Soviet leader would face opposition from many quarters, and Kohl did not want to add the uncertainty of a simultaneous NATO summit. Baker disagreed; responding to strong hints from Shevardnadze, the secretary thought that revamping NATO's goals and public relations would help Gorbachev defend himself at the congress. Washington prevailed. The summit would be scheduled for July 5–6.[47]

On top of the NATO meeting, Bush had also suggested to Gorbachev at Malta, back in December 1989, that he come to Washington for a bilateral summit. Gorbachev had agreed, and now it was time to finalize those plans. A date was set for the end of May 1990. As Hutchings, a member of the NSC at the time, remembers, "Gorbachev needed a successful summit, and we meant to give him one."[48] A great deal of spectacle would be involved, including a state dinner and a grandiose departure ceremony. The timing of the U.S.-USSR summit could be useful to the Americans as well. It would force Gorbachev to decide what kind of result he wanted to bring home to the congress afterward: happy accord in Washington, inconclusive results, or new confrontation? In other words, it would (ideally) pressure Gorbachev into making a decision on the big issues.

To help the White House prepare for the summit, Kohl and a large delegation, this time including Genscher, visited Washington in the middle of May 1990. Hutchings recalls that there was a real sense of camaraderie between the Americans and the West Germans who were working on the same issues. Kohl in particular was becoming an unusually frequent visitor to the United States for a foreign head of government, and would appear twice in three weeks during spring 1990. The mid-May trip was an especially successful one. Hutchings made the following notes at the time: "Atmosphere. Couldn't have been better. Kohl particularly, but all the Germans, were effusive in their gratitude for U.S. support. What a contrast to a year ago, when our mutual trust and confidence were slipping badly." Teltschik had similar recollections, saying that the spirit of cooperation was exceptional.[49]

Kohl emphasized to Bush the need to prevent Gorbachev from slowing down the $2+4$ talks since all other events were moving so quickly. Monetary union was now firmly scheduled for July 1, and Kohl had "not the least doubt that, in four years, the landscape would be blooming with economic success." National German elections should follow not long thereafter, Kohl felt: "the mood in both East and West Germany is to vote soon." Kohl explained that he felt like a farmer who was trying to get his harvest in before a storm, implying that he meant complete disintegration in the GDR—or the Soviet Union, given the challenges facing Gorbachev. The chancellor was also concerned about the Lithuanian factor. There was a lot of public sympathy in both Europe and the United States for its attempt to break away, but "people cannot live on sympathy." Bush agreed, although he pointed out that every man had his pride, and Gorbachev would be particularly sensitive ahead of the contentious party congress, so they would have to move carefully. Moreover, the U.S. president was not willing to give the Soviet Union large loans, or even "Most Favored Nation" trading status, while the Baltic crisis was still going on and economic reforms stalled.[50] The U.S. president was coming under criticism for doing too little for Lithuania—George Will's cutting remark that the president's timid response proved "Bushism is Reaganism minus the passion for freedom" had stung—and did not want to seem to be favoring Moscow at a delicate time. Still, the president did consider a trade deal, and one would eventually emerge from the Washington summit.[51]

Bush and Kohl felt that the trickiest issue would be to find a way to get rid of Soviet troops without parallel requests for NATO troop withdrawals. A concept that had been raised already by Baker on his visits to Moscow seemed like it might be the solution: use the "Helsinki Principle." This phrase was a shorthand way of saying that Bush, at the summit, should once again cite the Helsinki Final Act of 1975 that had produced the CSCE. The Final Act, which the United States, the Soviets, both of the Germanies, and thirty-one others had signed, declared that a signatory must respect the right of each state "to define and conduct as it wishes its relations with other States." In other words, signatories had "the right to belong or not to belong to international organizations, to be or not to be a party to bilateral or multilateral treaties including the right to be or not to be a party to treaties of alliance"; they also had "the right to neutrality." Put bluntly, Helsinki signatories had the right to choose their own military alliances. As a result, if Germany united democratically and then chose to be in NATO, Western troops could stay there, thanks to Helsinki. Of course, the Final Act also explicitly gave the Germanies the right to choose neutrality, something that Washington wanted very much to avoid; discussion of the Helsinki Principle avoided this delicate topic. Instead, consensus emerged that getting Gorbachev to affirm his agreement with this principle would be very useful.[52]

Kohl believed that he had found another way to force Soviet troops to leave while allowing their Western counterparts to stay. The chancellor strongly suspected that if the continued presence of Soviet troops came to be seen popularly as an impediment to unification, then "anti-Soviet feelings" would arise. Public animosity toward their continued presence would compel Gorbachev to bring the troops home or risk a violent clash. The chancellor also repeated once again his belief that the appearance of the DM would demoralize Soviet troops. Kohl concealed his new knowledge of their field bank savings, however. Defense Minister Stoltenberg, who was also at the meeting, chimed in to encourage Bush to try to get arms control moving again as part of the process of assuaging Gorbachev. The CFE talks in Vienna were stalling. Stoltenberg hoped that the Bush administration would follow through on hints that it was willing to make concessions there.[53]

Even as the West Germans and Americans strategized for the summit in Washington, Baker and his delegation were back in Moscow yet again. There, the secretary found a Soviet leader trying to fend off opponents on both the Right and Left. On the Right, nationalistic unrest continued. Dozens of Armenians would soon die in clashes with police in Yerevan. On the Left, Gorbachev's rival Yeltsin was already well en route to being the elected leader of the new Russian republic at the end of May 1990. This would give Yeltsin an independent power base that would ultimately allow him to challenge Gorbachev's authority.[54] A RAND delegation, visiting the Soviet Union on the eve of Baker's arrival, found in particular that Falin, Akhromeyev, and Defense Minister Dmitri Yazov were pushing for a much harder line toward the United States. Of these, Falin was the most assertive vocally during the visit, telling RAND President James Thomson that the United States should not treat Soviet leaders "like kids."[55] Akhromeyev and Yazov had increasingly serious doubts of their own. Originally willing to work with Gorbachev in the late 1980s, they were becoming despondent about the actions of their boss; both of them would eventually support the coup of 1991. Yazov would be actively involved in planning it, and Akhromeyev would take his own life when it failed, leaving a suicide note for Gorbachev that read "beginning in 1990, I was convinced, as I am today, that our country is heading for ruin." Since Akhromeyev had devoted his life to the cause of the Soviet Union, he saw no other recourse but to share in its demise.[56]

Although Baker could not know that there would be a coup in 1991, he could clearly see that his counterpart, the Soviet foreign minister, was under more pressure than ever from military hard-liners. Baker noted in a report to Bush that Shevardnadze had even felt "compelled to start off reading his whole arms control brief in front of his whole delegation—as if to show he could be trusted to make the points." The secretary tried to make progress on arms control with him, but his Soviet counterpart seemed unwilling to show initiative anymore. Baker's visit got more curious when, after one meeting, Shevardnadze took him to hear an archbishop preach at the Zagorsk Monastery, an important site for Russian Orthodox believers. The archbishop's remarks emphasized that people needed to believe in something; Baker took the point to be that if Communist ideology failed, others would fill the gap.[57]

It did not bode well for Baker's talks the next day with Shevardnadze's boss. Under siege at home, the Soviet leader was in no mood to be conciliatory to Baker. Gorbachev kept questioning the need for a united Germany to be in NATO, and accused Washington of game playing and not taking his concerns seriously. He worried that U.S. and Russian relations could become dramatically worse as a result. Baker reassured Gorbachev that he was not game playing.[58] He called Gorbachev's idea of a pan-European security institution "an excellent dream, but only a dream"; NATO was a reality, and a Germany solidly implanted in it would be in the interest of the Soviet Union. To make NATO more palatable, Baker echoed much of what Kohl had been offering and added more: he told Gorbachev that he was willing to offer nine assurances, including a future limitation on the size of the Bundeswehr, a prohibition against a united Germany developing nuclear weapons of its own, talks on tactical nuclear armaments, a transitional period for the Soviet troops to withdraw, changes to NATO itself, and finally, guarantees that the economic interests of the Soviet Union would be respected during the unification process.[59]

Gorbachev was still not convinced. If the continued existence of NATO was truly in the Soviet interest, he asked, then why couldn't the Soviet Union just join it as well? He emphasized that this was not a "hypothetical point, not some absurdity," but a serious question. Baker countered with the Helsinki Principle. Under it, he stressed, the Germans were allowed to choose their own alliance. But Gorbachev kept pressing his point, saying that Soviet membership in NATO was not a "wild fantasy or absurd idea." The United States and the USSR had been allies previously, so why shouldn't it be possible now? Baker repeated that some kind of pan-European security structure was just a dream and that it would be more realistic to address Soviet concerns as Germany joined NATO instead. He played on residual Soviet fears to bolster his point: given what disasters a standalone Germany had caused in the past, a quick and secure link to NATO would be in the Soviets' interest. Gorbachev gave up his line of argument, indicating that he would pursue it at the summit.[60]

In a telegram to Bush the next day, Baker recounted how Gorbachev, for "the first time," had accused Washington of taking advantage of "Soviet troubles." As Baker put it, "he almost seemed to be saying that in his hour of need, he didn't need us to complicate his life." Baker concluded that "Germany definitely overloads his circuits right now" and guessed that any breakthroughs were off the table until Gorbachev calmed down.[61]

Between the meeting with Baker and his arrival in Washington, Gorbachev kept articulating the same concerns, both in public and private. He gave a cover-story interview for the May 22 issue of *Time* magazine, which would hit the newsstands in the United States just before the start of the summit. In it, Gorbachev complained that for the Soviet people, "NATO is associated with the Cold War . . . as an organization designed from the start to be hostile to the Soviet Union, as a force that whipped up the arms race and the danger of war." He continued that regardless of the promises that he was hearing about its transformation, it remained "a symbol of the past, a dangerous and confrontational past." He concluded that "we will never agree to assign it the leading role in building a new Europe. I want us to be understood correctly on this."[62]

He also emphasized his opposition to NATO enlargement in a private conversation with Mitterrand on May 25, just before he left for Washington. Gorbachev told the French president that NATO "must not move into the Eastern part of the future united Germany." In response, Mitterrand was sympathetic yet cautious; he agreed that the result of German unification "must not be an isolated Soviet Union. France will not agree to it." If it were up to France, some kind of European confederation would have been the way forward, one that included the USSR. However, the French leader tried to point out delicately that the time for bargaining was rapidly disappearing. In Mitterrand's opinion, unification had already happened in the minds of the German people, so now it was just a matter of practicalities. Kohl intended to unify Germany by the end of the year, and he had U.S. support in doing so.[63]

Gorbachev did not take Mitterrand's point, emphasizing instead that the four powers retained final say over unification, so the issue of unification was still open. The Soviet leader indicated that he understood that Americans wanted a permanent role in Europe, and indeed that excluding them entirely would be destabilizing, but he was still unhappy with the idea of expanding NATO as the mechanism whereby they would stay. Rather, Gorbachev mentioned his quick-fix solution—a united Germany in both alliances—and also speculated about

Fig. 5.1. President Bush with his wife, Barbara, and Soviet leader Mikhail Gorbachev and his wife, Raisa, at the Washington Summit State Dinner. Courtesy of Time and Life Pictures/Getty Images.

demilitarizing the country. His goal was to make the united Germany, by whatever means, the link between East and West.

Mitterrand demurred, saying that there was little he could do to help Gorbachev in implementing this vision. If the French president opposed Germany's desire to join NATO, he would become isolated among his Western allies. "What can I do? Send a division?" Mitterrand asked. Gorbachev replied that he already had a division in East Germany.[64] After the conversation was over, Mitterrand sent a summary of it to Kohl. The French president's conclusion was that Gorbachev's attitude was "not sensible."[65]

Aware of Gorbachev's reticence about NATO, the White House had limited hopes for the summit. Rather than aiming for an absolute resolution of the matter, Washington would instead focus on components. Bush would agree to a renunciation by the united Germany of all "ABC" (atomic, biological, and chemical) weapons, and to a time period during which Soviet troops could stay. But there would be no massive financial aid, which is what Gorbachev really wanted. The briefing papers for the summit concluded that as a result, expectations should be low. In particular, one CIA preparatory paper concluded that the president should "not anticipate major movement on Germany."[66] Bush even said as much in his first of many phone calls to Kohl during the event. Bush's goal was simple: to have Gorbachev "come out feeling he has had a good summit, even though there are no major breakthroughs."[67]

The CIA and indeed Bush were right in this prediction. The Washington summit did not resolve the question of whether a united Germany could be in NATO, despite later claims that it had. Gorbachev voiced once again, this time to Bush directly, his quick-fix idea of Germany joining both NATO and the Warsaw Pact. The U.S. side rejected this notion as "schizophrenic."[68]

The closest the summit got to movement on German issues was when Gorbachev, in response to a direct question from Bush, confirmed his respect for the Helsinki Principle. In other words, the Soviet leader allowed that nations could choose their own military alliances under it. This acknowledgment did in fact represent an important achievement of the Washington summit. Both delegations knew that it was a critical point. On the Soviet side of the negotiating table, Gorbachev's concession on this point caused a great deal of consternation among his team, which included the rebellious Akhromeyev and Falin. Gorbachev let Falin take over the negotiations while he withdrew to a corner to whisper heatedly with a number of his unhappy advisers. There was some note passing on the U.S. side too. Bush's advisers wanted to confirm the concession and urged the president to ask Gorbachev about the matter again when he got back. Once Gorbachev had finished whispering and returned to the table, Bush repeated the question of whether the Soviet leader still supported the Helsinki Principle, hoping that all the theatrics had not changed the answer. They had not. Gorbachev, showing his delegation who was boss, said that he still did.[69]

No specific agreements about Germany or NATO resulted, however. This omission was not just due to Gorbachev's reluctance. As Baker noted to Bush at one point during the talks, they needed to make it clear to the Soviets that on the subject of Germany, "we are *not* agreeing to any of this now—even a *transition period* [for Soviet troop withdrawal]. OK to talk further—but only to EXPLORE."[70]

Gorbachev had received an invitation to visit Camp David as part of his summit package. He and Bush flew from the White House to the Maryland mountains in the same helicopter. They sat together, watching the summer countryside roll by, with the military aides carrying the nuclear codes that still allowed the two leaders to render each other's countryside lifeless.[71]

The short trip away from DC was meant to show hospitality and respect to the Soviet leader, and serve as a respite from formal talks. As a result, the agenda included such items as a tour of the grounds in golf carts and a coffee break. Gates recalls that the tour almost turned into disaster when Gorbachev, who was driving a cart with Bush in it, nearly drove into a tree, "lurching sharply to avoid it and nearly turning the golf cart over." Gates speculated that he could have made a great deal of money from photos of their faces, had he snapped some at the time.[72]

Afterward, Gorbachev distracted attention from his bad driving with even worse jokes. When offered a cup of decaf, he complained that "drinking decaffeinated coffee is like licking sugar through glass." The group laughed heartily, and Gorbachev decided to toss out a little macho banter. "We're all men here?" he observed, so he could say what he had really meant: "Having intercourse with condom is same thing as licking sugar through glass." The line was a hit. As Gates remembers, Bush liked smutty remarks: "You could always get his attention with a good dirty joke—as long as it wasn't really gross, and as long as only men were present." Baker thought it was so hilarious that it was worth mentioning in his memoirs years later—although his ghostwriter, Thomas DeFrank, had to leave readers guessing what the punch line was, because Baker deemed it unsuitable for publication.[73] But the secretary did have DeFrank describe Baker's own condom joke to Gorbachev in return. When the secretary was in Moscow for a 2 + 4 meeting later that year after Saddam Hussein invaded Kuwait, he took with him a condom to show the Soviet leader. Its packet had a picture of the Iraqi leader on the front. The secretary rather remarkably let DeFrank quote verbatim in Baker's memoirs, which are otherwise sober in tone, exactly what the packet said on the front: "For big pricks who don't know when to withdraw."[74]

These displays of masculinity in diplomacy are interesting not just because they add Bush and Baker to the long list of U.S. leaders–Johnson and Nixon were notorious in this regard—who enjoyed them, or for what they reveal about the memories cherished by the powerful.[75] Gorbachev's one-liner was more than just a random example of male bonding. Whether intentionally or unintentionally, it served as an expression of his feelings about the summit as a whole. To be certain, there were a number of significant accords signed, on chemical weapons, nuclear testing, and how to proceed in the CFE as well as the previously mentioned trade agreement. And the press conference afterward publicized the fact that Gorbachev had confirmed the Helsinki Principle.[76] But despite subsequent claims of Bush era officials that this meeting was "the most important U.S.-Soviet summit ever held" and the "turning point," the event had not really come to a satisfactory conclusion. As Zelikow and Rice remember, at the press conference afterward, there "was nothing to announce on Germany."[77] And Matlock reported from Moscow that the summit had hardly even registered there. It could "not compete with concerns over food supplies and the election of Yeltsin to the . . . presidency" of the new Russian republic. Most people had written it off as part of a "Gorbachev political campaign to gain support at home."[78]

In short, the U.S. team had not secured Soviet permission to build Germany into a new NATO, and its best chance for doing so was now past. They had made headway, but Bush indicated to Kohl that he would have to carry the ball now on that topic. The president and his team would focus on the important task of changing NATO while Kohl took over the lead on personal salesmanship to Gorbachev of a united Germany in the alliance.[79] It was clear that until Kohl could go to Russia in July and make the sale in person, everything remained open.

THE SECOND CARROT: NATO REFORM

There were a large number of sideshows, rumors, and confusion in the time between Bush's and Kohl's respective May and July summits with Gorbachev. For starters, it was not apparent until three days before Kohl's departure for Russia whether he was going to be favored with an invitation to Gorbachev's hometown in the Caucasus or not. Such an invitation was an important signal as to whether or not the visit would go well. Bonn pushed hard for a Caucasus visit, but only succeeded at the last minute, just seventy-two hours before departure.[80]

In the meantime, Baker and Shevardnadze saw each other frequently in June and July 1990, not least at the 2 + 4 meetings. Baker was repeatedly mystified at the Soviet foreign minister's vacillations between harder and softer lines. Shevardnadze's retreat on particular details in June infuriated the secretary. Baker reported to Bush that he went to see Shevardnadze to complain about this and "hit him hard." Baker was certain that Gorbachev and Shevardnadze were zigging and zagging to dodge fire at home. "They were under attack for making unilateral concessions—e.g., for having lost Eastern Europe, for being soft on Germany, etc."[81] Bush and Kohl concluded that the Soviet leadership was improvising from one day to the next, as the struggle between Gorbachev's supporters and enemies raged on.[82] The British came to the same conclusion. Reporting back to London on the same June meeting, the UK delegation discussed the talks in a telegram: "New and unacceptable Soviet paper tabled . . . probably with domestic Soviet factors principally in mind."[83]

In short, in the run-up to the Caucasus meeting, there was a lot of sound and noise, but little of it was significant. What still mattered most were the two carrots offered to Gorbachev: money and NATO reform. The money carrot consisted of the credits offered to Gorbachev as a result of Teltschik's secret mission, and the concessions being negotiated in response to Falin's pressure on East Berlin.[84] The biggest concern for all involved in the latter enterprise was, put bluntly, to make the Red Army happy. Soviet soldiers in East Germany were demoralized, living in deteriorating barracks, badly fed, and selling equipment for personal gain. Locals complained that they seemed hungry, helpless, and potentially dangerous. It was not clear whether they would continue to obey remote political leaders in Moscow. If they suddenly became penniless once a hard currency was introduced, the consequences could become unpleasant.

In other words, participants in the talks understood, without saying so openly, that the goal was to prevent the military taking matters into its own hands, both in East Germany and at home in Moscow. There were even rumors floating around that the withdrawing Soviet troops from Czechoslovakia and Hungary might decide of their own will to relocate to East Germany because they faced such a terrible housing shortage back in the USSR.[85] In Moscow, a plan by Ryzhkov for economic reform was going badly wrong in the course of June 1990, so there seemed little hope that conditions back in the Soviet Union would improve soon.[86] The attitude of Soviet military leaders to events in East Germany therefore was a matter of great concern. Ryzhkov personally got involved to insist that the Soviet troops should be no worse off than East Germans as a result of monetary union.[87]

Bonn saw the point. On June 25, the West German side agreed to pay 1.25 billion DM in stationing costs for Soviet troops in the second half of 1990. Moreover, Soviet soldiers and dependents would be allowed to exchange their East German savings (which were essentially worthless) at a rate of two to one into Western DM. There were also favorable terms set up for the exchange rate that would apply to GDR-USSR trade. On top of all this, both the West and East German governments agreed that legally held property confiscated during the initial wartime occupation—that is, during the initial Soviet occupation, before the 1949 founding of both the FRG and GDR—could not be subject to legal action in a united Germany. (The agreement did not cover property that was illegally expropriated under National Socialist rule.)[88] This pronouncement would shield Moscow from legal challenges dating back to the early occupation period. In short, while the Soviet negotiators did not get everything they wanted, they got a lot, and they consoled themselves that Kohl would clearly still have to bargain with Gorbachev later, so they could presumably secure more then.[89] For its part, the West German side made an attempt to limit future exposure by saying that these generous terms applied only to the second half of 1990, but that restraint would disappear in the final rush to unity.[90]

The money carrot had grown as big as it was going to get, at least for the time being. Now it was time to focus on the military alliance. The NATO "public relations" relaunch—targeted at participants in the Soviet Communist Party Congress of mid-July 1990—depended on successful close U.S.–West German management of the process. First, the two countries had to make sure that their own allies did not derail their efforts. Thatcher remained skeptical about making dramatic changes, which the West German mission to NATO had already started proposing.[91] In a speech to the North Atlantic Council in Turnberry on June 7, she declared that "you do not cancel your home insurance policy just because there have been fewer burglaries in your street in the last twelve months." In her opinion, the discussion should be about "how to extend NATO's role."[92] Thatcher even told Gorbachev in mid-June of her worry about changing NATO to facilitate German unification. According to the Russian record, Thatcher informed Gorbachev that Mitterrand agreed with her, but would not say so publicly because of his need to work closely with the new Germany in the EC. In her opinion, Kohl was using the process of unification merely as part of his election campaign.[93]

Meanwhile, to Kohl's consternation, both the East German prime minister, de Maizière, and the foreign minister, Meckel, continued to contradict him. The chancellor sent a sharply worded letter to de Maizière at the end of May, complaining about independent East German contacts with Poland at a time when he was trying to resolve border issues.[94] Poland wanted a border treaty before unification, and East Berlin was sympathetic to that desire, in contrast to Bonn. Feelings of solidarity among the newly elected leaders of Eastern Europe, many of whom had long shared the struggle against dictators together as outlaws and become friends, were hard for Bonn to suppress.[95] Kohl did not want a border treaty before the December elections for the same reasons that he had not wanted one before the March elections. Instead, the chancellor persuaded both the Bundestag and the Volkskammer to issue a joint declaration confirming that the existing border between East Germany and Poland was permanent.[96] But the Poles were not satisfied; they wanted a treaty. Warsaw's finance minister was also looking for a "radical solution to the problem of Polish foreign debt."[97] Kohl would have preferred to postpone dealing with Poland until after unity, but he was under pressure not just from Warsaw but also Washington, Paris, and London to address Polish concerns. Teltschik worried that Polish demands might prove to be a major stumbling block when the unification process moved to its close.[98]

Kohl became even more upset in June about comments, yet again, from both de Maizière and Meckel questioning the desirability of NATO membership (to the applause of the Soviet Union). Meckel mused to Baker, whom he was seeing regularly at the 2 + 4 foreign ministers' sessions, that the former GDR, Czechoslovakia, Hungary, and Poland should all become one big demilitarized zone.[99]

Meckel followed this up with comments to reporters to the effect that NATO had to compromise over Germany.[100] As already discussed, Meckel, along with de Maizière and Eppelman, disliked both military alliances, and genuinely hoped for a future in which Central European nations would work together to become a kind of neutral, peaceful bridge between the East and West.[101]

For his part, de Maizière was still promoting Gorbachev's heroic vision of a pan-European security architecture as late as a Warsaw Pact summit in Moscow on June 7. This pact was now fatally weakened. Those still interested in reviving it—the Hungarian minister president would soon tell Kohl that he did not want the pact to dissolve—tried to beat NATO at its own game of transformation.[102] At their urging, the Warsaw Pact summit announced that its "ideological image of its enemy" was outdated; it wanted to begin a new era.[103] De Maizière also suggested to his fellow pact members that an updated NATO with a special military status for GDR territory would be just a transitional solution—one that would expire when a European security system was set up. Gorbachev echoed many of the same sentiments, telling the crowd that he was certain Europe did not want to tie its future to the existing block structure.[104]

De Maizière subsequently accepted an invitation to Washington, and spoke at Georgetown University, where he repeated many of these views.[105] He also indicated that these issues should be discussed in the 2 + 4 talks—something that Bush and Kohl were trying hard to avoid. When de Maizière went to the White House for a meeting with Bush and Baker, he heard how unhappy they were with these kinds of remarks. Presumably, the main reason he received the invitation to the White House was to give the two U.S. leaders a chance to persuade him to change his mind. They succeeded in convincing him to tone down his rhetoric, which followed the FRG line much more closely afterward.[106] As de Maizière would explain to Gorbachev when it was all over, by summer 1990 he had decided to follow a German saying: "*lieber ein Ende mit Schrecken als ein Schrecken ohne Ende*" (better to end with horror than to have horror without end).[107]

With East Berlin's idealism diminishing, Kohl could focus on his upcoming meeting with Gorbachev. Just as he and Bush had met in Washington to strategize for the May U.S.-USSR summit, they met in Washington yet again to strategize for the July FRG-USSR summit. Without large delegations this time, they could discuss even the most sensitive issues. In a session attended only by Bush, Baker, Scowcroft, and Kohl, the chancellor explained how he and Teltschik had arranged for the five billion DM in credit for Gorbachev. The implication was that the United States should act similarly, but Bush and Baker remained consistent in their refusal to help Gorbachev in this way, saying that U.S. laws prohibited Soviet access to its capital markets as a result of outstanding debts from the revolutionary era of 1918.[108] This reason was one of a number that they cited over spring and summer 1990; but if the reasons varied, the conclusion did not. The United States was not going to fund Gorbachev; that would be up to Kohl.

The group then discussed the timing of the first all-German elections, which (as already mentioned) Kohl envisioned happening early in December and wanted to turn into the first all-German vote.[109] Yet that would require unifying before December, and he was keeping quiet about that idea for now. The upcoming monetary union, just three weeks away, was the focus of his attention instead. He still needed the blessing of both the EC and his own parliament for it (and would secure both in June). In addition, he needed to reassure East Germans that they would survive in their new capitalist world.[110] Kohl's hope was that after they had DM in their hands, East Germans themselves would call for a quick unification and full elections, to seal the deal. His goal was to do everything that he could to promote unification, without obviously being the initiator of it. His behind-the-scenes orchestration of events demanded a public contrapuntal line of self-effacement.[111]

And of course the issue of German membership in NATO remained unresolved, and that could derail everything. Kohl underscored that he would not sacrifice NATO membership for unification, but exactly what concessions he might need to make remained unclear, and push was coming to shove on that issue. The alliance had decided not to modernize the short-range Lance weapons in West Germany, designed to strike targets in East Germany and Eastern Europe, but that was not enough.[112] The 2 + 4 talks were bogging down. Gorbachev kept speaking about Soviet membership in NATO and he seemed serious. Kohl felt that Moscow simply did not know what it wanted. The chancellor immodestly repeated a comment from Mitterrand: "Helmut, now everything is in your hands." Bush and Baker did not disagree openly, although they knew that Kohl could not make deals on NATO without them.[113]

As a result of this meeting, the Americans and West Germans began working even more closely and confidentially together to choreograph every critical part of the July NATO summit well in advance. Although NATO was de jure an alliance of many nations, de facto Scowcroft, Teltschik, and the advisers they called on sorted out its transformation between themselves, with the support of NATO Secretary General Wörner. They did so (with Bush's and Kohl's blessings) through an exchange of draft communiqués in late June. Bush specified that Wörner, along with Andreotti, Mitterrand, and Thatcher, might be personally consulted as needed, but no one else was allowed to have a hand in this drafting of the communiqué before the summit.[114] The idea was to produce a press release unlike any preceding it—one that would make it clear that NATO was serious about transforming.

Its main goal was to help Gorbachev over the domestic political hurdles that he was facing at the Communist Party Congress.[115] Nothing was going to happen until it was evident that he had survived with his authority intact.[116] The decision of Lithuania to revoke its troublesome declaration of independence at the end of June helped, but more was needed. To that end, Bush and Kohl saw the communiqué as utterly crucial, and wanted it nailed down well before the gavel fell on the first session of the summit.

Scowcroft's initial draft communiqué proposed extensive changes to the offensive structure of the alliance. It called for the introduction of more multinational corps to replace national ones; they would report to the Supreme Allied Commander for Europe. But Teltschik's team thought that the U.S. draft did not go far enough and had a number of critiques. The White House draft linked its changes to the complete withdrawal of Soviet troops, which was still some indefinite number of years off. Moreover, it did not sufficiently acknowledge the importance of CSCE. It also did not offer to limit the size of German conventional forces. It talked only about dealing with members of the Warsaw Pact, not directly with the pact itself as Gorbachev was indicating that he wanted. And it lacked some kind of immediate headline move, such as a promise to withdraw, say, a thousand nuclear artillery warheads when talks on SNF began.[117]

Scowcroft agreed with some of these criticisms, but insisted that NATO and the Warsaw Pact were no longer equals, so it made more sense to talk to individual members of what would soon be a former alliance than to the group as a whole. In a later interview, Zelikow suggested that this practice—dealing with individual countries rather than pact to pact—was a way of opening NATO's door to Eastern European states, creating various opportunities for expanding in the future.[118] Teltschik recognized the U.S. objection to dealing with the dying Warsaw Pact, but still sought at least some kind of joint declaration, since Moscow had hinted that this was strongly desired. The Americans pushed back on the idea of withdrawing nuclear artillery; they felt that it should only happen after all Soviet troops in Central Europe had gone home.[119] Finally, the national security adviser also thought that it was too soon for Germany to make concessions on its overall troop numbers; that should be saved for later.[120]

On the same weekend that Gorbachev's Communist Party Congress opened, Bush assembled all senior members of the NSC and the State Department for a final briefing on the communiqué before the NATO summit. As it was the July 4 holiday weekend, they met at his vacation home on scenic Walker's Point in Ken-

nebunkport, Maine. Baker explained how the White House had successfully prevented the draft from going through the usual NATO bureaucratic machinery.
Zoellick noted that since this was "NATO's last shot" to impress and make an
impact on the Soviet population, it was essential to get it right. Key points included the classification of nuclear weapons as an option of "last resort," an invitation to Gorbachev to address the North Atlantic Council, and a new conventional force structure. Cheney interjected that the proposed draft was "a helluva
lot" more important than any other arms control efforts the administration had yet
headed. Zoellick agreed, replying that "we really do have to start changing."
Baker added that it served the primary goal, which was to get a unified Germany
into NATO as soon as possible.[121]

The discussion turned to how to convince other members of NATO to agree.
Since Wörner was clearly reliable, he could once again be used as an intermedi-
ary to European leaders (and he would also go to Moscow right afterward to convince Gorbachev of the merits of the new NATO).[122] As usual, Thatcher needed
persuading. She was concerned that these reforms could dilute NATO's effective-
ness. Assistant Secretary of State Raymond Seitz used an Oscar Wilde quotation
to describe how Thatcher thought about the Yanks: Wilde's motto was that anything worth doing was worth overdoing, and Thatcher thought that this described
Americans perfectly, so she would need reassuring that they would not overdo
reform.

Baker suggested that the real future risk to NATO might come from the CSCE,
or to be more precise, French notions of building a new security structure around
it. Baker's comments were meant to suggest that decisive leadership of NATO
now would ensure that the U.S.-led security organization would maintain its significance in the post–Cold War world.[123] Bush asked, "do [the] French really want
to see us out of there?" Baker replied that the French did not exactly want Americans to disappear entirely, they would just prefer if they could become mercenar-
ies, available for hire only when needed. Zoellick pointed out that Mitterrand also
wanted assurances that NATO would not go "out-of-area." Cheney interjected
that there needed to be a "rethink" of what was "out-of-area." Chairman of the
Joint Chiefs of Staff Colin Powell joined the conversation at this point and spelled
out the practical impact that the proposed reforms would have on NATO war
planning. Powell did not anticipate one immediate consequence: Mitterrand, an-
noyed at the success of Washington in promoting NATO as the post–Cold War
security alliance in place of a European confederation, would soon show his
pique by pulling fifty thousand troops out of Germany and resisting the formation
of multinational units.[124]

The meeting concluded with agreement on the basic goal: to provide some kind of sense of security and perhaps even structure for the East once its international institutions—such as the Warsaw Pact and the Council for Mutual Economic Assistance—collapsed around it. It was also essential to provide a "halfway house" for East Europeans, to enable them to participate in a united Europe.[125]

The NATO summit began just after the July 4 holiday weekend. In London, the United States and West Germany succeeded in getting the approval of the alliance's members for their communiqué with hardly any changes. The press release proclaimed NATO to be "the most successful defensive alliance in history." The West Germans had added a sentence to the original U.S. draft saying that "a united Germany in the Atlantic alliance . . . will be an indispensable factor of stability," and it appeared in the final version verbatim. NATO promised that it would never "be the first to use force" and that reliance on nuclear weapons in planning for Europe's defense would be reduced. The West Germans got their joint declaration with the Warsaw Pact, but invitations to visit and establish permanent diplomatic missions were extended to individual member states, not the pact as a whole. The document also called for the CFE talks to go into "continuous session." A long section on the importance of the CSCE appeared at the close.[126] All of these provisions (and more) originated either in the first U.S. draft or subsequent West German edited versions; clearly, where Bonn and Washington led, NATO followed.

The sense of cooperation was reportedly marred only in trivial ways—namely, by ongoing sniping between Kohl and Thatcher. The West German and English football teams had faced each other in the semifinal round of the World Cup on July 4, and the FRG had won. Kohl gloated that the Germans had beat the English at their national game; Thatcher shot back that the English had beaten the Germans at theirs twice in the twentieth century.

Meanwhile, on the other side of the globe, there was sniping at the Congress of the Communist Party of the Soviet Union as well, which had started on July 2. In the course of it, Gorbachev's opponent Yeltsin, along with the mayor of Leningrad, Anatoly Sobchak, resigned from the party altogether and formed a new opposition group. Conservatives within the party mounted a challenge too. Despite fierce attacks, Gorbachev was able to win a vote to stay on as general secretary of the party.[127] Once the NATO summit got rolling, the news of its communiqué and planned reforms also helped. Shevardnadze would later thank Baker for getting the press release approved during the congress, saying it had enabled him and Gorbachev to defeat their enemies. The Soviet president emerged from the congress feeling, despite all of the setbacks, triumphant. Although he did not know it at the time, this was not much of a victory. His power would do nothing but continually erode afterward, hitting bottom with the coup in 1991.[128]

Kohl and Teltschik were on a roll, but they were also tired, given that they were facing four summits in as many weeks. First they had gone to the final EC summit in Ireland at the end of June. This meeting served to reinforce what had already been decided in April—that the member states supported German monetary union and, after that, unification. Kohl had also continued his efforts to get his allies to provide substantial loans and credits to Gorbachev, without success. The British foreign secretary, Hurd, summed up Western thinking when he said that "one doesn't help his friends by throwing a great deal of money down a hole."[129]

Then, following the successful rollout of the Western DM into East Germany on July 1, Kohl and Teltschik were in London for the NATO summit (July 5–6). They were cheered by the fact that the West German soccer team, after defeating England, went on to win the entire World Cup on July 8, 1990; but there was not much time for celebrating: next was a trip to Houston, for a meeting of the G-7 (July 9–11), Kohl's third visit to the United States in three months. In his memoirs, Teltschik remembered that his tie became an "instrument of torture" as the temperature of the Texas summer rose to 40 degrees Celsius, or 104 degrees Fahrenheit. He thought that the combination of "extreme" security and strict adherence to protocol inhibited actual work on the issues at hand by keeping even trusted aides away from the action and leaving little flexibility. Kohl did manage to get Bush to agree on a future Bundeswehr of 370,000 troops. But Kohl failed again to get others to support Gorbachev with major financial credits. At least he was clear on the fact that it would be up to him alone to provide such funding as he readied himself for his July 14 departure for the Soviet Union.[130]

BREAKTHROUGH IN RUSSIA

Late in the afternoon of that day, a Saturday, Kohl, his delegation, and an enormous number of journalists climbed into two Boeing 707s at Cologne Airport for their fateful weekend journey to Moscow.[131] Over dinner on board, the group speculated that this was possibly the most important foreign trip the chancellor had ever taken. The nervous energy on board erupted into a fight, sparked by the long-standing tensions between Kohl's and Genscher's aides. Kohl stated that in the venue of the CFE multilateral disarmament talks, he would offer to reduce the size of the Bundeswehr to 400,000 troops (having already agreed with Bush that he would go no lower than 370,000). Doing so in the CFE Vienna talks was meant to avoid singling West German forces out within NATO for special reductions, creating an awkward precedent.

Genscher argued for going lower, to 350,000. Kohl, unhappy with Genscher's number, insulted his foreign minister by accusing him of trying to turn the Bundeswehr into a professional army on the sly. Genscher was horrified, saying there was absolutely no one in his party who wanted that. In the country that produced the Nazi horrors of World War II, it was an article of faith that the draft would keep the country's military anchored in society and repress extremist tendencies.[132] By the time the dust had settled, it was apparent that a compromise at 370,000 was possible; but nerves were obviously on edge.

Shevardnadze met the plane personally as it landed at Vnukovo airport on Saturday night. He greeted the group warmly, which seemed to bode well. As the motorcade made its way downtown, Shevardnadze called for it to stop on the hillside from which Napoleon had watched Moscow burn. Teltschik remembers that the lights of the city reflected brightly off the streets, wet from a fresh rain. The view testified to Moscow's ability to endure whatever came its way.

After arriving at their guesthouse, the West Germans and their hosts enjoyed caviar and vodka together. Teltschik received a message for Kohl from Wörner, who had visited town earlier that day, saying that Gorbachev was pleased with the results of the London NATO summit. Gorbachev was also clearly happy that he had survived vicious attacks at the party congress. Surveying the convivial scenes at the table, Kohl had a strong sense that his meeting with Gorbachev the next morning would go well. He also knew a secret: although the five billion DM credit that had so thrilled Gorbachev was only recently finalized, Kohl learned just before leaving for Moscow that it had already been used up. Gorbachev was going to need another credit, and that would be to Kohl's advantage.[133]

Falin seems to have known this as well. Even as Kohl and his entourage were making merry, Falin tried one last-ditch effort to convince Gorbachev that he was being too conciliatory. He sent the Soviet leader a briefing paper, urging the hardest possible line and using whatever leverage the Soviet Union had left. Gorbachev should say that an overly ambitious plan for unification could not possibly be ratified by the Soviet Union. He should also say that if the West wanted to keep nuclear weapons in the FRG, then the Soviet Union would have to have a nuclear presence in the East as well. Falin had no idea whether or not Gorbachev would actually read this briefing paper, so he followed up with a number of phone messages. The Soviet leader finally called Falin back just before midnight, ten hours before the meetings with Kohl were to begin. Falin argued vehemently that West Germany was carrying out an Anschluss and Gorbachev should resist. Gorbachev was only moderately interested in the complaints of his untrustworthy adviser, however, and Falin made little headway.[134]

On the following morning, a Sunday, Kohl, Teltschik, and others went to the guesthouse of the Soviet Foreign Ministry. The critical initial session with Gorbachev, Chernyaev, and their translator would take place there. The chancellor and his aide would have about two hours alone with Gorbachev and his adviser before the rest of their delegations joined them. Meanwhile, Genscher and Shevardnadze as well as Finance Minister Waigel and his Soviet counterpart would meet at the same time and in the same building, but in different rooms.[135]

Gorbachev opened with reminiscences about World War II, and how much the world had changed to bring Kohl to Moscow. They agreed that their generation now had a chance to reshape the world. Kohl congratulated Gorbachev on surviving his "ride on the tiger" as he tried to reshape the Communist Party; Gorbachev agreed that it was a challenge. Trying to move from generalities to practicalities, Kohl again offered to sign a wide-ranging bilateral treaty with the Soviet Union, as he had signaled in correspondence before the conference. It had to be before the German elections at the end of the year, Kohl insisted, because he was not sure what kind of authority he would have after them.[136] This theme was one Kohl would use often throughout his visit: deal with me, because you don't know what comes next. Kohl was, of course, trying hard to do the same himself, since he did not know what would come after Gorbachev.

The Soviet leader then revealed that he had thought quite a lot about a treaty, because he handed Kohl a draft of what it might contain: a nonaggression pact, and "compensation to the citizens of the USSR who were forced into labor during the Second World War in Germany."[137] Gorbachev also brought up the uncertainty in the GDR about how long economic recovery would take. He joked that Kohl was experiencing "his own perestroika."[138]

Ignoring the draft treaty, Kohl kept emphasizing practicalities. He recalled the five billion DM in credit that he had organized and the concessions that had been made to maintain GDR-Soviet trade after monetary union. Kohl then explained what he needed: a plan for Soviet troop withdrawal and agreement that a united Germany could enter NATO. In return, he would be willing to talk about future limits on the size of the Bundeswehr as well as economic relations between the FRG and Soviet Union.

Gorbachev initially responded that military leaders and journalists were already howling that he was selling the Soviet gains in World War II for DM; but he was finally ready to talk about specifics, and tell Kohl what he needed.[139] First, the two of them had to agree that a united Germany would consist of the current FRG, GDR, and Berlin; in other words, it would stay within its current borders, so Poland would have no cause for alarm. Kohl concurred. Second, a united Germany could never have its own atomic, biological, and chemical weapons. Kohl said that his position was clear, as he was already on the record as agreeing with this. Then, with studied casualness, Gorbachev slipped in what sounded like the long hoped-for concession in a way that downplayed it. Without explicitly saying that Germany could join NATO, he simply proceeded to the details. He announced that, third, "NATO's structures" could not extend to what was now East Germany, and Soviet troops would remain there for a transitional period. Kohl asked whether this meant Germany would be fully sovereign, and Gorbachev confirmed that it would.[140]

Teltschik was scribbling furiously to make sure he had the translation down precisely. He knew these were the crucial minutes and wanted to make sure that he had every word right.[141] Outwardly, everyone kept their cool, but it was apparent that a breakthrough was in the offing. Kohl tried to clarify what had just transpired and asked whether Gorbachev meant that NATO's jurisdiction could spread to the GDR after Soviet troops left. Gorbachev answered somewhat indirectly, saying that "the united Germany will be a member of NATO." While Germany might belong to NATO de jure, however, "de facto it must look like the territory of the GDR does not come under NATO jurisdiction as long as Soviet troops are there." The two leaders then discussed how long the Soviet troops could stay, and agreed on three to four years.[142]

Kohl notes in his memoirs, although it does not appear in the official transcript, that at this point he pushed Gorbachev even further, asking for a clear statement that a united, sovereign Germany would belong to NATO; but he did not get one.[143] Instead, Gorbachev responded with a cryptic remark that does appear in the official transcripts: he recommended that the chancellor come with him to Stavropol to talk further, saying that it would "be possible to think more clearly" in the fresh mountain air.[144] Kohl was in the mood for a showdown, though. He threatened to break off his trip right then and there, and not go to the Caucasus at all, because he saw little point in doing so without clear agreement. He looked right at Gorbachev and said that he would only go to Stavropol if he knew that at the end, a united Germany could be in NATO. Gorbachev repeated that he should come to the Caucasus. At that moment, Kohl recalls, he knew that he had his breakthrough.[145]

When Gorbachev's and Kohl's delegations joined them shortly thereafter, Kohl announced to the assembled group that "at the end of the year, according to everything that we know now and plan to do, Germany will reunify."[146] The group enjoyed a lavish lunch together to celebrate, complete with more vodka. Even as he was eating, however, Kohl was considering how to ensure that what he had just achieved did not slip away. Once again, using his old and proven method of publicizing an agreement as soon as it was reached to legitimate it, solidify it, and make it difficult to reverse, Kohl pressed for a quick and unscheduled press conference. He was uncertain about how rapidly journalists could report from the mountain villages where they were going, so he wanted to get the message out while they were all still in Moscow, with better communications technology. The Soviets agreed, and a press conference was held on short notice. Gorbachev announced that NATO issues were in flux. Kohl told journalists that he was now optimistic that the 2 + 4 talks would wrap up soon and German unity could be achieved within the year.[147]

After the press event, the delegations took a two-hour flight to humid Stavropol, about a thousand miles south of Moscow. Gorbachev took the West Germans on a tour of his old hometown, where he had worked as secretary of the Stavropol city party organization when he and Raisa were first married and sharing an apartment with a dozen other people years ago.[148] Nazi Germany had occupied the city from August 1942 until January 1943, and as a gesture of reconciliation, Kohl went with Gorbachev to a war memorial to lay a wreath. While looking on, Genscher mingled with a crowd of aging veterans who had assembled to watch. Their common desire seemed clear to him: they had not forgotten the brutal past but wanted to move forward into the future together with the Germans.

The senior members of both delegations then went onward by helicopter and finally car to the mountain village of Archys. As promised, the air was indeed much clearer, and the views were lovely. Local farm girls formed a welcoming party, and handed bread and salt to Gorbachev and Kohl as they arrived. Waigel remembers that the welcome, even though staged, was nonetheless extremely moving in its beauty, hospitality, and simplicity. Genscher once again had the same feeling as he had had with the veterans: it was as if a door to the future was being opened.[149] The mood was one of happy optimism, Teltschik recalls, as they walked by a nearby river in the evening.

Still, there were hints of trouble ahead. Waigel, making small talk, commented on the agricultural bounty of the region and asked about the absence of barns, assuming that the harvest was transported by truck elsewhere for storage. He was shocked to learn that there were neither sufficient barns nor trucks anywhere in the region, and most of the harvest was simply left in the open to rot; it impressed on him how far the Soviet Union had to go.[150]

Meanwhile, a private conversation between Genscher and Gorbachev's wife, Raisa, who had joined the group, also struck a note of warning. Pulling Genscher aside, she asked him in a low voice if he was fully aware of what her husband was risking. The Gorbachevs' marriage seems to have been an exceptionally happy one, and it pained Raisa greatly to see Mikhail in danger. Essentially, she asked Genscher to save her trusting husband from himself. She made Genscher swear to deliver on any promises made there in the mountains. Genscher, taking her hand, replied solemnly that "we have learned the lessons of history in every aspect. I know very well what your husband is doing here. Everything will work out fine."[151] Another hearty meal followed later, with yet more good Russian vodka for all.[152]

Monday, July 16, was less harmonious. Meeting in a large group, the delegation members went back and forth on the exact terms under which Moscow would let a united Germany join NATO. The biggest open questions surrounded the Soviet troops there: How long would they be allowed to stay? How much financial aid would Moscow get for their withdrawal? What limits would there be on NATO activity in the regions that they vacated? To the frustration of the West Germans, when they thought they had an agreement, suddenly a new statement would seem to contradict it. Kohl was certain that he and Gorbachev had agreed on a three to four year withdrawal period the day before, but in Archys the Soviet leader began speculating about five to seven years. Kohl pushed back, saying that they had agreed on three to four years already, and Gorbachev relented.[153]

Less evident was what kind of financial aid the Soviet Union would receive for the withdrawal. The West German delegation did not pay sufficient attention to strong hints from Gorbachev and his aides that it was to be an enormous amount. The Soviets suggested that it should cover many areas of the troops' withdrawal, resettlement, and retraining back at home as well as the loss of Defense Ministry property. Genscher cut in to ask what, exactly, that property was, but Gorbachev responded only vaguely.[154] Kohl, impatient to move on and thinking that it could be handled at a lower level—he would be proved wrong, as he and Gorbachev would have to settle the amount in contentious phone calls in September—replied that West Germany might be willing to help with some of these areas. Their two countries should set up teams to negotiate a bundle of accords.[155] He thereby de facto delegated the details of funding for troop withdrawal to his finance minister, Waigel.

Kohl did focus, however, on trying to figure out the status of East German territory after troops withdrew and, by extension, what NATO could do there. At first, Gorbachev declared flatly that "NATO's military structures" could not extend eastward.[156] Genscher interjected that Germany had the right to select its

Fig. 5.2. Kohl and Gorbachev in the Caucasus. © Régis Bossu/Sygma/Corbis.

own alliance (according to the Helsinki Principle, which Gorbachev had confirmed at the Washington summit) and that it would choose to join NATO.[157]
Gorbachev agreed, but it became clear in the course of the conversation that he
did not want this agreement explicitly codified. He wanted as little as possible
about the future of NATO to be put in writing.[158] Why he felt this way is unclear.
Perhaps he wanted to make sure that his enemies did not have written evidence,
or perhaps he wanted to keep open some possibility for changes later. Whatever
the reason, this hesitancy would have far-reaching consequences. His successors
would search in vain for written guarantees that the price for German unity was a
preemptive repudiation of any kind of NATO enlargement.

Genscher asked a number of detailed questions; in response to them, Gorbachev modified his position to say that NATO structures could not extend to the GDR as long as Soviet troops were there.[159] But Shevardnadze seemed to contradict his boss when he interjected that even after Soviet troop withdrawal, there should be no NATO structures and especially no nuclear weapons.[160] Gorbachev suggested a compromise, saying that he could envision both sides living with some kind of bilateral agreement that left the limits of NATO's role in East German territory vague, but guaranteed that no steps would be taken to "diminish the security of the Soviet Union."[161] He added that NATO's nuclear weapons must be specifically banned from the area.[162] German NATO troops could go in after withdrawal, as long as they had no nuclear weapons.[163] For their part, Kohl and Genscher indicated that they would agree to a future ceiling of 370,000 troops in the Bundeswehr; as they had anticipated, this would eventually be codified in an annex to the CFE treaty.[164]

Kohl decided that he had enough to go public. He had conceded in only two respects: there would be no foreign troops and no nuclear weapons in East German territory. Otherwise, he had gotten everything that he wanted.[165] There was still lingering uncertainty about exactly what NATO could do in the East German territory after Soviet troop withdrawal, but Kohl felt that it was not going to be a deal breaker down the road. Ironically, at the last minute, he would have more trouble with the Americans than with the Russians over this question.[166]

Even without complete clarity on that point, the press release would still be a sensation, once Kohl and his team could get it into the hands of their journalists. Reporters had been taken to a different location from the talks, were not happy about it, and were ravenous for news. When they all assembled for a press conference in the nearby Zheleznovodsk sanatorium later than afternoon, Kohl did not disappoint them. The chancellor started by asserting that the new Germany would maintain the existing borders of East and West Germany and include Berlin; this was aimed at Mazowiecki. Next, he explained that the four occupying powers would retire their remaining occupation rights and united Germany would regain full sovereignty. It would, according to the Helsinki Principle agreed on at the Washington summit, be able to choose its own alliance, but there would be a transition period of three to four years before Soviet withdrawal, and all occupying powers would stay in Berlin during the transition. A united Germany would renounce atomic, biological, and chemical weapons, and not send NATO troops to former East German territory while the Soviets were still there; but Bundeswehr and territorial defense forces that were not part of NATO could move in. There would be an upper limit on German forces after unity of 370,000. Kohl would make sure that East Germany was in accord with all of these terms. Finally, there would be bilateral talks about economic cooperation.[167]

This was big news. Television stations rushed to broadcast the story. "Germany Can Go into NATO" flashed the headline on one talk show, displaying happy images of Kohl and Gorbachev in casual clothing and scenic surroundings.[168] The broadcast inspired a wide range of reactions; the farther away a viewer was from the site of the press conference, the happier he or she was about it. Halfway across the globe, Washington was thrilled. The press conference was the first that any Americans had heard of Kohl's success; the White House would have to wait for details until Kohl was back in Bonn with secure communications. Bush issued an immediate statement nonetheless, in which he—apparently unintentionally— overstated what had in fact happened. The president welcomed the news, noting that he and Kohl had decided five months before that NATO's military structures should extend to Eastern Germany. In fact, Kohl and Gorbachev had just agreed that almost none of NATO's military structures could extend. There was thus a discrepancy between what transpired in Archys and what Bush told the world had happened there. This discrepancy would cause problems once it became obvious in the final days of the 2 + 4 talks. Meanwhile Baker, who was in transit to Europe for a newly important 2 + 4 meeting the next day in Paris, did his best to brief journalists on the basis of what he knew.[169]

In Warsaw, the Polish leadership realized that German unity now had Soviet blessing, and Poland had less leverage as a result. Mazowiecki and his advisers decided to reduce their demands correspondingly. At the Paris session of the 2 + 4, to which Poland had succeeded in getting an invitation, the Polish delegation dropped its calls for a peace treaty to World War II. It also agreed that a border treaty with the united Germany, which Warsaw had sought before unification, could be signed immediately afterward instead.[170] Kohl would later invite Mazowiecki to visit Bonn on November 8, 1990, signaling that they could finalize the treaty then, and that the united Germany would remove Article 23 entirely from its Basic Law. Bonn also showed a willingness to forgive more debt and ease payment terms on the remainder. The Polish border issue was finally going to be solved.[171]

As for Gorbachev's colleagues and opponents watching in the Soviet Union itself, they were utterly aghast. They were already upset at receiving little or no information about the negotiations in Archys other than what was released to the public. Falin complained that the only papers that mattered were those exchanged between Chernyaev and Teltschik; he, Ryzhkov, Kryuchkov, and indeed all institutions of the Soviet Union and Warsaw Pact were in the dark. Gorbachev had wanted to wave his magic wand once again, Falin concluded, and wondered aloud whether the Soviet leader had agreed with Kohl because he was a "masochist."[172] Another adviser thought that by this point, Gorbachev was behaving like an emperor.[173]

Meanwhile, Kohl, Genscher, and their colleagues, flying home in their Boeing 707s with scores of journalists, popped the corks on bottles of German champagne. Genscher, who was not a well man, said that the exhilaration made him feel strong enough to "rip trees out of the ground with just bare hands."[174] Teltschik was impressed at how well Kohl and Genscher had cooperated to win Gorbachev over. When the stakes could not be higher, these two leaders of German politics could put aside their differences and pull in harness together.[175]

Once they all got back to Bonn, Genscher went onward to Paris to meet Baker before the next 2 + 4 session, while the chancellor received a round of thunderous applause from journalists at a press conference.[176] He also got hearty congratulations from Bush, with whom he spoke on Tuesday, July 17. (Scowcroft also sent a handwritten congratulatory note to Wörner, thanking him for all his help.)[177] Kohl reported to Bush that Gorbachev had a lot of authority as a result of the party congress and he was willing to use it even when his advisers disagreed. Neither he nor Bush knew, of course, that Gorbachev would never have that much authority again, and his compromises in Archys would hasten his downfall. For now, the chancellor focused on what he had said at his sanatorium press conference (and sent a note about it to Mitterrand as well).[178] Discussing what Gorbachev might expect in return, Kohl foolishly said that Gorbachev could not possibly expect another five billion DM.[179] Kohl was right. Gorbachev did not expect another five. He expected more.

But for now, it felt very much as if the carrots had worked, and Kohl had found his happy ending.[180] He had gotten all the necessary top-level decisions made, he thought. Now he could trust subordinates to solve the detailed problems. The 2 + 4 delegations would write a treaty that would restore sovereignty to Germany; joint East-West German talks would complete the internal legal documents needed for unification; and Waigel would figure out how much they would have to pay the Soviet Union for its permission. In the meantime, he and Teltschik went off on month-long vacations.

PAY ANY PRICE

It only looked like the end. There was, in fact, much drama left in the final act of 1990. In Moscow, Gorbachev's opponents were not willing to accept what he had done in the Caucasus, especially with Ukraine and Belorussia causing new problems by trying to assert their own laws and sovereignty.[181] Through a variety of means, hard-liners sought to extract as much advantage as possible in negotiations with the West before giving their final blessing to unity.

One day after Kohl's triumphant press conference in the sanatorium, seemingly a high point in East-West relations, a CIA investigation concluded that Soviet military leaders were transferring billions of dollars worth of military equipment east of the Urals. Doing so exempted such equipment from the CFE Treaty that was still under negotiation, because that treaty would only cover the "Atlantic-to-Urals" (or ATTU) zone. These measures had begun possibly as early as January 1989 and seemed like the start of a long process.[182] The investigatory report estimated that "7,700 tanks, 13,400 artillery pieces, and several hundred armored combat vehicles and aircraft that would be subject to destruction under [the] CFE" had already been sequestered out of the relevant zone. The problem was that proving it at the Vienna talks would be difficult. Given that negotiators were talking about an upper limit of just twenty thousand tanks and artillery pieces in the ATTU region, the amounts being moved were certainly nontrivial.[183]

And just two days after the sanatorium press conference, Ryzhkov sent Bonn the price tag for Gorbachev's concession: over twenty billion DM. This amount would ostensibly fund the costs of keeping troops in the GDR until 1994, removing them to the Soviet Union bit by bit, building new homes for them and retraining them for civilian life, and compensating the USSR for the loss of its property in East Germany. Ryzhkov was already on record as saying that the united Germany should compensate the Soviet Union for all possible economic disadvantages that might result from unification, and his demands showed it.[184] Gorbachev followed this up a few days later with yet another draft of a bilateral treaty.[185]

Kohl took advantage of his vacation to delay in responding to either of them for over a month. This gave the teams of people in Bonn working on internal unification issues more time to make unity a reality.[186] Those teams needed to move as quickly as possible, since not only the economy but also the ruling coalition in East Germany were both deteriorating. Internal divisions were tearing de Maizière's government apart, since he was more willing to follow Kohl's lead than his partners were. The SPD was threatening to pull out altogether, and would eventually do so. The foreign minister, Meckel, remained stubbornly unwilling to give up his vision of a nuclear-free Germany as a neutral bridge between the East and West. De Maizière would eventually replace Meckel with himself.[187] By the end of July, Schäuble was seriously concerned that he could become unable to complete the unity treaty at all, since there might be no government in East Berlin to sign it.[188]

As if that were not enough, at the start of August 1990, Iraq shocked the world by invading Kuwait. The United Nations rapidly passed Resolution 660, condemning the aggression and sending a green light to the Americans who wanted a decisive military response.[189] Suddenly, Europe moved dramatically lower on the Bush administration's priority list. Instead of Kohl looking to Bush for support, now the president would be sending Baker to ask for financial help in repelling the invasion. Kohl would respond generously, giving even more to the Gulf War effort than the Americans asked for.[190]

Kohl realized that he needed to push down hard on the accelerator. He sought unity as fast as possible, because otherwise he might lose it to a combination of hard-line resistance in Moscow, squabbling in East Berlin, and U.S. distraction. Whatever issues could not be resolved quickly must now be pushed aside and left for a united Germany to decide. The mission was to unite as quickly as possible. In his memoirs, Hurd recalls that he "never blamed [Kohl] for driving ahead with unification as fast as he could. That was legitimate leadership; in his position Thatcher would have done the same."[191]

Kohl was convinced that no cost would be too high. As Teltschik remembers, by this point Kohl and his advisers were clear that they would pay just about any price short of withdrawing from NATO to make unity happen. Teltschik was amazed that Moscow did not sense this and make more extensive demands at the eleventh hour, such as the removal of all U.S. nuclear weapons from German soil. Teltschik believes that even if Gorbachev had asked for a hundred billion DM as the price for unity at this point, Bonn would have found a way to pay it, so great was the opportunity at hand and the desire to seize it.[192] It was also a matter of no small importance that all of this was taking place with an election just months away.[193] The timing provided motivation, but also risks; the Soviet Union could have forced the West German electorate to choose between NATO and their national unity in an election year, and many FRG politicians would have been willing to let NATO go. In brief, Kohl's worry was that if he did not get unity now, under known conditions, future alternatives would be much worse.[194]

Kohl moved forward quickly and on a variety of fronts, even though he was ostensibly still on vacation. He struck an agreement with Delors to prevent any possible opposition in the EC. The two agreed that West Germany would be paying the costs for unification.[195] This move had both European and domestic motivations; on the one hand, it was to prevent poorer EC members from complaining that they would lose out; on the other hand, it addressed domestic complaints from West Germans that they paid too much into the EC already, and would have to pay twice if they supported unity with both their domestic taxes and their EC contributions.[196] Earlier that year, Kohl had confided in UK Foreign Minister Hurd that he thought the West German population was being greedy and churlish on this issue, and was simply unwilling to give up its luxurious lifestyle; as he put it, "people in the FRG were unwilling to make sacrifices for unification."

There were also worrying signs of a developing backlash against East Germans. A poll in early 1990 showed a majority of West German respondents in favor of stopping immigration from the East entirely. The SPD's candidate for chancellor, Lafontaine, played on that sentiment by saying that Easterners should only be allowed to come to the West if they could provide proof of a job offer and housing. He had won a record reelection victory in his home state of Saarland earlier in 1990 after famously deriding the chancellor's aspirations as "Kohlonialism," and believed that questioning the desirability of a German-German merger was a ticket to national success. He also doubted whether the West German status quo should be extended to the East without any thought as to whether the West "was on the right course."[197]

Concerns about the cost of subsidizing Easterners who came West had caused the CDU to drop nineteen thousand votes in a state election in Lower Saxony. In fact, the costs were more than the voters knew. Kohl estimated that tending to the GDR would cost thirty to forty billion DM in 1990. If he let West Germans know that he expected it to cost another sixty billion in 1991, Kohl explained to Hurd, unification would lose all of its popularity. As a result, his goal "was to accelerate the process and to hold pan-German elections" as soon as possible before all this bad news became public. Kohl felt that his mission was clear; as he put it, "the German train was now arriving at the station. Either the Germans got on or they let it go, in which case there would not be another opportunity during his lifetime."[198]

The chancellor also summoned de Maizière and other East Germans to his holiday lake house to try to resolve their coalition's concerns. The group discussed timing and agreed to aim for unification in early October, just two months away, so that the West German elections in December would definitely become the first national ones. An October date created various problems, however. It meant that the 2 + 4 talks absolutely had to conclude in a matter of weeks, ideally at the meeting scheduled for September 12 in Moscow. Waigel would have to give the Soviets what they wanted before then. Finally, Kohl could not maintain his public relations plan of having the CSCE summit in November bless unity before it happened. He decided that it did not matter, considering the dangers; now, a meeting merely of CSCE foreign ministers in New York on October 1–2 would suffice.[199]

De Maizière, fulfilling his end of the bargain even though he had personal doubts and his coalition was fracturing, managed to secure parliamentary approval of the use of Article 23 to unify the Germanies. It came after a long debate ending just before 3:00 a.m. on August 23. The date on which East Germany would formally merge with its larger Western sibling was now set for October 3.[200] De Maizière also began the process of withdrawing formally from the Warsaw Pact. Such a withdrawal was technically unnecessary, but he felt that it was essential to have one anyway, to show respect to former allies and to avoid creating even more Soviet resentment.[201] Buoyed by de Maizière's success, Schäuble managed to push the unity treaty through, getting approval from both Bonn and East Berlin on August 31, once again in the wee hours of the morning.[202]

The last remaining obstacle was now final Soviet agreement, which had to come in two shapes: first, to some kind of final 2 + 4 accord, whereby the Soviet Union along with the other three powers would give up all quadripartite rights remaining from 1945; and second, to a bundle of accords designed to commit the Soviets to withdrawing their troops by 1994 in return for some undetermined amount of compensation.[203] Although Waigel and Teltschik were working hard on the latter bundle, the Soviet delegation had no desire to match the West German's breakneck tempo. A particular problem was that half of the Soviet delegation was from the military, not at all inclined to compromise, and indeed actually opposed what they were supposed to be negotiating.[204] Shevardnadze seemed by now to be in a state of open warfare with the military, which did not help matters either. Waigel was refusing to accede to Ryzhkov's request for twenty billion DM, and the military was digging in its heels in response.[205]

In addition, new problems were emerging. Russia simply refused to admit how many soldiers and dependents were living in East Germany, hinting that the number could be anywhere between 600,000 and 1.2 million, depending on how "dependents" was defined. (Both sides would later agree that it was 600,000.)[206] The Red Army also wanted to continue to apply its own justice to its troops after unity. That justice included the death penalty, which was illegal under the West German law that was about to extend to the territory they inhabited. And the military wanted to know how it could monitor restrictions on Western troops in East Germany. On top of all this, a new issue arose during the drafting of the German unification treaty, concerning restrictions on foreign troop movements in the East German area. The West Germans were now proposing to include in the treaty a formal written guarantee that allied forces would "not cross a line" corresponding to the FRG-GDR border. Hutchings remembers that in the minds of the U.S. and British negotiating teams, this raised the question of whether a united Ger-

many would be half-in and half-out of NATO. This open question caused Hutchings to send Scowcroft a memo entitled "German Unification: New Problems at
End-Game." The issue of whether the Western allies could enter the territory of
the former GDR, he wrote, "cast serious doubt on the agreement we thought was
at hand for the united Germany's remaining a full member of NATO."[207] Yet Kohl
resisted the U.S. desire to expand the possibilities for non-German troops to enter
East German regions.[208]

The chancellor got personally involved in Waigel's negotiations. Waigel had
managed to talk the Soviet side down somewhat, to 18.5 billion DM, but it was
pointless as the finance minister was simply not willing to offer more than 5 or
6 billion at most. He felt that more would have dangerous consequences for the
economies of both Germany and the EC. For their part, the Soviets were unwilling to sign the 2 + 4 accord until this issue was cleared up. Waigel threw up his
hands and told Kohl that he had gone to the limits of the West German ability to
pay. Agreeing even to 6 billion would, in his opinion, stretch the finances of the
FRG painfully thin.[209]

Kohl decided that he needed to talk to Gorbachev personally once again to settle the matter and called him on Friday, September 7. The chancellor opened the
conversation by offering the Soviet leader 8 billion DM. Gorbachev vehemently
rejected this amount as a "dead end." Indeed, he felt that such an insulting offer
undermined everything that the two of them had achieved together. The Soviet
leader, sounding desperate, said that he felt "like he had fallen into a trap."[210]
The implication was that his country would suffer a humiliating loss of status
and standing if he accepted that amount.[211] Gorbachev's eyes had been opened to
the duplicity of the West; he was the leader of a proud nation that had defeated
Germany by force of arms, yet now he was falling prey to unscrupulous negotiations and a legal wrong as bad as a violent wrong. Kohl emphatically refused to
indulge these emotions, insisting that the two of them could not and would not
speak to each other that way. He calmed Gorbachev down by assuring him that
he would think about matters again and call back at 4:30 p.m. Moscow time on
Monday.

A feverish weekend ensued. Kohl tracked status reports on all of the ongoing
talks. The upshot was that almost of the deals were done, but awaiting top-level
approval from Moscow. In particular, the 2 + 4 accord was close to being a
done deal. It contained the promises that Kohl had made Gorbachev in Archys,
but there were two outstanding disagreements, mostly with the Americans and
the British. First, the Americans wanted to make sure that even though nuclear
weapons would not be allowed, "dual-capable" systems that could support either

conventional or nuclear weapons, such as most planes, could still enter the GDR. Second, Scowcroft left a phone message for Teltschik on September 8 saying that the United States, as part of the accord, would insist on the right of Western troops to enter former GDR territory. In an interview in 2008, Zoellick, who had been the lead U.S. negotiator of the settlement agreement, recalled that he wanted to keep the door open for non-German NATO forces to cross the former GDR in the event that Poland and others would someday join NATO, although that possibility was not discussed and was only anticipatory. Scowcroft, on the other hand, said that enlargement was not an issue then and all negotiations related to Germany only.[212]

Whatever the longer-term implications, in September 1990 these two issues boiled down to the same fundamental question: What amount and kind of access would non-German NATO troops have to GDR territory after unification? Answering this required the three Western powers plus West Germany to come to some agreement not only between themselves but also with the Soviet Union. But Western negotiators had realized by September that they easily could outmaneuver the Soviet delegation in the 2 + 4 talks. The British team had reported home as early as May that "the Russians are clearly still trying to get their act together," and the situation had not improved by the fall. Soviet negotiators seemed to have no clear instructions and to be improvising their responses by this time.[213] So if the West Germans could find agreement with the Americans and the British on the issue, talks with the Soviet team could be managed afterward. And other than that outstanding question, the 2 + 4 accord was basically done. If Kohl could find a sum that would make Gorbachev happy, it would be over.[214]

Kohl pressed his advisers to tell him how far he could go without destroying the West German economy. According to the rushed internal estimates that he received over that fateful weekend, the absolute maximum would be eleven billion DM in payments over four years. He could only offer that at the risk of seriously damaging the FRG's financial health, however.[215] Kohl was willing to run that risk for the cause of unity. He decided this with little regard for the future impact on the EC, which would prove to have fateful consequences in 1992.[216]

The chancellor called Gorbachev on September 10 as promised and offered him eleven to twelve billion DM. Ostensibly this sum would serve to build thirty-six thousand apartments for returning Soviet solders in the USSR, but essentially it was payment for unity. Gorbachev was not satisfied. He told Kohl that fifteen to sixteen billion was the least that he could accept, snapping that this was not just a handout; Germans would benefit from a healthy Soviet Union, so "you are helping yourself." Kohl proposed an alternative: twelve billion for the troop housing, plus an interest-free line of credit to the tune of three billion. Kohl added that he hoped Gorbachev and Bush would be willing to attend the unity ceremonies on October 3. Gorbachev gave in, saying, "I shake your hand" over the phone to signify that the deal was done, but refused to say whether he would appear in October. He and Bush had met briefly over the previous weekend at a hastily arranged summit in Helsinki, where the focus had been the Gulf.[217] The leaders of the two superpowers had expressed mutual disinterest in showing up for Kohl's final ceremony in Helsinki, although Gorbachev did not tell Kohl this on the following Monday.[218]

Shortly thereafter, Teltschik received word that the Soviet Union was ready to sign off on the various outstanding accords. The Americans subsequently got what they wanted as well. The 2 + 4 treaty gained an insertion that explicitly permitted dual-capable systems. And after some last-minute, late-night negotiating that involved Genscher waking up Baker at midnight for talks in pajamas, the issue of non-German NATO troop access got settled as well. An "agreed minute," tacked on to the document at the end, stated that the united Germany could interpret the phrase "deployed" within reasonable boundaries, meaning that some deployments and exercises by the Western allies—that is, some crossing of the line between the former West and the former East Germany—would be permitted by non-German NATO troops.[219] The alliance had begun to move eastward.

CONCLUSION

The 2 + 4 treaty was done. There was a signing ceremony in Moscow on September 12. Shortly thereafter, the four powers would formally relinquish their occupation rights, and NATO's guarantees would come into force in the former GDR.[220] Genscher assured Gorbachev—echoing his words to Raisa—that the Germans understood how hard this was for the USSR. The Soviet people, Genscher solemnly intoned, would never be disappointed by what they had done.[221]

Gorbachev invited the representatives of the six countries to a lavish lunch after the signing. Sitting at the table, Hurd was struck by the strange contrast between the mood inside and the one outside. Gorbachev was jovial and self-confident presiding over the table; but "outside all is slipping."[222]

Kohl had his building permits. The twin carrots of money and NATO reform had worked. There was still a great deal of paperwork to go—the various bilateral German-Soviet accords now had top-level blessing but still had to be finalized, and everything needed ratification from the parliaments of the countries involved—but the essentials were now in place.[223] The regions of East Germany

Fig. 5.3. Gorbachev (center right) presides over the final signing of the 2 + 4 accord in Moscow by the six representatives of the countries involved (from left to right, the United States, the United Kingdom, the Soviet Union, France, the GDR, and the FRG) on September 12, 1990. Courtesy of Vitaly Armand/AFP/Getty Images.

went about forming themselves into "Länder," or states, in preparation for merger with the existing West German Länder and national elections.

In short, in the second half of 1990, Kohl got the building permits that he needed to move the prefabricated structures that had served West Germany well—its alliance, constitution, currency, and market economy—eastward to replace the ruins of Eastern socialism. The two halves of Germany carried out an economic merger in July 1990, and then completed political and legal union on the following October 3.

Neither Bush nor Gorbachev attended the celebration in Berlin, as they had discussed in Helsinki.[224] The American had other priorities and the Russian did not find it wise to take part in the celebrations, given public opinion at home. While their absence dimmed the wattage of the celebrations—Kohl could not invite other world leaders as a result, because doing so would have drawn questions about Bush's and Gorbachev's absence from the ranks—it had no legal impact on the proceedings. The division of Germany was past. Kohl got his happy ending, at least for a while.

CONCLUSION

THE LEGACY OF 1989 AND 1990

My apologies to chance for calling it necessity
My apologies to necessity if I'm mistaken after all
—Wisława Szymborska, 1972

We were interested in any information about the "main opponent," as we called them, and the main opponent was considered NATO.
—Vladimir Putin, remembering his Cold War KGB work in Dresden[1]

Although unification was a done deal, there were still a number of loose ends to tie up after October 3. Kohl and his team worried about them mightily—U.S. attention, in contrast, was focused on the Gulf—but ultimately none seriously threatened German unity. The biggest outstanding problem was that the various treaties needed ratification by signatory countries. The one place where it seemed possible that they might not receive it was the Soviet Union, which could either oppose them or fall apart without conferring any final verdict. If it did the latter, the accords would forever be vulnerable to legal questions about their validity. Nevertheless, German willingness to pay up front much of what it had originally promised to provide during the years 1991–94, plus hints of future aid, helped to carry the day.[2] The USSR, facing severe food shortages and massive unrest, could not afford to alienate the only reliable source of lending still available to it—namely, Bonn. Ratification succeeded.[3]

The Soviet Union, along with the other members of the Warsaw Pact and all NATO states, also signed the multilateral CFE accord on November 19, 1990. As discussed previously, united Germany agreed to a ceiling of 370,000 troops as part of the package. The CSCE summit in Paris approved German unity around the same time as well.[4] Questions about the willingness of the Red Army to comply with the CFE and its movement of material beyond the Urals poisoned the atmosphere almost immediately afterward. In the USSR, military opponents of Shevardnadze would contribute to his resignation in December. But the CFE had already served its uses for German unification, so these events no longer endangered it.

In Germany itself, the Basic Law still had to endure minor surgery and Kohl still had to win another election on December 2. A series of edits were made to the old West German Basic Law that effectively ruled out any future territorial acquisitions, as Schäuble had promised Baker. The most important was the removal of the original Article 23. Later, it was replaced with a new version, endorsing what unity had expedited—that is, the creation of the EU. Article 146 also received alterations to make it clear that unification had been completed and that the Basic Law now covered the former GDR. In other words, the overall effect was to ensure that there would be no question of further German territorial expansion.[5]

On the electoral front, Kohl's main opponent was the SPD candidate Lafontaine, who was (rightly) convinced that the rapid unification process would soon cost West Germans more than Kohl was letting on.[6] And the attention of the nation was taken away from unification altogether when a deranged man shot Schäuble twice from behind. The minister's bodyguard leaped in front of a third bullet. Both men survived, but Schäuble was paralyzed from the chest down as a result. Ultimately, however, neither the shock of the assassination attempt nor the efforts of the opposition prevented Kohl from securing another big victory. His ruling coalition won well over half of the popular vote and secured 306 out of 507 seats in the first Bundestag elected after unity.[7]

In short, by the end of 1990, Kohl (with the support of his leading Western partners) had defeated all other models of the future and won another full term in office to oversee the long-term implementation of his own. Germany had unified; NATO and the EC had extended themselves eastward; the U.S. presence in Europe was solidly guaranteed; and the Soviet Union had failed to secure a lifesaving package in return. The post–Cold War era had begun.

COUNTERFACTUALS

Before speculating on the legacy of these events, it is worth stepping back for a moment to review how the model favored by Bonn and Washington prevailed while the others did not. All four of the alternative models for order in Europe were viable ones, although to varying degrees; the success of prefab was not a foregone conclusion. How could the three other models—or counterfactuals—have won the competition to define order after the collapse of the Cold War, and why did they not?

First, the restoration model—or reassertion of the status of 1945—could have succeeded if the brush with a stage of terror in January 1990 had escalated into massive bloodletting. It is particularly surprising that such bloodletting did not occur. Given the extent of domestic repression in the former GDR (to repeat, roughly 1 Stasi agent per 180 East Germans), it is remarkable that there were so few attempts to extract bloody vengeance after the wall came down. If victims had decided to attack members of the secret police, the latter may well have sought the protection of Soviet troops. Certainly when the Dresden KGB office where Putin worked in the second half of the 1980s came under direct threat, the future Russian leader called the Soviet group of forces in the GDR for armed support, and the group provided it. Indeed, it is possible that former Stasi agents intentionally tried to incite violence in 1990 for that reason; that is, they wanted to set off a chain of events that could lead to the forceful reimposition of hard-line control.[8] Moreover, the clear tension between Gorbachev and the Soviet military raised the question of whether or not he could command it in a crisis.

Both Bonn and Washington worried constantly about what would happen if Soviet soldiers in East Germany—who were demoralized, hungry, and selling weaponry for cash in 1990—began using violence. The beginning of widespread bloodshed in East Germany, particularly if it involved Soviet troops killing civilians, would have caused the Western powers to put their own troops on high alert, especially the U.S., British, and French forces in West Berlin. The end result might not have been the restoration of 1945-style occupation (indeed full restoration was unlikely), but it certainly would have caused a reassertion of quadripartite authority unseen in decades.

Or, recognizing that he did not have enough support among his Western partners to re-create quadripartitism fully, Gorbachev could have tried to take advantage of Soviet status as a major victor of the Second World War to restore the legal status of 1945 by rapidly convening a peace conference in Moscow in 1990. Such a conference would have attracted a number of the 110 states that had been at war with the Third Reich in 1945. The chance of receiving reparations, the main issue such a conference would have addressed, would have inspired a number of countries to attend and cooperate with Moscow.

Reverting to 1945, however, required either that Gorbachev choose the path of confrontation with West Germany, which was the desire of some of his advisers but not Gorbachev himself, or that the Soviet leader manage to convince the three Western powers to restore quadripartitism. But his advisers failed to convince him, and he failed to convince the West. Mitterrand decided that the greater opportunity was to focus on the future of the EC, rather than on the past of European conflict; and Washington was always strongly in favor of solutions that did not involve active decision-making roles for Moscow.[9] Absent the kind of violence described above, the restoration model faded.

The second model of order—the concept of reviving confederative structures but updating them for the twenty-first century—appeared viable precisely because there were a number of successful precedents for it. As discussed above, the creation of a German nation-state was a relatively recent invention. Before Bismarck accomplished it, a number of different German-speaking entities had existed in a variety of loosely confederative configurations. Moreover, confederationism remained a live political tradition. The notion of "two states in a German nation" had rested at the core of Brandt's efforts to create a sense of unity in divided Germany in the 1960s and 1970s. Mitterrand found the concept appealing as well and thought that a confederative Europe, or a Europe of confederations at different levels, would be the best manner for structuring post–Cold War international relations.

In other words, it was precisely because they were convinced of the concept's viability that Kohl and his advisers proposed confederative structures via the Ten-Point-Program in November 1989. They came to the conclusion that such structures were a reasonable way to proceed in the midst of chaos. In many ways, a slow merger of the two German economies would have avoided a number of the problems that actually occurred when Eastern businesses suddenly had to face market conditions. But the revival model never got a full airing. Kohl himself withdrew it, once he went to East Germany after the collapse of the wall and got a personal picture of the fervor in the East for rapid unity. The negotiations that he had scheduled with counterparts in the GDR to create a confederation became empty exercises as a result. East Germans from both the old ruling SED party and the new round table realized that their carefully prepared requests to Kohl about this confederation were falling on deaf ears.

Finally, how could the third model—Gorbachev's vague vision of pan-European structures (largely excluding the United States)—have succeeded? Even as Gorbachev and his advisers were searching for new ways to structure political, economic, and military alliances across all of Europe, East European leaders were also struggling to find new national paths forward. The desire of the East German round table, acting in concert with its East European peers, to create property pluralism and a demilitarized zone in post–Cold War Eastern Europe could have been useful to Gorbachev, had he made more of it. Even after the GDR round table disbanded in March 1990, the new East German leaders kept the dream of a neutral Central Europe alive well into summer 1990 despite opposition in Bonn. Meckel in particular, a pacifist and devout Christian, felt strongly that the enormous opportunity created by 1989 should not be wasted; it should result in widespread disarmament in Central Europe and denuclearization in Germany. Coordinated action among these disparate voices calling for a new, pan-European, post–Cold War

Fig. C.1. Gorbachev receiving the Nobel Peace Prize in 1990. Courtesy of Getty Images.

order never truly emerged, though. If those voices had produced a well-thought-out blueprint for a common European home, with Eastern and Western wings, and a militarily neutral bridge linking the two at its center, it would have enjoyed the support of a number of leading figures in Europe. Coming from a leader of Gorbachev's international stature at that time (*Time* magazine's "Man of the Decade," not just of the year, and soon to be the 1990 winner of the Nobel Prize for Peace), it would have required serious attention in capitals around the world.

Indeed, if Gorbachev had been thinking more strategically, he would have pushed harder to enlist not just East European but also West European leaders in his planning. His tentative efforts in this direction with Mitterrand failed, but they were not doomed from the start. The lineup of West European characters dubious about German unification early on, from Andreotti to the Dutch to Thatcher to a not insignificant portion of the West German population in an election year, was long. There existed realistic counterfactual scenarios in which coordinated, no-holds-barred criticism by West European leaders about Kohl's nationalist dreams—"the death of the European project"—would have had a good chance at swaying West German voters in an election year.

Alternatively, if Gorbachev had listened to Falin and his other hard-line advisers at home, he could have pushed harder in negotiations. That is, he could have insisted that German unification could occur only at the price of participation in his new pan-European structures, with, at a minimum, a firm limit to NATO. If the Soviet leader had made a request for a written guarantee that NATO would not move eastward (which he had heard as a proposition in oral form) early enough, he might well have gotten it.

Yet Gorbachev's advisers failed to convince him that he needed to negotiate harder on behalf of the Soviet Union. A number of them would become despondent over this failure, and the coup in 1991 would be the ultimate expression of their despair. And above and beyond any questions of tactics, Gorbachev's ideas suffered from the pace of events and the sheer number of unfolding issues, which were moving too quickly to permit the kind of new conceptualizing that he wanted. In talks with the Americans at the time, Gorbachev would repeatedly say that creativity was needed in devising a new European order, without understanding that timing was critical as well. He simply had too many balls in the air and too little time to deal with them.

In contrast, one of the greater successes of Kohl's team and the Bush administration was that they both sensed the need for swift action, although Washington was initially slower to realize it than Bonn. The chancellery and the White House guessed, correctly, that the speed of the implementation of change was critical, not least because Gorbachev's time was limited. Kohl repeatedly used the metaphor of trying to get a harvest in before a storm. As a result, the transfer of known commodities to the East—such as Article 5 of the North Atlantic Treaty, the Basic Law of West Germany, and last but not least the DM—became the favored route to transformation. Such a transfer wasted no time on conceptualizing new accords and institutions. Prefab conferred a strong element of predictability on the chaotic and disorderly overhaul of both domestic and international order, and succeeded for that reason. People knew what they were getting.

The success of the prefab model was also due to the tactical savviness of the West German chancellor. In 1989–90, he displayed a talent for knowing when he should submit his visions to authentic and credible legitimizing moments. In other words, he knew when he needed popular support, but realizing that did not mean either that he should completely stage an appropriate event or be at its mercy. Rather, by influencing the East German vote with promises about the one-to-one exchange rate, scheduling the FRG's own election early in December 1990, and ensuring that it would be the first all-German national election, he improved the chances that both elections would produce results favorable to himself and his party, yet remain credible. He thereby made a virtue out of necessity. Kohl knew that he would have to put his visions to a democratic test, but he made sure to do so in ways that would enhance their standing. On top of this, the chancellor had a great talent for using the media to his advantage, which he shared with Baker. Kohl, like the secretary of state, was skilled at locking in his diplomatic gains through clever, selective, and well-timed press disclosures. Easterners, who had much less experience with a free press, had lacked an incentive to acquire the same skills. They were therefore at a disadvantage.

In short, working together with Washington, the chancellor was able to market his vision successfully to all audiences: East and West Germany, EC and NATO allies, and Gorbachev, if not his opponents in the Soviet leadership. Of course, the marketing process cost West Germany a great deal: an extremely generous exchange rate when the currencies merged, a long series of credits, payments, and subsidies to Moscow, and the ongoing costs of propping up the economy in former East German regions after unity, to name a few expenses.[10] Such costs would ultimately lead to Kohl's own electoral downfall, but not for another eight years.

CONSEQUENCES

The consequences of these events for the post–Cold War world were to be far-reaching. A political theorist (Fukuyama) speculated in 1992 that the single biggest one for the United States and its liberal democratic allies would be the challenge of dealing with the magnitude of their own success. They had created a new world, he thought, which was "less and less the old one of geopolitics," and increasingly a "post-historical" one in which the old "rules and methods" were not appropriate. They would have to learn politics anew.[11] The irony, of course, is that Bonn and Washington had achieved exactly the opposite. Rather than bringing an end to the history that had culminated in the Cold War, they had perpetuated key parts of it instead. As British Foreign Minister Hurd concluded, they did not remake the world. Rather, the struggle to recast Europe *after* the momentous upheaval of 1989 resulted in prefabricated structures from *before* the upheaval moving eastward and securing a future for themselves. Americans and West Germans had successfully entrenched the institutions born of the old geopolitics of the Cold War world—ones that they already dominated, most notably NATO—in the new era. This success was deserved, but not without costs. It is thus necessary to ask, what is the legacy of the way that they restored order?[12]

Stepping back from all the details presented in this book to look at the overarching themes that link them, four prominent components of the legacy emerge.

The first component is also the most commonplace. A close examination of 1989 and 1990 shows that the people who brought the previous order to an end enjoyed no particular claim to run matters after the dust settled. This is the core meaning of the old saying that the revolution eats its children. It is worth reviewing how this became apparent in 1989: it was nearly inevitable after a certain point that the old Soviet regime would collapse. But there was nothing at all inevitable about what would follow. The dynamics of the competition to create order yielded a triumph above all for Kohl, thanks to his penchant for quick, spare-no-expense action, but little for the East European revolutionary leaders who had opened the door to change in the first place. Former Czech and East German dissidents in particular had no interest in contributing to a project to promote NATO in the post–Cold War world. Their priority was less military security than new forms of democracy and property pluralism. They saw their dreams thwarted by Kohl's success.

Likewise, the brave Polish protesters who had done so much of the hard, frightening work of destroying the old Cold War order, rising from the dockyards and jails to the halls of power in Warsaw, saw their justifiable hopes for massive West German financial infusions dashed when the wall opened and Kohl's priorities shifted. Instead, they had to settle for less than they wanted. They had to participate in a bitter exchange of recriminations over border guarantees. They had to endure Kohl's use of Stalin era treaties as clubs to beat down their hopes of a peace treaty to World War II. The ironies of history were such that for a time in 1989–90, Polish leaders aligned with Moscow to see if they could force a peace treaty on Bonn; as mentioned, one State Department analyst thought that Stalin's ghost got a good laugh out of that.

The situation of the Polish dissidents-turned-leaders paralleled that of the man most responsible for destroying the sorry stability provided by the old order: Gorbachev. He received accolades abroad but hostility at home for his decision to hand over territory soaked in Soviet blood to NATO. Events in divided Germany and Eastern Europe subsequently had a toxic spillover effect in the Soviet Union. Scholars have rightly argued that this spillover exacerbated the "political instability and intra-elite divisions in the USSR . . . and made it far more difficult for Mikhail Gorbachev to prevent the Soviet Union from unraveling." As the Soviet leader would write to Kohl on that Christmas in 1991 when the union was no more and his long fall from grace finally concluded, ever since becoming general secretary he had sought one goal. He wanted to bring Russia into the fold of "modern democratic countries." This concept was somewhat of a flattering self-portrait, since he had not sought to introduce completely democratic politics into the Soviet Union. But his disappointment was genuine; although "events did not go in the manner that I considered correct and most expedient, I do not lose hope for the final success of the matter."[13]

In short, an examination of 1989 and 1990 suggests that we need to understand the ending of the Cold War, and the process of constructing the post–Cold War Europe, as distinct and dichotomous events. The figures involved in tearing down the previous order—Gorbachev, Reagan, and masses of East European dissidents—were not those who ultimately built the new. A relatively small number of policymakers in Bonn, Paris, and Washington secured that role for themselves.

A second component of the legacy of 1989–90 is the conundrum of imperfect choices. Because the contest to define order in post–Cold War Europe took place at a blisteringly fast pace, there was not much time for perfecting plans and ideas. As a number of observers noted at the time, life simply speeded up. Gates described it as follows: "We shot the rapids of history, and without a life jacket." J. D. Bindenagel, an American diplomat, remembered his experience working in the U.S. embassy in East Berlin in 1989–90 as the feeling of living in a video on which someone had pressed the fast-forward button. Falin said that it felt as if history were "pressing a hundred years into a hundred days."[14] Questions needed answers right away; but the quickest answers were not always the ideal ones. Once the speedy process of selecting and laying the foundation for the future was complete, however, it became hard to challenge, even if it was less than perfect. In the process of exporting Western order to the East—an understandable response to events on the ground—Bonn and Washington sowed the seeds of future problems, to reuse Baker's phrase.

Within Germany, the sudden imposition of Western currency and standards on the East caused dramatic difficulties. Optimistic predictions about how well former East German firms would fare quickly proved to be illusory. At one point early on, Bonn estimated that the privatization of state-run businesses in the East would create a profit of 600 billion DM. Instead, taxpayers had to subsidize the process to the tune of 230 billion DM.[15] Official unemployment rates in the former GDR hit 10.9 percent for men and 21.5 percent for women by 1994. Joblessness remained stubbornly high and productivity in the region peaked at little more than half that of the West for most of the 1990s. Former property owners from prewar, Nazi, and socialist eras gained the ability to fight out legal claims over real estate extensively. The costly and extensive litigation that resulted tied up buildings and land for years or even decades, scared off investors, and exacerbated the economic difficulties of the former East Germany. Former West Germans soon came to call the GDR territory a "barrel without a bottom," into which unending Western subsidies disappeared; one expert estimates that Germany's reconstruction of the East cost roughly 120 billion dollars per year starting in 1990–91.[16] These costs soured not only the economy of Germany as a whole but also had an impact on all of East and West Germany's former trading partners. The chancellor spent huge sums of money against the advice of his financial advisers, driving up German borrowing and setting off a sequence of events that later contributed to the severe European currency crisis of 1992. Of course, Kohl and his advisers were aware at the time that they were making costly choices, but the alternative—missing the chance to unify—seemed worse to them.[17]

Outside of Germany in the international arena, NATO was subject to the same dilemma of imperfect choices. The alliance began creeping eastward in response to the demands of the day, but without much assessment of the long-term consequences. Even Kohl's own East German coalition partners balked at the swift installation of the Western military pact on the still-smoking ruins of the old Eastern one. They hoped instead that in a peaceful post–Cold War world, neither of the old military blocs would be necessary. They wanted to move beyond the East-West divide, not move its front eastward. An ideal model for the future would have been one that included a clear vision for *both* Eastern Europe *and* the former Soviet countries. But the path to this alternative future was not nearly as clear as the one to Bush's and Kohl's. The West German foreign minister, Genscher, was right to warn continually about Russian resentment as a result of the western plan, and Gorbachev's wife, Raisa, was right to be worried about its costs for her husband.

Summarizing the legacy of 1989–90 this way requires a corollary: a clear discussion of its implications for NATO enlargement. No less a figure than George Kennan may have termed such enlargement a "'strategic blunder of potentially epic proportions,'" but his judgment requires context.[18] Strategy is the calculated relation of means to ends. When assessing whether or not NATO enlargement was a blunder, it is necessary to ask first what ends it was meant to achieve: was post–Cold War NATO supposed to serve political or military goals? The answer to this question seems to have varied both over the years since 1990 and among the alliance's leading members; but it is crucial, because it results in widely divergent assessments of expansion.

If the alliance's goal became a political one—namely, to provide an umbrella of stability to new East European democracies after the end of the Cold War, thereby reducing their external worries and allowing them to prioritize internal reform— then it was not a blunder. Nor was it illegitimate. As described above, NATO first began moving eastward when it absorbed former East German territory as a result of a democratic election there on March 18, 1990, and in accordance with signed and ratified treaties. After that, freely elected leaders in Central and Eastern Europe sought further enlargement of the alliance. Legitimate government entities on both sides of the Atlantic approved NATO expansion (such as the U.S. Senate, which ratified NATO's addition of Poland, Hungary, and the Czech Republic by a vote of eighty to nineteen on April 30, 1998). Baker himself would later argue that under a political understanding of NATO's mission, Russia itself should be considered eligible for NATO membership—as long as it definitively "embraced democracy and free markets." [19] In short, if the alliance's mission was to be a political one, then the possibility of Soviet membership in NATO should have been seriously considered; failing that, the mission should have been given to an institution, possibly a new one, that could have included Russia.

If the highest goal remained military security for alliance members even after the end of the Cold War, though, then the strategy of NATO enlargement starts to look more dubious. Strictly speaking, a military pact is supposed to increase the security of its members; but by converting new areas into territory covered by Article 5, the alliance increased its liabilities without a corresponding increase in capabilities. New members could not become equal military partners quickly. (The alliance in some ways thereby recapitulated its founding in 1949, when the United States had taken on West European countries still ravaged by war.) There were benefits, of course, such as increased options for troop and missile defense placements, but there were also new problems. The expansion perpetuated the military dividing line between NATO and its biggest strategic threat, Russia, into the post–Cold War world, which did not have to be the outcome of 1990.

And regardless of which view is accurate, it is fair to ask questions about the implementation of NATO enlargement. There was an unfortunate lack of success in limiting Russian hostility toward the process. Such prevention was essential, if expansion were not to create new strategic problems. An ideal policymaker in the West would have recognized that the implementation of expansion created the greatest possible duty of care; Russia had only episodically shown interest in cooperation with the West, so a rare window of opportunity opened in 1989–90. An ideal policymaker in the East would have bargained much harder before implementation began; Moscow had opportunities during the unification process to seek written prohibitions on NATO movement eastward but did not do so.

Instead, the evidence presented here about the early origin of NATO expansion reveals a gap between public expressions and private thinking. In the West, while Bonn and Washington publicly expressed sympathy for Gorbachev's reformist goals in 1989–90, they privately sensed that they did not really need to accommodate him. To repeat what Baker wrote in a summary of U.S.-Soviet relations: the

Russians "have to make hard choices. *We do Gorbachev no favors when we make it easier to avoid choices.*" Bonn and Washington realized that they could outmaneuver him. The discrepancy between what Kohl in particular suggested to Gorbachev in February—that NATO would not move eastward if the Soviet leader let Germany unite, which Gorbachev then agreed to let happen internally—and what transpired afterward created ill will in the long term. In other words, the goal of Bonn and Washington was, as Gates put it, to bribe the Soviets out of Germany, not to set up long-term cooperation or structures in which Gorbachev and his successors would be full partners. Gorbachev eventually came to feel that he had walked into a trap, and told Kohl so in those words in September 1990. Presumably the Soviet leader was also angry at himself for failing to have gotten more out of unification, particularly with regard to NATO, since the issue was such a toxic one for any Soviet or Russian leader. The Clinton administration, seeing how difficult NATO expansion could be for Yeltsin in terms of domestic politics, waited until after the Russian leader secured reelection in July 1996 before enlarging beyond former East Germany. It also, together with the NATO secretary general at the time, Javier Solana, organized a multinational conference in Paris in May 1997 to provide Yeltsin with a public relations boost. At this conference, the "Founding Act on Mutual Relations, Cooperation, and Security between the Russian Federation and NATO" was signed. This act created a Permanent Joint Council that included Russia, but neither it, nor its successor organization, the NATO-Russia Council, ever really lived up to expectations. Russians saw the new relationship as a counterintelligence opportunity. Western policymakers gave Russia only token consultative rights.[20] The window of opportunity closed. Lacking some kind of successful Western-Russian consultation to smooth over the disagreements, NATO enlargement continued to increase tension between Washington and Moscow.

As opportunities for cooperation dwindled in the course of implementation, Russian worry about NATO enlargement intensified. During the Cold War, Leningrad was roughly twelve hundred miles away from the nearest border of NATO. By 2008, the membership of Estonia meant that the border had moved to within a hundred miles of the city, renamed Saint Petersburg.[21] Any country would be concerned about such a development, but Russia was particularly angry about it. It insisted that in implementing expansion, the United States and the West had thereby broken what Moscow perceived to be their promises; Ron Asmus, a Clinton State Department official who helped to enlarge NATO, remembers being continually confronted by such claims.[22] U.S. government officials have responded to Moscow's worries by trying to clarify what happened in February 1990. In the Clinton era, a memorandum written by Assistant Secretary of State John Kornblum

Fig. C.2. Ceremonial signing of the NATO-Russia Founding Act in Paris, with Russian President Boris Yeltsin (left) and NATO Secretary General Javier Solana, May 1997. © Pascal Le Segretain/Corbis Sygma.

and approved by the State Department legal team argued that Baker's words applied only to divided Germany. In other words, when the secretary suggested to Gorbachev that NATO's jurisdiction would not shift one inch eastward from its present position, he was speaking solely in his authority as a representative of one of the four powers still occupying Germany in 1990. Baker meant only that NATO's jurisdiction would not move eastward within a united Germany; he did not have the authority to speak for other regions, let alone NATO itself.[23] On top of this, Zelikow published an article titled "NATO Expansion Wasn't Ruled Out" in 1995. This op-ed contended that whatever Baker may have said, Gorbachev was informed about changes to the U.S. view afterward and signed a number of accords consistent with those later changes.[24]

Yeltsin's eventual successors, Putin and Dmitri Medvedev, were not swayed by these explanations. They saw the failure to resist NATO expansion as a massive strategic error on the part of their predecessors. Putin in particular, used to thinking of NATO as the "main opponent" from his days in Dresden, felt strongly that the alliance was an impediment to Russia assuming its full role in Europe. He felt that "no matter where our people live, in the Far East or in the south, we are Europeans." Russians "would have avoided a lot of problems if the Soviets had not made such a hasty exit from Eastern Europe."[25] Medvedev, Putin's handpicked successor, followed his mentor's lead by speaking sarcastically about "the unbridled expansion of NATO and other gifts to Russia." He especially resented the decision in August 2008 to base ten U.S. interceptor missiles in Poland and the corresponding radar equipment in the Czech Republic as part of a planned missile defense; Medvedev suspected that the equipment could also have offensive uses. Even Gorbachev himself emerged from retirement to blame the 2008 Russian invasion of Georgia—which he thought was justified—on the "unending expansion of NATO . . . set against the backdrop of sweet talk about partnership." To counter it, Gorbachev endorsed a plan by Medvedev: to set up a new "security architecture" for Europe as NATO celebrated its sixtieth birthday.[26]

The evidence and analysis offered in this book indicate that the controversy over February 1990 needs to be understood not just in terms of U.S.-Soviet history but also in terms of the relations of both with West Germany at the time, and subsequent events that same year. Baker suggested in a highly speculative way at the American-Soviet bilateral of February 9 that NATO would not expand eastward if Gorbachev allowed Germany to unite. It might have become a deal if the Soviet leader had insisted at the time, but their bilateral meeting ended without action or agreement. More problematic was the Soviet–West German bilateral of the next day, where Kohl echoed Baker despite receiving different U.S. wording directly from Bush. Unlike the previous day, the FRG-USSR meeting did end with action: Gorbachev allowed Germany to unify internally on the basis of what Kohl said. Unwisely, the Soviet leader neither sought nor received written agreement about NATO in return. But by the end of the month, Kohl would be at Camp David, agreeing to Bush's language on NATO. Since there was nothing in writing, the wording was fluid. The accords that would be signed in late 1990 ultimately would be ones consistent with the Camp David position. Attempts by Falin and others to force Gorbachev to seek written guarantees failed, as the Soviet leader decided to accept vague promises in the Caucasus in July 1990 instead. By the end of 1990, Gorbachev himself would be bitterly unhappy, and later his successors would cry foul about these proceedings as well.

Hence, when looking specifically at the legacy of 1989–90 for the issue of NATO enlargement, what emerges is not a *formal* prohibition against such an expansion; rather, it is Russian resentment—both at the West and former Soviet leaders for conceding in negotiations—arising from the *informal* proceedings. Such resentment has generated its own strategic problems. In December 2008, NATO Secretary General Jaap de Hoop Scheffer would complain about how hard it was to conduct dialogue with Russia, especially in the wake of Putin's decision to suspend compliance with the CFE treaty and the Russian invasion of Georgia.

"It's not easy to know how to approach someone, in daily life or in foreign policy, who feels themselves victimized," the NATO leader complained. This sense of victimization is a large component of the legacy of 1989–90 and the rushed, imperfect choices available to policymakers at the time. The West should have thought harder in the wake of 1990 about how it felt, longer term, to live in a once-great country that had to bring its soldiers home for lack of money.[27]

This leads to a third component: Russia was not the only great power struggling to react to events in 1989–90. A close look at the imperfect choices of 1989–90 shows that little was under superpower control. Clearly, the United States and the Soviet Union were the two most important countries during the Cold War, but they were not the only important countries in the shaping of the post–Cold War European order. Consider the following questions: Why did the Berlin Wall become suddenly and unexpectedly obsolete on November 9? Why did Gorbachev agree to let Germany unify internally? Why did he assent to NATO membership for the united country, allowing its precedent-setting enlargement to former Warsaw Pact territory to begin? It is not possible to answer these questions, other than with generalities, solely by talking about the superpowers. The long-term contest between the U.S. and Soviet visions of the future assuredly provided the context for all of these developments. But as previously asserted, the endgame was heavily European.

Because of this, it was fortunate for Washington that the German in charge was so deeply committed to NATO, and that he was able to win over the French leader. Of course, the United States was not without leverage. Quadripartite rights remaining from World War II gave it a veto over all changes in divided Germany. Simply stalling would have increased the likelihood of unification failing (if that were desired), because both Bonn and Washington knew that Gorbachev's authority was slipping, and it was unlikely that anyone more cooperative would succeed him.

Yet a number of other bargains for post–Cold War Europe could still have been struck between the Germans and Moscow. Knowing this, Scowcroft remembered in his memoirs how anxiously he waited for calls from Kohl whenever the chancellor had visited Moscow. At one point Scowcroft had one of his NSC staffers, Hutchings, prepare a memo for the U.S. president listing eighteen possible final scenarios to the drive for German unity, ranked in order of desirability for Washington. The scenario that actually emerged was outcome number two—number one would have been no restrictions on NATO in East Germany whatsoever—but a large number of less desirable outcomes were highly possible. Understanding how the process came to the result that it did requires looking beyond super-power shores.[28]

A corollary to this is that Washington's true talent in 1989–90 rested in its ability to recognize the significance of Bonn, not in its ability to direct all events itself. Indeed, Bush's willingness to let Kohl lead on the issue of German unification was remarkable. As the U.S. president himself stated in his memoirs, Bush—rather amazingly—did not have strong feelings about how to proceed when the chaos of 1989 in Germany demanded a response. Thatcher reportedly complained that the problem with Bush was that he did not have strong feelings about anything at all.

But Bush did have strong feelings about the future of NATO, to the anguish of not only the Soviet Union but also France at points. As the president said to Kohl at Camp David: "We prevailed, they didn't." United Germany would have full NATO membership as a result. Indeed, at times, Mitterrand's aide Védrine wondered if NATO was "the *only* issue" that truly concerned Bush. Whether it was or was not, the American president clearly understood the alliance's significance. It kept the United States in Europe, but it was also an organization created to contain a Soviet threat. NATO therefore needed new relevance as that threat seeped away; otherwise, it might disappear as well. The alliance had to change to survive. It is not surprising that Bush made time to go to Europe repeatedly for the NATO summits in 1989 and 1990, but did not attend the final ceremony for German unification, despite Kohl's strong desire that he do so. The pressure of the contemporaneous Gulf crisis was of course part of the reason for his absence, but a major event celebrating the triumph of Western unity could also have been useful, if Bush had wanted one.[29]

This finding yields a fourth and final component: the legacy of 1989–90 shows the power of chance and contingency. At many points, all state leaders, superpower and otherwise, were simply reacting to change. They had to propose models of order for the future precisely because they were overwhelmed by disorder. Often they were not so much designing events as simply surviving them. The challenge was to make the best use of events, no matter how unexpected they might be.

The most unexpected was the opening of the wall on November 9, 1989, which shocked everyone, and might easily not have happened at all. The severely sleep-deprived East German spokesman Schabowksi could have forgotten the piece of paper with incomprehensible new travel rules until after the end of his November 9 press conference. As it was, he got around to it only in the fifty-fifth minute of an hour-long session, when his memory was jogged by a journalist's question on a related topic. Had he not remembered, the wall would not have fallen that night.

Of course, the wall would have opened eventually, but not as easily, not for free, not when all East German leaders of any significance were incommunicado in a meeting, not when all Soviet leaders of any significance were asleep, and above all, not as soon and not at a time when a cooperation-minded Gorbachev still had sufficient authority to manage the Soviet reaction. If the wall had fallen when the separatist movement in the Soviet Union and the erosion of Gorbachev's power were much more advanced, it could have played into the hands of opponents contemplating a coup. Or there may simply not have been enough time to complete the unification process before chaos engulfed the USSR. The process could easily have become fatally mired in the infighting of the Soviet elite, with U.S. attention diverted to the Gulf.[30] Once the Soviet Union definitively fell apart, questions about the fractured legal successors to its rights would have gotten messy indeed.

Instead, Kohl seized his chance between November 9, 1989, and October 3, 1990, to establish a durable, democratic order in united Germany, and to anchor the new nation in the EC and NATO. He sensed, rightly, that it was necessary to act quickly. But did the balancing act between chance and necessity require stopping there? Was there not a real opportunity to take advantage of the unexpected opportunities and accomplish more at a pan-European level? The eventual outcome of NATO expansion was already unfolding in 1990. But was there some form of international economic support or guidance, other than large handouts from Kohl, that would have eased the transit of the Soviet Union into the company of modern democracies and economies in exchange for its consent to peaceful German unification in NATO? Did the West "lose" Russia, and did it do so as early as 1990?[31]

Clear answers to these questions are elusive. Any speculation about them must start with Gorbachev's hopes for a better economic future, however. As described in the text, both Teltschik and Genscher noted a strong desire on the part of the Soviet leader in 1990 and a number of his advisers to move ahead, not in confrontation, but in cooperation with West Germany. Gorbachev's hope was to achieve prosperity at home via close links with Bonn. This desire for cooperation was obviously not universally shared, as the bitter resentment of Gorbachev's actions among his enemies shows. But the Soviet leader recalled the squalor of life in the Gorkaya River valley, with the pitiful huts and the endless barking of stray dogs, until the end of his career, and wanted better. It was not entirely unreasonable to hope that extensive cooperation with wealthy West Germany, traded for its unity, could provide help in reaching that goal; Teltschik thinks this was his main motivation.[32]

Gorbachev's desire to negotiate such a future peacefully rested at the heart of his willingness to approve German unification. For this reason, he gave his approval for both unity and NATO membership to Kohl (who was willing to provide credits and cash) rather than Bush and Baker (who were not, in part because of the weakening domestic economy in the United States at the time). The Soviet leader seemed to have accepted that it was too costly for the USSR to try to direct political events in regions, whether in Afghanistan or Europe, that clearly had goals other than those set for them by Moscow, and decided to cut his losses. In keeping with this view, he set in motion a truly astonishing amount of disarmament. Between 1990 and 2008, the number of Russian nuclear warheads on ICBMs was cut almost 70 percent, and four thousand of its tanks left Europe.[33]

Teltschik feels strongly that Gorbachev thought he could completely transform the Soviet Union with the German help that he would receive in return for cooperation over unification. Gorbachev's hope may have been naive, and structured far too much as a pedantic top-down initiative. Yet it appears to have been a sincere desire to improve the daily life of the broad mass of his people, and as such, laudable. As Gorbachev's biographer has rightly argued, the Soviet leader's goal was "the creation of a better society and system than that which he inherited." The "democratic shortcomings of post-Soviet Russia notwithstanding, the country Gorbachev bequeathed to his successors was freer than at any time in Russian history."[34]

As a result, it is hard not to regret Kohl's failure in his repeated, insistent, but largely fruitless efforts to create some kind of international coalition in 1990 for providing comprehensive financial aid and advice to Gorbachev. Opponents of such aid pointed out, both at the time and afterward, that there was no good reason for the West to prop up Gorbachev's Soviet empire, and that incompetent governance would have wasted any aid. Indeed, help in setting up competent domestic authorities early on may even have been more valuable than aid to Moscow. Gorbachev would complain to Baker in 1991 that the money from Kohl had already vanished: "'Things disappear around here. We got a lot of money for German unification, and when I called our people, I was told they didn't know where it was. Yakovlev told me to call around, and the answer is no one knows.'" Clearly, Moscow needed more than just credits to ease its transition to being a modern market economy, but (other than from Bonn) it got little. Western advisers would descend on Russia later en masse, of course. But they arrived after fatal resentments had already piled up.[35]

Kohl's efforts seem to have been undone by a contest between deterritorialization and provinciality churning away beneath the public surface of events.[36] In

Fig. C.3. The concert hall on Gendarmenmarkt in Berlin, decorated to celebrate the extension of the EU to Eastern Europe in May 2004. © Langevin Jacques/Corbis Sygma.

other words, 1989–90 was a time when, on one level, multilateral institutions like the EC and NATO began to expand eastward. They therefore blurred the borders between, or deterritorialized, states in their ambit. On another and more old-fashioned level, however, wagons still circled. Deterritorialize the West, but get as much property into it as possible before you do so, and then protect the united province from the crumbling though still dangerous East, ran the argument. This animus represented the thinking of Bonn and Washington; it contrasted badly with Gorbachev's hope that deterritorialization could extend from the Atlantic to the Urals. The Soviet leader's advisers kept trying to make the contrast clear to him, without success.[37]

The heart of the problem seems to be that Moscow did not understand to what extent, and for how little time, international order would be up for grabs during 1989–90. Indeed, historians arguing that the end of the Cold War was a transition of little importance are retrospectively making the same mistake that Gorbachev did at the time: failing to grasp what was at stake. Gorbachev and his advisers did not comprehend the chance that had opened up, and the necessity of moving quickly to seize it. In 1990, they thought that they had more time to sort out big issues for post–Cold War Europe, whether it was domestic reforms or new pan-European economic and security structures.

They did not. The negotiations about German unification were already shaping politics far beyond that country's borders in ways both ideological and material. By achieving German unity, the major actors involved—and there were many, working first from below throughout Eastern Europe and then from above in the West—fabricated the future on a number of levels. They opened up new doors of possibility for the residents of the half of Europe that had paid the heaviest price for the Cold War. They negated the Chinese example of violent suppression as a model for the future. They created hope in the hearts of all those facing ideologically and physically repressive regimes around the world. They made it clear that the market economy vision of the future would dominate the vast majority of world economies afterward, even ones still calling themselves Communist. They cemented plans to create a common European currency, now one of the world's strongest. They ensured that NATO would endure and remain the dominant international military alliance. They forced both the EC/EU and NATO to evolve, and in doing so, to lay the groundwork for later rapid enlargement. They ironically began creating a common European home of many rooms—just without one for Russia. Last but not least, they taught a lasting lesson to Putin, who had experienced the events of 1989–90 in divided Germany firsthand. Having prevented a sacking of the Soviet Union's KGB office in Dresden, he did not want to find himself or, by extension, his country in such a position again.[38]

For all of these reasons, the collapse of the Berlin Wall and the subsequent struggle to re-create order in post–Cold War Europe represent truly major turning points in modern history. It is essential to understand the legacy of the successes of 1989–90: Berlin did indeed gain the ability to understand the dream of freedom. Its peaceful transition from its former state to its present one, negotiated diplomatically with its international partners, holds hope for the many places that are just at the beginning of the same journey. It is equally essential to understand the legacy of the failings of 1989–90: the speed with which it happened resulted in imperfect choices and costly consequences. The chance to foster enduring cooperation with an unusually willing, if weak, Russian leadership passed, and it will not appear again soon. Looking back at the choices that defined the post–Cold War international order, we should strive to be clear-eyed about both their benefits and their costs.

ACKNOWLEDGMENTS

Although I discharged my professional debts at the outset of this book, I would like to close by expressing my personal thanks. Going back many years, I acknowledge the German Academic Exchange Service (or DAAD) for funding a year of study abroad at the Free University of West Berlin in 1988 and 1989. At the time I was simply trying to improve my German, but I learned much more than that. Once I began historical research into the end of the Cold War, I received support from Yale University's International Security Studies Program, its contributing sponsors, the DAAD once again and, most importantly, the Alexander von Humboldt Foundation. After some initial investigations into and publications based on East European archives and interviews in the 1990s—I am grateful to the editors of *German Politics* for letting me reuse portions of an article here—I decided that I would prefer to wait for the availability of Western sources before proceeding and turned my attention to other topics. In the interim, I had the opportunity to serve as a White House Fellow, which gave me much more insight into politics than scholarship alone could provide. I am grateful to the Presidential Commission for granting me that experience.

Once the requisite Western sources became available years later, fellowship and research support from the Humboldt Foundation once again, St. John's College of the University of Cambridge, the Mershon Center of The Ohio State University, and the University of Southern California enabled me to work through them. The Institute for Advanced Study in Princeton provided the ideal setting for thinking through my findings during a year of sabbatical. I am grateful to the faculty of the Institute's School of Historical Studies for selecting me and to the National Endowment for the Humanities for supporting my stay there.

On top of these institutions, I am also indebted to a number of individuals. I benefited from more help and good humor than I had any right to expect over the years of work on this study. The staff members of archives and other institutions from Moscow to California and a dozen places in between worked hard to connect me to the sources that I wanted to see, and I thank them for their efforts. In particular, I would like to acknowledge Manfred Bolz, Dr. Günter Buchstab, Mary Curry, Jörg Filthaut, Pascal Geneste, Dietmar Haak, Buffie Hollis, Dr. Robert Holzweiss, Petra Jakobik, Shajaat Jalil, Sergei Kuznetsov, Dan Linke, Mircea Munteanu, Kathy Olson, Zachary Roberts, Professor Patrick Salmon, Dan Santamaria, Jennifer Sternaman, Alice Tkar, Anne Vogel, Roberto Welzel, Deborah

Wheeler, Dr. Claudia Zenker-Oertel, and particularly Karin Göpel and Sylvia Gräfe, both former East Germans who have served for over a decade now as my incomparable guides to the written remains of long-gone regimes.

My agent, Bruce Hunter of David Higham Associates, has been a source of good counsel from the moment we met. Dr. Chuck Myers of Princeton University Press encouraged this project from its first days to its last and improved it greatly with his knowledgeable suggestions. At the press, Taira Blankenship, Nathan Carr, Dmitri Karetnikov, Cindy Milstein, Blythe Woolston, and two anonymous reviewers helped enormously, and I am grateful to the board for selecting the book for inclusion into the Studies in International History and Politics series.

I must also thank my student research assistants: Nick Reves, Bethsabee Sabah, Cate Veeneman, Jonathan Willbanks, and above all Mariya Grinberg, who was (fittingly) born in the Soviet Union in November 1989. Mariya was clearly a major scholar in a previous life, and, now that she is once again at a university, is picking up where she left off. My colleague in art history, Professor Kenneth Breisch, and my friend Jan Otakar Fischer helped with the architectural terminology. They and others have saved me from a number of errors; any that remain are, of course, my responsibility.

In various locations around the world, I received help and support from colleagues, friends, and elders. Going (roughly) from East to West, these are Professor Alexander Polunov (Moscow); Professor Greg Domber (Warsaw); Dr. Hans-Hermann Hertle and his colleagues at the Center for Contemporary History, or ZZF (Potsdam); the Richter family and the Raskob family (Berlin); the Hadshiew-Tetu family (Hamburg); Dr. Georg Schütte and Dr. Steffen Mehlich (Bonn); Lieutenant Colonel Rich and Christy Morales, and the Rödder family (Mainz); Professor Frédéric Bozo (Paris); Peter Chapman and Christopher Fowler, the Choi-Undheim family, John Logan Nichols (who deserves special thanks for reading the entire manuscript twice), Dr. Sveta Rajak, and Professor Odd Arne Westad (London); the Drezner family and Dr. Mark Kramer (Boston); Professor Paul Kennedy and the late Professor Henry Turner (New Haven, CT); William Scot Murray (New York); Terrie Bramley, Professor Peter Goddard, Professor Robert Hutchings, Professor Andrew Moravcsik, and Professor Heinrich von Staden (Princeton, NJ); Captain Bill Cameron (retired), Colonel Kathy Conley (retired), Luke Faraone, Professor James Goldgeier, Dr. Jeffrey Richter, Dr. Svetlana Savranskaya, Colonel Terry Taylor (retired) and Mi Ae Geoum (Washington, DC); Professor Richard Herrmann, Professor Geoffrey Parker, Professor Bob McMahon, and the staff of the Mershon Center (Columbus, OH); Dr. Hillary Hahm (Atlanta); Professor Rory Rapple (South Bend, IN); Professor Mike Desch, the Engel family, and Professor Jason Parker (College Station, TX); the Lynn family (San Francisco); and finally my colleagues and friends in Los Angeles, especially Professor Laurie Brand, Professor Robert English, Professor Pat James, Sheri-Lyn Jones, Dean Steve Lamy, Professor John Odell, Petar Toshev, Professor Carol Wise, and the teaching assistants who stuck with me for multiple semesters dominated by this book, Christina Faegri, Dr. Kosal Path, and Sahra Sulaiman. My friend and colleague ever since our days at Yale, the wondrous Professor Jennifer Siegel, deserves special commendation for offering (1) useful archival advice, (2) excellent restaurant suggestions, and (3) a sofa to sleep on, in no fewer than three different countries.

Finally, throughout the writing of this study, I was sustained by the love of my family, old and new: Frank, Gail, and Steven Sarotte; Dianne and Al Minicucci; Marc, Sylvia, and Timmy Scheffler; Claus and Rita Wulf; Jack and Mary Ann Schiefsky; and all the furry critters who bring so much warmth to our homes. This book is dedicated to my fiancé Mark Schiefsky, a classicist, despite his disapproval of many aspects of the story and his general belief that all history gets repetitive after about AD 200. As children in Detroit years ago (before we knew each other), we were both inspired by Carl Sagan's magnificent television series *Cosmos* to commence our own intellectual journeys. It is now a great happiness to join together on this journey with someone who is at once so wise and so loving. I cannot express the feeling better than the dedication from the book version of *Cosmos*: In the vastness of space and the immensity of time, it is my joy to share a planet and an epoch with you.

NOTES

ADDITIONAL ABBREVIATIONS IN THE NOTES

BPL   George H. W. Bush Presidential Library

BP   Baker Papers (Mudd Library, Princeton University)

BRD   Bundesrepublik Deutschland (German name for West Germany)

BStU   Bundesbeauftragte für die Unterlagen des Staatssicherheitsdienstes der ehemaligen Deutschen Demokratischen Republik (German name for the Stasi Archive, Germany)

CAB   Cabinet Office (United Kingdom)

CWIHPPC   Cold War International History Project Paris Conference

DCI   Director of Central Intelligence (United States)

DDR   Deutsche Demokratische Republik (German name for East Germany)

DESE   *Deutsche Einheit Sonderedition* (*German Unity Special Edition*, published West German documents)

FCO   Foreign and Commonwealth Office (United Kingdom)

FOI, FOIA   Freedom of Information (United Kingdom), Freedom of Information Act (United States)

GC   Georgia Conference (see bibliography for details)

GDE   *Geschichte der Deutschen Einheit* (*History of German Unity*, four-volume official history)

JAB   James A. Baker III

KADE   Kabinettausschuß Deutsche Einheit (West German Cabinet Committee on Germany Unity)

KASPA   Konrad Adenauer Stiftung Pressearchiv (Konrad Adenauer Foundation Press Archive, Germany)

Memcon   Memorandum of Conversation (United States)

MfS   Ministerium für Staatssicherheit (Ministry for State Security, official name of the East German Stasi)

МГ   *Михаил Горбачев и германский вопрос* (*Mikhail Gorbachev and the German Question*, published Soviet documents)

NIC   National Intelligence Council (United States)

PC   Prague Conference (see bibliography for details)

RHG	Robert-Havemann Gesellschaft (Robert Havemann Foundation, archive of the former East German dissident movement)
SAPMO	Stiftung/Archiv der Parteien und Massenorganisationen der DDR (Archive of Former GDR Parties and Mass Organizations)
ZRT	Zentraler Runder Tisch (Central Round Table, East Germany)
ZRT-WD	*Der Zentrale Runde Tisch der DDR: Wortprotokolle und Dokumente* (Central Round Table of the GDR, transcripts and published documents)

NOTES TO PREFACE

1. Francis Fukuyama originally published "The End of History?" as a *National Interest* article in summer 1989, but subsequently expanded it into a book, *The End of History and the Last Man* (New York: Penguin Books, 1992). Detailed popular accounts have come from Michael R. Beschloss and Strobe Talbott, *At the Highest Levels: The Inside Story of the End of the Cold War* (Boston: Little, Brown, 1993); James Mann, *The Rebellion of Ronald Reagan: A History of the End of the Cold War* (New York: Viking, 2009); Don Oberdorfer, *The Turn: From the Cold War to a New Era* (New York: Simon and Schuster, 1991). Some of the more interesting scholarly accounts are the following: Frédéric Bozo, *Mitterrand, la fin de la guerre froide et l'unification allemande: De Yalta à Maastricht* (Paris: Odile Jacob, 2005); Stephen G. Brooks and William Wohlforth, "Power, Globalization, and the End of the Cold War," *International Security* 25, no. 3 (Winter 2000–2001): 5–53, and "From Old Thinking to New Thinking," *International Security* 26, no. 4 (Spring 2002): 93–111; Archie Brown, "Perestroika and the End of the Cold War," *Cold War History* 7, no. 1 (February 2007): 1–17, and *Seven Years That Changed the World: Perestroika in Perspective* (New York: Oxford University Press, 2007); Robert D. English, *Russia and the Idea of the West: Gorbachev, Intellectuals, and the End of the Cold War* (New York: Columbia University Press, 2000), and "Power, Ideas, and New Evidence on the Cold War's End: A Reply to Brooks and Wohlforth," *International Security* 26, no. 4 (Spring 2002): 70–92; John Lewis Gaddis, *The Cold War* (New York: Penguin, 2006); Timothy Garton Ash, *In Europe's Name: Germany and the Divided Continent* (New York: Vintage Books, 1993); Richard K. Herrmann and Richard Ned Lebow, eds., *Ending the Cold War* (New York: Palgrave Macmillan, 2004); Hans-Hermann Hertle, *Der Fall der Mauer: Die unbeabsichtigte Selbstauflösung des SED-Staates* (Opladen: Westdeutscher Verlag, 1996); see also Hans-Hermann Hertle, *Chronik des Mauerfalls: Die dramatischen Ereignisse um den 9. November 1989* (Berlin: Links, September 1996), "The Fall of the Wall: The Unintended Self-Dissolution of East Germany's Ruling Regime," *Cold War International History Project Bulletin* 12–13 (Fall–Winter 2001): 131–40, "Germany in the Last Decade of the Cold War," in *The Last Decade of the Cold War: From Conflict Escalation to Conflict Transformation*, ed. Olav Njølstad, 265–87 (London: Frank Cass, 2004), and his television documentary, *When the Wall Came Tumbling Down*, Sender Freies Berlin, 1999. The Njølstad volume contains a number of useful papers resulting from a conference on the end of the Cold War, as does Odd Arne Westad, ed., *Reviewing the Cold War* (London: Routledge, 2000); Westad was editing, together with Melvyn P. Leffler, a multivolume history of the entire Cold War for Cambridge University Press as this book went to press. Robert L. Hutchings, *American Diplomacy and the End of the Cold War: An Insider's Account of US Policy in Europe, 1989–1992* (Washington, DC: Wilson Center, 1997); Konrad Jarausch, *The Rush to German Unity* (New York: Oxford University Press, 1994); Mark Kramer, "Ideology and the Cold War," *Review of International Studies* 25 (1999): 539–76; Melvyn P. Leffler, *For the Soul of Mankind: The United States, the Soviet Union, and the Cold War* (New York: Hill and Wang, 2007); Charles S. Maier, *Dissolution: The Crisis of Communism and the End of East Germany* (Princeton, NJ: Princeton University Press, 1997); Gerhard A. Ritter, *Der*

NOTES

Preis der deutschen Einheit: Die Wiedervereinigung und die Krise des Sozialstaats (Munich: Beck, 2006), which is a popular version of his *1989–1994 Bundesrepublik Deutschland: Sozialpolitik im Zeichen der Vereinigung,* vol. 11, *Geschichte der Sozialpolitik in Deutschland seit 1945* (Baden-Baden: Nomos Verlag, 2007); Andreas Rödder, *Deutschland Einig Vaterland* (Munich: Beck, 2009), see also his "Zeitgeschichte als Herausforderung: Die deutsche Einheit," *Historische Zeitschrift* 270 (2000): 669–87, "'Breakthrough in the Caucasus'? German Reunification as a Challenge to Contemporary Historiography," *German Historical Institute London Bulletin* 24, no. 2 (November 2002): 7–34, *Die Bundesrepublik Deutschland, 1969–1990* (Munich: Oldenbourg Verlag, 2004); Angela Stent, *Russia and Germany Reborn: Unification, the Soviet Collapse, and the New Europe* (Princeton, NJ: Princeton University Press, 1999); Bernd Stöver, *Der Kalte Krieg, 1947–1991: Geschichte eines radikalen Zeitalters* (Munich: Beck, 2007); Stephen Szabo, *The Diplomacy of German Unification* (New York: St. Martin's Press, 1992); Philip Zelikow and Condoleezza Rice, *Germany Unified and Europe Transformed: A Study in Statecraft* (Cambridge, MA: Harvard University Press, 1995). There is also a multivolume study that was produced by a group of German professors who received early access to West German documents. Their resulting publication runs to a cumulative 3,008 pages. See *Geschichte der deutschen Einheit* (hereafter GDE) (Stuttgart: Deutsche Verlags-Anstalt, 1998): Karl-Rudolf Korte, vol. 1, *Deutschlandpolitik in Helmut Kohls Kanzlerschaft: Regierungsstil und Entscheidungen 1982–1989*; Dieter Grosser, vol. 2, *Das Wagnis der Währungs-, Wirtschafts- und Sozialunion: Politische Zwänge im Konflikt mit ökonomischen Regeln*; Wolfgang Jäger, vol. 3, *Die Überwindung der Teilung: Der innerdeutsche Prozeß der Vereinigung 1989/90*; most relevant to this study and also the longest, at 952 pages, Werner Weidenfeld, Peter M. Wagner, and Elke Bruck, vol. 4, *Außenpolitik für die deutsche Einheit: Die Entscheidungsjahre 1989/90.* An online chronology is available in both English and German at http://www.chronik-der-mauer. de, produced by Hertle at the Zentrum für Zeitgeschichtliche Forschung in Potsdam together with the Bundeszentrale für politische Bildung and Deutschlandradio; see also, in a similar vein, http://www.chronik-der-wende.de. On the first George Bush era more generally, see Christopher Maynard, *Out of the Shadow: George H. W. Bush and the End of the Cold War* (College Station: Texas A&M Press, 2008). Finally, a collection of documents and essays about 1989 edited by Thomas Blanton, Svetlana Savranskaya, and Vladislav Zubok was forthcoming as this book went to press.

2. John Lewis Gaddis, "History, Theory, and Common Ground," *International Security* 22, no. 1 (Summer 1997): 84.

3. Ikenberry himself has produced one of the finest studies of major international reordering moments in *After Victory* (Princeton, NJ: Princeton University Press, 2001). See also his article, together with Daniel Deudney, "Who Won the Cold War?" *Foreign Policy* 87 (Summer 1992): online.

4. Ellen Schrecker, ed., *Cold War Triumphalism: The Misuse of History after the Fall of Communism* (New York: New Press, 2004), 2.

5. Particularly useful was the video archive of the West German television station ARD in Hamburg and the Robert Havemann-Gesellschaft (hereafter RHG) in Berlin, to which a number of former East German dissidents have donated their private materials.

6. A limited number of issues of the edited Gorbachev documents were published in Moscow in late 2006: *Михаил Горбачев и германский вопрос* (hereafter МГ) (Moscow: Весь Мир, 2006). The documents, however, have since become available online at http://rodon.org/other/mgigv/ index.htm; I am grateful to Victor Grinberg for calling my attention to this site. Gorbachev's aide, Chernyaev, has made materials available both via the Gorbachev Foundation and online via the National Security Archive. Chernyaev's memoirs are also available in an excellent translation: Anatoly Chernyaev, *My Six Years with Gorbachev,* trans. and ed. Robert English and Elizabeth Tucker (University Park: Pennsylvania State University Press, 2000). There is also a German version: *Die letzten Jahre einer Weltmacht* (Stuttgart: Deutsche-Verlagsanstalt, 1993);

however, I have relied on the English-Tucker translation. The Fond 89 is now available in various archives and libraries. I have used the copy at Harvard University, in the U.S. Government Documents section of Lamont Library; I am grateful to Mark Kramer for his help with this collection and other sources. I must also thank Dr. Alexander (Sasha) Polunov of Moscow State University and particularly Mariya Grinberg of the University of Southern California for their help in processing Russian sources.

7. Some of Kohl's papers on the process of German unification, or to be more precise, the records of the Bundeskanzleramt from late 1989 to late 1990 on the subject, were released and published in the truly remarkable volume edited by Hanns Jürgen Küsters and Daniel Hoffman, *Dokumente zur Deutschlandpolitik: Deutsche Einheit, Sonderedition* (hereafter DESE) *aus den Akten des Bundeskanzleramtes 1989/90* (Munich: R. Oldenbourg Verlag, 1998). Despite the use of small fonts and the combination of many pages of original documents into shorter continuous typescripts, the volume still runs to 1,667 pages. While it does not contain every single item produced by the Bundeskanzleramt in this time period, it represents a remarkable selection of 430 central documents, many involving bilateral contacts with countries that have kept their own copies from the same meetings still secret. On top of this, the decision of the Bundeskanzleramt and the Bundesarchiv to grant me access to still-closed documents allowed me to read the published items in fuller context, although I could not cite the unpublished sources. These sources will inform the analysis that follows without explicit mention. The Bundesarchiv staff in Koblenz and the Bundeskanzleramt staff in Berlin have been helpful in this process; I am grateful to Jörg Filthaut, Katja Neuman, and Dr. Claudia Zenker-Oertel in particular. For more on the published documents, see Hartmut Mayer, Review of *Dokumente zur Deutschlandpolitik: Deutsche Einheit, International Affairs* 74, no. 4 (October 1998): 952–53.

8. Especially useful were the FOIA requests filed by James Goldgeier and Christian Ostermann. Ostermann essentially requested all of the documents cited in Zelikow and Rice, *Germany Unified*, so that independent scholars can assess them. I am grateful to the staff of the Bush Presidential Library (hereafter BPL) for their help with these and other relevant FOIA requests. In particular, I appreciate their assistance in filing hundreds of mandatory review requests (covering every redacted or removed document in the relevant FOIAs). On the Zelikow and Rice account, already cited in note 1, see also Zelikow and Rice, "German Unification," in Kiron K. Skinner, *Turning Points in Ending the Cold War* (Stanford, CA: Hoover Institution Press, 2008), 229–54.

9. I would like to thank Secretary Baker for granting me both an interview and permission to view and copy his papers, which are held by the Mudd Library of Princeton University. Furthermore, I am grateful to Daniel Linke and Daniel Santamaria for their help with these materials. Emphasis in the original Baker documents, whether shown via the use of underlining or italics, is shown with italics in this text.

10. I am grateful to Patrick Salmon of the Foreign and Commonwealth Office (FCO) for a number of consultations on these sources. I also thank Shajaat Jalil of the FCO for his help with my numerous British FOI requests. At the Cabinet Office (CAB) I am grateful to John Jenkins for his aid. Ian Brown of the UK Information Commissioner's office helped with my successful appeal of a CAB denial, and I thank him for his support.

11. The documents published by Mitterrand will be cited in the text to follow, when they are quoted. French historian Frédéric Bozo succeeded in his attempt to receive early access to extensive Mitterrand records; see Bozo, *Mitterrand*. My own petition (or *dérogation*) for an early viewing of the documents succeeded as well, although mostly too late for incorporation into this book, and will be the subject of future writing. I thank Bozo and Pascal Geneste for their help with French sources.

12. Andrew J. Nathan, Perry Link, and "Zhang Liang," eds., *The Tiananmen Papers: The Chinese Leadership's Decision to Use Force against Their Own People—in Their Own Words* (New York:

Public Affairs, 2001). Zhang Liang is the pseudonym of the Chinese collaborator who supplied the Western scholars with document copies. It is worth noting the concerns raised about these smuggled document copies, voiced by China scholar Jonathan Spence, "Inside the Forbidden City," *New York Times Book Review*, January 21, 2001, 10–11. Spence suggests that the name chosen by the Chinese collaborator may be a hint. The real Zhang Liang was a historical figure from the third century BC who, according to Spence, was "a strategist of the highest order, a man whose subtlety at analyzing the nuances of political life, military realities and personal relationships was exceptional." He was also known to sometimes "sharpen" stories, however, by writing lengthy confidential dialogue as if he were repeating it verbatim. As a result, Spence guesses that while the gist of the documents may be accurate, the "verbatim" quotations may not be as reliable.

13. The translations from French, German, and Russian are my own unless otherwise indicated. For other languages, I often relied on the translations provided by these two organizations, and sometimes used them for German and Russian if I agreed with their translations.

14. A full list of interviews starts on p. 290.

15. As Jack Levy has pointed out, narrative is a method. Jack Levy, "Too Important to Leave to the Other," *International Security* 22, no. 1 (Summer 1997): 22–33.

16. Alexander L. George, "Case Studies and Theory Development: The Method of Structured Focused Comparison," in *Diplomacy: New Approaches in History, Theory, and Policy*, ed. Paul Gordon Lauren (New York: Free Press, 1979), 43–68. See also Alexander L. George, "The 'Operational Code': A Neglected Approach to the Study of Political Decision-Making," *International Studies Quarterly* 12 (June 1969): 190–222.

17. Theda Skocpol, *States and Social Revolutions: A Comparative Analysis of France, Russia, and China* (Cambridge: Cambridge University Press, 1979), 36.

18. John Lewis Gaddis, *Strategies of Containment: A Critical Appraisal of Postwar American National Security Policy* (Oxford: Oxford University Press, 1982). It is a testament to the durability of this work that the publisher issued a twenty-fifth anniversary edition in 2007, with additions by the author; see the discussion of the revised version in Robert L. Jervis, "Containment Strategies in Perspective," *Journal of Cold War Studies* 8, no. 4 (Fall 2006): 92–97. Paul Kennedy, *The Rise and Fall of the Great Powers* (New York: Random House, 1987). Odd Arne Westad, *The Global Cold War: Third World Interventions and the Making of Our Times* (Cambridge: Cambridge University Press, 2005).

NOTES TO INTRODUCTION

1. Barack Obama, "A World That Stands as One" (speech delivered in Berlin, Germany, July 24, 2008), video and text at http://my.barackobama.com/page/content/berlinvideo; Jana Hensel, *Zonenkinder* (Reinbek bei Hamburg: Rowohlt, 2004), 160.

2. Nicholas Kulish and Jeff Zeleny, "Prospect of Obama at Brandenburg Gate Divides German Politicians," *New York Times*, July 10, 2008, online. For the content of the speech, see Obama, "A World That Stands as One."

3. "Transcript of Barack Obama's Victory Speech," November 5, 2008, available at http://www.npr.org; also available on a number of other news websites. For insightful analysis focusing on the power of memory about the collapse of the Berlin Wall, see the chapter by Mel Leffler in Jeffrey Engel, ed. *The Fall of the Berlin Wall: The Revolutionary Legacy of 1989* (Oxford: Oxford University Press, 2009).

4. As Stephen Kotkin has concluded, 1989 signaled the end of "the death agony of an entire world comprising non-market economics and anti-liberal institutions." Stephen Kotkin, *Armageddon Averted: The Soviet Collapse, 1970–2000* (New York: Oxford University Press, 2001), 2. For more on the collapse of the Soviet Union, see Michael Ellman and Vladimir Kontorovich, eds.,

The Disintegration of the Soviet Economic System (New York: Routledge, 1992), and *The De-struction of the Soviet Economic System: An Insiders' History* (Armonk, NY: M. E. Sharpe, 1998). On the discrediting of Marxism-Leninism, see Mark Kramer, "The Collapse of East European Communism and the Repercussions within the Soviet Union (Part 2)," *Journal of Cold War Studies* 6, no. 4 (Fall 2004): 3–64. For more on the decline of Communism and socialism generally, see François Furet, *The Passing of an Illusion: The Idea of Communism in the Twentieth Century* (Chicago: University of Chicago Press, 1999); Tina Rosenberg, *The Haunted Land: Facing Europe's Ghosts after Communism* (New York: Random House, 1995); Adam B. Ulam, *The Communists: The Story of Power and Lost Illusions, 1948–1991* (New York: Scribner's, 1992). See also the personal account in Slavenka Drakulic´, *How We Survived Communism and Even Laughed* (New York: Harper Perennial, 1993); see also Alan Greenspan, *The Age of Turbulence* (New York: Penguin, 2007), 12. Greenspan argues that 1989 was the most significant single year in the history of the global economy. "The defining moment for the world's economies was the fall of the Berlin Wall in 1989, revealing a state of economic ruin behind the iron curtain," and this event, more so than any other, exposed Communism "as an unredeemable failure."

5. In her autobiography, she described the wonder and challenge of entering into an adulthood unexpectedly rich in new opportunities, individual freedoms, and consumer goods, but at the price of leaving behind all the familiar certainties and identities of her parents' world. In particular, Hensel still recalls the first moment that she knew nothing would ever be the same again: when her usually apolitical mother took her to a protest march in their hometown of Leipzig in October 1989. Up until then, she remembers a life concerned mainly with hitting the marks set for her by socialist teachers and peers. That night, as she marched with her mother and university students, "I thought, for the first time in my life, that something was happening to the country that had always been my homeland, that I did not know anything about it, and that no adult could tell me where it would lead." Hensel's book, *Zonenkinder* (Hamburg: Rowohlt, 2004) or "Children of the Zone," was published in English as *After the Wall* (New York: Public Affairs, 2004). For a discussion of the controversy caused by the book, disliked by those who did not agree with her characterization of a new generation, see Tom Kraushaar, ed., *Die Zonenkinder und Wir: Die Geschichte eines Phänomens* (Hamburg: Rowohlt, 2004). For an account from an East German woman of a similar age, but with a different and much more politicized upbringing, see Claudia Rusch, *Meine freie deutsche Jugend* (Frankfurt: Fischer, 2003).

6. See the preface for the names of specific scholars who have argued this way. In general, I have tried to keep the scholarly apparatus out of the main text, so that the lay reader may follow the story without digressions for experts' debates.

7. A number of works suggest that the East German government intentionally opened the wall; to cite one example, see the analysis in Joseph Held, ed. *The Columbia History of Eastern Europe in the Twentieth Century* (New York: Columbia University Press, 1992), 376ff. For the argument that German unification is a closed chapter with no further relevance for NATO expansion, see Mark Kramer, "The Myth of a No-NATO-Enlargement Pledge to Russia," *Washington Quarterly* 32, no. 2 (April 2009): 39–61. The American policymaker quoted above is Robert Hutchings, although he is not alone in holding this view; see Robert Hutchings, "The European Question, Revisited," in *The Legacy of 1989,* ed. German Marshall Fund (Washington, DC: German Marshall Fund, 2009), 6. Finally, interview with Lord Douglas Hurd, London, March 17, 2009. The full hour-long interview that I conducted with Lord Hurd was recorded, and is available to researchers at the Mudd Library, Princeton University, thanks to Lord Hurd's generous decision to open it with no restrictions.

8. As John Lewis Gaddis has put it, "The most striking anomaly of the Cold War was the existence of a divided Europe, within which there resided a divided Germany, within which there lay a divided Berlin." John Lewis Gaddis, *We Now Know: Rethinking Cold War History* (Oxford: Clarendon Press, 1997), 115.

9. As Raymond L. Garthoff has argued, "While the end of the Cold War was virtually assured by the end of 1989, there remained the very important and difficult task of negotiating the terms of the liquidation of the division of Germany, and thereby of Europe. This was the 'endgame' in winding down the Cold War." See Raymond L. Garthoff, "The U.S. Role in Winding Down the Cold War, 1980–9," in *The Last Decade of the Cold War: From Conflict Escalation to Conflict Transformation*, ed. Olav Njølstad, 191 (London: Frank Cass, 2004), 191.

10. I use this metaphor of an architectural competition as a "problematizing redescription" of the issue at hand, to highlight the most important aspects. This term comes from Ian Shapiro, *The Flight from Reality in the Human Sciences* (Princeton, NJ: Princeton University Press, 2005), 202.

11. Hannes Adomeit, *Imperial Overstretch: Germany in Soviet Policy from Stalin to Gorbachev* (Baden-Baden: Nomos Verlagsgesellschaft, 1998), 560, uses it in a particularly insightful manner.

12. This understanding of a competition is superior to other frequently used metaphors, such as a ball game or Russian roulette. In these, contests take place on an empty field, the results are final when the whistle blows or the last gun fires, and the next contest begins de novo. None of this is true of politics. As Alexander George has argued, the critical question of any simplifying device "is whether the loss of information and condensation of the explanation jeopardizes the validity of the generic knowledge and its utility for diagnosing and dealing with new instances of that phenomenon." The architectural concept allows for condensation but also for nuance. Alexander L. George, "Case Studies and Theory Development: The Method of Structured Focused Comparison," in *Diplomacy: New Approaches in History, Theory, and Policy*, ed. Paul Gordon Lauren (New York: Free Press, 1979).

13. Westad observed that he was repeatedly struck "by how instructive the European example is for understanding what happened in the Third World." Odd Arne Westad, "Devices and Desires: On the Uses of Cold War History," *Cold War History* 6, no. 3 (August 2006): 373–76; quotation is on 374. Westad is agreeing on this point with comments made by William Wohlforth. See Stephen G. Brooks and William Wohlforth, "Power, Globalization, and the End of the Cold War," *International Security* 25, no. 3 (Winter 2000–2001): 5–53; William Wohlforth, *The Elusive Balance: Power and Perceptions during the Cold War* (Ithaca, NY: Cornell University Press, 1993). For more on the consequences of the end of the Cold War, see Bernd Stöver, *Der Kalte Krieg, 1947–1991: Geschichte eines radikalen Zeitalters* (Munich: Beck, 2007), 471–75.

14. The concept of competing visions of modernity comes from James C. Scott, as interpreted by Odd Arne Westad; see Odd Arne Westad, "Bernath Lecture: The New International History of the Cold War: Three (Possible) Paradigms," *Diplomatic History* 24, no. 4 (Fall 2000): 551–65; and *The Global Cold War: Third World Interventions and the Making of Our Times* (Cambridge: Cambridge University Press, 2005), introduction, especially 4. Harold James and Marla Stone similarly see 1989–91 as the end of a contest that started with World War I and the creation of the Soviet Union; see Harold James and Marla Stone, eds., *When the Wall Came Down* (New York: Routledge, 1992), 9.

15. For an insightful discussion of the fluid nature of sovereignty, see Stephen Krasner, *Sovereignty: Organized Hypocrisy* (Princeton, NJ: Princeton University Press, 1999).

16. French scholar Marie-Pierre Rey is right to suggest that this concept has not received enough attention; see Marie-Pierre Rey, "'Europe Is Our Common Home': A Study of Gorbachev's Diplomatic Concept," *Cold War History* 2 (January 2004): 33–65. See also Jacques Lévesque, "In the Name of Europe's Future: Soviet, French, and British Qualms about Kohl's Rush to Unity," in *Europe and the End of the Cold War*, ed. Frédéric Bozo, Marie-Pierre Rey, N. Piers Ludlow, and Leopoldo Nuti (London: Routledge, 2008), 95–106.

17. I am grateful to Jan Otakar Fischer for his insights on the subject of heroic modernism.

18. I am grateful to Piers Ludlow for this and many other points on the interaction between German and European unification. For more on the role of large, multinational institutions in international relations, see Michael Barnett and Martha Finnemore, *Rules for the World: International Organizations in Global Politics* (Ithaca, NY: Cornell University Press, 2004).

19. James A. Baker with Thomas A. DeFrank, *The Politics of Diplomacy* (New York: G. P. Putnam's Sons, 1995), 84. See also Dimitri K. Simes, "Losing Russia: The Costs of Renewed Confrontation," *Foreign Affairs* (November–December 2007), online; and Stephen F. Cohen, *Soviet Fates and Lost Alternatives: From Stalinism to the New Cold War*. (New York: Columbia University Press, 2009).

20. This sentence echoes Jeff Legro's discussion of work by Juan Linz: "The fate of new regimes depends on their ability to fulfill expectations relative to the claims of the opponents to be able to do so better." See Jeff Legro, *Rethinking the World: Great Power Strategies and International Order* (Ithaca, NY: Cornell University Press, 2005), 37; Juan Linz, *The Breakdown of Democratic Regimes* (Baltimore: Johns Hopkins University Press, 1978).

NOTES TO CHAPTER 1

1. T. S. Eliot, "East Coker," *Four Quartets* (New York: Harcourt Brace, 1943).

2. Irina Scherbakova, interview with author, July 12, 2005, Moscow. Scherbakova became a leader of the Memorial Institute in Moscow, dedicated to collecting evidence on former Soviet gulags and protest movements.

3. Don Oberdorfer, *The Turn: From the Cold War to a New Era* (New York: Simon and Schuster, 1991), 24; Christopher Andrew and Oleg Gordievsky, *KGB: The Inside Story of Its Foreign Operations from Lenin to Gorbachev* (New York: HarperCollins, 1990), 601. On Jahn, see notes 11 and 32, below. For more on the 1980s, see John Ehrman, *The Eighties: America in the Age of Reagan* (New Haven, CT: Yale University Press, 2005); John Lewis Gaddis, *The Cold War* (New York: Penguin, 2006), chapter 6.

4. For a description of Christian Gueffroy's death, see the entry for February 5, 1989, at the online documentation site http://www.chronik-der-mauer.de, available in both English and German.

5. Christopher Andrew and Vasili Mitrokhin, *The Sword and the Shield: The Mitrokhin Archive and the Secret History of the KGB* (New York: Basic Books, 1999), 331.

6. Elaine Tyler May, *Homeward Bound: American Families in the Cold War Era*, rev. ed. (New York: Basic Books, 2008). For more on both the United States and Germany during the Cold War, see Detlef Junker, ed., *Die USA und Deutschland im Zeitalter des Kalten Krieges 1945–1990: Ein Handbuch*, 2 vols. (Stuttgart: Deutsche Verlags-Anstalt, 2001).

7. Robert M. Collins, *Transforming America: Politics and Culture during the Reagan Years* (New York: Columbia University Press, 2007), 200. The film also reportedly had a dramatic effect on Reagan personally, inspiring him to rethink his approach to the Soviet Union after seeing an advance screening. See Beth A. Fischer, *The Reagan Reversal: Foreign Policy and the End of the Cold War* (Columbia: University of Missouri Press, 1997), 115. For a discussion of Warsaw Pact fears about the West, see Vojtech Mastny and Malcolm Byrne, eds., *A Cardboard Castle? An Inside History of the Warsaw Pact* (New York: Central European University Press, 2005), 73.

8. Herbert Grönemeyer's successful hit song "Amerika" was written in 1984 and appeared on the album *4630 Bochum* (see http://www.groenemeyer.de); videos from performances of "Amerika" in concert tour still attract viewers on YouTube's website today. For more on protests about nuclear weapons, see Lawrence S. Wittner, *Toward Nuclear Abolition: A History of the World Disarmament Movement: 1971 to the Present* (Stanford, CA: Stanford University Press, 2003), 3:145; see also Matthew Evangelista, *Unarmed Forces: The Transnational Movement to End the Cold War* (Ithaca, NY: Cornell University Press, 1999); Jonathan Haslam, *The Soviet Union and the Politics of Nuclear Weapons in Europe, 1969–1987: The Problem of the SS-20* (London: Macmillan, 1989).

9.   The lens quotation comes from Matthew Connelly, "Taking off the Cold War Lens: Visions of North-South Conflict during the Algerian War for Independence," *American Historical Review* 105 (June 2000): 739–69. On the question of whether the Cold War is a useful construct or not, to cite just a few authors in alphabetical order, see Benedict Anderson, *The Spectre of Comparisons* (London: Verso, 1998); Dipesh Chakrabarty, *Provincializing Europe: Postcolonial Thought and Historical Difference* (Princeton, NJ: Princeton University Press, 2000); Walter Hixson, *The Myth of American Diplomacy: National Identity and US Foreign Policy* (New Haven, CT: Yale University Press, 2008); the H-DIPLO discussion thread on this work, 2008; the discussion of some of these works in Jeremi Suri, "The Cold War, Decolonization, and Global Society Awakenings: Historical Intersections," *Cold War History* 6, no. 3 (August 2006): 353–63. For a discussion of the Cold War as a "radical age," see Bernd Stöver, *Der Kalte Krieg, 1947–1991: Geschichte eines radikalen Zeitalters* (Munich: Beck, 2007).

10. Stephen Kotkin, *Armageddon Averted: The Soviet Collapse, 1970–2000* (New York: Oxford University Press, 2001), 61; Jens Gieseke, *Der Mielke-Konzern: Die Geschichte der Stasi 1945–1990* (Munich: Deutsche Velags-Anstalt, 2006), 71–72, 107, 248. For further basic information on the Stasi and the history of East Germany, see Hermann Weber, *Die DDR 1945–1990* (Munich: Oldenbourg Verlag, 1993). On the technology of espionage, see Kristie Mackrakis, *Seduced by Secrets: Inside the Stasi's Spy-Tech World* (Cambridge: Cambridge University Press, 2008).

11. Ilko-Sascha Kowalczuk and Tom Sello, eds., *Für ein freies Land mit freien Menschen: Opposition und Widerstand in Biographien und Fotos* (Berlin: Robert-Havemann-Gesellschaft, 2006), 312 (photo), 321–24; online biographical information about Jahn at http://www.chronik-der -wende.de.

12. Jacques Lévesque, "The Messianic Character of 'New Thinking': Why and What For?" in *The Last Decade of the Cold War: From Conflict Escalation to Conflict Transformation*, ed. Olav Njølstad (London: Frank Cass, 2004), 159–76. For more on the development of socialist thought in postwar Europe, see Tony Judt, *Postwar: A History of Europe since 1945* (New York: Penguin, 2005).

13. See "The President's Private Meeting with Gorbachev," December 7, 1988, 1:05 to 1:30 p.m., Governor's Island, New York; Memorandum of Conversation (hereafter Memcon), drafted by T. J. Simons, executive secretariat, NSC, records 8890931, system file, vertical file, "Governor's Island," Reagan Library, Simi Valley, California. For more on Reagan's background, see Matthew Dallek, *The Right Moment: Ronald Reagan's First Victory and the Decisive Turning Point in American Politics* (New York: Oxford University Press, 2000).

14. See Kotkin, *Armageddon Averted*, 67, 88; Raymond Garthoff, *The Great Transition: American-Soviet Relations and the End of the Cold War* (Washington, DC: Brookings Institution Press, 1994), 390–91.

15. Csaba Békés and Melinda Kalmár, "The Political Transition in Hungary, 1989–90," *Cold War International History Project Bulletin* 12–13 (Fall–Winter 2001): 78. For more on 1968, see Carole Fink, Philipp Gassert, and Detlef Junker, eds., *1968: The World Transformed* (New York: Cambridge University Press, 1998).

16. On the significance of anniversary dates as a mobilization factor, see Steven Pfaff and Guobin Yang, "Double-Edged Rituals and the Symbolic Resources of Collective Action: Political Commemorations and the Mobilization of Protest in 1989," *Theory and Society* 30, no. 4 (August 2001): 539–89.

17. Andrew J. Nathan, Perry Link, and "Zhang Liang," eds., *The Tiananmen Papers: The Chinese Leadership's Decision to Use Force against Their Own People—in Their Own Words* (New York: Public Affairs, 2001), 359.

18. The Chinese Red Cross estimate, and Gorbachev's reaction, is given in Mark Kramer, "The Collapse of East European Communism and the Repercussions within the Soviet Union (Part 2),"

Journal of Cold War Studies 6, no. 4 (Fall 2004): 33–34, see in particular footnotes 86, 88. See also Nancy Bernkopf Tucker, "China as a Factor in the Collapse of the Soviet Empire," *Political Science Quarterly* 110, no. 4 (Winter 1995–96): 501–19. For more on the Chinese leadership, see Renee Chiang, Adi Ignatius, and Bao Pu, eds., *Prisoner of the State: The Secret Journal of Zhao Ziyang* (New York: Simon and Schuster, 2009).

19. Erich Mielke's orders of June 10, 1989, are reprinted and translated in *Cold War International History Project Bulletin* 12–13 (Fall–Winter 2001): 209.

20. Egon Krenz was on a trip to the West German city of Saarbrücken at the time. He informed West German television reporters that the Chinese Communists had only done what was necessary "to restore order" and remarked that the images of the massacre were simply fictional nightmares produced by Western media. Quoted in "Am Leben bleiben," *Der Spiegel* 24 (June 12, 1989): 27. See also Egon Krenz's memoirs, Egon Krenz, *Wenn Mauern fallen* (Vienna: Neff, 1990).

21. Krenz quoted him verbatim: the problem had been a lack of education, but now it had been addressed; as a result, "it was possible to turn a bad thing into a good thing." Egon Krenz, "Vorlage für das Politbüro des ZK der SED, Betr.: Besuch der Partei- und Staatsdelegation der DDR [Deutsche Demokratische Republik] unter Leitung des Genossen Egon Krenz in der VR China vom 25. September bis 2. Oktober 1989," Bek. Protokoll Nr. 43/5 vom 17.10.1989, J IV 2/2A/3247, Stiftung/Archiv der Parteien und Massenorganisationen (hereafter SAPMO).

22. Tucker, "China as a Factor."

23. Vladimir Putin, with Nataliya Gevorkyan, Natalya Timakova, and Andrei Kolesnikov, *First Person: An Astonishingly Frank Self-Portrait by Russia's President Putin*, trans. Catherine A. Fitzpatrick (New York: Public Affairs, 2000), 69–76.

24. "East European Independent News Agency report," July 13, 1989, samizdat, Czechoslovak Documentation Center, Scheinfeld, VIA Collection, copy translated and distributed as document 26 to the National Security Archive Prague Conference (hereafter PC).

25. For Socialist Unity Party (SED) Politburo assessments of protests in Leipzig and elsewhere, see IV 2/2.039/317, Büro Krenz, SAPMO. For more on October 9, see Günter Hanisch et al., eds., *Dona nobis pacem: Fürbitten und Friedensgebete Herbst '89 in Leipzig* (Berlin: Evangelische Verlagsanstalt, 1990); Martin Janowski, *Der Tag, der Deutschland veränderte: 9. Oktober 1989* (Leipzig: Evangelische Verlagsanstalt, 2007); Reiner Tetzner, *Leipziger Ring: Aufzeichnungen eines Montagsdemonstranten Oktober 1989 bis 1. Mai 1990* (Frankfurt: Luchterhand, 1990). For an insightful journalistic account, suggesting that Honecker was considering a "Chinese solution" in Berlin on October 7–8, 1989, as well as in Leipzig, see Cordt Schnibben, "Chinesische Lösung," *Der Spiegel* 51, December 18, 1989, 42–44.

26. Hans-Hermann Hertle, *Der Fall der Mauer: Die unbeabsichtigte Selbstauflösung des SED-Staates* (Opladen: Westdeutscher Verlag, 1996), 114–15; see also Gieseke, *Mielke-Konzern*, 257.

27. Interview with Pfarrer Christian Führer, in Ekkehard Kuhn, *Der Tag der Entscheidung: Leipzig, 9. Oktober 1989* (Berlin: Ullstein, 1992). See also Christian Führer, *Und wir sind dabei gewesen* (Berlin: Ullstein, 2009); Jürgen Grabner, Christiane Heinze, and Detlef Pollack, *Leipzig im Oktober* (Berlin: Wichern-Verlag, 1990); Uwe Thaysen, "Wege des politischen Umbruchs in der DDR: Der Berliner und der Dresdner Pfad der Demokratiefindung," in *Berlin*, ed. Karl Eckart and Manfred Wilke (Berlin: Duncker and Humblot, 1998), 69–90, an interesting article in which Thaysen discusses the difference between the protest movement of Saxony and that of Berlin; see also Eckhard Jesse, ed., *Friedliche Revolution und deutsche Einheit: Sächsische Bürgerrechtler ziehen Bilanz* (Berlin: Links, 2006).

28. Reported on the ARD channel's news program *Tagesschau*, October 8–9, 1989 (ARD-NDR Videoarchiv, Hamburg). Journalists who had tried to film at the Brandenburg Gate in Berlin days earlier were told that it was now a closed zone and they could not film. See also the biographical information page on Siegbert Schefke at http://www.chronik-der-wende.de.

NOTES

29. The full story of why that night did not produce the German Tiananmen Square remains to be investigated. A good place to start would be the local archives, not only in Leipzig, but also in the capital of Saxony, Dresden. On a visit to the Sächsisches Hauptstaatsarchiv in Dresden, I found Abt. Sicherheit, A 13155–13157, 60 20 00 20, Lageberichte Oktobertage 1989, Okt./Nov. 1989 and A 13680, Sicherheitspolitik, Einschätzungen, 1987–89, to be helpful; similar documents exist in the Sächsisches Staatsarchiv Leipzig. I am grateful to Thoralf Handke, Bestandsreferent für Parteien und Massenorganisationen, for help during my visit. See also the memoirs of Wjatscheslaw Kotschemassow, *Meine letzte Mission* (Berlin: Dietz, 1994), 169, where he claims that he was responsible for telling Soviet troops in the region to stay in their barracks, but this claim still needs independent confirmation.

30. Gorbachev's obvious criticism of Honecker in front of the other Politburo members—"he who comes late will be punished by life"—did not escape their notice. Rather, it made them aware that Moscow was giving them a mandate for change. See "Из беседы М.С. Горбачева с членами Политбюро ЦК СЕПГ," October 7, 1989, МГ, 209–14; an English translation is available in the briefing book for the "End of the Cold War in Europe, 1989 Conference," document 57, Musgrove, Saint Simons Island, Georgia, May 1–3, 1998 (hereafter GC, for Georgia Conference). The "asshole" comment appears in the Russian volume, albeit with a few key letters missing ("Из дневника А.С. Черняева," October 9–11, 1989, МГ, 215–16), and also in GC. See also the footage from the fortieth-anniversary celebrations broadcast in episode 23 of the CNN *Cold War* series and Mark Kramer, "The Collapse of East European Communism and the Repercussions within the Soviet Union (Part 1)," *Journal of Cold War Studies* 5, no. 4 (Fall 2003): 201.

31. See the footage of the *Tagesschau* from October 9–10, 1989, available at the ARD-NDR Videoarchiv, Hamburg.

32. Kowalczuk and Sello, *Für ein freies Land*, 321–24; biographical information about Jahn, Radomski, and Schefke, available at http://www.chronik-der-wende.de. For more information on East German dissident history, see Erhard Neubert, *Geschichte der Opposition in der DDR 1949–1989* (Bonn: Bundeszentrale für politische Bildung, 1997).

33. See the footage of *Tagesthemen*, October 10, 1989, available at the ARD-NDR Videoarchiv, Hamburg.

34. Tom Sello, interview with author, August 30, 2006, Berlin.

35. Timothy Garton Ash terms this the "crucial breakthrough" that made the East German revolution possible; see his *In Europe's Name: Germany and the Divided Continent* (New York: Vintage Books, 1993), 345.

36. Tucker, "China as a Factor."

37. Chinese scholar Tao Wenzhou, paraphrased in Olav Njølstad, ed., *The Last Decade of the Cold War: From Conflict Escalation to Conflict Transformation* (London: Frank Cass, 2004), xvii–xviii.

38. Schnibben, "Chinesische Lösung," 44.

39. See Njølstad, *The Last Decade of the Cold War*, xvii; see also Geir Lundestad, "The European Role at the Beginning and the End of the Cold War," in *The Last Decade of the Cold War: From Conflict Escalation to Conflict Transformation*, ed. Olav Njølstad (London: Frank Cass, 2004), 60–79.

40. For earlier eras in which independent West German initiative mattered to the superpowers, see the initial chapters of my *Dealing with the Devil* (Chapel Hill: University of North Carolina Press, 2001). On the friction that Willy Brandt's independence caused with the Western allies, see my "The Frailties of Grand Strategies: A Comparison of Détente and Ostpolitik," in *Nixon in the World: American Foreign Relations, 1969–1977*, ed. Fredrik Logevall and Andrew Preston (Oxford: Oxford University Press, 2008), 146–65.

41. See Robert L. Hutchings, *American Diplomacy and the End of the Cold War: An Insider's Account of US Policy in Europe, 1989–1992* (Washington, DC: Wilson Center, 1997), 6; Jack F. Matlock Jr., *Autopsy on an Empire: The American Ambassador's Account of the Collapse of the Soviet Union* (New York: Random House, 1995), 183. For a broader overview of U.S. foreign policy in the twentieth century and the various transitions between administrations, see Robert Schulzinger, *US Diplomacy since 1900* (New York: Oxford University Press, 2008).

42. Comment made in an on-air discussion of his book: Paul Light, *A Government Ill Executed* (Cambridge, MA: Harvard University Press, 2008), in "Massive Reorganization Awaits New President," National Public Radio, July 27, 2008; transcript available at http://www.npr.org.

43. Robert M. Gates, *From the Shadows: The Ultimate Insider's Story of Five Presidents and How They Won the Cold War* (New York: Touchstone, 1996), 460.

44. Note on "U.S.-Soviet Relations," February 1989, box 108, folder 2, 8c monthly files, series 8, James A. Baker III Papers, Mudd Library, Princeton University, Princeton, NJ (hereafter BP); Cheney and Shevardnadze quoted in James A. Baker with Thomas A. DeFrank, *The Politics of Diplomacy: Revolution, War, and Peace, 1989–1992* (New York: G. P. Putnam's Sons, 1995), 70–75. Also in February, Jack Matlock cabled his estimate of what the next four years would hold for Soviet foreign policy: " . . . its external policy is more likely to resemble a sulk in the corner more than a rampage through the neighborhood." See "Amembassy Moscow to Secstate Washdc," February 13, 1989, document circulated as part of the Princeton conference, March 29–30, 1996.

45. At the meeting in New York in December 1988, Gorbachev had suggested the former USSR ambassador to the United States, Anatoly Dobrynin, as a confidential back-channel contact. Bush felt that it would be appropriate to tap Dobrynin's old sparring partner Kissinger in response, although he had misgivings. As he commented in George Bush and Brent Scowcroft, *A World Transformed* (New York: Knopf, 1998), 26: "I was wary. I wanted to be sure we did not pass the wrong signals to Moscow, with some in our Administration saying one thing while others were conducting secret negotiations that might be sending out contradictory signals. Although helpful, back channels can leave critical people in the dark on either a forthcoming policy decision or on the details of some conversation between the President and a foreign leader." On the role of back channels during Kissinger's own time in office, see (to name just a few) William Bundy, *A Tangled Web: The Making of Foreign Policy in the Nixon Presidency* (New York: Hill and Wang, 1998); Jussi Hanhimäki, *The Flawed Architect: Henry Kissinger and American Foreign Policy* (New York: Oxford University Press, 2004); Logevall and Preston, *Nixon in the World*; Sarotte, *Dealing with the Devil*; Jeremi Suri, *Henry Kissinger and the American Century* (Cambridge: Belknap Press, 2007).

46. "Основное содержание беседы с Г. Киссинджером (США) 16 января 1989 г.," 4, conversation between Kissinger and Yakovlev, Russian and East European Archival Documents Database, National Security Archive. Some short excerpts from the next day's conversation between Gorbachev and Kissinger were circulated as "Record of Main Conversation between M.S. Gorbachev and H. Kissinger," document 17, in GC, 4.

47. Fax from Henry Kissinger, Kissinger Associates, New York, January 21, 1989, 9:05 a.m., titled "Meeting with Gorbachev—January 17, 1989, 12:00–1:20 p.m.," folder 1, box 108, 8c monthly files, series 8, BP.

48. In the past the roles had been reversed, and Baker had to apologize to Kissinger. See Baker with DeFrank, *The Politics of Diplomacy*, 22–29, 40; "time-honored" is on 23; the joking response is on 29. On Baker outmaneuvering Kissinger, see Beschloss and Talbott, *At the Highest Levels*, 45–46.

49. Letter from Henry A. Kissinger to James A. Baker III, January 24, 1989, folder 49, box 100, 8b correspondence, series 8, BP.

50. Interestingly, the tension that existed between the Reagan and Bush foreign policy teams is replicated in the historical and memoir writing about the period. Gaddis, a strong admirer of President Reagan, finds it extremely fortunate for U.S. foreign policy that Reagan did not die in the assassination attempt on his life. This would have made Bush president in 1981 instead of 1989. Had that happened, argues Gaddis, Bush's lack of creativity would have precluded "an American challenge to the Cold War status quo. Bush, like most foreign policy experts of his generation, saw that conflict as a permanent feature of the international landscape." Gaddis compliments Reagan for thinking that it was not; see Gaddis, *The Cold War*, 188. In contrast, Bush's biographer titles the chapter in which Bush becomes president "Cleaning Up Reagan's Mess"; see Timothy Naftali, *George H.W. Bush* (New York: Times Books, 2007), chapter 3. See also Jack F. Matlock Jr., *Reagan and Gorbachev: How the Cold War Ended* (New York: Random House, 2004); on Reagan in particular, see Paul Lettow, *Ronald Reagan and His Quest to Abolish Nuclear Weapons* (New York: Random House, 2005).

51. On the conversation with Kohl: "Gespräch des Bundeskanzlers Kohl mit Generalsekretär Gorbatschow, Bonn, 12. Juni 1989," document 2, DESE, 281. Both the federal chancellery and Gorbachev have released records of this conversation; they duplicate each other on these points, with some minor variations in wording. See "Беседа М.С. Горбачева с Г. Колем один на один," June 12, 1989, МГ, 156–65. A partial English translation of the Gorbachev Foundation's notes on this meeting was circulated in GC and is available from the National Security Archive. On the conversation with Mitterrand, this account draws on a Russian summary. Gorbachev chose not to include it in the documents that he released, but an English translation of the document appeared in GC.

52. Garthoff, *The Great Transition*, 376.

53. Scowcroft's view is summarized in Michael Beschloss and Strobe Talbott, *At the Highest Levels: The Inside Story of the Cold War* (Boston: Little, Brown, 1993), 45; Garthoff, *The Great Transition*, 377; Gates, *From the Shadows*, 460.

54. Baker with DeFrank, *Politics of Diplomacy*, 68.

55. Gates, *From the Shadows*, 460. Gates's statement about the source of ideas, if accurate, is useful for historians because the BPL and Baker have released materials on 1989–90, and most members of the inner circles have written accounts, including the useful Philip Zelikow and Condoleezza Rice, *Germany Unified and Europe Transformed: A Study in Statecraft* (Cambridge, MA: Harvard University Press, 1995), which was based on extensive documentation. What is not available are more standard governmental papers (although FOIA requests have brought a number into the public domain), but if Gates is right, these materials will be of secondary importance.

56. See "Vermerk des Bundesministers Genscher über das Gespräch des Bundeskanzlers Kohl mit Ministerpräsident Németh und Außenminister Horn, Schloß Gymnich, 25. August 1989," document 28, DESE, 378.

57. "Telephone Call from Helmut Kohl, Chancellor of the Federal Republic of Germany, June 23, 1989, 7:26 a.m.–7:42 a.m. EDT, The Oval Office," NSC Pres. Telcons, 6/23/89, FOIA Request 1999-0393-F, BPL. The German note taker, or perhaps translator, of the same conversation was more cautious, summarizing Bush's comments as "One should avoid making mistakes and possibly spending money for things that do not achieve anything for the population." See also "Telefongespräch des Bundeskanzlers Kohl mit Präsidenten Bush, Bonn, 23.06.89, 13.30 bis 13.50 Uhr," document 10, DESE, 315.

58. Point 13 in telegram, "Amembassy Warsaw to Secstate Washdc," June 27, 1989, copy distributed to Cold War International History Project Paris Conference, The End of the Cold War in Europe, June 15–17, 2006 (hereafter CWIHPPC).

59. "President Bush's Address to the Polish Parliament," in *Europe Transformed: Documents on the End of the Cold War—Key Treaties, Agreements, Statements, and Speeches*, ed. Lawrence Freedman (New York: St. Martin's Press, 1990), 333–35; see especially 334.

60. Robert Pear, "U.S. Aid for Poland: Long on Incentives, Short on Dollars," *New York Times,* November 19, 1989, online. This article points out that the biggest offer of aid, also in November 1989, came from West Germany, which promised $2.2 billion. The lesson of Polish indebtedness was a cautionary one to Havel, soon to be the leader of Czechoslovakia. According to VIA, a Czech news agency, he made remarks to this effect to Hans-Dietrich Genscher: "Havel expressed fear that the loans might be issued, and that he would not be happy if Czechoslovakia's children were forced in fifteen years to pay back a many billion-crown debt, as was now the case in Poland. Loans should be furnished only for specific investments." "East European Independent News Agency Report," July 13, 1989, samizdat, Czechoslovak Documentation Center, Scheinfeld, VIA Collection, copy translated and distributed in PC.

61. Andrej Paczkowski, *The Spring Will Be Ours: Poland and Poles from the Occupation to Freedom,* trans. by Jane Cave (University Park: Pennsylvania State University Press, 2003), 507. For a broader overview of the transition in Eastern Europe, see Piotr S. Wandycz, *The Price of Freedom* (London: Routledge, 1992).

62. Andrei Grachev displays this view at various points in his *Gorbachev's Gamble: Soviet Foreign Policy and the End of the Cold War* (London: Polity Press, 2008).

63. "Gespräch des Bundeskanzlers Kohl mit Präsident Bush, Bonn, 30. Mai 1989, 17.30 bis 18.30," document 1, DESE, 272.

64. The exact numbers of Soviet troops in Germany, together with their dependents, was a matter of some controversy in 1989–90, but was eventually clarified in a treaty between West Germany and the Soviet Union. See "Zum Vertrag zwischen der Bundesrepublik Deutschland und der UdSSR über die Bedingungen des befristeten Aufenthalts und die Modalitäten des planmäßigen Abzuges der sowjetischen Truppen aus dem Gebiet der Bundesrepublik Deutschland," document 59 in Auswärtiges Amt, ed., *Deutsche Aussenpolitik 1990/91: Auf dem Weg zu einer europäischen Friedensordnung eine Dokumentation* (Bonn: Auswärtiges Amt, April 1991), 231–32. See also Henry Ashby Turner Jr., *Germany from Partition to Unification,* 2nd ed. (New Haven, CT: Yale University Press, 1992), 174.

65. Stephen Szabo, *The Diplomacy of German Unification* (New York: St. Martin's Press, 1992), 12.

66. Quoted in GDE, 4:34.

67. "Proposed Agenda for Meeting with the President, Wednesday, March 8, 1989, 1:30–2:00 p.m.," folder 6, box 115, 8e White House Meetings and Notes, series 8, BP.

68. Pointing out that forward defense "wasn't the US preference 30 years ago," he argued that the United States "held to it" because it was critical to the FRG and because "such a conventional defense is only tenable if backed up by a full range of nuclear response." "JAB [James A. Baker] Notes from 4/24/89 meeting w/FRG FM Genscher & DM Stoltenberg, WDC," folder 4, box 108, 8c Monthly Files, series 8, BP.

69. GDE, 4:34.

70. On the nature of the Thatcher-Gorbachev partnership, see Archie Brown, "The Change to Engagement in Britain's Cold War Policy: The Origins of the Thatcher-Gorbachev Relationship," *Journal of Cold War Studies* 10, no. 3 (Summer 2008): 3–47.

71. "Record of Conversation between Gorbachev and Margaret Thatcher," September 23, 1989, notes of Anatoly Chernyaev, Archive of the Gorbachev Foundation, copied and translated for GC. I received a copy of the British record of this conversation via FOI; it did not include these comments, but it was redacted. "Prime Minister's Meeting with Mr. Gorbachev, 24 September 1989," released by CAB via FOI. See also notes of Anatoly Chernyaev, October 9, 1989, Archive of the Gorbachev Foundation, copied and translated in GC as well. Rumors of Thatcher's comments seem to have reached Bonn, because in an unusually pointed way, a chancellery official, Peter Hartmann, asked Thatcher's close aide Charles Powell about her September visit with

Gorbachev. Hartmann reported back that Powell evaded giving him any answer. "Vermerk des MD Hartmann, Bonn, 13. Okt. 1989, Betr.: Meine Gespräche in London (FCO and Cabinet Office)," document 61, DESE, 450. See also comments about Thatcher in "Беседа М.С. Горбачева с Вилли Брандтом," October 17, 1989, МГ, 228–29.

72. Egon Krenz, "An alle Mitglieder und Kandidaten des Politbüros des ZK der SED," November 5, 1989, JIV 2/2A/3255, SAPMO. This document summarizes what Jaruzelski told Krenz.

73. Some of the analysis in the next few pages is drawn from my "Elite Intransigence and the End of the Berlin Wall," *German Politics* 2 (August 1993): 270–87. I am grateful to Wade Jacoby, one of the editors of *German Politics*, for his permission to reuse some of this article here. Gareth Dale sees a similar force at work, which he refers to as a "radicalising dynamic." See Gareth Dale, *The East German Revolution of 1989* (Manchester: Manchester University Press, 2006); see also his *Popular Protest in East Germany, 1945–1989* (London: Routledge, 2005). See also Padraic Kenney, *A Carnival of Revolution: Central Europe 1989* (Princeton, NJ: Princeton University Press, 2002).

74. For more on the rigidity of the SED, see Catherine Epstein, *The Last Revolutionaries: German Communists and Their Century* (Cambridge, MA: Harvard University Press, 2003), 262. See also various elements of the press coverage of Gorbachev's visit to the GDR for its fortieth-anniversary celebrations on October 7, 1989, which are available in many places; a few citations follow here. His major speech on the occasion was published under the title "Uns vereinen die Ideale des Sozialismus und des Friedens," *Neues Deutschland*, October 9, 1989, 3–4. Remarks to journalists were reproduced in many places; see in particular Christian Schmidt-Häuer, "Die Widerspenstigen Lähmung," *Die Zeit*, October 13, 1989, 3. Other public signs during his visit that Gorbachev had abandoned the Brezhnev doctrine were cited in "'Die Geduld ist zu Ende,'" *Der Spiegel*, October 9, 1989, 18. Günter Mittag published the transcript of Gorbachev's address to the East German Politburo in Günter Mittag, *Um jeden Preis* (Berlin: Aufbau-Verlag, 1991). Finally, contemporary analysis of Gorbachev's personal role can be found in, for example, Michael Howard, "1989: A Farewell to Arms?" *International Affairs* 65 (Summer 1989): 407; see also J. F. Brown, *Surge to Freedom* (Durham, NC: Duke University Press, 1991), 55.

75. Jonathan Zatlin, *The Currency of Socialism: Money and Political Culture in East Germany* (Cambridge: Cambridge University Press, 2007), 155–56, 323. For more on the status of the late 1989 East German economy, see Hans-Hermann Hertle, "Staatsbankrott: Der ökonomische Untergang des SED-Staates," *Deutschland Archiv* 10 (October 1992): 1019–30, and *Fall der Mauer*. See also Jeffrey Kopstein, *The Politics of Economic Decline in East Germany, 1945–1989* (Chapel Hill: University of North Carolina Press, 1997).

76. The conduct of local elections in May 1989 was one such issue. Despite monitoring by opposition groups and reports of widespread abuses, election director Krenz declared that the proceedings had been "in order" and that the incumbent government had garnered 98.85 percent of the vote. See contemporaneous press coverage in the West in "Zeugnis der Reife," *Der Spiegel*, May 15, 1989, 24–25. See also A. James McAdams, *Germany Divided: From the Wall to Reunification* (Princeton, NJ: Princeton University Press, 1993), which argues that "displays of self-satisfaction also seem to have played a key role in compounding the East German leadership's inability to contend with the very specific challenges that were to haunt the GDR in the late 1980s" (178–79).

77. Albert O. Hirschmann, "Exit, Voice, and the Fate of the German Democratic Republic: An Essay in Conceptual History," *World Politics* 45 (January 1993): 173–202. For more on the daily lives of East Germans, see Mary Fulbrook, *The People's State: East German Society from Hitler to Honecker* (New Haven, CT: Yale University Press, 2005); Jeannette Z. Madarász, *Conflict and Compromise in East Germany, 1971–1989* (London: Palgrave Macmillan, 2003).

78. Conversation between Gorbachev and Németh on March 3, 1989, reprinted in "The Political Transition in Hungary, 1989–90," *Cold War International History Project Bulletin* 12–13 (Fall–Winter 2001): 77.

NOTES

79. The opening was soon to become a violation of a 1969 treaty with the GDR forbidding the unauthorized passage of citizens of either country into third countries. For contemporary comment on its significance, see Günter Schabowski, Frank Sieren, and Ludwig Koehne, eds., *Das Politbüro Ende eines Mythos: eine Befragung Günter Schabowskis* (Reinbek bei Hamburg: Rowohlt Verlag, December 1990), 51; "Ich bin das Volk," *Der Spiegel*, April 16, 1990, 90; "The Great Escape," *Time*, September 25, 1989, 30.

80. A contemporary journalistic report on the conditions in Hungary may be found in "Eine Zeit geht zu Ende," *Der Spiegel*, September 4, 1989, 16–21.

81. Zelikow and Rice, *Germany Unified*, 66.

82. The Németh quotation can be found in Helmut Kohl, Kai Diekmann, and Ralf Georg Reuth, *Ich wollte Deutschlands Einheit* (Berlin: Ullstein, 1996), 74, which is essentially an extended interview with Kohl. In it, the chancellor quotes Németh to Diekmann and Reuth; he also publishes a similar description in Helmut Kohl, *Erinnerungen 1982–1990* (Munich: Droemer, 2005), 922. Németh's declaration of his intent to open the border to East Germans does not actually appear in the Bundeskanzleramt's official summary of the conversation, only in Kohl's various remarks; see documents 28 and 29 from August 25, 1989, in DESE, 377–82. On the five hundred million DM credit to Hungary, see "Gespräch des Bundeskanzlers Kohl mit Präsident Delors, Bonn, 5. Oktober 1989," document 58, DESE, 443–47.

83. Zelikow and Rice, *Germany Unified*, 68.

84. "Verleihung der Stresemann-Medaille an den Außenminister der Republik Ungarn, Gyula Horn, in Mainz, Rede des Bundesministers des Auswärtigen, Genscher, am 10.1.1990 (Auszüge)," document 1 in Auswärtiges Amt, *Deutsche Aussenpolitik*, 64–65.

85. "Information on the Security Situation in the CSSR," memorandum, Czechoslovak Federal Ministry of Interior, October 17, 1989, CWIHPPC, 5.

86. On the negotiations, see "Gespräch des Ministerialdirigenten Duisberg mit dem Ständigen Vertreter der DDR, Neubauer, Bonn, 1 Oktober 1989," document 51, DESE, 429–30; "Telefongespräch des Bundeskanzlers Kohl mit Ministerpräsidenten Adamec, 3. Oktober 1989," document 55, DESE, 437; "Gespräche und Kontakte des Chefs des Bundeskanzleramtes Seiters und des Ministerialdirigenten Duisberg, 3–5 Okt. 1989," document 56, DESE, 438–41; Richard Kiessler and Frank Elbe, *Ein runder Tisch mit scharfen Ecken: Der diplomatische Weg zur deutschen Einheit* (Baden-Baden: Nomos Verlagsgesellschaft, 1993), 34–41. In an interview in Wachtberg-Pech on June 2, 2009, Genscher recalled that his September 1989 talks with Shevardnadze in New York at the UN General Assembly meeting were crucial in producing agreement to let the embassy refugees leave. After the deal was struck, Genscher thought that he would ride on a train himself, but as he was leaving for Prague, East Berlin notified him that he did not have permission to do so. He sent lower-ranking diplomats on the trains instead as a result.

87. These details come from Frank Elbe, phone conversations, June 10 and 11, 2009.

88. See interview with a train passenger broadcast in episode 23 of the CNN *Cold War* video series; "Fernschreiben des Staatssekretärs Bertele an den Chef des Bundeskanzleramtes Berlin (Ost), 2. Oktober 1989," document 52, DESE, 430–32. Franz Bertele was on the train leaving from Warsaw. Bertele's account accords well with that of Frank Elbe, in transit from Prague, on events such as the appearance of more refugees at stopping places along the transit route.

89. I am grateful to Richard Kiessler for discussion of these events. The chancellery received the following report: "Nach Berichten von Reisenden gebe es erhebliche Menschenansammlungen entlang der Strecke." "Gespräche und Kontake des Chefs des Bundeskanzleramtes Seiters und des Ministerialdirigenten Duisberg, 3–5 Okt. 1989," document 56, DESE, 440. For reporting to

NOTES

Washington, DC, by the U.S. embassy in East Berlin, see "Amembassy Embberlin to Secstate Washdc," October 4, 1989, in CWIHPPC.

90. On October 9, the Politburo decided, in essence, that all of the property of those who had left the GDR should be confiscated; see the various papers on this subject prepared for the Politburo, J IV 2/2A/3245, SAPMO. I am also grateful to Frank Elbe for discussing these events in phone conversations on June 10 and 11, 2009.

91. "Vorlage des Ministerialdirigenten Duisberg an Bundesminister Klein, Bonn, 2. Oktober 1989," document 54, in DESE, 435–36.

92. Much of the account above comes from Kiessler and Elbe, *Ein runder Tisch*, 42–44; see also Baker with DeFrank, *The Politics of Diplomacy*, 199.

93. "Freedom Train," *Time*, October 16, 1989, 40.

94. "Из дневника А.С. Черняева," October 5, 1989, МГ, 204.

95. This comment is not in the version of the diary released by Gorbachev, cited above; rather, it appears in a translated copy of the same source and date in GC.

96. "Telefongespräch des Bundeskanzlers Kohl mit Generalsekretär Gorbatschow, 11. Oktober 1989," document 60, DESE, 449–50; "Телефонный разговор М.С. Горбачева с Г. Колем," October 11, 1989, МГ, 220–22.

97. In a singularly insipid move, the party-run media tried to suggest that some of the emigrants had been kidnapped. If so, they certainly looked happy about it. See the coverage of the emigration in the party newspaper, *Neues Deutschland*, in the months of September and October 1989.

98. On the role of churches in the GDR, see Gary Lease, "Religion, the Churches, and the German 'Revolution' of November 1989," *German Politics* 1 (August 1992): 264–73; Bernd Schäfer, *Staat und katholische Kirche in der DDR* (Cologne: Böhlau, 1999).

99. Comments made by Bärbel Bohley in a radio broadcast on RIAS, October 12, 1989. A transcription of this interview is in the Stasi archive, SED-KL 5009, 32–34, Ministerium für Staatssicherheit (hereafter MfS), Bundesbeauftragte für die Unterlagen des Staatssicherheitsdienstes der ehemaligen Deutschen Demokratischen Republik (hereafter BStU).

100. "Fernschreiben des Staatssekretär Bertele an den Chef des Bundeskanzleramtes, Berlin (Ost), den 20 Sept. 1989," document 43, DESE, 409–10. See also "Fernschreiben des Staatssekretär Bertele an den Chef des Bundeskanzleramtes, Berlin (Ost), den 22 Sept. 1989," document 45, DESE, 413–16.

101. Grabner, Heinze, and Pollack, *Leipzig im Oktober*, 150–51; Deutscher Bundestag, ed., *Bundestag Report* (Bonn: Bundestag, August 1, 1990), 47; "Von den Arbeitern verlassen," *Der Spiegel*, November 27, 1989, 19.

102. See the letters in IV 2/2.039/323 Büro Krenz, SAPMO.

103. Schabowski, Sieren, and Koehne, *Das Politbüro Ende eines Mythos*, 113; SED Bezirksleitung, Leipzig, 20 30 30 10, 8 November 1989, in the Sächsisches Staatsarchiv, Leipzig; *Newsweek's* description of the November 4 demonstrations in "Egon, Here We Come," *Newsweek*, November 13, 1989, 52.

104. *DDR Journal zur November Revolution August bis Dezember 1989, vom Ausreisen bis zum Einreißen der Mauer*, a compilation produced by the Western newspaper *taz*, 1990, 73–75.

105. In his study *Revolutionary Change*, Chalmers Johnson observes the costs of elites failing to meet popular goals, arguing that "elite intransigence . . . always serves as an underlying cause of revolution," and his insight aptly characterizes the East German episode. Chalmers Johnson, *Revolutionary Change*, 2nd ed. (Stanford, CA: Stanford University Press, 1982), 92.

106. *Der Spiegel* estimated at the time that the number of "non-approved demonstrations" (the Stasi term for them) went from 24 involving 140,000 participants between October 16 and 22, to 210 involving 1.35 million between October 30 and November 5. See "Genosse, schlagen die uns tot?" *Der Spiegel*, April 30, 1990, 199.

107. Ilse Spittmann, "Eine Übergangsgesellschaft," *Deutschland Archiv* 22 (November 1989), 1204.

108. For documents from and a detailed analysis of the events of November 9, see Hertle, *Fall der Mauer*, and his documentary film, *When the Wall Came Tumbling Down*, Sender Freies Berlin, 1999. See also Walter Süß, "Weltgeschichte in voller Absicht oder aus Versehen?" *Das Parlament* (November 9–16, 1990): 9; Hartmut Zimmermann, *DDR Handbuch*, 3rd ed. (Cologne: Verlag Wissenschaft und Politik, 1985), 975; for more general analysis, see Gesamtdeutsches Institut, Bundesanstalt für gesamtdeutsche Aufgaben, *Analysen, Dokumentationen und Chronik zur Entwicklung in der DDR von September bis Dezember 1989* (Bonn: Bundesanstalt 1990), 86.

109. "Schreiben von Gerhard Schürer an Egon Krenz, 27.10.1989: Zur Zahlungsunfähigkeit der DDR," reprinted as document 8 in Hertle, *Fall der Mauer*, 461. In the Soviet Union, Valentin Falin appears to have prepared a largely similar document: "An A.N. [Jakowlew], Zur Devisensituation in der UdSSR," reprinted in German in Valentin Falin, *Konflikte im Kreml: Zur Vorgeschichte der deutschen Einheit und Auflösung der Sowjetunion* (Munich: Blessing Verlag, 1997), 289–93.

110. Documents to this effect may be found in various locations. The East German version, available in J IV 2/2A/3255, ZPA-SED, SAPMO, has been reprinted as "Niederschrift des Gesprächs von Egon Krenz und Michail Gorbatschow am 01.11.1989 in Moskau," document 9 in Hertle, *Fall der Mauer*, 462–82. The Russian version is also available, translated in GC. See also the analysis of the GDR-USSR trading relationship in Randall W. Stone, *Satellites and Commissars: Strategy and Conflict in the Politics of Soviet-Bloc Trade* (Princeton, NJ: Princeton University Press, 1996); Angela Stent, *Russia and Germany Reborn: Unification, the Soviet Collapse, and the New Europe* (Princeton, NJ: Princeton University Press, 1999), 125. Philip Zelikow has argued that this conversation suggests that Gorbachev did have a plan for moving forward with East Germany; see his comments in Fred I. Greenstein and William C. Wohlforth, eds., *Cold War Endgame: Report of a Conference*, Center of International Studies Monograph Series No. 10 (Princeton, NJ: Center of International Studies, 1997).

111. Douglas J. MacEachin, *CIA Assessments of the Soviet Union: The Records versus the Charges: An Intelligence Monograph* (Washington, DC: Central Intelligence Agency, May 1996), 8–9.

112. Comments made on camera in, respectively, the CNN *Cold War* series and the documentary film *When the Wall Came Tumbling Down*.

113. On this topic, see Sarotte "Elite Intransigence," 270–87; relevant documents in Detlef Nakath and Gerd-Rüdiger Stephan, eds., *Countdown zur deutschen Einheit: Eine dokumentierte Geschichte der deutsch-deutschen Beziehungen 1987–1990* (Berlin: Dietz, 1996).

114. Transcripts of the press conference exist in a number of versions. See, for example, Albrecht Hinze, "Versehentliche Zündung," *Süddeutsche Zeitung*, November 9, 1990, 17; and Hertle, *Fall der Mauer*, 170–73 (other key documents from the same day may be found in Hertle as well). Hertle's documentary film *When the Wall Came Tumbling Down* includes video from it; the Brokaw quotations come from the video. An English-language transcript appears in CWIHPPC; however, in the paragraphs above I have produced my own translation, which is not identical to the CWIHPPC one. See also Cordt Schnibben, "'Diesmal sterbe ich, Schwester,'" *Der Spiegel*, October 8, 1990, 107; Schabowski, Sieren, and Koehne, *Das Politbüro Ende eines Mythos*, 136.

115. Hinze, "Versehentliche Zündung," 17; Hertle, *Fall der Mauer*, 170–73. For more on the overall significance of this event, see Manfred Görtemaker, *Unifying Germany, 1989–1990* (New York: St. Martin's Press, 1994).

NOTES

116. For a study of media impact in a different era, see Todd Gitlin, *The Whole World Is Watching: Mass Media and the Making and Unmaking of the New Left* (Berkeley: University of California Press, 1980). For more on the Stasi and television, see Jochen Staadt, Tobias Voigt, and Stefan Wolle, *Operation Fernsehen: Die Stasi und die Medien in Ost und West* (Göttingen : Vandenhoeck and Ruprecht, 2008).

117. The Brokaw interview with Schabowski is reprinted in both English and German in Hertle, *Fall der Mauer*, 173–74. Schabowski was in transit home afterward until 8:00 p.m. and did not know the consequences of what he had said until he received a phone call later that night. See Günter Schabowski, "Wie ich die Mauer öffnete," *Die Zeit*, March 13, 2009, online. I am grateful to Sylvia Gneiser-Castonguay for drawing my attention to this *Zeit* article.

118. *Tagesthemen*, November 11, 1989, ARD Video-Archiv Hamburg.

119. "Kohl-Gorbachev Conversation," June 12, 1989, notes by Anatoly Chernyaev, copied and translated in GC.

120. John C. Torpey, *Intellectuals, Socialism, and Dissent: The East German Opposition and Its Legacy* (Minneapolis: University of Minnesota Press, 1995), 97.

121. See "Berlin Border Guards Stunned by the News," *New York Times*, November 10, 1989, A15.

122. For more on the end of the practice of shooting border crossers, see the entry for April 3, 1989, on http://www.chronik.der.mauer.de.

123. The account in the five paragraphs above comes largely from "Kontrollen eingestellt—nicht mehr in der Lage.—Punkt," published transcript of an interview with Harald Jäger, in Hertle, *Fall der Mauer*, 380–89; Gerhard Haase-Hindenberg and Harald Jäger, *Der Mann, der die Mauer öffnete: Warum Oberstleutnant Harald Jäger den Befehl verweigerte und damit Weltgeschichte schrieb* (Munich: Heyne, 2007), 194–201; comments, images, and analysis from Hertle's documentary film *When the Wall Came Tumbling Down*.

124. For more contemporary press coverage of the events, see "Einmal Ku'damm und zurück," *Der Morgen*, November 11–12, 1989); "Eine friedliche Revolution," *Der Spiegel*, November 13, 1989, 19. *Der Spiegel* described the situation at the border crossings as follows: "Die Grenzer blieben zunächst stur. Jeder, so belehrten sie die Menge, müsse sich zunächst bei der Volkspolizei ein Visum besorgen, sonst gehe hier nichts. . . . Dann geriet die Lage, wie so manches in der vergangenen Wochen, der SED außer Kontrolle. Plötzlich war die Grenze offen—für alle. Hunderte stürmten, nach flüchtiger Kontrolle ihrer Ausweise durchs uniformierte Personal, hinüber." See also Christoph Links and Hannes Bahrmann, *Wir sind das Volk* (Berlin: Links, 1990), 91: "Die Grenzsoldaten sind kulant, stellen angesichts des enormen Ansturms und der unklaren Regelungen einfach jede Kontrolle ein. DDR-Bürger können völlig ungehindert hinüber und wieder zurück."

125. For more on Jäger's experience that night, see Hertle, *Der Fall der Mauer*, 387–89; Haase-Hindenberg and Harald Jäger, *Der Mann*. See also the press discussion of the release of Jäger's book: Lothar Heinke, "'Macht den Schlagbaum auf!'" *Tagesspiegel*, November 8, 2007, online; Peter Pragal, "Der Druck auf die Ventile," *Berliner Zeitung*, July 17, 2007, online.

126. The statistics in the above three paragraphs appear in "Information über die Entwicklung der Lage an den Grenzübergangstellen der Hauptstadt zu Westberlin sowie an den Grenzübergangsstellen der DDR zur BRD, Berlin, 10. November 1989," Arbeitsbereich Mittig 30, 96–106, BStU.

127. Hertle, *Fall der Mauer*, 232–40.

128. "'Ein Alleingang der DDR war politisch nicht denkbar und militärisch nicht vertretbar': Gespräch mit Manfred Grätz," in Hertle, *Fall der Mauer*, 390–98; see also 230–40.

129. "Opposition: DDR-Behörden von der Reisewelle überrollt," *Tagesspiegel*, November 14, 1989, 4. Eventually the requirement was dropped; see Spittmann, "Eine Übergangsgesellschaft," 1204.

130. "DDR-Reisebüro beklagt Mangel an Devisen," *Frankfurter Allgemeine Zeitung*, November 10, 1989, 4.

131. Spittmann, "Eine Übergangsgesellschaft," 1204.

132. For more on changing Soviet attitudes toward military intervention, see Andrew Bennett, *Condemned to Repetition? The Rise, Fall, and Reprise of Soviet-Russian Military Intervention, 1973–1996* (Cambridge, MA: MIT Press, 1999); Matthew J. Ouimet, *The Rise and Fall of the Brezhnev Doctrine in Soviet Foreign Policy* (Chapel Hill: University of North Carolina Press, 2003).

133. Anton W. DePorte, *Europe between the Superpowers: The Enduring Balance* (New Haven, CT: Yale University Press, 1979), was an example of that consensus. DePorte believed that the division of Germany and Europe was durable, because it solved the German problem in a way "that is now, and will probably remain, generally acceptable or at least tolerable to most Europeans." He also found that the Soviet Union "is likely to maintain its strategic and political dominance over Eastern Europe" (243–44).

134. The phrase "a good Cold War" belongs to William I. Hitchcock, *The Struggle for Europe: The Turbulent History of a Divided Continent, 1945–2002* (New York: Doubleday, 2003), 2.

NOTES TO CHAPTER 2

1. François Mitterrand, *Ma part de vérité: De la rupture à l'unité* (Paris: Fayard, 1969), 20. Translation from David Bell, *François Mitterrand* (Cambridge: Polity, 2005), 7–8. Daniel Kehlmann, *Die Vermessung der Welt* (Reinbek: Rowohlt, 2005), 13. Published in English as *Measuring the World* (New York: Pantheon Books, 2006).

2. The significance of the East German street has been recognized by a number of scholars. Samuel F. Wells finds that the "central actors were the people of the German Democratic Republic who expressed an overwhelming desire to improve their political and economic condition and Chancellor Helmut Kohl, who saw an opportunity to achieve rapid unification of his nation." See Samuel F. Wells, *The Helsinki Process and the Future of Europe* (Washington, DC: Wilson Center Press, 1990). Charles Maier has written that it was the collective action of dissidents and the public, "no matter how hesitant at first, and how filled with doubts later," that "impelled decisive accommodations or allowed new initiatives." He continues that he is "not claiming heroism; but I am defending agency." Charles S. Maier, *Dissolution: The Crisis of Communism and the End of East Germany* (Princeton, NJ: Princeton University Press, 1997), xiv. Lothar Probst, "Zu wenig 'wind of change' im fernen Westen," *Deutschland Archiv* (January 1994): 128–30, criticizes the Philip Zelikow and Condoleezza Rice account for paying too little attention to East Germany: "Das revolutionäre Treiben auf den Straßen von Leipzig, Berlin und Rostock löste sich z.B. in dem Diskurs des Harvard-Historikers Philip Zelikow ganz in den gewohnten Bahnen der diplomatischen Strippenzieher auf, die hinter den Kulissen die eigentlichen Weichen für die deutsche Einheit gestellt hätten. Das Volk war in dieser Lesart eigentlich nur Manövriermasse im Spiel der führenden Politiker der Groß- und Mittelmächte und kam als eigenständig handelndes Subjekt nur am Rande vor, eine Sichtweise, die in der Diskussion u.a. von Konrad Jarausch (Univ. of NC) zu Recht wegen ihrer Einseitigkeit kritisiert wurde."

3. On the necessity for clearly defining terms, see Stephen H. Haber, David M. Kennedy, and Stephen D. Krasner, "Brothers under the Skin: Diplomatic History and International Relations," *International Security* 22, no. 1 (Summer 1997): 34–43, especially 40.

4. This definition obviously owes a debt to existing theories, such as Alexander Wendt's claim that "the identities and interest of purposive actors are constructed by . . . shared ideas rather than given by nature." Alexander Wendt, *Social Theory of International Politics* (Cambridge: Cambridge University Press, 1999), 1–2, 20. Another useful concept comes from Charles Tilly. He sees "trust networks" as crucial to revolutions. Charles Tilly, *Contention and Democracy in Europe, 1650–2000* (Cambridge: Cambridge University Press, 2004), 257.

NOTES

5. For more background on key actors and context, see Henry Ashby Turner Jr., *Germany from Partition to Unification*, 2nd ed. (New Haven, CT: Yale University Press, 1992), 175. I am also grateful to Jürgen Chrobog for a discussion of Genscher's role.

6. "Gespräch des Bundeskanzlers Kohl mit dem Vorsitzenden der Gewerkschaft 'Solidarität,' Wałęsa, Warschau, 9. November 1989," document 76, DESE, 492–96. The summary prepared by Kohl's staffers notes that the conversation took place from 6:05 to 7:00 p.m.

7. Eduard Ackermann, *Mit feinem Gehör: Vierzig Jahre in der Bonner Politik* (Bergisch Gladbach: Lübbe Verlag, 1994), 310; Helmut Kohl, Kai Diekmann, and Ralf Georg Reuth, *Ich wollte Deutschlands Einheit* (Berlin: Ullstein, 1996), 126–27; Horst Teltschik, *329 Tage: Innenansichten der Einigung* (Berlin: Siedler, 1991), 14–16. See also Hanns Jürgen Küsters, "Entscheidung für die deutsche Einheit," DESE, 54.

8. A useful biographical summary of his life may be found at http://www.helmut-kohl.de/index.php?key=&menu_sel=15&menu_sel2=38.

9. There is some disagreement between Teltschik's memoir written in 1991, and later comments by Kohl in 1996 and afterward, as to whether he wanted to go to Bonn or Berlin first. Kohl later said that he wanted to go to the "German capital," a vague term because technically at that point there was no German capital, only a West German capital (Bonn) and an East German capital (East Berlin); see Kohl, Diekmann, and Reuth, *Ich wollte*, 128. The Teltschik account is more convincing because it was written closest to the time and provides extensive substantiating details. For more on the Kohl era generally, see Clay Clemens and William E. Paterson, eds., *The Kohl Chancellorship* (London: Frank Cass, 1998).

10. Philip Zelikow and Condoleezza Rice, *Germany Unified and Europe Transformed: A Study in Statecraft* (Cambridge, MA: Harvard University Press, 1995), 103.

11. Teltschik, *329 Tage*, 18–19.

12. The text of the public remarks is in "Vor dem Schöneberger Rathaus in Berlin am 10. November 1989," in Auswärtiges Amt, ed., *Aussenpolitik der Bundesrepublik Deutschland: Dokumente von 1949 bis 1994* (Cologne: Verlag Wissenschaft und Politik, 1995), 618–22. For behind-the-scenes details, see Kohl, Diekmann, and Reuth, *Ich wollte*, 132–33; Teltschik, *329 Tage*, 19–20. Press reports from that evening (both written and video) are available in the Konrad Adenauer Stiftung Pressearchiv (hereafter KASPA); see also the press reports delivered to James Baker, folder 11, box 108, 8c monthly files, series 8, BP. Zelikow and Rice, *Germany Unified*, 103, say that the crowds were jubilant in front of the Schöneberger Rathaus—an accurate description earlier, but not the case when Kohl started speaking.

13. "Auch für Herrn Kohl gilt: 'Wer zu spät kommt, den bestraft das Leben,'" *taz*, November 13, 1989, in KASPA. See also Harold James and Marla Stone, eds., *When the Wall Came Down* (New York: Routledge, 1992), 46.

14. For more on the poll results and concepts of West German identity, see Andreas Rödder, *Deutschland Einig Vaterland* (Munich: Beck, 2009), chapter 4.

15. "Mündliche Botschaft des Generalsekretärs Gorbatschow an Bundeskanzler Kohl, 10. November 1989," document 80, DESE, 505. Copies of the similar messages that Gorbachev sent to Bush, Kohl, Mitterrand, and Thatcher were given to the SED, and are in DY 30/IV 2/2.039/319, SAPMO.

16. In his own work on German unification, Charles Maier pointed out the following: "Speaking personally, since much of my work as a twentieth-century historian has involved examining the pressures that lead to choices for submission, it has been exhilarating to focus this time on choices for freedom." Maier, *Dissolution*, xv.

17. Claudia Rusch, *Meine freie deutsche Jugend* (Frankfurt: Fischer, 2003), 35, 75.

18. Note from J. Stapleton Roy to James A. Baker, November 9, 1989, folder 11, box 108, 8c monthly files, series 8, BP.

19. Baker wrote this note on top of a press report from November 9; see folder 11, box 108, 8c monthly files, series 8, BP. For the original text of Bush's Mainz speech, see "A Europe Whole and Free, Remarks to the Citizens in Mainz. President George Bush. Rheingoldhalle. Mainz, Federal Republic of Germany, May 31, 1989," on the website of the U.S. Diplomatic Mission to Germany, available at http://usa.usembassy.de/etexts/ga6-890531.htm.

20. See in particular transcripts of Baker interviews, folder 34, box 160, series 11, BP.

21. See the press reports, folder 11, box 108, 8c monthly files, series 8, BP. Bush's biographer, Timothy Naftali, praises the president for his restraint; summarizing Bush and unification, Naftali concludes that "George H.W. Bush, for a moment at least, became a great president." See Timothy Naftali, *George H.W. Bush* (New York: Times Books, 2007), chapter 4.

22. Zelikow and Rice, *Germany Unified*, 105.

23. For the Baker comments, see press reports, folder 11, box 108, 8c monthly files, series 8, BP. For more on the centrality of NATO to Washington's thinking, see Frank Costigliola, "An 'Arm around the Shoulder': The United States, NATO, and German Reunification, 1989–90," *Central European History* 3, no. 1 (1994): 87–110.

24. Wörner had impressed Bush on a German visit in 1983, when the former was defense minister and the latter was vice president. Bush had seen the inner-German border for himself and then shared a long train ride with Wörner afterward, and the friendship stuck. George Bush and Brent Scowcroft, *A World Transformed* (New York: Knopf, 1998), 184.

25. Mitterrand's remarks were broadcast in German on *Tagesschau* at 8:00 p.m. (ARD Videoarchiv) and reproduced in his memoirs in French: François Mitterrand, *De l'Allemagne, de la France* (Paris: Editions Odile Jacob, April 1996), 201.

26. Philip Zelikow, interview with author, July 27, 2008, phone conversation and subsequent emails.

27. Fred I. Greenstein and William C. Wohlforth, eds., *Cold War Endgame: Report of a Conference*, Center of International Studies Monograph Series No. 10 (Princeton, NJ: Center of International Studies, 1997), 7.

28. I agree with Frédéric Bozo about this, although disagreements about the finer points of Mitterrand's strategy will be developed in the text. See Frédéric Bozo, *Mitterrand, la fin de la guerre froide et l'unification allemande: De Yalta à Maastricht* (Paris: Odile Jacob, 2005). For more on Franco-German relations, see Georges-Henri Soutou, *L'alliance incertaine: Les rapports politico-stratégiques franco-allemands, 1954–1996* (Paris: Fayard, 1996).

29. For an assessment of Bousquet, see Daniel Singer, "Death of a Collaborator," *The Nation*, July 19, 1993, online.

30. This paragraph draws heavily from David Bell, *François Mitterrand* (Cambridge, UK: Polity, 2005), see especially 165; Frédéric Bozo, "Mitterrand's France, the End of the Cold War, and German Unification: A Reappraisal," *Cold War History* 7, no. 4 (2007): 457–59; Mitterrand, *De l'Allemagne*, which was published posthumously.

31. Eduard Shevardnadze, *The Future Belongs to Freedom* (London: Sinclair-Stevenson, 1991), 13, 132. See also Pavel Palazchenko, *My Years with Gorbachev and Shevardnadze: The Memoir of a Soviet Interpreter* (University Park: Penn State University Press, 1997).

32. Horst Teltschik, interview with author, June 13, 2008, phone conversation.

33. Mikhail Gorbachev, *Memoirs* (New York: Doubleday, 1995), 31.

34. On Mitterrand and unification, see Tilo Schabert, *Wie Weltgeschichte gemacht wird: Frankreich und die deutsche Einheit* (Stuttgart: Klett-Cotta, 2002).

NOTES

35. Stephen Szabo, *The Diplomacy of German Unification* (New York: St. Martin's Press, 1992), 36, says that "suddenly, the Soviets received notice of the decision from the East German leadership just before it was announced to the public." He cites a 1992 interview with Foreign Ministry officials as the source. This contradicts comments repeatedly made by Gorbachev that he received no information; see, for example, the on-air interview in the CNN *Cold War* television series, episode 23. The Foreign Ministry officials may have been overstating an earlier event, when they were advised of further updates to the misbegotten travel regulations; the East German foreign minister, Oskar Fischer, informed the Soviet ambassador in East Berlin, V. I. Kochemasov, that the SED was planning on liberalizing travel rules on November 7, 1989. Fischer explicitly stated that the border would not be opened, however ("Die Grenze DDR/BRD werde nicht geöffnet, weil sie unkontrollierbare Wirkung hätte"). See "Vermerk über ein Gespräch zwischen Genossen Oskar Fischer und dem sowjetischen Botschafter Genossen W. I. Kotschemassow am 7.11.989, 11.45 Uhr, Berlin," DDR Staatsarchiv, DC20-4933; also reprinted as document 13 in Hans-Hermann Hertle, *Der Fall der Mauer: Die unbeabsichtigte Selbstauflösung des SED-Staates* (Opladen: Westdeutscher Verlag, 1996), 487–88.

36. "Из дневника А.С. Черняева," November 10, 1989, МГ, 246. Translated as "Notes of Anatoly Chernyaev," November 10, 1989, in GC; GC translation used here.

37. Gorbachev, *Memoirs*, 516.

38. "Telefongespräch des Bundeskanzlers Kohl mit Präsident Bush, 10. November 1989," document 82, DESE, 507; see the U.S. version of the same document, FOIA 1999-0393-F, BPL. On Geremek, see his obituary, written by Nichols Kulish, in the *New York Times*, July 14, 2008. For more on the Polish revolution, see Bernd Schäfer, "The Catholic Church and the Cold War's End in Europe: Vatican Ostpolitik and Pope John Paul II," in *Europe and the End of the Cold War*, ed. Frédéric Bozo, Marie-Pierre Rey, N. Piers Ludlow, and Leopoldo Nuti (London: Routledge, 2008), 64–77.

39. "Delegationsgespräch des Bundeskanzlers Kohl mit Ministerpräsident Mazowiecki, Warschau, 10. November 1989," document 77, DESE, 498.

40. Bernhard Kempen, *Die deutsch-polnische Grenze nach der Friedensregelung des Zwei-plus-Vier-Vertrages* (Frankfurt: Peter Lang, 1997), 288, argues as follows: "Ungeachtet der Verpflichtungen, die der Bundesrepublik und der DDR aus den von ihnen mit Polen und der Sowjetunion abgeschlossenen Verträgen des Jahres 1970 erwachsen sind, hat sich an dem territorialen Status der Ostgebiete nach der Rechtslage von 1937 nichts geändert. Diese Gebiete sind aus der territorialen Souveränität des fortbestehenden deutschen Gesamtstaats zu keiner Zeit ausgegliedert worden. Es bestand kein Erwerbstitel zugunsten Polens und der Sowjetunion, als im Zuge der deutschen Vereinigung im Jahr 1990 grenzbezogenen Regelungen über die jenseits von Oder und Neiße gelegenen Gebiete getroffen worden sind."

41. Mazowiecki press conference, February 21, 1990, reported to Condoleezza Rice, National Security Council (hereafter NSC) PRS files, 1989–1900 [*sic*] subject file, 2 + 4—Germany #1 [2], CR00721-009, FOIA 2001-1166-F, BPL.

42. The Margaret Thatcher Foundation has secured the release of a number of documents via FOI and posted them on its website, www.margaretthatcher.org. Papers produced by her domestic political advisors in late 1989, available on the site, express concern that she was focusing too much on foreign policy when she was in difficulty at home.

43. John Campbell, *Margaret Thatcher* (London: Pimlico, 2004), 303.

44. On this point, see Bozo, "Mitterrand's France," footnote 42; Douglas Hurd, *Memoirs* (London: Little, Brown, 2003), 383.

45. Peter Heinacher, "Parteien ohne Konzept," *Handelsblatt*, November 13, 1989, KASPA. See also Konrad Jarausch, *Die Umkehr: Deutsche Wandlungen, 1945–95* (Munich: Deutsche Verlags-Anstalt, 2004), 291.

NOTES

46. "Telefongespräch des Bundeskanzlers Kohl mit Premierministerin Thatcher, 10. November 1989," document 81, DESE, 505–6; November 10 Bush-Kohl conversation cited above in note 38. My request for the British CAB copy of the same document was approved in 2009: Report entitled "East Germany," from Charles Powell, 10 Downing Street, to J.S. Wall, FCO, November 10, 1989, released by CAB under FOI.

47. "Telefongespräch des Bundeskanzlers Kohl mit Staatspräsident Mitterrand, 11. November 1989," document 85, DESE, 511; "Telefongespräch des Bundeskanzlers Kohl mit Staatsratsvorsitzenden Krenz, 11. November 1989," document 86, DESE, 513–15; "Telefongespräch des Bundeskanzlers Kohl mit Generalsekretär Gorbatschow, 11. November 1989," document 87, DESE, 515–17, also available as "Из телефонного разговора М.С. Горбачева с Г. Колем," November 11, 1989, МГ, 247–50. The quotation is from Kohl's version of the conversation.

48. Teltschik, *329 Tage*, 22–27.

49. "Vorlage an Bundeskanzler Kohl, ohne Datum," document 95, DESE, 548–49; "Schreiben des Bundesministers Waigel an Bundeskanzler Kohl, Bonn, 10. November 1989," document 84, DESE, 510–11.

50. "Predigt des Bischofs von Oppeln (Opole), Alfons Nossel, während der Heiligen Messe, in Gegenwart von Bundeskanzler H. Kohl und Ministerpräsident T. Mazowiecki, Kreisau, 12. November 1989," document 135 in Hans-Adolf Jacobsen, ed., *Bonn-Warschau 1945–1991* (Cologne: Verlag Wissenschaft und Politik, 1992), 498–501; Kohl, Diekmann, and Reuth, *Ich wollte*, 144–46.

51. "Gemeinsame deutsch-polnische Erklärung vom 14. November 1989," in Auswärtiges Amt, *Aussenpolitik*, 623–31.

52. Bush's priority was clear: do not do anything that might provoke the Soviet Union. On this point, see Küsters, "Entscheidung für die deutsche Einheit," 57.

53. Kohl had a series of briefing papers prepared for him the day before this dinner; see documents 94, 94a, and 94b, DESE, 541–48.

54. "European Community Heads of Government Meeting in Paris 18 November," summary sent by C. D. Powell, 10 Downing Street, to Stephen Wall, FCO, released by CAB under FOI; Helmut Kohl, *Erinnerungen 1982–1990* (Munich: Droemer, 2005), 984; Jacques Attali, *C'était François Mitterrand* (Paris: Fayard, 2005), 317, and *Verbatim, Tome 3, Chronique des années 1988–1991* (Paris: Fayard, 1993), 342–45. The veracity of Attali's memoirs has been challenged (see Bozo, "Mitterrand's France," 458), and Kohl's memoirs also deviate from primary sources in parts, so neither source is entirely reliable, but they provide more details of the emotions of the event than the British summary.

55. Kohl, Diekmann, and Reuth, *Ich wollte*, 151–52.

56. "Speech of President Mitterrand to the European Parliament, Strasbourg, 22 November 1989," in Lawrence Freedman, ed., *Europe Transformed: Documents on the End of the Cold War—Key Treaties, Agreements, Statements, and Speeches* (New York: St. Martin's Press, 1990), 367.

57. Copies of the formal 1945 surrender and the subsequent legal modifications can be found in Karl Kaiser, *Deutschlands Vereinigung: Die internationalen Aspekte* (Bergisch-Gladbach: Lübbe Verlag, 1991).

58. The so-called Deutschlandvertrag, or "Vertrag über die Beziehungen zwischen der Bundesrepublik Deutschland und den drei Mächten in der Fassung des am 23. Oktober 1954 in Paris unterzeichneten Protokolls über die Beendigung des Besatzungsregimes . . . ," had, as its name indicates, technically ended the occupation regime; see DESE, 546n30. On the history of the four powers in Germany, see Hanns Jürgen Küsters, *Der Integrationsfriede: Viermächte-Verhandlungen über die Friedensregelung mit Deutschland 1945–1990* (Munich: R. Oldenbourg Verlag, 2000); for

more on the United States specifically, see Klaus-Dietmar Henke, *Die amerikanische Besetzung Deutschlands* (Munich: Oldenbourg, 1995).

59. Teltschik, *329 Tage*, 23; Zelikow and Rice, *Germany Unified*, 106–7, 140–41; my concept of "restoration" as applied to Moscow's plans is paraphrased from James Stevens Curl, *Oxford Dictionary of Architecture and Landscape Architecture* (Oxford: Oxford University Press, 1999), 634.

60. "Verbal Message from Mikhail Gorbachev to François Mitterrand, Margaret Thatcher and George Bush," November 10, 1989, in CWIHPPC, original source DY 30/IV 2/2.039/319, SAPMO. Interestingly, the document is not reprinted in МГ.

61. Zelikow and Rice, *Germany Unified*, 106–7; Teltschik, *329 Tage*, 23.

62. However, it would revive before long; see Zelikow and Rice, *Germany Unified*, 140.

63. R. W. Apple, Jr., "Possibility of a Reunited Germany Is No Cause for Alarm, Says Bush," *New York Times*, October 25, 1989, online. Kohl made the request in a telephone call on October 23, 1989; the U.S. transcript is available in CWIHPPC.

64. Bush and Scowcroft, *A World Transformed*, 187–88.

65. Baker handwritten notes, "11/11," "Maggie," and press summaries from November 10, folder 11, November 1989, box 108, 8c monthly files, series 8, BP.

66. "Guildhall Speech: Major Extract from Text of a Speech Made by the Prime Minister the Rt Hon Margaret Thatcher FRS MP at the Lord Mayor's Banquet Guildhall on Monday 13 November 1989," faxed from the British Embassy, Washington, DC, to 202-395-5221, Zelikow files, NSC, FOIA 2001-1166-F, BPL. See also "Speech Made by Margaret Thatcher at the Lord Mayor's Banquet Guildhall," reprinted in Freedman, *Documents*, 359–60.

67. "Message from Prime Minister to Gorbachev," and cover note from Charles Powell, 10 Downing Street, November 15, 1989, released by CAB via FOI.

68. "Eastern Europe: Prime Minister's Talk with President Bush," note by Charles Powell, November 17, 1989, released by CAB via FOI.

69. "Prime Minister's Meeting with President Bush at Camp David on Friday 24 November," summary sent by C. D. Powell, 10 Downing Street, to Stephen Wall, FCO, November 25, 1989, released by CAB via FOI.

70. "11/12/89," folder 11, box 108, 8c monthly files, series 8, BP.

71. Letter from Gorbachev to Bush, received November 20, 1989, folder 12, box 108, 8c monthly files, series 8, BP.

72. "Schreiben des Ministers für Nationale Verteidigung, Heinz Keßler, an Egon Krenz vom 13.11.1989: Abschrift eines Fernschreibens des Chefs des Stabes der Westgruppe der Streitkräfte der UdSSR, W. Fursin, an Generaloberst Fritz Streletz, 12.11.1989," reprinted as document 35 in Hertle, *Der Fall der Mauer*, 555–57

73. "Record of Telephone Conversation between Mikhail Gorbachev and President of France François Mitterrand, 14 November 1989," notes of Anatoly Chernyaev, document 66 in GC, translation from GC.

74. Küsters, "Entscheidung für die deutsche Einheit," 61.

75. "Gespräch des Bundeskanzlers Kohl mit dem Regierenden Bürgermeister Momper, Bonn, 1. Dezember 1989," document 103, DESE, 578–86.

76. Zelikow and Rice, *Germany Unified*, 104, 119.

77. Victoria DeGrazia, *Irresistible Empire: America's Advance through Twentieth-Century Europe* (Cambridge, MA: Belknap Press, 2005).

78. On the topic of rape by the Red Army during its occupation of Germany, see Norman M. Naimark, *The Russians in Germany: A History of the Soviet Zone of Occupation, 1945–1949* (Cambridge, MA: Belknap Press, 1995), chapter 2.

79. David Childs, "Beate Uhse," *Independent*, September 10, 2001, online.

80. "Da rollt eine Lawine," *Der Spiegel*, November 20, 1989, 21–27.

81. Küsters, "Entscheidung für die deutsche Einheit," 61.

82. Jonathan R. Zatlin, "Hard Marks and Soft Revolutionaries: The Economics of Entitlement and the Debate about German Monetary Union, November 9, 1989–March 18, 1990," *German Politics and Society* 33 (Fall 1994): 1–28.

83. For information about Modrow's worldview, see Hans Modrow, ed., *Das Große Haus: Insider berichten aus dem ZK der SED* (Berlin: edition ost, 1995).

84. The correspondence calling for the meeting is in the collection Zentraler Runder Tisch (hereafter ZRT), Ordner 1, RHG, Berlin.

85. "m.s.," *Frankfurter Allgemeine Zeitung*, November 14, 1989, KASPA. See also document 4 in Konrad H. Jarausch and Volker Gransow, eds., *Uniting Germany: Documents and Debates, 1944–1993* (Providence, RI: Berghahn Books, 1994), 109, where Grass says, "Yes, we are one people. But history has decreed that we live in two states"; see also John C. Torpey, *Intellectuals, Socialism, and Dissent: The East German Opposition and Its Legacy* (Minneapolis: University of Minnesota Press, 1995), 171.

86. The summary in the above paragraphs comes from Horst Teltschik, interview with author, June 13, 2008, phone conversation; Teltschik, *329 Tage*, 42–44; and the document cited below in note 87.

87. "SU und 'deutsche Frage,'" document 112A, DESE, 616–18.

88. Alexander von Plato, *Die Vereinigung Deutschlands—ein weltpolitisches Machtspiel: Bush, Kohl, Gorbatschow und die geheimen Moskauer Protokolle* (Berlin: Links, 2002), 113–15; Zelikow and Rice, *Germany Unified*, 118.

89. Zelikow and Rice, *Germany Unified*, 117–18; Jarausch, *Die Umkehr*, 292; Teltschik, *329 Tage*, 43, and interview with author.

90. "Zehn-Punkte-Programm zur Überwindung der Teilung Deutschlands und Europas: Rede von Bundeskanzler Kohl vor dem Deutschen Bundestag am 28. November 1989 (Auszüge)," in Auswärtiges Amt, *Aussenpolitik*, 632–38; Kohl, Diekmann, and Reuth, *Ich wollte*, 157–211; Teltschik, *329 Tage*, 42–54. An English version is available in "Speech by Chancellor Kohl to the Bundestag on Intra-German Relations," in Freedman, *Documents*, 372–76.

91. The definition of revivalism is paraphrased from Curl, *Oxford Dictionary of Architecture and Landscape Architecture*, 636.

92. See my book on this subject, Mary Elise Sarotte, *Dealing with the Devil* (Chapel Hill: University of North Carolina Press, 2001).

93. For a history of Germany before the Cold War period, see Gordon Craig, *Germany, 1866–1945* (Oxford: Oxford University Press, 1978); Hajo Holborn, *A History of Modern Germany*, 3 vols. (Princeton, NJ: Princeton University Press, 1959); James Sheehan, *German History, 1770–1866* (Oxford: Oxford University Press, 1989).

94. "Zehn-Punkte-Programm," in Auswärtiges Amt, *Aussenpolitik*, 635; Teltschik, *329 Tage*, 52; memorandum from Harvey Sicherman to S/P—Dennis Ross, "Subject: Europe: Triumph or Tragedy?" December 14, 1989, from personal collection of the memo's author. I am grateful to him for a copy of it.

95. Zelikow and Rice, *Germany Unified*, 123. The telcon appears neither in DESE nor FOIA 1999-0393-F at the BPL.

96. "Schreiben des Bundeskanzlers Kohl an Präsident Bush, Bonn, 28 November 1989," document 101, DESE, 568.

97. "Amembassy Bonn to Secstate Washdc," December 1, 1989, "Subject: Kohl's Ten-Point-Program—Silence on the Role of the Four Powers," telegram reprinted in CWIHPPC.

98. Put another way, the transnational ties between governmental subunits were, as Thomas Risse-Kappen has argued, indeed stronger than national ties. Thomas Risse-Kappen, "The Cold War's Endgame and German Unification," *International Security* 21, no. 4 (Spring 1997): online.

99. Horst Teltschik, interview with author, June 13, 2008, phone conversation.

100. "Zehn-Punkte-Programm," in Auswärtiges Amt, *Aussenpolitik*, 633.

101. "Из беседы М.С. Горбачева с Дж. Андреотти," November 29, 1989, МГ, 264–66; see also "Vorlage des Ministerialdirektors Hartmann an Bundeskanzler Kohl, Bonn, 1. Dezember 1989, Betr: Italienische Äußerungen zur deutschen Frage," document 107, DESE, 595–96.

102. "Soviet Spokesman," *International Herald Tribune*, November 30, 1989, reprinted in Freedman, *Documents*, 377.

103. At least two versions of Chernyaev's account of this meeting exist. The most complete is in "Из беседы М.С. Горбачева с Г.-Д. Геншером," December 5, 1989, МГ, 273–84. A shorter, translated version appears as document 70 in GC. Translation from GC. On this meeting, see also Teltschik, *329 Tage*, 68; Küsters, "Entscheidung für die deutsche Einheit," 70.

104. Hans-Dietrich Genscher, *Erinnerungen* (Berlin: Siedler, 1995), 683.

105. "Schreiben des Bundeskanzlers Kohl an Staatspräsident Mitterrand, Bonn, 27 Nov. 1989," document 100, DESE, 565–66; see also Bozo, *Mitterrand*, 145.

106. Teltschik, *329 Tage*, 60–61.

107. "Vorlage des Ministerialdirektors Teltschik an Bundeskanzler Kohl, Bonn, 30. November 1989, Betr.: Reaktion aus den wichtigsten Hauptstädten auf Ihren 10-Punkte Plan," document 102, DESE, 574–77.

108. Zelikow and Rice, *Germany Unified*, 117.

109. Note from the president to "JAB III, Brent, John S., cc VP Dan Quayle," November 18, 1989, with attachment of letter from Nixon to Bush, November 16, 1989, folder 10, box 115, POTUS notes, series 8, BP.

110. "Draft RBZ 11/27/89, Points for Consultation with European Leaders," filed with notes from "12/4/89 NATO Meeting following POTUS-Gorbachev Meeting," folder 12, box 108, series 3, BP.

111. Baker's notes from Malta are available in various places in BP as cited below. Gorbachev published a German-language version in Michail S. Gorbatschow, *Gipfelgespräche: Geheime Protokolle aus meiner Amtszeit* (Berlin: Rowohlt, 1993), 93–129. Chernyaev's notes have appeared in a variety of versions. They were published in Russian, and then translated into English for the limited-circulation CNN *Cold War* television series briefing book, Hutchings's private collection. This paragraph draws on those places where Baker and Chernyaev agree, with the quotations coming from Baker's version.

112. Opening statement, "Used by G.B. at initial session. 10 am to 11 am on board Soviet Cruise Ship MAXIM GORKI," handwritten on top by Baker, folder 9, box 176, 12c chapter files, series 12, BP.

113. Baker's handwritten notes from the Malta summit, "Page 4 of 2nd Day 12/3," folder 12, box 108, series 8, BP. I am also grateful to Ambassador Robert Blackwill for sharing his recollections of the summit.

NOTES

114. "Memorandum of Conversation, Subject: Meeting with Helmut Kohl, Chancellor of the Federal Republic of Germany, Participants: the President, John H. Sununu, Chief of Staff, Brent Scowcroft, Assistant to the President for National Security Affairs," December 3, 1989 in FOIA 1999-0393-F, also available in the NSA "End of the Cold War" boxes; "Gespräch des Bundeskanzlers Kohl mit Präsident Bush, Laeken bei Brüssel, 3. Dezember 1989, 20:30–22:30," document 109, DESE, 600–609.

115. Alexander Moens has argued that U.S. diplomacy was key at four points: first, at this point in December 1989, when it did not join in the chorus of criticism against Kohl's Ten-Point-Program; second, when it agreed to the 2 + 4; third, when it coordinated its position with Bonn on NATO; and fourth, in summer 1990, when it helped to reform NATO. See Alexander Moens, "American Diplomacy and German Unification," *Survival* 33, no. 6 (November–December 1991): 531–45.

116. Brent Scowcroft, interview with author, September 19, 2008, Washington, DC (in which he agreed that this meeting was more important than Malta); Bush and Scowcroft, *A World Transformed*, 199, 213; Philip Zelikow, interview with author, July 27, 2008, phone conversation and subsequent emails.

117. Bush and Scowcroft, *A World Transformed*, 255.

118. "Memorandum of Conversation" and document 109, DESE (cited above in note 114). "UKDel NATO, to Deskby 04213OZFCO, Tel No 375," December 4, 1989, p. 3, released by FCO under FOI. For more on the economic and social impact of East German immigration to the West, see A. James McAdams, *Germany Divided: From the Wall to Reunification* (Princeton, NJ: Princeton University Press, 1993), 204–6.

119. Letter from Shevardnadze to Baker, December 8, 1989, folder 12, box 108, 8c monthly files, series 8, BP.

120. "General Secretary Mikhail Gorbachev's Speech to Central Committee, 9 December 1989," in Freedman, *Documents*, 384–91; report entitled "Germany" from C.D. Powell to J.S. Wall, FCO, December 8, 1989, released by CAB under FOI; "Vorlage des Ministerialdirigenten Hartmann an Bundeskanzler Kohl, Bonn, 18. Dez. 1989," document 127, DESE, 660–61. See also Vojtech Mastny, ed., *The Helsinki Process and the Reintegration of Europe, 1986–1991: Analysis and Documentation* (New York: New York University Press, 1992), 194–96.

121. "12/9," folder 12, box 108, 8c monthly files, series 8, BP, written in the margins of the letter from Shevardnadze from December 8, 1989, cited above.

122. "Information von Wjatschleslaw Kotschemassow, UdSSR-Botschafter in der DDR, an Hans Modrow, DDR-Ministerpräsident, über ein Treffen mit den Bonner Botschaftern der USA, Großbritanniens und Frankreichs am 11. Dezember 1989 in Westberlin (Auszüge)," reprinted as document 10 in Detlef Nakath, Gero Neugebauer, and Gerd-Rüdiger Stephan, *"Im Kreml brennt noch Licht" Spitzenkontakte zwischen SED/PDS und KPdSU 1989–1991* (Berlin: Dietz, 1998), 93–97; "Gespräch des Bundesministers Seiters mit den Botschaftern der Drei Mächte, Bonn, 13. Dez.1989," document 121, DESE, 641–42. For more on the context of this meeting, see GDE, 4:179–87.

123. Zelikow and Rice, *Germany Unified*, 140–41; GDE, 4:922.

124. For Baker's materials from this visit, see folder 12, box 108, 8c monthly files, series 8, BP; for Baker's memory of Kohl, see *Politics of Diplomacy*, 171–72. Baker's speech is available in CFO1337-010, December 12, 1989, Susan Koch files, NSC, FOIA 2001-1166-F, BPL. See also "A New Europe, a New Atlanticism: Architecture for a New Era," address by James A. Baker, Berlin Press Club, Berlin, December 12, 1989, from State Department press release, reprinted as document 59 in Mastny, *Helsinki Process*, 196–97; "Speech by US Secretary of State James Baker to Berlin Press Club," in Freedman, *Documents*, 397–98. Freedman has mistakenly

dated the press conference one day later; Baker's schedule confirms that it took place on December 12.

125. Baker's note is available only in German translation so the text above is my English version of "Schreiben des Außenminister Baker an Bundeskanzler Kohl," document 125, DESE, 658; see also footnote 1 to this document for a summary of the media coverage of Baker's press conference. Television coverage of Baker's visit, including Dan Rathers's CBS report, is available in BP by date.

126. Mitterrand, *De l'Allemagne*, 205–11, pointedly reproduces notes from his meetings "avec des étudiants, intellectuels et artistes" in Leipzig as well.

127. "Из беседы М.С. Горбачева с Ф. Миттераном," December 6, 1989, МГ, 286–91; a translated version appears in GC.

128. "Gespräch des Bundeskanzlers Kohl mit Präsident Delors, Bonn, 5. Okt. 1989," document 58 in DESE, 443.

129. See Bozo, *Mitterrand*, 145–66; Küsters, "Entscheidung für die deutsche Einheit," 71–72; Zelikow and Rice, *Germany Unified*, 137–38. For further details on France, see Robert L. Hutchings, *American Diplomacy and the End of the Cold War: An Insider's Account of US Policy in Europe, 1989–1992* (Washington, DC: Wilson Center, 1997), 15ff.

130. Kohl, *Erinnerungen 1982–1990*, 1012–13.

131. Kohl, *Erinnerungen 1982–1990*, 1015–16; "European Council: European Political Cooperation Declaration on Central and Eastern Europe, 10 Dec. 1989," in Freedman, *Documents*, 395–96; Kaiser, *Deutschlands Vereinigung*, 171–73. On the significance of this deal, see Bozo, *Mitterrand*, 25.

132. See "Schreiben des Staatspräsidenten Mitterrand an Bundeskanzler Kohl, vom 1. Dez. 1989," document 108A, DESE, 599–600; "Vorlage des Vortragenden Legationsrats I Bitterlich an Bundeskanzler Kohl, Bonn, 2./3. Dezember 1989," document 108, DESE, 596–98; "Schreiben des Bundeskanzlers Kohl an Staatspräsident Mitterrand, Bonn, 5 Dez. 1989," document 111, DESE, 614–15; Horst Teltschik, interview with author, June 13, 2008, phone conversation. See also GDE, 4:422–23; Gerhard A. Ritter, *Der Preis der deutschen Einheit: Die Wiedervereinigung und die Krise des Sozialstaats* (Munich: Beck, 2006), 60; Hans Stark, *Helmut Kohl, l'Allemagne et l'Europe: La politique d'intégration européenne de la République fédérale 1982–1998* (Paris: L'Harmattan, 2004), 151.

133. "European Council: Conclusions of the Presidency, 10 December 1989," in Freedman, *Documents*, 392–94. For more on the timing of the intergovernmental conference, see also Rawi Abdelal, *Capital Rules: The Construction of Global Finance* (Cambridge, MA: Harvard University Press, 2008), 78–79. For more on the evolution of the EC, see Barry Eichengreen, *The European Economy since 1945: Coordinated Capitalism and Beyond* (Princeton, NJ: Princeton University Press, 2007).

134. On the attitude of Mitterrand and his advisors, see in particular the following files in the Archives Nationales, Paris: 5 AG 4/4160, including papers from December 1989; 5 AG 4/CDM 36, dossier 2, and CDM48, including discussion of restoring quadripartitism. On the attitude of Delors, see Zelikow and Rice, *Germany Unified*, 138.

135. Bozo, *Mitterrand*, 26, correctly asks the following questions: "La transition démocratique et économique en Europe de l'Est, le retour de l'Allemagne à l'unité et à la pleine souveraineté, la désintégration de l'URSS et la recomposition de l'ordre européen : tout cela aurait-il pu se produire de manière ordonnée et stable sans la contribution majeure de la construction européenne et de la relation franco-allemande?"

136. For a detailed assessment of European monetary union, see Andrew Moravcsik, *The Choice for Europe: Social Purpose and State Power from Messina to Maastricht* (Ithaca, NY: Cornell

University Press, 1998); and David Marsh, *The Euro* (New Haven, CT: Yale University Press, 2009).

137. "Gespräch des Bundeskanzlers Kohl mit Außenminister Baker, Berlin (West), 12. Dez. 1989," document 120, DESE, 636–41. The copy of this document in the Bundesarchiv Koblenz version includes a cover note that is omitted from the DESE version. The cover note from Teltschik reads as follows: "Anliegend lege ich Vermerk über o.a. Gespräch zur Billigung vor. Ich gehe davon aus, daß dieser Vermerk nicht weitergegeben werden soll." Kohl wrote "Ja" by hand on the page as a response.

138. A State Department memorandum, from S/P Harvey Sicherman to S/P—Dennis Ross and C—Robert Zoellick, "Subject: Europe: Triumph or Tragedy?" May 1, 1990 (from the personal collection of the memo's author), suggests that Mitterrand started playing with an idea of a Europe of confederations.

139. "Gespräch des Bundeskanzlers Kohl mit Mitgliedern der Rüstungskontroll-Beobachtergruppe des amerikanischen Senats, Bonn, 1. Dezember 1989: Senatoren Pell, Lugar, Chafee, Warner, Sarbanes, Garn, Moynihan, Nickles," document 104, DESE, 586–90; Küsters, "Entscheidung für die deutsche Einheit," 75; Teltschik, *329 Tage*, 82. Kohl had visited the GDR privately in 1988, but made no public appearances at that time; see Jan Schönfelder and Rainer Erices, *Westbesuch: Die geheime DDR-Reise von Helmut Kohl* (Thuringia: Verlag Dr. Bussert and Stadeler, 2007).

140. Kohl, *Erinnerungen 1982–1990*, 1020. The phrase in German is "die Sache ist gelaufen."

141. Records of Kohl's various Dresden conversations are available in DESE, 668–75; see also "Arbeitsbesuch von Bundeskanzler Kohl in Dresden am 19./20. Dezember 1989," in Auswärtiges Amt, *Aussenpolitik*, 647–51.

142. There is a contradiction here between Kohl's memoirs and Teltschik's. Kohl said that he had not planned to give a speech but rather decided to do so on the spot; Teltschik, however, recounts the meeting that took place in Bonn the night before their departure to prepare his remarks. Kohl, *Erinnerungen 1982–1990*, 1020; Teltschik, *329 Tage*, 86.

143. Video footage of Kohl's speech is available from both ARD and ZDF in KASPA; video excerpts and the text of the speech is available at http://www.2plus4.de.

144. See "Schreiben des Bundeskanzlers Kohl an Premierminister Shamir, Bonn, 1. Dezember 1989," document 106, DESE, 594–95; "Schreiben des Premierministers Shamir an Bundeskanzler Kohl, Jerusalem, 10. Dez. 1989," document 118, DESE, 632.

145. Vladimir Putin, with Nataliya Gevorkyan, Natalya Timakova, and Andrei Kolesnikov, *First Person: An Astonishingly Frank Self-Portrait by Russia's President Putin*, trans. Catherine A. Fitzpatrick (New York: Public Affairs, 2000), 76.

NOTES TO CHAPTER 3

1. Federalist Papers, no. 4, in James Madison, Alexander Hamilton, and John Jay, *The Federalist Papers,* ed. Isaac Kramnick (New York: Penguin Books, 1987), 100. "I am not one of those who left the land," in *Poems of Akhmatova,* trans. Stanley Kunitz and Max Hayward (New York: Houghton Mifflin, 1973), 75. Robert Havemann, *Fragen Antworten Fragen: Aus der Biographie eines deutschen Marxisten* (1990; repr., Berlin: Piper, 1970), 270.

2. Havemann joined the Righteous among Nations in 2005; Yad Vashem, the Martyrs' and Heroes' Remembrance Authority, available at http://www.yadvashem.org.

3. Havemann's son Florian would later write a controversial memoir about the burden of being Robert's soon, called simply *Havemann*; for more about Florian's life and career, see his website, available at http://www.florian-havemann.de.

NOTES

4. Robert Havemann, *Fragen Antworten Fragen: Aus der Biographie eines deutschen Marxisten* (Berlin: Piper, 1970), 7–16; Dieter Hoffmann, "Robert Havemann—eine deutsche Biographie," in Havemann, *Fragen*, 281–93; John C. Torpey, *Intellectuals, Socialism, and Dissent: The East German Opposition and Its Legacy* (Minneapolis: University of Minnesota Press, 1995), 58–59. For an overview of the context of Havemann's life—namely, twentieth-century German history—see Eberhard Jäckel, *Das deutsche Jahrhundert* (Stuttgart: DVA, 1996).

5. Ilko-Sascha Kowalczuk and Tom Sello, eds., *Für ein Freies Land mit freien Menschen: Opposition und Widerstand in Biographien und Fotos* (Berlin: Robert-Havemann-Gesellschaft, 2006), 136–39, 306–9; Torpey, *Intellectuals*, 96. The foundation, or RHG, is in Berlin, where it maintains an archive and organizes events to commemorate the protest movement in East Germany.

6. The preceding paragraphs are drawn largely from Havemann, *Fragen*, especially 280; and Torpey, *Intellectuals*, especially 90, 124, 144, 156.

7. Uwe Thaysen, *Der Runde Tisch, oder: Wo blieb das Volk? Der Weg der DDR in die Demokratie* (Opland: Westdeutscher Verlag, 1990), 28. On the significance of the founding or refounding of parties in the GDR, see Gerhard A. Ritter, *Der Preis der deutschen Einheit: Die Wiedervereinigung und die Krise des Sozialstaats* (Munich: Beck, 2006), 35ff; the refounding of the SPD was a particular slap in the face of the SED, which considered itself to be the heir to the SPD in the East, after having forced it to merge in the 1940s.

8. The RHG maintains a list of attendees at all round table, or ZRT, meetings; see ZRT Ordner 9, "Sonstiges," RHG.

9. The RHG holds a set of copies of the issues of *Grenzfall*; see also Ilko-Sascha Kowalczuk, ed., *Freiheit und Öffentlichkeit: Politischer Samisdat in der DDR 1985–1989* (Berlin: Robert-Havemann-Gesellschaft, 2002); Ilko-Sascha Kowalczuk, *Endspiel: Die Revolution von 1989 in der DDR* (Munich: Beck, 2009). For more on the Poppes and other leading East German intellectuals, see Torpey, *Intellectuals*, 94. For discussion of the break with the past close relationship between the church and dissident movements, see Reinhard Schult, "Offen für alle—das 'Neue Forum,'" in *Aufbruch in eine andere DDR: Reformer und Oppositionelle zur Zukunft ihres Landes*, ed. Hubertus Knabe (Rowohlt: Hamburg, 1989), 163–70.

10. Kowalczuk and Sello, *Für ein freies Land*, 297–301, 310–13; see also Erhard Neubert, *Geschichte der Opposition in der DDR 1949–1989* (Bonn: Bundeszentrale für politische Bildung, 1997); Ulrike Poppe et al., eds., *Zwischen Selbstbehauptung und Anpassung* (Berlin: Links, 1995).

11. Thaysen, *Der Runde Tisch*, 40–45.

12. The transcripts of the round table meetings have been published in five volumes: Uwe Thaysen, ed., *Der Zentrale Runde Tisch der DDR: Wortprotokolle und Dokumente* (hereafter ZRT-WD), (Wiesbaden: Westdeutscher Verlag, 2000).

13. ZRT-WD, 1. Sitzung, 56–60; Thaysen, *Der Runde Tisch*, 50.

14. ZRT-WD, 1. Sitzung, "Selbstverständnis," 62.

15. ZRT-WD, 1. Sitzung, 66–89. A decision was taken at the second meeting, December 18, 1989, to follow the work of the independent control commission for dissolving the former Stasi; see ZRT-WD, 2. Sitzung, 131. See also Friedrich Schlomann, *Die Maulwürfe: Die Stasi-Helfer im Westen sind immer noch unter uns* (Frankfurt: Ullstein, 1994), 66–68.

16. "Ausführungen von Ministerpräsident Hans Modrow anläßlich der Dientseinführung von Generalleutnant Wolfgang Schwanitz als Leiter des Amtes für Nationale Sicherheit in Berlin am 21. November 1989," document 54 in Gerd-Rüdiger Stephan and Daniel Küchenmeister, eds., *"Vorwärts immer, rückwärts nimmer!"* (Berlin: Dietz, 1994), 253–67.

17. Vladimir Putin, with Nataliya Gevorkyan, Natalya Timakova, and Andrei Kolesnikov, *First Person: An Astonishingly Frank Self-Portrait by Russia's President Putin*, trans. Catherine A. Fitzpatrick (New York: Public Affairs, 2000), 76–78.

NOTES

18. "Fernschreiben des Staatssekretärs Bertele an Bundesminister Seiters, Berlin (Ost), 7 Dezember 1989," document 114, DESE, 621. By this point, Bohley had become one of the most prominent figures in East Germany, so she knew that her message would receive attention.

19. "Telegram to MfS Berlin Stellv. des Ministers, Gen. Generaloberst Mittig, Information ueber das Stimmungsbild unter den Mitarbeitern der Bezirksverwaltung fuer Staatssicherheit Karl-Marx-Stadt, insbesondere in den Kreisdienststellen," November 10, 1989, 76–78, in Arbeitsbereich Mittig 30, BStU.

20. "Arbeit für 10 000 Staatsanwälte: Die Auflösung des Stasi-Überwachungsapparates stellte die DDR-Regierung vor kaum lösbare Probleme," *Der Spiegel*, December 18, 1989, 35–42.

21. ZRT-WD, 1. Sitzung, 62; Torpey, *Intellectuals*, 157.

22. For basic information on the setup of the round table, see ZRT-WD, 1:xii.

23. ZRT-WD, 1. Sitzung, 48–53; Poppe comment is on 53. See also Thaysen, *Der Runde Tisch*, 52–53. Letters from private citizens (a common form of communication in a country widely lacking phone service) started coming in almost as soon as the round table started meeting, and many seconded Poppe in questioning the extent of the round table's legitimacy. See DA 3–67, Briefe der Bevölkerung, letters from December 28, 1989, SAPMO. The East German government was also trying to edit the existing GDR constitution by removing the primacy of the SED and allowing private property, but neither the government nor the existing constitution retained sufficient authority to be taken seriously in any way. See also Ursula Münch, "1990: Grundgesetz oder neue Verfassung?" available on the website of the Bundeszentrale für politische Bildung, http://www.bpb.de.

24. The leading SED member at the round table, Gregor Gysi, remained adept at maneuvering in committees and discussions, and his party retained control over most media outlets. Thaysen, *Der Runde Tisch*, 56, 136.

25. Intriguingly, hints that this "sale" might have been under consideration surfaced in the form of a November 6 conversation between the Bundeskanzleramt and the SED's behind-the-scenes negotiator, Alexander Schalck-Golodkowski. The idea got nowhere, however, because Kohl decided that any future payments to East Germany would require thoroughgoing domestic reform, including free elections. He announced this to the Bundestag on November 8; events the next day later rendered the entire discussion irrelevant. For more on the November 6 talk, see "Schreiben von Alexander Schalck an Egon Krenz, 6.11.89, mit der Anlage: 'Vermerk über ein informelles Gespräch des Genossen Alexander Schalck mit dem Bundesminister und Chef des Bundeskanzleramtes der BRD, Rudolf Seiters, und dem Mitglied des Vorstandes der CDU, Wolfgang Schäuble, am 06.11.1989," document 11, in Hans-Hermann Hertle, *Der Fall der Mauer: Die unbeabsichtigte Selbstauflösung des SED-Staates* (Opladen: Westdeutscher Verlag, 1996), 483–6; a partial English translation appears in CWIHPPC. For more on Kohl's November 8 speech, see "Bericht der Bundesregierung zur Lage der Nation, Erklärung von Bundeskanzler Kohl am 8. November 1989 vor dem Deutschen Bundestag (Auszüge)," in Auswärtiges Amt, *Aussenpolitik der Bundesrepublik Deutschland: Dokumente von 1949 bis 1994* (Cologne: Verlag Wissenschaft und Politik, 1995), 605–16.

26. Thaysen, *Der Runde Tisch*, 51.

27. ZRT-WD, 2. Sitzung, 126.

28. "Gespräch des Bundeskanzlers Kohl mit Staatspräsident Mitterrand, Latché, 4. Jan. 1990," document 135, DESE, 682–90; see also Frédéric Bozo, "Mitterrand's France, the End of the Cold War, and German Unification: A Reappraisal," *Cold War History* 7, no. 4 (2007): 455–78; Hanns Jürgen Küsters, "Entscheidung für die deutsche Einheit," DESE, 79–80; Hélène Miard-Delacroix, "Latché," in *Tour de France*, ed. Armin Heinen and Dietmar Hüser (Stuttgart: Franz Steiner Verlag, 2008), 283–92.

NOTES

29. Ritter, *Der Preis der deutschen Einheit*, 21.

30. Thaysen, *Der Runde Tisch*, 57.

31. Stephen Szabo, *The Diplomacy of German Unification* (New York: St. Martin's Press, 1992), 55–56.

32. *"Neues Deutschland,"* January 3, 1990, document 19 in Konrad H. Jarausch and Volker Gransow, eds., *Uniting Germany: Documents and Debates, 1944–1993* (Providence, RI: Berghahn Books, 1994), 96–98.

33. "Fernschreiben vom 9.12., 11.00h," authored by "das kollektiv des bezirkamtes für Nationale Sicherheit Gera und die Kreisämter," discussed in ZRT, 6. Sitzung, January 8, 1990, reprinted in Thaysen, *Der Runde Tisch*, 60–61.

34. ZRT-WD, 6. Sitzung, 334–35, 343. See also ZRT-WD, 5. Sitzung, January 3, 1990, 290–95; Thaysen, *Der Runde Tisch*, 58–62.

35. "Vermerk über ein Gespräch zwischen Hans Modrow und UdSSR-Ministerpräsident, Nikolai Ryshkow am 10. Januar 1990," document 58 in Detlef Nakath and Gerd-Rüdiger Stephan, eds., *Countdown zur deutschen Einheit: Eine dokumentierte Geschichte der deutsch-deutschen Beziehungen 1987–1990* (Berlin: Dietz, 1996), 271–73.

36. Thaysen, *Der Runde Tisch*, 64–66 (Modrow quotation appears on 64).

37. "Stellungnahme der Bürgerkomitees 'Auflösung der Kreis- und Bezirksämter des ehemaligen MfS/AfNS' zur Vorlage der Arbeitsgruppen des ZRT," January 15, 1990, in ZRT Ordner 2, RHG. An interesting account of a successful plan to stop Stasi document destruction at a branch in Frankfurt/Oder in December 1989 may be found in Christoph Links, Sybille Nitsche, and Antje Taffelt, *Das wunderbare Jahr der Anarchie* (Berlin: Links, 2004), 109–14.

38. The materials calling for the protest are in DA 3/8, SAPMO.

39. Memorandum from Harvey Sicherman to S/P—Dennis Ross, "Subject: Europe: Triumph or Tragedy?" December 14, 1989, from Sicherman's personal collection; interview with Charles Powell, London, March 19, 2009.

40. ZRT-WD, 7. Sitzung, 346–48, 408–9; Thaysen, *Der Runde Tisch*, 66–67.

41. The East German Ministry of the Interior and the New Forum would later prepare somewhat contradictory reports on what had gone wrong on January 15; this paragraph is drawn from what seems to be agreed between them. See "Erklärung NF: Zur Demonstration am 15. Januar 1990," in ZRT-WD, 8. Sitzung, 412–13; "Ergebnisse des Rundtischgesprächs am 18. Januar 1990," DA 3/8, SAPMO; "MdI, Betr.: Gewaltsame Besetzung der Zentrale des ehemaligen Amtes für Nationalen Sicherheit in Berlin-Lichtenberg," DA 3/8, SAPMO.

42. In keeping with German privacy laws, the names of the individual letter writers are not given here, but they are available at the RHG. See "Randale oder Provokation???" undated, ZRT Ordner 8, Korrespondenz, RHG; various letters of January 18, 1990, ZRT Ordner 8, Korrespondenz, RHG; "Beobachtungen eines Beobachters vom NF," January 22, 1990, ZRT Ordner 8, Korrespondenz, RHG; "Zur Demonstration in der Normannenstraße," presented to the round table on January 22, 1990, in ZRT-WD, 5:126–29. For more on the argument that Stasi agents in the crowd started the violence, see Anne Worst, *Das Ende des Geheimdienstes* (Berlin: Links, 1991), 38.

43. See the various materials resulting from the January 15 events in ZRT, Ordner 2, RHG; see also Armin Mitter and Stefan Wolle, eds., *Ich liebe euch doch alle! Befehle und Lageberichte des MfS Januar-November 1989* (Berlin: BasisDruck, 1990); Jens Gieseke, *Der Mielke-Konzern: Die Geschichte der Stasi 1945–1990* (Munich: Deutsche Velags-Anstalt, 2006), 261; Worst, *Das Ende*, 49–60.

44. "Beschluß über den Bericht und Schlußfolgerungen über die Begegnung des Vorsitzenden des Ministerrates der DDR, Hans Modrow, mit dem Bundesminister für besondere Aufgaben und Chef des BRD-Bundeskanzleramtes, Rudolf Seiters, am 25.1.1990," DDR Ministerrat. I am grateful to Hans-Hermann Hertle for a copy of this document.

45. "Niederschrift des Gesprächs zwischen Hans Modrow und KPdSU-Generalsekretär und Vorsitzender des Obersten Sowjets der UdSSR, am 30. Januar 1990," in Nakath and Stephan, *Countdown*, 288–98; "Из беседы М.С. Горбачева с Х. Модровым," January 30, 1990, МГ, 312–24.

46. Modrow announcement on January 29, 1990, to the Volkskammer der DDR, 9. Wahlperiode, Okt. 89–März 90; DESE, 712n12. I am grateful to Hans-Hermann Hertle for a copy of Modrow's comments.

47. "Gespräch des Bundeskanzlers Kohl mit Botschafter Walters, Bonn, 24. Januar 1990," document 141, DESE, 699–701.

48. See "Gespräch des Bundeskanzlers Kohl mit Ministerpräsident Modrow, Davos, 3. Februar 1990," document 158, DESE, 753–56.

49. "Gespräch des Bundeskanzlers Kohl mit Ministerpräsident Modrow, Davos, 3. Februar 1990," 756.

50. "Vorlage des Ministerialdirigenten Hartmann, Bonn, 29. Januar 1990," document 151, DESE, 727–35. Teltschik started looking into the legal justification for Soviet troop stationing in the GDR, seeing if there was any useful information there; see "Vorlage des Ministerialdirektors Teltschik an Bundeskanzler Kohl," n.d., document 166, DESE, 771–76. Hartmann worked on foreign policy, but Kohl's domestic politics and public opinion experts agreed: Kohl needed to be on the cutting edge of developments, yet also ensure that his leadership did not antagonize those who mattered. See documents 157, 157a, and 157b, all February 2, 1990, DESE, 749–53.

51. Robert Keatly, Glynn Mapes, and Barbara Toman, "Thatcher Sees Eastern Europe Progress as More Urgent Than Germans' Unity," *Wall Street Journal*, January 26, 1990, A12.

52. "President François Mitterrand, interviewed on Italian television, January 27, 1990," in Lawrence Freedman, ed., *Europe Transformed: Documents on the End of the Cold War— Key Treaties, Agreements, Statements, and Speeches* (New York: St. Martin's Press, 1990), 428–29.

53. "Vorlage des Ministerialdirektors Teltschik an Bundeskanzler Kohl, Bonn, 25. Januar 1990, Betr.: Interview der britischen Premierministerin Margaret Thatcher in der Wall Street Journal am 25. Jan 1990," document 148, DESE, 719–20.

54. "Speech by UK Foreign Secretary Douglas Hurd, Bonn, 6 February 1990," in Freedman, *Documents*, 458–61.

55. Douglas Hurd, *Memoirs* (London: Little, Brown, 2003), 384; "Internal Minute," February 1, 1990, released by the FCO via FOI. The FCO went so far as to suggest to the prime minister that she should make some kind of positive remarks about German unification; see "Note from J.S. Wall, Private Secretary, FCO to Charles Powell," February 5, 1990, released by CAB via FOI. Pyeongeok An has argued that Hurd and the FCO were trying to undercut Thatcher, but that they did so quietly; see Pyeongeok An, "Obstructive All the Way? British Policy toward German Unification, 1989–90," *German Politics* 15, no. 1 (March 2006): 111–21. See also Patrick Salmon, "The United Kingdom and German Unification," in *Europe and the End of the Cold War*, ed. Frédéric Bozo, Marie-Pierre Rey, N. Piers Ludlow, and Leopoldo Nuti (London: Routledge, 2008), 177–90; Küsters, "Entscheidung für die deutsche Einheit," DESE, 83–84.

56. Report entitled "Germany" from C.D. Powell to J.S. Wall, February 8, 1990, released by CAB under FOI.

NOTES

57. Horst Teltschik, *329 Tage: Innenansichten der Einigung* (Berlin: Siedler, 1991), 102.

58. The CIA estimated on January 29, 1990, that Gorbachev would not use force to make Lithuania stay in the Soviet Union; see "Executive Brief," Director of Central Intelligence (hereafter DCI), National Intelligence Council (hereafter NIC) 00095/90, released by the CIA via the FOIA. See also Robert L. Hutchings, *American Diplomacy and the End of the Cold War: An Insider's Account of US Policy in Europe, 1989–1992* (Washington, DC: Wilson Center, 1997), 360.

59. According to GDE, 4:215, and based on documents not available to the public, the Soviet Union sent a request for another four-power meeting to the three other powers on January 10, 1990.

60. There is some dispute about the exact date of this meeting. The source of information about it, in all cases, is a set of handwritten notes by Chernyaev. They have "GDR-FRG" written at the top and an unclear handwritten date that looks like 27.1.90 (these notes are reproduced in the handwritten original in CNN's *Cold War* briefing book, along with a translation dated January 27, 1990, by Nina Khrushcheva). The notes are also reprinted in Russian, in typed format, as "Обсуждение германского вопроса на узком совещании в кабинете Генерального секретаря ЦК КПСС," МГ, 307–11, but with the date of January 26, 1990. Finally, in an interview with the German scholar Alexander von Plato, Chernyaev said that the correct date was really January 25, 1990; see Alexander von Plato, *Die Vereinigung Deutschlands—ein weltpolitisches Machtspiel: Bush, Kohl, Gorbatschow und die geheimen Moskauer Protokolle* (Berlin: Links, 2002), 188. Unfortunately Chernyaev canceled an interview on the day that it was scheduled to occur due to a family illness, so it was not possible to ask him directly. The paragraphs below summarize what seems consistent between these sources. For more on Chernyaev's thinking, see Anatoly Chernyaev, "Gorbachev and the Reunification of Germany: Personal Recollections," in *Soviet Foreign Policy, 1971–1991*, ed. Gabriel Gorodetsky (London: Routledge, 1994), 166. For more on Gorbachev's personality and thinking, see Stephen Kotkin, *Armageddon Averted: The Soviet Collapse, 1970–2000* (New York: Oxford University Press, 2001), 67, 88; Vladislav Zubok, *A Failed Empire: The Soviet Union in the Cold War from Stalin to Gorbachev* (Chapel Hill: University of North Carolina Press, 2007), 326–27.

61. DESE, 747n4; see also the day entry for February 9, 1990, on the chronology available at http://www.chronik-der-mauer.de.

62. For more on this topic, see Raymond Garthoff, *The Great Transition: American-Soviet Relations and the End of the Cold War* (Washington, DC: Brookings Institution Press, 1994), 423; Jack F. Matlock Jr., *Autopsy on an Empire: The American Ambassador's Account of the Collapse of the Soviet Union* (New York: Random House, 1995), 382; Angela Stent, *Russia and Germany Reborn: Unification, the Soviet Collapse, and the New Europe* (Princeton, NJ: Princeton University Press, 1999), 104–8. Stent points out that the option of using force to restore order was not seriously considered. For more on Falin in particular, see Hannes Adomeit, *Imperial Overstretch: Germany in Soviet Policy from Stalin to Gorbachev* (Baden-Baden: Nomos Verlagsgesellschaft, 1998), 567–68.

63. In a summary of West German–Soviet relations written just after the brainstorming session, Teltschik advised Kohl of his sense that Gorbachev appeared to be deciding to work with the chancellor, but it is not clear if this was based on knowledge of the meeting. "Vorlage des Ministerialdirektors Teltschik an Bundeskanzler Kohl, Bonn, 29. Januar 1990, Betr.: Stand und Perspektiven der deutsch-sowjetischen Beziehungen," document 150, DESE, 722–26.

64. Gorbachev wrote to Kohl on February 2, inviting him to Moscow as early as February 9, in the evening after talks with Baker that day; Kohl would subsequently request that he visit on the weekend of February 10–11 instead, and Gorbachev would agree. See "Schreiben des Generalsekretärs Gorbatschow an Bundeskanzler Kohl, 2. Februar 1990," document 156, DESE, 748–49; "Gespräch des Bundeskanzlers Kohl mit Botschafter Kwizinskij, Bonn, 2. Februar 1990," document 155, DESE, 747–48.

65. Gorbachev complained to the West German ambassador in Moscow, Klaus Blech, that the speech left open many questions. "В.В. Загладин о беседе с послом ФРГ в СССР К. Блехом," February 1, 1990, МГ, 327–29.

66. "Schreiben des Ministerpräsiden Mazowiecki an Bundeskanzler Kohl, Warschau, 30. Januar 1990," document 154, DESE, 744–47.

67. For copies of the relevant treaties and accords from 1945 to 1975, see Karl Kaiser, *Deutschlands Vereinigung: Die internationalen Aspekte* (Bergisch-Gladbach: Lübbe Verlag, 1991).

68. Ritter, *Der Preis der deutschen Einheit*, 31; Wolfgang Schäuble, *Der Vertrag: Wie ich über die deutsche Einheit verhandelte* (Munich: Knaur, 1991), 293.

69. "Rede des Bundesministers des Auswärtigen, Hans-Dietrich Genscher, zum Thema 'Zur deutschen Einheit im europäischen Rahmen,' bei einer Tagung der Evangelischen Akademie Tutzing, 31. Jan. 1990," reprinted in Richard Kiessler and Frank Elbe, *Ein runder Tisch mit scharfen Ecken: Der diplomatische Weg zur deutschen Einheit* (Baden-Baden: Nomos Verlagsgesellschaft, 1993), 245–46. The translation is my own, but an English version with the same comment appears in Freedman, *Documents,* 436–45. See also Szabo, *Diplomacy,* 57–58; GDE, 4:256.

70. "JAB notes from 2/2/90 press briefing following 2 ½ hr meeting w/FRG FM Genscher, WDC," folder 14, box 108, 8c monthly files, series 8; Hans-Dietrich Genscher, *Erinnerungen* (Berlin: Siedler, 1995), 716–19; Philip Zelikow and Condoleezza Rice, *Germany Unified and Europe Transformed: A Study in Statecraft* (Cambridge, MA: Harvard University Press, 1995), 174–77. The press conference quotation appears in Al Kamen, "West German Meets Privately with Baker," *The Washington Post,* February 3, 1990, A20.

71. "Gespräch des Ministerialdirektors Teltschik mit Botschafter Walters, Bonn, 4. Februar 1990," document 159, DESE, 756–57.

72. Baker's scheduling calendars from his time as secretary of state are available in BP. He departed on Monday, February 5, 1990, from Andrews Air Force Base for Czechoslovakia, where he met President Havel. He then went onward to Moscow on Wednesday, February 7.

73. See his comments at the "Konstituierende Sitzung der Arbeitsgruppe Außen- und Sicherheitspolitik des Kabinettausschusses Deutsche Einheit (hereafter KADE), Bonn, 14. Februar 1990," document 182, DESE, 830–31. Perhaps because of such comments, the KADE decided at its second meeting that its records would be secret; see "Zweite Sitzung der Arbeitsgruppe Außen- und Sicherheitspolitik des KADE, Bonn, 19. Februar 1990," document 189, DESE, 854. See also Stent, *Russia and Germany Reborn*, 117–19; GDE, 4:256–62.

74. David Childs, "Gerhard Stoltenberg," *Independent*, November 27, 2001, online.

75. Richard A. Falkenrath, *Shaping Europe's Military Order: The Origins and Consequences of the CFE Treaty* (Cambridge, MA: MIT Press, 1995). See also Andrei Grachev, "From the Common European Home to European Confederation," in *Europe and the End of the Cold War*, ed. Frédéric Bozo, Marie-Pierre Rey, N. Piers Ludlow, and Leopoldo Nuti (London: Routledge, 2008), 207–19.

76. Valentin Falin, *Konflikte im Kreml: Zur Vorgeschichte der deutschen Einheit und Auflösung der Sowjetunion* (Munich: Blessing Verlag, 1997), 160; Vojtech Mastny and Malcolm Byrne, eds., *A Cardboard Castle? An Inside History of the Warsaw Pact* (New York: Central European University Press, 2005), 70–71.

77. "За Германию, единое отечество (концепция к дискуссии о пути к германскому единству)," МГ, 325–26. Washington did not like the phrase "common European home" because it excluded the United States, but Shevardnadze would nonetheless float this balloon again publicly to the Central Committee on February 6; see "Shevardnadze's Remarks at Central Committee Plenum February 6," folder 13, box 176, 12b chapter files, series 12, BP. Report entitled "German

Unification: The Wider Consequences," from Charles Powell to J.S. Wall, February 23, 1990, released by the CAB under FOI.

78. Falin, *Konflikte im Kreml*, 187; Vladislav Zubok, "New Evidence on the End of the Cold War: New Evidence on the 'Soviet Factor' in the Peaceful Revolutions of 1989," *Cold War International History Project Bulletin* 12–13 (Fall–Winter 2001): 5–14.

79. Memorandum from S/P Harvey Sicherman to S/P—Dennis Ross and C—Robert Zoellick, "Subject: Europe: Triumph or Tragedy?" May 1, 1990, from Sicherman's personal collection.

80. On its later impact on NATO expansion, see Ronald D. Asmus, *Opening NATO's Door: How the Alliance Remade Itself for a New Era* (New York: Columbia University Press, 2002), 4–5.

81. Mikhail Gorbachev, *Memoirs* (New York: Doubleday, 1995), 24–26. Gorbachev is apparently telling this story from memory, and it may therefore be prey to any errors he made, but its broad outlines conform to numerous other stories of the experience of prisoners of Stalin's purges. See Zbigniew Brzezinski, *The Grand Failure: The Birth and Death of Communism in the Twentieth Century* (New York: Charles Scribner's Sons, 1989), 24–26; Robert Conquest, *The Great Terror* (New York: Oxford University Press, 1968); Stéphane Courtois et al., *Le livre noir du Communisme: Crimes, terreur, répression* (Paris: Laffont, 1997), published in English as *Black Book of Communism* (Cambridge, MA: Harvard University Press, 1999).

82. James A. Baker, with Thomas A. DeFrank, *The Politics of Diplomacy: Revolution, War, and Peace, 1989–1992* (New York: G. P. Putnam's Sons, 1995), 61–62.

83. Gorbachev, *Memoirs*, 56–66.

84. Archie Brown, *The Gorbachev Factor* (New York: Oxford University Press, 1997), 29–40; Gorbachev, *Memoirs*, 59.

85. Baker with DeFrank, *The Politics of Diplomacy*, 18, 37–38, 72–77.

86. Garthoff, *The Great Transition*, 420; Baker with DeFrank, *The Politics of Diplomacy*, 79. On the impact of nationalism, see Mark R. Beissinger, *Nationalist Mobilization and the Collapse of the Soviet State* (Cambridge: Cambridge University Press, 2002); Garthoff, *The Great Transition*, 419–20; Ronald Grigor Suny, *The Revenge of the Past: Nationalism, Revolution, and the Collapse of the Soviet Union* (Stanford, CA: Stanford University Press, 1993). Suny insightfully points out (160) that Soviet nationalities did not just awake from slumber after seventy-four years but rather were constantly being nurtured during the Soviet period; "their pasts were constructed and reconstructed; traditions were selected, invented, and enshrined, and even those with the greatest antiquity of pedigree became something quite different from past incarnations."

87. Robert M. Gates, *From the Shadows: The Ultimate Insider's Story of Five Presidents and How They Won the Cold War* (New York: Touchstone, 1996), 456; Baker with DeFrank, *The Politics of Diplomacy*, 80, 134.

88. Mastny and Byrne, *A Cardboard Castle?* 63. For more information on the Soviet nuclear arsenal, see Pavel Podvig, ed., *Russian Strategic Nuclear Forces* (Cambridge, MA: MIT Press, 2004).

89. "President George Bush: State of the Union Address, 31 January 1990 (Excerpts)," in Freedman, *Documents*, 446–47; *NBC Today Show*, highlights of Thursday morning television newscasts, February 8, 1990, telegram, "Secstate Washdc to USDEL Secretary Immediate," State Department, released via FOIA. He had informed his leading NATO allies of this ahead of time, by sending the deputy secretary of state, Lawrence Eagleburger, to Europe with Gates. See "Gespräch des Bundeskanzlers Kohl mit dem stellvertretenden Außenminister Eagleburger Bonn, 30. Januar 1990," document 153, DESE, 739–43. On this conversation, see also Falkenrath, *Shaping Europe's Military Order*, 62–63; Gates, *From the Shadows*, 463–64, 485–88.

90. Garthoff, *The Great Transition*, 413–14. By the end of their talks, they would also release a statement saying that they had agreed on numerical limits on certain "non-deployed ballistic missiles and the warheads attributable to them"; see "Soviet-American Joint Statement, 10 February 1990," in Freedman, *Documents*, 469–71.

91. Baker with DeFrank, *The Politics of Diplomacy*, 204; on CFE, see Falkenrath, *Shaping Europe's Military Order*.

92. For an in-depth study of USSR attitudes to unity, see Rafael Biermann, *Zwischen Kreml und Kanzleramt: Wie Moskau mit der deutschen Einheit rang* (Paderborn: Ferdinand Schöningh, 1997).

93. "JAB notes from 2/7–9/90 Ministerial Mtgs., w/ USSR FM Shevardnadze, Moscow USSR," note "GERMANY 2/8/90," folder 14, box 108, 8c monthly files, series 8; see information about U.S.-USSR bilaterals, folder 13, box 176, 12b chapter files, series 12. Despite the fact that some of these documents are in the files used by the team of people drafting his autobiography, the final version of the book does not mention them. See the discussion of the February 7–9 meetings, Baker with DeFrank, *The Politics of Diplomacy*, 202–6.

94. "Из беседы М.С. Горбачева с Дж. Бейкером," February 9, 1990, МГ, 333–34, 338. Excerpt published and translated in GC. Original, Gorbachev: Разумеется, ясно, что расширение зоны НАТО является неприемлемым. Baker: Мы согласны с этим. (These documents are also summarized in Gorbachev, *Memoirs*, 528–29.) They agree with the summary of the conversation that Baker gave Kohl the next day; see "Schreiben des Außenministers Baker an Bundeskanzler Kohl, 10. Februar 1990," document 173, DESE, 793–94. See also "JAB notes from 2/9/90 mtg. w/USSR Pres. Gorbachev, Moscow, USSR," folder 12, box 176, 12b chapter files, series 12. Gates, who went to Moscow with Baker, also remembers Gorbachev saying that any "extension of the zone of NATO is unacceptable." Gates, *From the Shadows*, 490. Similar comments are in von Plato, *Die Vereinigung Deutschlands*, 244, based on his access to Soviet sources. See also Asmus, *Opening NATO's Door*, 4–5.

95. Gorbachev, *Memoirs*, 529.

96. Asmus, *Opening NATO's Door*, 4; Stent, *Russia and Germany Reborn*, 140–41, states that the U.S. position remained constant: "The record shows that no explicit promises on NATO expansion were made, but what was implied during the negotiations ultimately lies in the eyes of the beholder."

97. Dennis Ross, interview with author, November 17, 2008, Washington, DC; Baker with DeFrank, *The Politics of Diplomacy*, 206; Helmut Kohl, Kai Diekmann, and Ralf Georg Reuth, *Ich wollte Deutschlands Einheit* (Berlin: Ullstein, 1996), 268–69; Teltschik, *329 Tage*, 137. The full text of the letter appears in English in DESE, 793–94; citations to particular passages appear in the endnotes to the related text discussions.

98. "Schreiben des Außenministers Baker an Bundeskanzler Kohl," 793–94. This private note described in detail what Baker summarized for journalists at a midnight briefing the same day. As reported by Thomas Friedman in *The New York Times,* Baker "suggested for the first time that Washington might be prepared to accept a reunification of East and West Germany in which the unified country would not be a full member of NATO. . . ." Thomas Friedman, "Some Link to NATO," *The New York Times,* February 10, 1990, A1.

99. "Schreiben des Präsidenten Bush an Bundeskanzler Kohl, 9. Februar 1990," reproduced in English as document 170, DESE, 784–85; "Speech by NATO Secretary General Manfred Worner [*sic*], Hamburg, 8 February 1990," in Freedman, *Documents*, 462–66, especially 466. Zelikow remembers that Baker had not "internalized" the fact that "special military status" was the preferred wording in time for his conversation with Gorbachev, but that he would later. Zelikow and Rice, *Germany Unified*, 186–87, especially 423n62.

NOTES

100. Philip Zelikow, interview with author, July 27, 2008, and subsequent emails.

101. Teltschik, *329 Tage*, 135; J.D. Bindenagel, interview with author, June 28, 2008, phone conversation.

102. Both the Russian and West German records from this conversation are available, and they agree on the points cited above. See "Из беседы М.С. Горбачева с Г. Колем один на один," February 10, 1990, МГ, 339–55; "Gespräch des Bundeskanzlers Kohl mit Generalsekretär Gorbatschow, Moskau, 10. Februar 1990," document 174, DESE, 795–807. Kohl's exact statement was: "Natürlich könne die NATO ihr Gebiet nicht auf das heutige Gebiet der DDR ausdehnen." He asked Gorbachev if he could describe their talks as follows: "Sie seien sich darüber einig, daß die Entscheidung über die Einigung Deutschlands eine Frage sei, die die Deutschen jetzt selbst entscheiden müßten." Gorbachev replied only that the chancellor's summary was "sehr nahe an seinen Ausführungen." This was not the same as agreeing (see also DESE, 805); so it is not surprising that Kohl wanted to lock in this somewhat uncertain gain via publicizing it. On the subject of Chernobyl as a reference for what could go wrong with a nuclear power program, see Scott Sagan, *The Limits of Safety: Organizations, Accidents, and Nuclear Weapons* (Princeton, NJ: Princeton University Press, 1993).

103. *Tagesschau* and *heute journal* spezial, February 10, 1990, ZDF, KASPA. See also "Soviet-German Joint Statement, 10 February 1990," in Freedman, *Documents*, 472–75; "Delegationgespräch des Bundeskanzlers Kohl mit Generalsekretär Gorbatschow, Moskau, 10. Februar 1990," document 175, DESE, 808–11.

104. The text of Kohl's comments at the February 10, 1990 Moscow press conference is reproduced in DESE, 812–13. See also GDE, 4:247; Teltschik, *329 Tage*, 141–43.

105. James A. Baker III, interview with author, February 11, 2009, Houston; Philip Zelikow, "NATO Expansion Wasn't Ruled Out," *International Herald Tribune*, August 10, 1995; Zelikow and Rice, *Germany Unified*, 182–87 (quotation from 187).

106. For more on the origins and consequences of NATO enlargement, see Asmus, *Opening NATO's Door*, 4–5; Gates, *From the Shadows*, 490; John Kornblum and Michael Mandelbaum, "NATO Expansion, a Decade On," *American Interest* 3–5 (May–June 2008): 56–62; von Plato, *Die Vereinigung Deutschlands*, 244.

107. The GDR delegation was still working on the assumptions from the Dresden meeting—that there would be movement toward a confederative structure, and that considerable aid would come from the West in the meantime. However, reports that Kohl was no longer interested in what had been discussed in Dresden made it to the delegation before the trip. See "Anlage, Ergebnisse der 12. Sitzung des Rundtischgesprächs am 12. Februar 1990," in DA 3-12, and Ergänzung, DA 3-94, SAPMO. See also the round table preparations, ZRT-WD, 12. Sitzung, 703–20; GDE, 4:211.

108. The former dissidents would campaign under the play-on-words slogan "Artikel 23: Kein Anschluß unter dieser Nummer," but without success among the voters. For more on their campaign, see Andreas Rödder, *Deutschland Einig Vaterland* (Munich: Beck, 2009), chapter 4.

109. "Gespräch des Bundeskanzlers Kohl mit Ministerpräsident Modrow, Bonn, 13. Februar 1990," document 177, DESE, 814–19; "Gespräch des Bundesministers Seiters mit den Ministern ohne Geschäftsbereich der DDR, Bonn, 13. Februar 1990," document 178, DESE, 819–20; "Delegationsgespräch des Bundeskanzlers Kohl mit Ministerpräsident Modrow, Bonn, 13. Februar 1990," document 179, DESE, 821–26; "Positionen des RUNDEN TISCHES für die Verhandlungen Modrow/Kohl am 13./14. Februar 1990," Antrag 12/6, 12. Sitzung, 12.02.1990, in RHG, ZRT, Ordner 3.

110. Thaysen, *Der Runde Tisch*, 16, 91; ZRT-WD, 10. Sitzung. See also "Beschluß der AG Sicherheit des ZRT zur weiteren Auflösung der Hauptverwaltung Aufklärung," RHG, ZRT, 14. Sitzung, Ordner 4.

111. A draft of the resolution is available in "Vorlage 13/14, 13. Sitzung, 19. Februar," RHG, ZRT, Ordner 3; ZRT-WD, 13. Sitzung, 839.

112. On the role that the vision of a third way played in the East German opposition movement, see Christof Geisel, *Auf der Suche nach einem dritten Weg: Das politische Selbstverständnis der DDR-Opposition* (Berlin: Links, October 2005). The concept of competing visions of modernity comes, as mentioned in the Introduction, note 14, from James C. Scott, as interpreted by Odd Arne Westad; see Odd Arne Westad, "Bernath Lecture: The New International History of the Cold War: Three (Possible) Paradigms," *Diplomatic History* 24, no. 4 (Fall 2000): 551–65. In addition to its goal of devising a third way, the draft constitution that resulted also addressed the practicalities of designing a parliament and other law-giving bodies. For the sections of the draft containing information about the future parliament, see ZRT-WD, document 16/8, 5:679–711.

113. ZRT-WD, 16. Sitzung, March 12, 1990, 1100.

114. These sections of the draft constitution are in ZRT-WD, document 16/7, 5:673–78.

115. "Arbeitsgruppe 'Neue Verfassung der DDR' des Runden Tisches, Brief an alle Abgeordneten, 04.04.1989," RHG, ZRT, Ordner 9.

116. The SED saved some in its archive (see citations below), although it is hard to know how complete the collection is. Nonetheless, it mirrors popular attitudes at the time.

117. First two letters in DA 3-69, SAPMO, Briefe der Bevölkerung zur Wiedervereinigung, dated February 8 and 9, 1990. The names of the authors are deleted here, in compliance with German privacy laws for individuals who are not public figures, but are available at the archive. The last letter is anonymous, February 15, 1990, in DA 3-71, SAPMO.

118. Also in DA 3-69, SAPMO, dated February 9, 1990 and February 13, 1990.

119. DA 3-71, SAPMO, dated February 15, 1990.

120. DA 3-71, SAPMO, dated February 2, 1990; anonymous, DA 3-69, undated, SAPMO.

121. See Joachim Scholtyseck, *Die Aussenpolitik der DDR* (Munich: R. Oldenbourg Verlag, 2003), 45–46, which argues the following: "Immer klarer zeichnete sich ab, dass Gorbatschow seine politischen Visionen nicht einmal ansatzweise in die Tat umsetzen konnte." See also the critical comments by Valentin Falin in an interview with David Pryce-Jones, reprinted in David Pryce-Jones, *The Strange Death of the Soviet Empire* (New York: Metropolitan Books, 1995), 291.

122. Jacques Lévesque argues in his *The Enigma of 1989: The USSR and the Liberation of Eastern Europe* (Berkeley: University of California Press, 1997), 257, that "a somewhat slower transition in Prague and Berlin, which a more activist Soviet policy could have supported, would have allowed Gorbachev to better push ahead with his European policy. His prospects were excellent in the summer of 1989."

123. Charles S. Maier, *Dissolution: The Crisis of Communism and the End of East Germany* (Princeton, NJ: Princeton University Press, 1997), 57.

124. I am grateful to Jan-Werner Müller for these insights. His forthcoming chapter in the *Cambridge History of the Cold War* on intellectuals and the end of the German division promises to be very interesting.

NOTES TO CHAPTER 4

1. Max Weber, *Schriften zur Sozialgeschichte und Politik* (Stuttgart: Reclam), 320. Translation from Peter Lassmann and Ronald Speirs, eds., *Weber: Political Writings* (Cambridge: Cambridge University Press, 1994), 352. James Stevens Curl, *Oxford Dictionary of Architecture and Landscape Architecture* (Oxford: Oxford University Press, 1999), 602. Michael Frayn, *Democracy* (New York: Faber and Faber, 2003), 86.

NOTES

2. On the elections, see Jürgen W. Falter, "Wahlen 1990: Die demokratische Legitimation für die deutsche Einheit mit großen Überraschungen," in *Die Gestaltung der deutschen Einheit*, ed. Eckhard Jesse and Armin Mitter (Bonn: Bundeszentrale für politische Bildung, 1992), 163–88. The process of institutional transfer took place throughout Eastern Europe and has become a field of study in its own right. One of the best studies is Wade Jacoby, *The Enlargement of the European Union and NATO: Ordering from the Menu in Central Europe* (Cambridge: Cambridge University Press, 2004).

3. The definition of corporatism comes from Harold James, *Europe Reborn: A History, 1914–2000* (Harlow, UK: Pearson Longman, 2003.)

4. In this, Kohl was fulfilling the predictions of Eckart Kehr, author of *Der Primat der Innenpolitik* (Berlin: Gruyter, reprint 1970). For an overview of inner-German relations, see Heinrich Potthoff, *Im Schatten der Mauer: Deutschlandpolitik 1961 bis 1990* (Berlin: Ullstein, 1999). See also Robert Cooper, *The Breaking of Nations: Order and Chaos in the Twenty-First Century* (London: Atlantic Books, 2003), 102–13.

5. Acheson is cited in Charles A. Kupchan and Peter L. Trubowitz, "Grand Strategy for a Divided America," *Foreign Affairs* 86, no. 4 (July–August 2007): 82.

6. "Soviet Government Statement on Troop Withdrawal Pledge, 11 February 1990," TASS, translated and reprinted in Lawrence Freedman, ed., *Europe Transformed: Documents on the End of the Cold War—Key Treaties, Agreements, Statements, and Speeches* (New York: St. Martin's Press, 1990), 477–78.

7. See the calendars of Baker's travel schedule for February 1990, available in BP; Robert L. Hutchings, *American Diplomacy and the End of the Cold War: An Insider's Account of US Policy in Europe, 1989–1992* (Washington, DC: Wilson Center, 1997), 114; Philip Zelikow and Condoleezza Rice, *Germany Unified and Europe Transformed: A Study in Statecraft* (Cambridge, MA: Harvard University Press, 1995), 192. The trip, lasting February 5–13, included stops in Ireland, Czechoslovakia, the Soviet Union, Bulgaria, Romania, and Canada; it was followed immediately by another trip to the Andean Drug Summit in Cartagena, Colombia. On attendance at the conference, see "Treffen der Außenminister der NATO und der Warschauer Vertragsorganisation in Ottawa (12.-14.2.1990)," in Auswärtiges Amt, ed., *Deutsche Aussenpolitik 1990/91: Auf dem Weg zu einer europäischen Friedensordnung eine Dokumentation* (Bonn: Auswärtiges Amt, April 1991), 64–65.

8. See folder 11, box 176, 12b German unification, series 12, BP; Raymond Garthoff, *The Great Transition: American-Soviet Relations and the End of the Cold War* (Washington, DC: Brookings Institution Press, 1994), 414.

9. "Telefongespräch des Bundeskanzlers Kohl mit Präsident Bush, 13. Februar 1990," document 180, DESE, 826–28.

10. George Bush and Brent Scowcroft, *A World Transformed* (New York: Knopf, 1998), 240–41. The letter, published in English, reads as follows: "In no event will we allow the Soviet Union to use the Four Power mechanism as an instrument to try to force you to create the kind of Germany Moscow might want, at the pace Moscow might prefer." In "Schreiben des Präsidenten Bush an Bundeskanzler Kohl, 9. Februar 1990," document 170, DESE, 784–85.

11. "Executive Brief," DCI, NIC, March 1, 1990, 3: "The Kremlin will continue to work directly with Bonn in talks we will not be fully privy to. It has few, if any, blandishments to offer, and its ability to threaten lacks credibility. Nonetheless, the Soviets are likely to try to make Bonn think there is a strong possibility they will refuse to remove their troops from East Germany unless their security concerns are fully addressed. Moscow probably would also back any popularly-supported move by a new East German government for a neutral East Germany, hoping this would stall intra-German discussion on the future alignment of Germany." Released via FOIA.

12. Memo by Valentin Falin, "An M.S. [Gorbatschow] (Zum geplanten Treffen mit Helmut Kohl)," reprinted in German in Valentin Falin, *Konflikte im Kreml: Zur Vorgeschichte der deutschen Einheit und Auflösung der Sowjetunion* (Munich: Blessing Verlag, 1997), 314–16; discussion in text, 154. Falin dates this document as March 1990, but given its title—for the planned meeting with Kohl—and content, it seems to be from February of that year.

13. Memcon, the White House, "Telephone Call from Chancellor Helmut Kohl of the Federal Republic of Germany," February 13, 1990, 1:49 p.m., in FOIA 1999-0393-F, BPL; also available at the NSA and in CWIHPPC.

14. Hans-Dietrich Genscher, *Erinnerungen* (Berlin: Sielder, 1995), 726.

15. "Telefongespräch des Bundeskanzlers Kohl mit Präsident Bush, 13. Februar 1990," 828. The phrase "non-starter" appears in English in quotation marks in the German version; the U.S. version merely has Bush saying that the "35 won't work."

16. Memcon, the White House, "Telephone Call from Chancellor Helmut Kohl of the Federal Republic of Germany," February 13, 1990, 3:01–3:10 p.m. EST, in FOIA 1999-0393-F, BPL; also available at the NSA.

17. "Prime Minister's Meeting with the German Foreign Minister," summarized by her private secretary, n.d., but document explains that Genscher was visiting on his way back from Ottawa, released by the FCO via FOI. The Italians, in particular, would complain about being excluded. "Interview with Italian Foreign Minister, Gianni De Michelis, 15 February 1990," in Freedman, *Documents*, 489.

18. Genscher, *Erinnerungen*, 726; James A. Baker with Thomas A. DeFrank, *The Politics of Diplomacy: Revolution, War, and Peace, 1989–1992* (New York: G. P. Putnam's Sons, 1995), 214

19. Dennis Ross, interview with author, November 17, 2008, Washington, DC.

20. Baker with DeFrank, *The Politics of Diplomacy*, 215–16; "Statement by the Foreign Ministers Attending the 'Open Skies' Conference, Ottawa," in Freedman, *Documents*, 480.

21. Anatoly Chernyaev's introduction to МГ, xix.

22. Handwritten note from Baker to Gorbachev, March 28, 1990, folder 15, box 108, 8c monthly files, series 8, BP.

23. "EUR Daily Press Guidances—February 14, 1990," run by Margaret Tutwiler, in NSC, Wilson, FOIA 2001-1166-F, BPL. It is not clear who provided the answer cited above; not all of the commentators present were identified.

24. Philip Zelikow, interview with author, July 27, 2008, phone conversation and subsequent emails; "В.В. Загладин о своей беседе с К. Райс," February 12, 1990, МГ, 365–66. For more information on Zagladin, see his memoirs: Vadim Sagladin, *Und Jetzt Welt-Innen Politik: Die Außenpolitik der Perestroika* (Rosenheim: Horizonte, 1990).

25. Report entitled "Germany and NATO," from Charles Powell to Stephen Wall, February 10, 1990, released by CAB under FOI; and Briefing Papers, prepared by Security Policy Department, FCO, entitled "Nuclear Weapons on German Territory," March 1, 1990, released by CAB under FOI. "Konstituierende Sitzung der Arbeitsgruppe Außen- und Sicherheitspolitik des Kabinettausschusses Deutsche Einheit, Bonn, 14. Feb. 1990," document 182, DESE, 830–31; "Vermerk des Vortragenden Legationsrats I Kaestner, Bonn 15. Februar 1990," document 184, DESE, 833–34. See also Stephen Szabo, *The Diplomacy of German Unification* (New York: St. Martin's Press, 1992), 103; Hanns Jürgen Küsters, "Entscheidung für die deutsche Einheit," DESE, 111.

26. Philip Zelikow, interview with author, July 27, 2008, phone conversation and subsequent emails. See also Zelikow and Rice, *Germany Unified*, 186–87; James M. Goldgeier, *Not Whether but When: The US Decision to Enlarge NATO* (Washington, DC: Brookings, 1999), 15.

NOTES

27. Bush and Scowcroft, *A World Transformed*, 243.

28. Handwritten notes on side of "Moscow Domestic Service in Russian 1900 GMT 20 Feb 90," Condoleezza Rice, NSC, PRS files, FOIA 2001-1166-F, BPL.

29. Szabo, *Diplomacy*, 59.

30. For a detailed and insightful discussion of the conduct of the 2 + 4 talks in the context of German unification, see Andreas Rödder, *Deutschland Einig Vaterland* (Munich: Beck, 2009), chapter 5.

31. The Thatcher quotation comes from a report entitled "German Unification: NATO and Security Aspects," from C.D. Powell to J.S. Wall, March 5, 1990, released by CAB under FOI.

32. "Memorandum for William Sittmann, From Philip Zelikow, Subject: Memorandum of Conversation between the President and Prime Minister Margaret Thatcher of the United Kingdom in Bermuda on April 13," forwarded on May 3, 1990, available at www.margaretthatcher.org. Bush and Mitterrand met on April 19, 1990, in Key Largo. Just before the meeting, Bush sent a telegram to Mitterrand, summarizing what he wanted to discuss. This telegram duplicated nearly word-for-word the language used with Thatcher: ". . . the two plus four should not negotiate over Germany's right to remain a full member of NATO; should not decide the fate of allied conventional or nuclear forces on the territory of the current FRG; should not agree on the future size of united Germany's armed forces; and should not replace the old four power rights with new discriminatory limits on German sovereignty—a prescription for future instability." Bush added that "NATO is the only plausible justification in my country for the American military presence in Europe. If NATO is allowed to wither because it has no meaningful political place in the new Europe, the basis for a long-term U.S. military commitment can die with it." Telegram from White House to Elysée Palace, 17 April 1990, in 5 AG 4/EG 170, Archives Nationales, Paris; telegram in English language. The French Foreign Ministry interpreted this telegram as evidence of the German and American desire to reduce the role of the 2 + 4 to the absolute minimum: see "NOTE POUR LE DIRECTEUR," Direction d'Europe, 17 April 1990, in 5 AG 4/CDM 36, dossier 2, Archives Nationales, Paris.

33. All of the Baker quotations in the paragraphs above come from "Proposed Agenda for Meeting with the President, Friday, February 16, 1990, 1:30pm," with handwritten notes by Baker, folder 7, box 115, 8e White House meetings and notes, series 8, BP. See also Hutchings, *American Diplomacy*, 109–14.

34. Helmut Kohl, *Erinnerungen 1982–1990* (Munich: Droemer, 2005), 1080.

35. Horst Teltschik, *329 Tage: Innenansichten der Einigung* (Berlin: Siedler, 1991), 159.

36. On Polish questions, see letter from Charles Powell to Richard Gozney, FCO, February 23, 1990, released from CAB by FOI; "Schreiben des Ministerpräsident Mazowiecki an Bundeskanzler Kohl, Warschau, 30. Januar 1990," document 154, DESE, 744–45; "Artikel von Prof. Dr. Krzystof Skubiszewski, Minister für Auswärtige Angelegenheiten der Republik Polen, in der Zeitschrift 'Europa-Archiv,' 'Die völkerrechtliche und staatliche Einheit des deutschen Volkes und die Entwicklung in Europa,' Bonn, 7. Februar 1990," with postscript from March 25, 1990, document 137 in Hans-Adolf Jacobsen, ed., *Bonn-Warschau 1945–1991* (Cologne: Verlag Wissenschaft und Politik, 1992), 510–18. See also Timothy Garton Ash, *In Europe's Name: Germany and the Divided Continent* (New York: Vintage Books, 1993), 353; report entitled "German Unification: The Role of the CSCE 35," from J.S. Wall to C.D. Powell, February 19, 1990, released by CAB via FOI.

37. "Gespräch des Bundeskanzlers Kohl mit Präsident Bush, Camp David, 24. Feb. 1990," document 192, DESE, 860–73, especially 863–64; Helmut Kohl, *Erinnerungen 1990–1994* (Munich: Droemer, 2007), 36.

38. See "Federal Chancellor Kohl on 'The German Question and European Responsibility,' Paris, 17 January 1990," in Freedman, *Documents*, 416–17; "Speech by Tadeusz Mazowiecki, Prime

Minister of Poland," February 21, 1990, in Freedman, *Documents*, 488; "Vorlage des Regierungsdirektors Mertes und des Legationsrats I Hanz an Bundeskanzler Kohl, Bonn, 27. Feb. 1990," document 195, DESE, 878–79; see also Zelikow and Rice, *Germany Unified*, 215.

39. "Gespräch des Bundeskanzlers Kohl mit Präsident Bush," DESE, 863.

40. See Hutchings, *American Diplomacy*.

41. Bush and Scowcroft, *A World Transformed*, 253. The quotations in this book correspond closely to the documents that have been released, so presumably the quotations from unreleased documents, such as this one (the U.S. version of the Camp David meeting is not yet available in full) may be used with a high degree of confidence. For an analysis of this particular comment, see Stephen G. Brooks and William C. Wohlforth, "Economic Constraints and the Turn towards Superpower Cooperation in the 1980s," in *The Last Decade of the Cold War: From Conflict Escalation to Conflict Transformation*, ed. Olav Njølstad (London: Frank Cass, 2004), 105–6.

42. Interviews by the author (anonymity requested); "Gespräch des Bundeskanzlers Kohl mit Präsident Bush, Camp David, 24. Feb. 1990," 868–69. See also Zelikow and Rice, *Germany Unified*, 215; GDE, 4:269, 466.

43. Kohl, *Erinnerungen 1982–1990*, commentary on photos between 688 and 689; Teltschik, *329 Tage*, 161.

44. Teltschik, *329 Tage*, 162.

45. "Comments at Joint Press Conference by Chancellor Kohl and President Bush," in Freedman, *Documents*, 503; see also Küsters, "Entscheidung für die deutsche Einheit," 120.

46. He complained to Bush in particular about Kohl's evasiveness on the Polish border question when the U.S. president called a few days later to give him a summary of events at Camp David. For information on the call, see "Из телефонного разговора М.С. Горбачева с Дж. Бушем," February 28, 1990, МГ, 376–78; Bush and Scowcroft, *A World Transformed*, 257. Scowcroft briefed Teltschik on it afterward: "Mitteilung des Sicherheitsberaters Scowcroft an Ministerialdirektor Teltschik," February 28, 1990, document 199, DESE, 898.

47. "Gespräch des Bundeskanzlers Kohl mit Präsident Bush, Camp David, 25. Feb. 1990," document 194, DESE, 874–77. See also Zelikow and Rice, *Germany Unified*, 212–15.

48. The text of Articles 23 and 146, both before and after 1990, is on the website of the Bundeszentrale für politische Bildung, available at http://www.bpb.de. The expert commentary comes from Henry Ashby Turner Jr., *Germany from Partition to Unification*, 2nd ed. (New Haven, CT: Yale University Press, 1992).

49. Schäuble was attacked on October 12, 1990, in Oppenau/Südbaden; for more details, see his autobiography, dictated to coauthors from his hospital bed where he was recovering from the assassination attempt: Wolfgang Schäuble, *Der Vertrag: Wie ich über die deutsche Einheit verhandelte* (Munich: Knaur, 1991). For extensive details on the inner-German process of unification, see GDE, vol. 3.

50. "Aufzeichnung des Bundesministers des Innern, 27. Februar 1990, Überlegungen zu verfassungsrechtlichen Fragen im Zusammenhang mit der Einigung Deutschlands," document 196, DESE, 879–86.

51. Turner, *Partition to Unification*, 127–28; Adrian Webb, *Germany since 1945* (London: Longman, 1998), 26.

52. "Aufzeichnung des Bundesministers des Innern," DESE, 880.

53. "Aufzeichnung des Bundesministers des Innern," DESE, 883.

54. "Konstituierende Sitzung der Arbeitsgruppe Außen- und Sicherheitspolitik des Kabinettausschusses Deutsche Einheit," document 182, DESE, 830–31.

NOTES

55. Teltschik, *329 Tage*, 164; interview with Eduard Shevardnadze by TASS, March 7, 1990, in NSC, PRS, Condoleezza Rice files, FOIA 2001-1166-F, BPL. This interview was highlighted by Zelikow for Robert Blackwill's attention. Teltschik scrutinzed this interview as well; see "Vorlage des Ministerialdirektors Teltschik an Bundeskanzler Kohl, Bonn, 9. März 1990," document 211, DESE, 921–23.

56. Schäuble, *Der Vertrag*, 59–60.

57. Kohl, *Erinnerungen 1990–1994*, 40–42,

58. Kohl, *Erinnerungen 1990–1994*, 37–47; Helmut Kohl, Kai Diekmann, and Ralf Georg Reuth, *Ich wollte Deutschlands Einheit* (Berlin: Ullstein, 1996), 283–84; Gerhard A. Ritter, *Der Preis der deutschen Einheit: Die Wiedervereinigung und die Krise des Sozialstaats* (Munich: Beck, 2006), 35–37; Schäuble, *Der Vertrag*, 293; Szabo, *Diplomacy*, 26. Information about Ulrich and Thomas de Maizière, respectively, is available on the current websites of the Bundeswehr and the Bundeskanzleramt, http://www.bundeswehr.de and http://www.bundeskanzler.de. For more on the election campaign, see GDE, 3: 159–65.

59. "Schreiben des Staatssekretärs Köhler an Bundesminister Seiters, Bonn, 14. März 1990," documents 219–19A, DESE, 947–50. On the way in which Kohl made this decision, see David Marsh, *The Euro* (New Haven, CT: Yale University Press, 2009), 139–46. As Marsh puts it, the decision "suspended the principles of financial probity on which West Germany had built its forty-year post-war success. . . . It was the moment when Germany served notice that the D-Mark, the cornerstone of Europe's currency stabilisation arrangements, would become . . . a force for disturbance rather than stability." The head of the Bundesbank would eventually resign, in May 1991, as a belated protest over what he considered to be "Kohl's reckless financing of German unification."

60. Kohl, *Erinnerungen 1990–1994*, 42; Ritter, *Der Preis der deutschen Einheit*, 31; Angela Stent, *Russia and Germany Reborn: Unification, the Soviet Collapse, and the New Europe* (Princeton, NJ: Princeton University Press, 1999), 117; Teltschik, *329 Tage*, 129.

61. "Vorlage des Ministerialdirektors Teltschik an Bundeskanzler Kohl, Bonn, 28. Feb. 1990," documents 198, 895, in DESE, 893–97; see also 771n1.

62. The troop numbers come from Garthoff, *The Great Transition*, 413. On the Hungarian troop withdrawal in particular, see Csaba Békés, "Back to Europe: The International Background of the Political Transition in Hungary, 1988–90," in *The Roundtable Talks of 1989: The Genesis of Hungarian Democracy, Analysis and Documents*, ed. András Bozóki (Budapest: Central European University Press, 2002); "Agreement concerning the Withdrawal of Soviet Troops Temporarily Stationed on the Territory of the Hungarian Republic," in Freedman, *Documents*, 510–12. See also "Из беседы М.С. Горбачева с А. Дубчеком," May 21, 1990, МГ, 446–47; "Gespräch des Bundeskanzlers Kohl mit Staatspräsident Mitterrand, Paris, 15. Februar 1990," document 187, DESE, 842–52.

63. "55. Deutsch-französischen Konsultationen, Paris, 26. April 1990," document 257, DESE, 1056–59. A telegram from Bonn confirms these events and provides part of the information quoted above; "Telegram, from Amembassy Bonn to Secstate Washdc," May 4, 1990, released by the State Department via FOIA.

64. Kohl made remarks to this effect in "Gespräch des Bundeskanzlers Kohl mit Außenminister Arens, Bonn, 15. Feb. 1990," document 186, DESE, 839–42.

65. The East German Volkskammer, in its February 20–21, 1990 session, finally approved an election law; the records from the debate are available in the Bundesarchiv, Berlin. See also Kohl, *Erinnerungen 1990–1994*, 47. Kohl told the UK foreign minister that he believed that East Germans had intentionally delayed passage of an election law. See "Gespräch des Bundeskanzlers Kohl mit Außenminister Hurd, Bonn, 12. März 1990," document 214, DESE, 932–35.

66. The letters and *Bild* clipping were sent to the round table. See DA 3-70, ZRT, Briefe der Bevölkerung, Wahlredner, SAPMO.

67. "Telefongespräch des Bundeskanzlers Kohl mit Premierminister Mulroney, 21. Feb. 1990," document 190, DESE, 855–57.

68. Teltschik, *329 Tage*, 154.

69. The Polish government had reacted to hints that this announcement might be coming: "Polish Government Statement, 1 March 1990," in Freedman, *Documents*, 504.

70. Ritter, *Der Preis der deutschen Einheit*, 48; Horst Teltschik, interview with author, June 13, 2008, phone conversation.

71. "Vorlage des Ministerialdirektors Teltschik an Bundeskanzler Kohl," document 198, DESE, 896; for the details of the agreements from 1950 and 1953, see document 92, DESE, 534n9; for its use in an "Entschließungsantrag . . . der Fraktionen der CDU/CSU und der FDP," see document 204A, DESE, 913. See also Teltschik, *329 Tage*, 165–66; "The Polish Border: Text of Bundestag Resolution, 8 March 1990," in Freedman, *Documents*, 513. For historical background on Stalin's relations with Eastern Europe, see Joseph P. Held, ed., *The Columbia History of Eastern Europe in the Twentieth Century* (New York: Columbia University Press, 1992); Melvyn P. Leffler, *For the Soul of Mankind: The United States, the Soviet Union, and the Cold War* (New York: Hill and Wang, 2007); Andrej Paczkowski, *The Spring Will Be Ours: Poland and Poles from the Occupation to Freedom*, trans. Jane Cave (University Park: Pennsylvania State University Press, 2003); Vladislav Zubok, *A Failed Empire: The Soviet Union in the Cold War from Stalin to Gorbachev* (Chapel Hill: University of North Carolina Press, 2007).

72. "Entwurf eines Entschließungsantrages der Fraktionen der CDU/CSU und der FDP," Bonn, n.d., but from context between March 2 and 6, 1990, document 204a, DESE, 913.

73. "Vorlage des Vortragenden Legationsrats I Ueberschaer an Ministrialdirektor Teltschik, Bonn, 6. März 1990," document 206, DESE, 915–16.

74. See "Интервью М.С. Горбачева газете «Правда»," March 7, 1990, МГ, 381–84; "President Gorbachev Interview to Soviet and German Journalists," in Freedman, *Documents*, 507. Teltschik thought that this was just a negotiating tactic and that really the Soviet position still contained flexibility; see "Vorlage des Ministerialdirektors Teltschik an Bundeskanzler Kohl," DESE, 921–23.

75. For more on the domestic political resistance to Kohl's actions toward Poland, see Rödder, *Deutschland Einig Vaterland*, chapter 5.

76. See DESE, 912n1.

77. Teltschik, *329 Tage*, 166–70.

78. "Vermerk über ein Gespräch von UdSSR-Außenminister Eduard Schewardnadse mit Ibrahim Böhme, Vorsitzender der SPD in der DDR, am 2. März 1990," document 65, in Detlef Nakath and Gerd-Rüdiger Stephan, eds., *Countdown zur deutschen Einheit: Eine dokumentierte Geschichte der deutsch-deutschen Beziehungen 1987–1990* (Berlin: Dietz, 1996), 313–19.

79. "Vermerk über die Begegnung einer DDR-Regierungsdelegation unter Leitung von Hans Modrow mit Michail Gorbatschow, KPdSU-Generalsekretär, am 6. März 1990," document 67, in Nakath and Stephan, *Countdown*, 320–25; quotation from 322. "Интервью М.С. Горбачева газете «Правда»," March 7, 1990, МГ, 381–84.

80. "Conférence de presse conjointe, March 9, 1990, in François Mitterrand, *De l'Allemagne, de la France* (Paris: Editions Odile Jacob, April 1996), 213–18. For the West German reaction to this press conference, see "Vorlage des Ministerialdirigenten Hartmann an Kohl, Bonn, 13. März 1990," document 216, DESE, 937–41.

81. "Gespräch des Bundeskanzlers Kohl mit Staatspräsident Mitterrand," DESE, 849; "Telefongespräch des Bundeskanzlers Kohl mit Staatspräsident Mitterrand, 5. März 1990," document 203, DESE, 909–12, quotation from 911; "Telefongespräch des Bundeskanzlers Kohl mit Staatspräsident Mitterrand, 14. März 1990," document 218, DESE, 943–47.

NOTES

82. "Interview by the French President, M. Francois [*sic*] Mitterrand, with French Regional News-papers," in Freedman, *Documents*, 481–84.

83. Mitterrand cited in Bush and Scowcroft, *A World Transformed*, 256.

84. "Telefongespräch des Bundeskanzlers Kohl mit Staatspräsident Mitterrand," DESE, 943–47; Kohl, *Erinnerungen 1990–1994*, 45.

85. On Soviet attitudes to Article 23, see Küsters, "Entscheidung für die deutsche Einheit," 135; Teltschik, *329 Tage*, 185.

86. Memorandum from Harvey Sicherman to S/P—Dennis Ross and C—Robert Zoellick, March 12, 1990, folder 14, box 176, series 12, BP. This memo is the source of all of the Sicherman quotations in these pages. See also "Erste Gesprächsrunde Zwei plus Vier auf Beamtenebene, Bonn, 14. März 1990," document 220, DESE, 950–52.

87. Percy Cradock, *In Pursuit of British Interests: Reflections on Foreign Policy under Margaret Thatcher and John Major* (London: John Murray, 1997), 115; interview with Lord Douglas Hurd, London, March 17, 2009.

88. As Angela Stent rightly points out, it is remarkable that Gorbachev never made such an offer. See Stent, *Russia and Germany*, 121.

89. Gyula Horn's comment is discussed in Mastny and Byrne, *Cardboard Castle,* 71; the direct quotation from Horn is in Mark Kramer, "The Myth of the No-NATO-Enlargement Pledge to Russia," *Washington Quarterly* 32 no. 2 (April 2009), 41; see also 58n16 in Kramer for a de-scription of the Polish proposal by Jan Rylukowski.

90. Harvey Sicherman, interview with author, December 12, 2008, phone conversation.

91. Reuters news release, March 13, 1990, NSC files, Wilson, FOIA 2001-1166-F, BPL; Teltschik, *329 Tage*, 170.

92. Teltschik, *329 Tage*, 173.

93. See my "A Small Town in (East) Germany: The Erfurt Meeting of 1970 and the Dynamics of Cold War Détente," *Diplomatic History* 25, no. 1 (Winter 2001): 85–104.

94. See Mary Elise Sarotte, *Dealing with the Devil* (Chapel Hill: University of North Carolina Press, 2001). The play was Michael Frayn, *Democracy* (quoted and cited in the epigraph to this chapter). See also Willy Brandt, *". . . was zusammengehört"* (Bonn: Dietz, 1993), and *My Life in Politics* (New York: Viking, 1991); GDE, 3:159–64.

95. For more about the campaign, see GDE, 3:160; Teltschik, *329 Tage*, 173–77.

96. Memcon, the White House, "Telephone Call from Chancellor Helmut Kohl," March 15, 1990, 8:37–9:01 a.m., in FOIA 1999-0393-F, BPL. The German version of the conversation contains similar comments; see "Telefongespräch des Bundeskanzlers Kohl mit Bush, 15. März 1990," document 211, DESE, 952–55.

97. "Gespräch des Ministerialdirektors Teltschik mit Botschafter Karski und dem stellvertretenden Abteilungsleiter Sulek, Bonn, 19. März 1990," document 223, DESE, 956–60.

98. For the exact election results, see DESE, 956n1; Ritter, *Der Preis der deutschen Einheit*, 37–39.

99. ZDF, March 18, 1990, KASPA. For more on the history of socialism in the twentieth century, see Donald Sassoon, *One Hundred Years of Socialism: The West European Left in the Twentieth Century* (London: Tauris, 1996).

100. Kohl, Diekmann, and Reuth, *Ich wollte*, 136–37.

101. Küsters, "Entscheidung für die deutsche Einheit," 135; Teltschik, *329 Tage*, 182–83.

102. The U.S. and the West German versions, the basis of this and the preceding paragraph, are largely but not entirely identical. See Memcon, "Telephone Call from Chancellor Helmut Kohl

of West Germany," March 1990, 8:31–8:59 a.m., in FOIA 1999-0393-F, BPL; "Telefongespräch des Bundeskanzlers Kohl mit Bush, 20. März 1990," document 224, DESE, 961–63. The direct English quotations here are taken from the U.S. original in that language. See also Teltschik, *329 Tage*, 176–79. For more information on West German dealings with Poland after the election, see "Gespräch des Ministerialdirektors Teltschik mit Botschafter Karski und dem stellvertretenden Abteilungsleiter Sulek," DESE, 956–60.

103. "Schreiben des Bundeskanzlers an Ministerpräsiden Mazowiecki, Bonn, 4. April 1990," document 242, DESE, 1007–9; "Vorlage des Ministerialdirektors Teltschik an Bundeskanzler Kohl, Bonn, 30. April 1990," document 263, DESE, 1069–71.

104. "Vorlage des Vortragenden Legationsrats I Kastner an Bundeskanzler Kohl, Bonn, 11. Mai 1990," document 275, DESE, 1106–7, reports on the criticism of a member of parliament about what Kohl's government was doing. For more on the final German-Polish treaty, see Jacobsen, *Bonn-Warschau*, 21, 48.

105. President Bush's restrained response to the Lithuanian declaration of independence was calculated to support Gorbachev, but he was criticized at home for it. See Timothy Naftali, *George H.W. Bush* (New York: Times Books, 2007), 92.

106. "Vorlage des Ministerialdirektors Teltschik an Bundeskanzler Kohl, Bonn, 23. März 1990," document 228, DESE, 970–75.

107. Telegram, "US Del Secretary Namibia, to White House Wash DC, 20 March 1990," "Memorandum for the President," State Department, released via FOIA.

108. Zelikow and Rice, *Germany Unified*, 246; Schäuble, *Der Vertrag*, 297.

109. "Schreiben des Bundesministers Blüm an Bundeskanzler Kohl, Bonn, 27. März 1990," document 231, DESE, 979–80; "Schreiben des Bundesbankpräsidenten Pöhl an Bundeskanzler Kohl, Frankfurt (Main), 30. März 1990," document 239, DESE, 1002–3; "Vorlage des Ministerialdirigenten Duisberg an Bundeskanzler Kohl, Bonn, 19. April 1990," document 248, 1018–20; Ritter, *Der Preis der deutschen Einheit*, 202–4.

110. "Address by the President of the European Commission, Jacques Delors, to the European Parliament," in Freedman, *Documents*, 418–23; N. Piers Ludlow, "Naturally Supportive," 161–73; and Hans Stark, "Helmut Kohl and the Maastricht Process," both in *Europe and the End of the Cold War*, ed. Frédéric Bozo, Marie-Pierre Rey, N. Piers Ludlow, and Leopoldo Nuti (London: Routledge, 2008), 220–58; GDE, 4:420–42; Ritter, *Der Preis der deutschen Einheit*, 58–59. For more on the history of the German division and its impact on European integration, see N. Piers Ludlow, ed., *European Integration and the Cold War* (London: Routledge, 2007).

111. "Gespräch des Bundeskanzlers Kohl mit Staatspräsident Mitterrand," DESE, 849; Ritter, *Der Preis der deutschen Einheit*, 59.

112. "Gespräch des Ministerialdirigenten Hartmann und des Ministerialrats Ludewig mit Präsident Delors, Paris, 16. Feb. 1990," document 188, DESE, 852–53.

113. "Roland Dumas, French Foreign Minister, Interview 9 February 1990," in Freedman, *Documents*, 467. Rice particularly noted these remarks, saying that they were "worth reading carefully: Definitive French view." See Condoleeza Rice files, NSC, PRS, FOIA 2001-1166-F, BPL.

114. "Article by Roland Dumas, French Minister of Foreign Affairs, Published in the New York Times, 13 March 1990," in Freedman, *Documents*, 508–9; letter from Charles Powell to J. S. Wall, February 20, 1990, released by CAB via FOI.

115. Douglas Hurd, *Memoirs* (London: Little, Brown, 2003), 383.

116. "What the PM Learnt about the Germans," *Independent*, July 15, 1990. For accounts from participants, see Gordon Craig, "Die Chequers-Affäre," *Vierteljahresheft für Zeitgeschichte* 39, no. 4 (October 1991): 611–23; Fritz Stern, *Five Germanys I Have Known* (New York: Farrar,

Straus and Giroux, 2006), 474. Stern accuses Powell of attributing Thatcher's views to the group as a whole, when, Stern argues, the group actually disagreed with her. See also John Campbell, *Margaret Thatcher* (London: Pimlico, 2004), 634–35; and on the Thatcher era generally, see E.H.H. Green, *Thatcher* (London: Hodder Arnold, 2006). On the role of Chequers seminars in Thatcher's foreign policymaking, see Archie Brown, "The Change to Engagement in Britain's Cold War Policy: The Origins of the Thatcher-Gorbachev Relationship," *Journal of Cold War Studies* 10, no. 3 (Summer 2008): 4n2. I am also grateful to Charles Powell for a discussion of these events. A document that Powell sent to at least one participant in advance of the seminar (listing questions to be discussed) and a copy of the summary that he wrote afterward are both available on line at www.margaretthatcher.org.

117. "Proposed Agenda for Meeting with the President, Friday, February 16, 1990, 1:30 p.m.," BP.

118. GDE, 4:392–93; Zelikow and Rice, *Germany Unified*, 234–35.

119. "20. Deutsch-britisch Konsultationen, London, 30. März 1990," document 238, DESE, 996–1001; see also Küsters, "Entscheidung für die deutsche Einheit," 28–29.

120. Kohl, *Erinnerungen 1990–1994*, 61.

121. Telegram, "From Amembassy London to Secstate Washdc," "For the President and Secretary of State from Catto," April 11, 1990, "Subject: Your Meeting with Thatcher in Bermuda," released via FOIA to the State Department.

122. "JAB notes . . . mtgs. w/ POTUS & UK PM Thatcher," folder 16, box 108, 8c monthly files, series 8; "Note to Prime Minister dated 17 April 1990: Bermuda Meeting," released by the FCO under FOI.

123. Telegram, "From Amembassy Bonn to Secstate Washdc," April 5, 1990, released by the State Department via FOIA. On the significance of the Dublin meeting, see Frédéric Bozo, "France, German Unification, and European Integration," in *Europe and the End of the Cold War*, ed. Frédéric Bozo, Marie-Pierre Rey, N. Piers Ludlow, and Leopoldo Nuti (London: Routledge, 2008), 157; he argues against Zelikow and Rice, saying that Dublin did not constitute a hasty rearguard action by the French.

124. "Vorlage des Ministerialdirektors Teltschik an Bundeskanzler Kohl," Bonn, April 3, 1990, "Betr.: Vorbereitung Sonder-ER Dublin 28. April 1990," document 241, DESE, 1005–6. See also Küsters, "Entscheidung für die deutsche Einheit," 143–44.

125. "Initiative Kohl-Mitterrand zur Europäischen Union: Botschaft des Staatspräsidenten der Französischen Republik, François Mitterrand, und des Bundeskanzlers der Bundesrepublik Deutschland, Helmut Kohl, an den irischen Premierminister und amtierenden Präsidenten des Europäischen Rates, Charles Haughey, vom 18. April 1990," in Auswärtiges Amt, ed., *Aussenpolitik der Bundesrepublik Deutschland: Dokumente von 1949 bis 1994* (Cologne: Verlag Wissenschaft und Politik, 1995), 669–70. On the conflicts, see "Vorlage des Vortragenden Legationsrats I Bitterlich an Ministerialdirektor Teltschik, Bonn, 6 Apr. 1990," document 243, DESE, 1010–11.

126. GDE, 2:408–9; GDE, 4:377, 410–18; Philip Zelikow, interview with author, July 27, 2008, phone conversation and subsequent emails; Frédéric Bozo, *Mitterrand, la fin de la guerre froide et l'unification allemande: De Yalta à Maastricht* (Paris: Odile Jacob, 2005), 24–25, which points out that of all the factors determining Mitterrand's policies toward German unification, his hopes that he could use it to shape Europe's future was the most important. As Bozo puts it, this factor, "sans doute le plus déterminant pour expliquer la politique française face aux événements considérés, concerne les enjeux d'avenir : c'est au nom d'une certaine vision de l'après-guerre froide—et du rôle et des intérêts de la France dans celui-ci—que la diplomatie mitterrandienne aura mis en avant une volonté forte d'encadrer et de canaliser ces mêmes événements." On this topic, see also Elke Bruck, *François Mitterrands Deutschlandbild: Perzeption und*

Politik im Spannungsfeld deutschland-, europa-, und sicherheitspolitischen Entscheidungen, 1989–1992 (Frankfurt: Peter Lang, 2003); Samy Cohen et al., *Mitterrand et la sortie de la guerre froide* (Paris: Presses Universitaires de France, 1998).

127. Hubert Védrine, *Les mondes de François Mitterrand* (Paris: Fayard, 1996), 445; Frédéric Bozo, "Mitterand's France, the End of the Cold War, and German Unification: A Reappraisal," *Cold War History* 7, no. 4 (2007): 467. For more on West German foreign relations and the EC, see also Helga Haftendorn, "German Unification and European Integration Are But Two Sides of One Coin: The FRG, Europe, and the Diplomacy of German Unification," in *Europe and the End of the Cold War*, ed. Frédéric Bozo, Marie-Pierre Rey, N. Piers Ludlow, and Leopoldo Nuti (London: Routledge, 2008), 135–47, and *Coming of Age: German Foreign Policy since 1945*, trans. Deborah S. Kaiser (Lanham, MD: Rowman and Littlefield, 2006).

128. "Amembassy Paris to Secstate Washdc," April 27, 2008, released by State Department via FOIA.

129. Küsters, "Entscheidung für die deutsche Einheit," 157; Ludlow, "Naturally Supportive," 168–69; Teltschik, *329 Tage*, 211. On the impact of unification on West and united Germany's policies toward Europe, see Jeffrey Anderson, *German Unification and the Union of Europe* (Cambridge: Cambridge University Press, 1999); see also Eberhard Eichendorfer, "Internationale Sozialpolitik," in *1989–1994 Bundesrepublik Deutschland: Sozialpolitik im Zeichen der Vereinigung*, vol. 3, *Geschichte der Sozialpolitik in Deutschland seit 1945*, ed. Gerhard A. Ritter (Baden-Baden: Nomos Verlag, 2007), 1079–103.

130. Bayerischer Rundfunk, Munich, radio report on Kohl's speech to the Bundestag, May 10, 1990, copy in NSC Zelikow files, FOIA 2001-1166-F, BPL.

131. Ritter, *Der Preis der deutschen Einheit*, 19, 58–60; W. Suraska, *How the Soviet Union Disappeared: An Essay on the Causes of Dissolution* (Durham, NC: Duke University Press, 1998), 105; see also GDE, 4:141–48, 221.

NOTES TO CHAPTER 5

1. Thucydides, 1.774; Jürgen Habermas, *Die Neue Unübersichtlichkeit* (Frankfurt: Suhrkamp, 1985), 142.

2. Quoted anonymously in Angela Stent, *Russia and Germany Reborn: Unification, the Soviet Collapse, and the New Europe* (Princeton, NJ: Princeton University Press, 1999), 126.

3. Robert M. Gates, *From the Shadows: The Ultimate Insider's Story of Five Presidents and How They Won the Cold War* (New York: Touchstone, 1996), 492.

4. Gerhard A. Ritter, *Der Preis der deutschen Einheit: Die Wiedervereinigung und die Krise des Sozialstaats* (Munich: Beck, 2006), 39.

5. "Erklärung der Volkskammer der DDR vom 12.4.1990 (Auszug)," document 15, in Auswärtiges Amt, ed., *Deutsche Aussenpolitik 1990/91: Auf dem Weg zu einer europäischen Friedensordnung eine Dokumentation* (Bonn: Auswärtiges Amt, April 1991), 111.

6. "Из беседы М.С. Горбачева с Л. де Мезьером," April 29, 1990, МГ, 409–23; "Prime Minister's Meeting with the Prime Minister of the GDR," June 27, 1990, summary sent by Charles Powell, 10 Downing Street, to J. S. Wall, FCO.

7. Meckel became the leading figure of the East German SPD after his colleague, Ibrahim Böhme, resigned amid allegations that he had worked for the Stasi; GDE, 4:315.

8. Markus Meckel, *Selbstbewußt in die deutsche Einheit* (Berlin: Berlin Verlag, 2001), 140–41; Ilko-Sascha Kowalczuk and Tom Sello, eds., *Für ein freies Land mit freien Menschen: Opposition und Widerstand in Biographien und Fotos* (Berlin: Robert-Havemann-Gesellschaft, 2006), 212–15, 224–25; Stephen Szabo, *The Diplomacy of German Unification* (New York: St. Martin's Press, 1992), 26–27; "German Unification: Official Level Two Plus Four, Bonn, 22 May,

released by the FCO via FOI; Ritter, *Der Preis der deutschen Einheit,* 45; Eppelmann comments come from "Memorandum of the Eppelman-Iazov Conversation, April 29, 1990," document 152, in Vojtech Mastny and Malcolm Byrne, eds., *A Cardboard Castle? An Inside History of the Warsaw Pact* (New York: CEU Press, 2005), 670–73; and "Records of the Political Consultative Committee Meeting in Moscow, June 7, 1990" document 153, also in Mastny and Byrne, eds., *A Cardboard Castle?* 674–77. The Bush statement to Kohl was reported by Teltschik on a visit to Paris: see "COMPTE RENDU DU DEJEUNER DE JACQUES ATTALI AVEC HORST TELTSCHIK (jeudi 15 mars 1990)," Présidence de la République, Le Chargé de Mission, in 5 AG 4/CDM33, Archives Nationales, Paris.

9.   "Gespräch des Staatssekretärs Bertele mit Ministerpräsident Modrow," Berlin (Ost), 28. März 1990, document 233, DESE, 983–86.

10. Hanns Jürgen Küsters, "Entscheidung für die deutsche Einheit," DESE, 147; Ritter, *Der Preis der deutschen Einheit*, 203. See also David Marsh, *The Euro* (New Haven, CT: Yale University Press, 2009), 139–146.

11. "Из беседы М.С. Горбачева с Д. Хэрдом," April 10, 1990, МГ, 391–93; "From Private Secretary, Secretary of State's Meeting with President Gorbachev, Summary," n.d., released by the FCO via FOI. Redactions to the latter document remove the discussion of NATO and security alliances still present in the former, so the summary above comes mainly from the Russian source. For an interesting discussion of the concept of a "European Germany," by which Gorbachev understood something very different than the West did, see Robert Cooper, *The Breaking of Nations: Order and Chaos in the Twenty-First Century* (London: Atlantic Books, 2003), 143. The Western understanding was roughly as Cooper describes it: "The German question has been on the European agenda for more than 300 years. The original solution, Richelieu's creation of a weak Germany, gave way—thanks to time, Napoleon and Bismarck—to a strong Germany. The third way of a European Germany seems finally to have resolved this problem." Gorbachev's understanding, however, appears to have been of a Germany as a link between East and West, not as the anchor of the EC in the West.

12. "Из беседы М.С. Горбачева с В. Ярузельским," April 13, 1990, МГ, 394.

13. Ambassador Matlock sent a long cable to Washington on May 1, detailing how Moscow's many desires for the future; see telegram, "From Amembassy Moscow to Secstate Washdc," May 1, 1990, released by the State Department via FOIA.

14. See the correspondence in folder 1, box 109, 8c monthly files, series 8, BP.

15. "Moscow Embassy Cable," May 11, 1990, released by the State Department via FOIA and reproduced in the Mershon Conference volume (see bibliography for details).

16. Reported by Powell to the U.S. ambassador in London; see Telegram, "From Amembassy London to Secstate Washdc," "For the President and Secretary of State from Catto," April 22, 1990, released by the State Department via FOIA.

17. Jack Matlock, interview with author, April 18, 2007, Princeton, NJ; the other U.S. policymaker wishes to remain anonymous.

18. The leak appeared in the *Frankfurter Rundschau* on April 17, 1990; see DESE, 1023n1. See also Stent, *Russia and Germany,* 125, and "Из беседы М.С. Горбачева с Л. де Мезьером," 29 Apr. 1990, МГ, 409–423.

19. "Non-paper der Regierung der UdSSR," April 19, 1990, document 250, DESE, 1023–24; "Vermerk des Ministerialrats Ludewig," Bonn, April 20, 1990, document 252, 1025–26.

20. "Из беседы М.С. Горбачева с Л. де Мезьером," April 20, 1990, МГ, 409–23.

21. "Записка В.М. Фалина М.С. Горбачеву," April 18, 1990, МГ, 398–408; also reprinted in German in Valentin Falin, *Konflikte im Kreml: Zur Vorgeschichte der deutschen Einheit und*

Auflösung der Sowjetunion. Munich: Blessing Verlag, 1997, 164–78; see also Wolfgang Schäuble, *Der Vertrag: Wie ich über die deutsche Einheit verhandelte* (Munich: Knaur, 1991). I am grateful to Robert Hutchings for copies of relevant documents, including "Directives for Negotiations with the U.S. Secretary of State James Baker, 16–19 May 1990," a Russian document that he had in English translation.

22. GDE, 2:415–19.

23. Horst Teltschik, *329 Tage: Innenansichten der Einigung* (Berlin: Siedler, 1991), 198–99.

24. "Gespräch des Ministerialdirektors Teltschik mit Ministerpräsident de Maizière und Minister Reichenbach," Berlin (Ost), April 16, 1990, document 244, DESE, 1011–12. See also Schäuble, *Der Vertrag*.

25. GDE, 2:415–19.

26. "Gespräch des Bundeskanzlers Kohl mit Botschafter Kwizinskij," Bonn, April 23, 1990, document 253, DESE, 1026–30. Kvisinsky has published memoirs but they say little about 1989–90: J. A. Kwizinskij, *Vor dem Sturm: Erinnerungen eines Diplomaten* (Berlin: Siedler, 1993).

27. "Schreiben des Bundeskanzlers Kohl an Generalsekretär Gorbatschow," Bonn, April 24, 1990, document 255, DESE, 1033.

28. He explained as much to Hurd; see "Gespräch des Bundeskanzlers Kohl mit Außenminister Hurd," Bonn, May 15, 1990, document 278, 1119–20. Kohl also decided to see if he could get the G-7 to help him in his quest to buy acceptance of NATO membership, but would have little success in doing so. Teltschik, *329 Tage*, 204.

29. "Gespräch des Bundeskanzlers Kohl mit Ministerpräsidentin Prunskiene," Bonn, May 11, 1990, document 274, DESE, 1103–5.

30. "Из докладной записки А.С. Черняева М.С. Горбачеву," May 4, 1990, МГ, 424–25.

31. "Erstes Treffen der Außenminister der Zwei plus Vier," Bonn, May 5, 1990, document 268, DESE, 1090–94.

32. Telegram, "From USDel Secretary in Germany, to Secstate and White House," "Memorandum for the President," May 5, 1990, released by the State Department via FOIA.

33. Szabo, *Diplomacy*, 93.

34. "Vorlage des Ministerialdirektors Teltschik an Bundeskanzler Kohl," Bonn, May 8, 1990, document 270, DESE, 1096–98.

35. GDE, 2:418–20; see also Philip Zelikow and Condoleezza Rice, *Germany Unified and Europe Transformed: A Study in Statecraft* (Cambridge, MA: Harvard University Press, 1995), 258–59.

36. Küsters, "Entscheidung für die deutsche Einheit," 165.

37. Teltschik, *329 Tage*, 230.

38. Horst Teltschik, interview with author, June 13, 2008, phone conversation.

39. Both the Russian and German versions of the conversation are available, and they duplicate each other on substantive issues, although differ in exact wording (which is understandable, given the need for translators). "Из беседы М.С. Горбачева с Х. Тельчиком," May 14, 1990, МГ, 426–36; "Gespräch des Ministerialdirektors Teltschik mit Präsident Gorbatschow, Moskau, 14. Mai 1990," document 277, DESE, 1114–18.

40. A copy is in *Die Vereinigung Deutschlands im Jahre 1990: Verträge und Erklärungen* (Bonn: Presse- und Informationsamt der Bundesregierung, 1991), 13–42.

41. Elisabeth Noelle-Neumann and Renate Köcher, eds., *Allensbacher Jahrbuch der Demoskopie 1984–1992* (Munich: Saur, 1993), 9:423, 452–53.

42. "Schreiben des Bundeskanzlers Kohl an Präsident Gorbatschow, Bonn, 22. Mai 1990," document 284, DESE, 1136–37; Teltschik, *329 Tage*, 235.

43. "Schreiben des Bundeskanzlers Kohl an Präsident Gorbatschow, Bonn, 12. Juni 1990," document 309, DESE, 1207; "Schreiben des Präsidenten Gorbatschow an Bundeskanzler Kohl, 14. Juni 1990," document 315, DESE, 1224–25; Küsters, "Entscheidung für die deutsche Einheit," 170.

44. Teltschik, *329 Tage*, 249.

45. Quoted in Timothy Garton Ash, *In Europe's Name: Germany and the Divided Continent* (New York: Vintage Books, 1993), 352.

46. "Vorlage des Ministerialdirektors Teltschik an Bundeskanzler Kohl, Bonn, 3. Mai 1990," document 265, DESE, 1076–78; see also telegram, "From USMission USNATO, to Secstate Washdc," April 17, 1990, released by the State Department via FOIA.

47. "Gespräch des Bundeskanzlers Kohl mit Außenminister Baker," Bonn, May 4, 1990, document 266, DESE, 1079–84; for more on this topic, see also Andrei Grachev, *Gorbachev's Gamble: Soviet Foreign Policy and the End of the Cold War* (London: Polity, 2008).

48. Robert L. Hutchings, *American Diplomacy and the End of the Cold War: An Insider's Account of US Policy in Europe, 1989–1992* (Washington, DC: Wilson Center, 1997), 132–33.

49. Summary of May 17 meeting, reprinted in Hutchings, *American Diplomacy*, 130–31; Horst Teltschik, interview with author, June 13, 2008, phone conversation.

50. Zelikow and Rice, *Germany Unified*, 259, 272.

51. Timothy Naftali, *George H.W. Bush* (New York: Times Books, 2007), 92.

52. The text of the Final Act is on the website of the successor organization to the CSCE, the Organization for Security and Cooperation in Europe, available at http://www.osce.org/item/15661 .html. The full list of signatories, from the same location, is as follows: Austria, Belgium, Bulgaria, Canada, Cyprus, Czechoslovakia, Denmark, Finland, France, the GDR, the FRG, Greece, the Holy See, Hungary, Iceland, Ireland, Italy, Liechtenstein, Luxembourg, Malta, Monaco, the Netherlands, Norway, Poland, Portugal, Romania, San Marino, Spain, Sweden, Switzerland, Turkey, the Soviet Union, the United Kingdom, the United States, and Yugoslavia. I am also grateful to Robert Hutchings and Philip Zelikow for conversations and emails on this point.

53. "Delegationsgespräch des Bundeskanzlers Kohl mit Präsident Bush, Washington, 17. Mai 1990," document 281, DESE, 1126–32; Kohl also reported to Mitterrand about what had been discussed in "Schreiben des Bundeskanzlers Kohl an Staatspräsident Mitterrand, Bonn, 23. Mai 1990," document 286, DESE, 1143–45. See also the press clippings criticizing the Bush administration for not supporting Lithuania more strongly in folder 14, box 176, 12b chapter files, series 12, BP.

54. Don Oberdorfer, *The Turn: From the Cold War to a New Era* (New York: Simon and Schuster, 1991), 412; Raymond Garthoff, *The Great Transition: American-Soviet Relations and the End of the Cold War* (Washington, DC: Brookings Institution Press, 1994), 419–22. For more on Yeltsin, see Timothy J. Colton, *Yeltsin: A Life* (New York: Basic Books, 2008).

55. Memo from Jim Thomson, president and CEO of the RAND Corporation, "Subject: Soviet Views on Germany," May 24, 1990, NSC Zelikow files, FOIA 2001-1166-F, BPL.

56. Archie Brown, *The Gorbachev Factor* (New York: Oxford University Press, 1997), 301–2; Stephen Kotkin, *Armageddon Averted: The Soviet Collapse, 1970–2000* (New York: Oxford University Press, 2001), 211n26.

57. Telegram, "From USDel Secretary in USSR, to Secstate Washdc and the White House," May 18, 1990, released by the State Department via FOIA.

58. "Gorby Kremlin 5/18/90," handwritten notes, folder 1, box 109, 8c monthly files, series 8, BP.

59. "Из беседы М.С. Горбачева с Дж. Бейкером," May 18, 1990, МГ, 437–45, especially 438.

60. "Gorby Kremlin 5/18/90"; "Из беседы М.С. Горбачева с Дж. Бейкером," especially 442.

61. Telegram, "From USDel Secretary in USSR, to Secstate Washdc and the White House," May 19, 1990, released by the State Department via FOIA. As part of the planning for the Washington summit, Baker sent a note to Scowcroft, asking him to include in formal events those people who had been part of his delegation in Moscow; the secretary described this team as his "core" group on unification. In the order listed, these were Jack Matlock, Robert Gates, Ronald Lehmann, Reginald Bartholomew, Robert Zoellick, Paul Wolfowitz, Raymond Seitz, Margaret Tutwiler, Dennis Ross, Richard Clarke, Richard Schifter, Eugene McAllister, Steve Hadley, Reed Hanmer, Arnold Kanter, Richard Burt, David Smith, James Woolsey, Stephen Ledogar, C. Paul Robinson, Howard Graves, Curtis Kamman, Avis Bohlen, V. Kim Hoggard, Condoleezza Rice, Eric Edelman, Linton Brooks, James Collins, James Timbie, Alexander Vershbow, Victor Alessi, and Andrew Carpendale. See note from Baker to Scowcroft, May 24, 1990, folder 11, box 115, 8e White House meetings, series 8, BP.

62. "I Am an Optimist," *Time*, June 4, 1990; see also "Из интервью М.С. Горбачева американскому журналу «Тайм»," May 22, 1990, МГ, 448–49.

63. "Из беседы М.С. Горбачева с Ф. Миттераном," May 25, 1990, МГ, 450–53.

64. "Из беседы М.С. Горбачева с Ф. Миттераном один на один," May 25, 1990, МГ, 454–65.

65. "Vorlage des Ministerialdirigenten Hartmann an Bundeskanzler Kohl, Betr.: Treffen Mitterrand/Gorbatschow am 25. Mai 1990 in Moskau hier, Unterrichtung durch den Elysée," document 294, DESE, 1162–64; "Schreiben des Staatspräsidenten Mitterrand an Bundeskanzler Kohl, Paris, 30. Mai 1990," document 295, DESE, 1164–65.

66. "Theme Paper: German Unification," May 23, 1990, released by the State Department via FOIA; "Primary Objectives for the Summit," DCI, NIC 00562/90, May 24, 1990, released by the CIA via FOIA; "The President's Meetings with Soviet President Mikhail Gorbachev, May 30–June 3, 1990, Washington D.C., Book I, Scope Paper, Secretary Baker's Memorandum to the President," released and circulated in the Mershon Conference briefing book (see bibliography for details).

67. Memcon, "Telephone Call from Chancellor Helmut Kohl of West Germany," May 30, 1990, the White House, released via FOIA 1999-0393-F, BPL; "Telefongespräch des Bundeskanzlers Kohl mit Präsident Bush, Washington, 30. Mai 1990, 13:30–13:45," document 293, DESE, 1161–62. See also Kohl's remarks to a visiting congressional delegation in West Germany at the time: "Gespräch des Bundeskanzlers Kohl mit Vertretern der Studiengruppen über Deutschland des amerikanischen Kongresses, Bonn, 29. Mai 1990," document 291, DESE, 1155–59.

68. "Из второй беседы М.С. Горбачева с Дж. Бушем," May 31, 1990, МГ, 466–76; Baker's notes from the summit, folder 1, box 109, 8c monthly files, series 8.

69. Brent Scowcroft, interview with author, September 19, 2008, Washington, DC; Gates, *From the Shadows*, 493; see also Michael R. Beschloss and Strobe Talbott, *At the Highest Levels: The Inside Story of the Cold War* (Boston: Little, Brown, 1993), 219–21; Zelikow and Rice, *Germany Unified*, 278.

70. "5/31/90 5:50 p.m. to POTUS," folder 1, box 109, 8c monthly files, series 8, BP.

71. George Bush and Brent Scowcroft, *A World Transformed* (New York: Knopf, 1998), 286.

72. Gates, *From the Shadows*, 493.

73. "6/2/90 Camp David," folder 1, box 109, 8c monthly files, series 8, BP; Gates, *From the Shadows*, 455; James A. Baker with Thomas A. DeFrank, *The Politics of Diplomacy: Revolution,*

NOTES

War, and Peace, 1989–1992 (New York: G. P. Putnam's Sons, 1995), 254. Baker's memoirs said only that a Gorbachev "one-liner about . . . intimate functions" was "hilariously funny," but not appropriate for "publication in a book with 'Diplomacy' in its title."

74. Baker with DeFrank, *The Politics of Diplomacy*, 294.

75. For insights on diplomacy and gender, see Carol Cohn, "Wars, Wimps, and Women," in *Gendering War Talk*, ed. Miriam Cooke and Angela Woollacott (Princeton, NJ: Princeton University Press, 1993), 227–46; Robert D. Dean, "Masculinity as Ideology," *Diplomatic History* 22, no. 1 (Winter 1998): 29–62; J. Ann Tickner, *Gender in International Relations: Feminist Perspectives on Achieving Global Security* (New York: Columbia University Press, 1992.

76. "Выступление М.С. Горбачева на совместной с Дж. Бушем пресс-конференции по итогам визита в США," June 4, 1990, МГ, 477.

77. Zelikow and Rice, *Germany Unified*, 280–81; see also Hutchings, *American Diplomacy*, 132–33.

78. Telegram, "From Ambembassy Moscow, to Secstate Washdc," June 12, 1990, released by the State Department via FOIA. A State Department briefing cable instructed embassies on how to describe the summit: say that "no breakthroughs" were achieved. Department of State briefing cable, "Briefing Allies on the Washington Summit," June 15, 1990, released by the State Department via FOIA and available in the Mershon Conference briefing book.

79. "Fernschreiben des Präsidenten Bush an Bundeskanzler Kohl, Washington, 4. Juni 1990," document 299, DESE, 1178–80; Zelikow and Rice, *Germany Unified*, 256–57. Christopher Maynard, *Out of the Shadow: George H. W. Bush and the End of the Cold War* (College Station: Texas A&M Press, 2008), 72, suggests that Shevardnadze subsequently told Baker on June 5 that the Soviet Union "would accept a unified Germany in NATO" and that Baker was so excited, he woke Genscher up to tell him; Maynard quotes as sources Baker with DeFrank, *The Politics of Diplomacy*; Beschloss and Talbott, *At the Highest Levels*. However, the former says that Baker woke Genscher up to tell him about a breakthrough in CFE, not NATO (see Baker with DeFrank, *The Politics of Diplomacy*, 255); and the latter says only that Shevardnadze took a "giant step toward Soviet acceptance of the unification of Germany in NATO," not that he said the USSR would accept it (Beschloss and Talbott, *At the Highest Levels*, 230).

80. Teltschik, *329 Tage*, 310.

81. "EYES ONLY FOR THE PRESIDENT, 6/23/90, JAB III—Points on the Shevardnadze Meeting," folder 2, box 109, 8c monthly files, series 8, BP.

82. Küsters, "Entscheidung für die deutsche Einheit," 177; see also Stent, *Russia and Germany*, 122.

83. "German Unification: Two Plus Four Ministerial Meeting, East Berlin, 22 June Summary," telegram, released by the FCO via FOI.

84. Since the internal steps that would lead to unity—practical plans for introducing the DM into the East and the necessary legal documents—were well under way, it was becoming clear to Moscow that it needed to secure these concessions sooner rather than later. For discussion of the need to change the West German Basic Law after unification, most notably to get rid of the Article 23 option for adding more territory, see "Vorlage des Regierungsdirektors Lehnguth an den Chef des Bundeskanzleramtes Seiters, Bonn, 12. Juni 1990, Betr.: Überlegungen für Verfassungsänderungen im Zusammenhang mit dem Beitritt der DDR," document 310, DESE, 1208–9.

85. "Fernschreiben des Staatssekretärs Bertele an den Chef des Bundeskanzleramtes, Berlin (Ost), 25. Mai 1990," document 287, DESE, 1146–47.

86. Garthoff, *The Great Transition*, 422.

87. "Schreiben von UdSSR-Ministerpräsident Nikolai Ryshkow an Lothar de Maizière, 7. Juni 1990," document 73 in Detlef Nakath and Gerd-Rüdiger Stephan, eds., *Countdown zur deutschen Einheit: Eine dokumentierte Geschichte der deutsch-deutschen Beziehungen 1987–1990* (Berlin: Dietz, 1996), 347–48; "Schreiben von Lothar de Maizière an UdSSR-Ministerpräsident Nikolai Ryshkow, 15. Juni 1990," document 74 in Detlef Nakath and Gerd-Rüdiger Stephan, eds., *Countdown zur deutschen Einheit: Eine dokumentierte Geschichte der deutsch-deutschen Beziehungen 1987–1990* (Berlin: Dietz, 1996), 349–50.

88. "Совместное заявление правительств ФРГ и ГДР об урегулировании открытых имущественных вопросов," June 15, 1990, МГ, 488–91. For more on this agreement, see A. James McAdams, *Judging the Past in Unified Germany* (Cambridge: Cambridge University Press, 2001).

89. GDE, 2:420–22; "Information über ein Gespräch von DDR-Staatssekretär Günther Krause mit UdSSR-Ministerpräsident Nikolai Ryshkow, 26. Juni 1990," document 75 in Detlef Nakath and Gerd-Rüdiger Stephan, eds., *Countdown zur deutschen Einheit: Eine dokumentierte Geschichte der deutsch-deutschen Beziehungen 1987–1990* (Berlin: Dietz, 1996), 351–52. For the Central Committee's assessment of the outcome of these talks, see Фонд 89, перечень 8, дело 77, copy available in the Government Documents Collection at Harvard University.

90. "Vorlage Ministerialdirektors Teltschik an Bundeskanzler Kohl, Bonn, 19. Juni 1990, Betr.: Finanzierungsfragen der Westgruppe der sowjetischen Streitkräfte (WGS) in der DDR, Hier: 3. Konsultationsrunde Staatssekretär Dr. Lautenschlager/stv. AM Obminskij, Bonn, 19. Juni 1990," document 320, DESE, 1232–34; "Vorlage Ministerialdirektors Teltschik an Bundeskanzler Kohl, Bonn, 27. Juni 1990," document 327, DESE, 1275–76.

91. Telegram, "From USMission US NATO, to Secstate Washdc," May 31, 1990, released by the State Department via FOIA.

92. "Transcript of a Speech Given by the Prime Minister, Mrs. Margaret Thatcher, to the North Atlantic Council, Turnberry, on Thursday, 7 June 1990," released by the FCO via FOI.

93. "Из беседы М.С. Горбачева с М. Тэтчер," June 8, 1990, МГ, 478–85.

94. "Schreiben von Helmut Kohl an Lothar de Maizière vom 31. Mai 1990," document 70 in Detlef Nakath and Gerd-Rüdiger Stephan, eds., *Countdown zur deutschen Einheit: Eine dokumentierte Geschichte der deutsch-deutschen Beziehungen 1987–1990* (Berlin: Dietz, 1996), 334–36.

95. GDE, 4:318; Meckel, *Selbstbewußt*, 146.

96. "Entschließung des Deutschen Bundestags vom 21. Juni 1990 zur deutsch-polnischen Grenze," in *Vereinigung Deutschlands*, 90–91.

97. "Entschließung des Deutschen Bundestages zur deutsch-polnischen Grenze," in Auswärtiges Amt, ed., *Aussenpolitik der Bundesrepublik Deutschland: Dokumente von 1949 bis 1994* (Cologne: Verlag Wissenschaft und Politik, 1995), 676–77; "Gespräch des Bundeskanzlers Kohl mit dem stellvertretenden Ministerpräsidenten und Finanzminister Balcerowicz, Bonn, 22. Juni 1990," document 323, DESE, 1244–47.

98. "Vorlage Ministerialdirektors Teltschik an Bundeskanzler Kohl, Bonn, 28. Juni 1990, Betr.: Polnische Reaktion auf die Entschließung des Deutschen Bundestags vom 21. Juni 1990," document 332, DESE, 1282–83.

99. "Secstate Washdc to Amembassy Embberlin and All NATO Capitals," June 12, 1990, "Subject: Secretary's Meeting with GDR Foreign Minister, June 5, 1990," released by the State Department via FOIA.

100. His comments received attention in Washington; see clippings from June 24, 1990, NSC Wilson Files, FOIA 2001-1166-F, BPL.

101. Kohl and Teltschik had a less charitable interpretation; they suspected that Meckel was more loyal to the West German SPD and his own vision for the future than to what his government

had agreed to with the Bundeskanzleramt. "Vorlage Ministerialdirektors Teltschik an Bundeskanzler Kohl, Bonn, 28. Juni 1990, Betr.: DDR-Haltung zu den äußeren Aspekten der deutschen Einheit," document 331, DESE, 1281.

102. "Tischgespräch des Bundeskanzlers Kohl mit Ministerpräsident Antall, Bonn, 21. Juni 1990," document 322, DESE, 1241–43; Vojtech Mastny and Malcolm Byrne, eds. *A Cardboard Castle? An Inside History of the Warsaw Pact* (New York: Central European University Press, 2005), 71.

103. "Deklaration der Teilnehmerstaaten der Warschauer Vertragsorganisation in Moskau vom 7.6.1990," document 20 in Auswärtiges Amt, *Deutsche Aussenpolitik*, 120–22.

104. "Rede von Michail Gorbatschow, Präsident der UdSSR, auf dem Gipfeltreffen der Warschauer Vertragsstaaten am 7. Juni 1990," document 71, and "Rede von Lothar de Maizière auf dem Gipfeltreffen der Warschauer Vertragsstaaten am 7. Juni 1990," document 72, both in Detlef Nakath and Gerd-Rüdiger Stephan, eds., *Countdown zur deutschen Einheit: Eine dokumentierte Geschichte der deutsch-deutschen Beziehungen 1987–1990* (Berlin: Dietz, 1996), 336–47.

105. "Zum deutschen Einigungsprozeß: Rede von Ministerpräsident de Maizière vor der Georgetown University in Washington am 11.6.1990," document 23 in Auswärtiges Amt, *Deutsche Aussenpolitik*, 125–26.

106. This conclusion emerges from the paperwork surrounding his visit in folder 2, box 109, 8c monthly files, series 8, BP; "Schreiben des Präsidenten Bush an Bundeskanzler Kohl, Washington, 13. Juni 1990," document 313, DESE, 1212–14. The latter contains a discussion of the notion of a "bridge" function between the East and West.

107. "Из беседы М.С. Горбачева с Л. де Мезьером," September 12, 1990, МГ, 567–69.

108. Kohl had also tried to encourage European leaders to help Gorbachev with financial aid; see "Botschaft des Bundeskanzlers Kohl an die Staats- und Regierungschefs der Mitgliedstaaten der Europäischen Gemeinschaften und der G-7 Staaten, Bonn, 13. Juni 1990," document 312, DESE, 1211–12. See also Szabo, *Diplomacy*, 93ff.

109. On some of the issues surrounding the process of turning the next West German vote into a national election, see "Vorlage des Ministerialdirigenten Busse an den Chef des Bundeskanzleramtes Seiters, Bonn, 26. März 1990," document 229, DESE, 975–77.

110. "Zu den äußeren Aspekten der deutschen Einheit und den deutsch-deutschen Beziehungen: Regierungserklärung von Bundeskanzler Dr. Kohl vom 21. Juni 1990," in Auswärtiges Amt, *Aussenpolitik*, 673–75. Major churches in both East and West Germany joined to issue a reassuring declaration on the eve of monetary union; see "Zur aktuellen Entwicklung Deutschlands: Gemeinsame Erklärung der Katholischen und der Evangelischen Kirche in der Bundesrepublik Deutschland und der DDR an die Bürger Deutschlands vom 26.6.1990 (Auszüge)," document 26 in Auswärtiges Amt, *Deutsche Aussenpolitik*, 131–33.

111. Hartmut Mayer, "Review of *Dokumente zur Deutschlandpolitik: Deutsche Einheit*," *International Affairs* 74, no. 4 (October 1998): 953.

112. "Gespräch des Bundeskanzlers Kohl mit Mitgliedern der Rüstungskontroll-Beobachtergruppe des amerikanischen Senats, Bonn, 12. März 1990," document 213, DESE, 927–31; Kohl told the senators that he had just given a speech in Rostock, one of the cities that the Lance weapons could strike. See also Hutchings, *American Diplomacy*, 129.

113. "Gespräch des Bundeskanzlers Kohl mit Präsident Bush, Washington, 8. Juni 1990," document 305, DESE, 1191–99. GDE, 1:7, agrees strongly with the notion that Kohl was the central figure.

114. "Fernschreiben des Präsidenten Bush an Bundeskanzler Kohl, 21. Juni 1990," document 321, DESE, 1234–37; "Entwurf," document 312A, DESE, 1237–41. See also Garthoff, *The Great Transition*, 433. I am also grateful to Craig Dunkerley, who at the time was the political adviser

to the U.S. mission to NATO, for insight as to how this process looked from inside the transatlantic alliance.

115. Kohl expressed his view that a united Germany in NATO was primarily a domestic political problem for Gorbachev in a conversation with Mitterrand. See "Gespräche des Bundeskanzlers Kohl mit Staatspräsident Mitterrand, Assmannshausen und auf dem Rhein, 22. Juni 1990," document 324, DESE, 1247–49.

116. "Vorlage Ministerialdirektors Teltschik an Bundeskanzler Kohl, Bonn, 26. Juni 1990," document 327, DESE, 1262–65.

117. "Vorlage des Oberstleutnants i.G. Ludwigs und des vortragenden Legationsrats Westdickenberg an Ministerialdirektor Teltschik, Bonn, 25. Juni 1990," document 326, DESE, 1256–61; "Schreiben des Ministerialdirektors Teltschik an Sicherheitsberater Scowcroft, Bonn, 28. Juni 1990," document 330, DESE, 1276, and its attachment, "Entwurf NATO Gipfelerklärung," document 330A, DESE, 1276–80.

118. Philip Zelikow, interview with author, July 27, 2008, phone conversation and subsequent emails. For more on NATO enlargement, see Ronald D. Asmus, *Opening NATO's Door: How the Alliance Remade Itself for a New Era* (New York: Columbia University Press, 2002).

119. "Gesprächsunterlagen des Bundeskanzlers Kohl für das Gipfeltreffen der Staats- und Regierungschefs der Mitgliedstaaten der NATO, London, 5./6. Juli 1990, documents 344, 344A-I, DESE, 1309–23.

120. "Schreiben des Sicherheitsberaters Scowcroft an Ministerialdirektor Teltschik, 30. Juni 1990," document 355, DESE, 1285–86.

121. "Notes from Jim Cicconi [note taker] re: 7/3/90 pre-NATO Summit briefing at Kennebunkport," folder 3, box 109, 8c monthly files, BP. In their account, Zelikow and Rice say that no transcript of this meeting survived (which is not accurate, as the Cicconi notes did), but they agree that Zoellick's briefing was key, because it emphasized the Soviet audience. Zelikow and Rice, *Germany Unified*, 321.

122. "Из беседы М.С. Горбачева с М. Вернером," July 14, 1990, МГ, 492–94.

123. For discussion of the relative weights of CSCE and NATO in U.S. foreign policy at this point, see Garthoff, *The Great Transition*, 427.

124. "56. Deutsch-französische Konsultationen, München, 17./18. September 1990," document 424, DESE, 1544–46; Zelikow and Rice, *Germany Unified*, 323.

125. All of the above discussion comes from "Notes from Jim Cicconi [note taker] re: 7/3/90 pre-NATO Summit briefing at Kennebunkport."

126. A copy of the final communiqué is available in various languages and locations; the one cited here is in folder 3, box 109, 8c monthly files, series 8, BP.

127. "Vorlage Ministerialdirektors Teltschik an Bundeskanzler Kohl, Bonn, 4. Juli 1990, Betr.: Innere Lage in der Sowjetunion nach Beginn des 28. KPdSU-Parteitages," document 340, DESE, 1297–99; Ritter, *Der Preis der deutschen Einheit*, 46; Stent, *Russia and Germany*, 123–34.

128. Stent, *Russia and Germany*, 134.

129. Hurd quotation in Szabo, *Diplomacy*, 93. "Botschaft des Bundeskanzlers Kohl an die Staats- und Regierungschefs der Mitgliedstaaten der Europäischen Gemeinschaften und der G-7 Staaten, Bonn, 13. Juni 1990," document 312, DESE, 1211–12. Kohl's urgings, however, did prompt the EC to give Delors a mandate to speak to Gorbachev about the matter.

130. Teltschik, *329 Tage*, 305–11. See also note from Baker to Bush, July 11, 1990, folder 3, box 109, BP; Küsters, "Entscheidung für die deutsche Einheit," 187–8.

131. Helmut Kohl, *Erinnerungen 1990–1994* (Munich: Droemer, 2007), 164.

132. For a further discussion of this belief, see my *German Military Reform and European Security* (London: Oxford University Press, 2001). For a description of the travel to Russia, see Teltschik, *329 Tage*, 317–19; Hans Klein, *Es begann im Kaukasus: Der entscheidende Schritt in die Einheit Deutschlands* (Berlin: Ullstein, 1991).

133. Kohl, *Erinnerungen 1990–1994*, 164; Teltschik, *329 Tage*, 318–19.

134. Falin, *Konflikte im Kreml*, 192–99. See also Valentin Falin, *Politische Erinnerungen* (Munich: Knaur, 1995), 494; Küsters, "Entscheidung für die deutsche Einheit," 189. For more on the internal struggles in shaping Soviet attitudes toward the German question, see Rafael Biermann, *Zwischen Kreml und Kanzleramt: Wie Moskau mit der deutschen Einheit rang* (Paderborn: Ferdinand Schöningh, 1997), 768–73.

135. Hans-Dietrich Genscher, *Erinnerungen* (Berlin: Sielder, 1995), 831; Theo Waigel and Manfred Schell, eds., *Tage, die Deutschland und die Welt veränderten* (Munich: edition ferenczy, 1994), 24–28.

136. "Gespräch des Bundeskanzlers Kohl mit Präsident Gorbatschow, 15. Juli 1990," document 350, DESE, 1340–48; "Из беседы Горбачева с Г. Колем один на один," July 15, 1990, МГ, 495–503. The "ride on the tiger" comment is only in the German version; otherwise everything cited is in both.

137. "Überlegungen zum Inhalt eines Vertrages über Partnerschaft und Zusammenarbeit zwischen der Union der Sozialistischen Sowjetrepubliken und Deutschland, 15. Juli 1990," document 351, DESE, 1348–52. The draft is included only with the German transcript of the conversation.

138. "Gespräch des Bundeskanzlers Kohl mit Präsident Gorbatschow, 15. Juli 1990," 1343; "Из беседы Горбачева с Г. Колем один на один," 497.

139. "Gespräch des Bundeskanzlers Kohl mit Präsident Gorbatschow, 15. Juli 1990," 1343–44. This discussion is only in the German version, which is longer than the Russian one.

140. "Gespräch des Bundeskanzlers Kohl mit Präsident Gorbatschow, 15. Juli 1990," 1343–46; "Из беседы М.С. Горбачева с Г. Колем один на один," 500–501. Original phrasing: "Strukturen der NATO" and "структур НАТО."

141. Teltschik, *329 Tage*, 323–24.

142. "Gespräch des Bundeskanzlers Kohl mit Präsident Gorbatschow, 15. Juli 1990," 1346–47; "Из беседы М.С. Горбачева с Г. Колем один на один," 501–2.

143. Kohl, *Erinnerungen 1990–1994*, 169.

144. "Gespräch des Bundeskanzlers Kohl mit Präsident Gorbatschow, 15. Juli 1990," 1348; "Из беседы М.С. Горбачева с Г. Колем один на один," 503.

145. Kohl, *Erinnerungen 1990–1994*, 169–70. Teltschik also knew that he had just been witness to a historic moment, although both he and Kohl say that they tried hard not to let it show outwardly. Teltschik, *329 Tage*, 324.

146. "Delegationsgespräch des Bundeskanzlers Kohl mit Präsident Gorbatschow, Moskau, 15. Juli 1990," document 352, DESE, 1354.

147. Kohl, *Erinnerungen 1990–1994*, 170; Teltschik, *329 Tage*, 325–26.

148. See description of Gorbachev's younger years in chapter 3, herein; see also Teltschik, *329 Tage*, 327.

149. Waigel and Schell, *Tage*, 38; Genscher, *Erinnerungen*, 834.

150. Waigel and Schell, *Tage*, 38.

151. Genscher, *Erinnerungen*, 837.

152. Teltschik, *329 Tage*, 327–32.

153. Both the West Germans and the Russians produced long transcripts from this meeting, but they are not always identical. I have only cited material here that appeared in both transcripts. "Gespräch des Bundeskanzlers Kohl mit Präsident Gorbatschow im erweiterten Kreis, Archys/ Bezirk Stawropol, 16. Juli 1990," document 353, DESE, 1361; "Из беседы М.С. Горбачева с Г. Колем," July 16, 1990, МГ, 516.

154. "Gespräch des Bundeskanzlers Kohl mit Präsident Gorbatschow im erweiterten Kreis, Archys/ Bezirk Stawropol," 1363; "Из беседы М.С. Горбачева с Г. Колем," 520.

155. "Gespräch des Bundeskanzlers Kohl mit Präsident Gorbatschow im erweiterten Kreis, Archys/ Bezirk Stawropol," 1364; "Из беседы М.С. Горбачева с Г. Колсм," 522.

156. "Gespräch des Bundeskanzlers Kohl mit Präsident Gorbatschow im erweiterten Kreis, Archys/ Bezirk Stawropol," 1357; "Из беседы М.С. Горбачева с Г. Колем," 510. Original phrasing: "Präsident Gorbatschow fährt fort, daß mit der Herstellung der vollen Souveränität Deutschlands einige Hauptprinzipien festgestellt werden müßten, nämlich auch die Nichtausdehnung der militärischen Strukturen der NATO auf das Gebiet der heutigen DDR." "Прежде всего нераспространение на территорию ГДР военных структур НАТО и сохранение там на определенный согласованный период советских войск."

157. "Gespräch des Bundeskanzlers Kohl mit Präsident Gorbatschow im erweiterten Kreis, Archys/ Bezirk Stawropol," 1357, 1360; "Из беседы М.С. Горбачева с Г. Колем," 510, 514.

158. "Gespräch des Bundeskanzlers Kohl mit Präsident Gorbatschow im erweiterten Kreis, Archys/ Bezirk Stawropol," 1357; "Из беседы М.С. Горбачева с Г. Колем," 510. See also Kohl, *Erinnerungen 1990–1994*, 175.

159. "Gespräch des Bundeskanzlers Kohl mit Präsident Gorbatschow im erweiterten Kreis, Archys/ Bezirk Stawropol," 1358; "Из беседы М.С. Горбачева с Г. Колем," 511.

160. "Gespräch des Bundeskanzlers Kohl mit Präsident Gorbatschow im erweiterten Kreis, Archys/ Bezirk Stawropol," 1358; "Из беседы М.С. Горбачева с Г. Колем," 512.

161. "Gespräch des Bundeskanzlers Kohl mit Präsident Gorbatschow im erweiterten Kreis, Archys/ Bezirk Stawropol," 1358–59; "Из беседы М.С. Горбачева с Г. Колем," 513. Original phrasing: "Präsident Gorbatschow wirft ein, wenn in der bilateralen Vereinbarung gesagt werde, nach dem Abzug der sowjetischen Truppen werde nichts unternommen, was die Sicherheit der Sowjetunion beeinträchtige, so stelle dies keine Einschränkung der Souveränität Deutschlands dar." "В договоре должна присутствовать мысль, что уход советских войск не будет использован для создания угрозы безопасности Советскому Союзу."

162. "Gespräch des Bundeskanzlers Kohl mit Präsident Gorbatschow im erweiterten Kreis, Archys/ Bezirk Stawropol," 1360; "Из беседы М.С. Горбачева с Г. Колем," 514.

163. "Gespräch des Bundeskanzlers Kohl mit Präsident Gorbatschow im erweiterten Kreis, Archys/ Bezirk Stawropol," 1360; "Из беседы М.С. Горбачева с Г. Колем," 515; Kohl, *Erinnerungen 1990–1994*, 176.

164. "Gespräch des Bundeskanzlers Kohl mit Präsident Gorbatschow im erweiterten Kreis, Archys/ Bezirk Stawropol," 1365; "Из беседы М.С. Горбачева с Г. Колем," 523; Richard A. Falkenrath, *Shaping Europe's Military Order: The Origins and Consequences of the CFE Treaty* (Cambridge, MA: MIT Press, 1995), 74–75; the German concession was dependent on the treaty entering into force, which was delayed by the disintegration of the Soviet Union. A number of former Soviet socialist republics eventually ratified it, though, allowing it to go at least partially into force. Falkenrath, *Shaping*, 172ff.

165. Kohl, *Erinnerungen 1990–1994*, 181.

166. Genscher, *Erinnerungen*, 840.

NOTES

167. "Gespräch des Bundeskanzlers Kohl mit Präsident Gorbatschow im erweiterten Kreis, Archys/Bezirk Stawropol," 1366. The English-language summary of what Kohl actually said at this press conference indicates that he did not explicitly discuss the question of whether NATO's nuclear capacity could move to former East German soil after unification. See the copy in the Wilson files, BPL, released via FOIA.

168. "Im Brennpunkt," video, July 17, 1990, KASPA.

169. "Statement by the President," the White House, Office of the Press Secretary, July 16, 1990, folder 3, box 109, 8c monthly files, series 8; "Remarks by Secretary of State James Baker on the Kohl-Gorbachev Press Conference, Shannon, Ireland, en route to Paris, France, Monday, July 16, 1990," folder 3, box 109, 8c monthly files, series 8. See also the NSC Wilson files for clippings from this date, FOIA 2001-1166-F, BPL.

170. "Drittes Treffen der Außenminister der 2 + 4-Gespräche unter zeitweiliger Beteiligung Polens, Paris, 17. Juli 1990," document 354, DESE, and supporting documents, 1367–70; "Schreiben des Ministerpräsidenten Mazowiecki an Bundeskanzler Kohl, Warschau, 25. Juli 1990," document 371, DESE, 1418–21.

171. "Schreiben Bundeskanzler Kohl an Ministerpräsidenten Mazowiecki," document 412, DESE, 1523–24; "Vertrag zwischen der Bundesrepublik Deutschland und der Republik Polen über die Bestätigung der zwischen ihnen bestehenden Grenze vom 14. November 1990," in Auswärtiges Amt, *Aussenpolitik*, 744–49; Küsters, "Entscheidung für die deutsche Einheit," 225; GDE, 4:506–8; see also the *Grundgesetz für die Bundesrepublik Deutschland, Textausgabe, Stand: Oktober 1990* (Bonn: Bundeszentrale für politische Bildung, 1990).

172. Falin, *Konflikte im Kreml*, 188 and 200–201; Stent, *Russia and Germany*, 135.

173. Valery Boldin, *Ten Years That Shook the World: The Gorbachev Era as Witnessed by His Chief of Staff* (New York: HarperCollins, 1994).

174. Quoted in GDE, 4:564; Genscher, *Erinnerungen*, 836. Genscher had in fact sought out medical assistance the night before, after the dinner in Archys, from the medical team that traveled with the delegation.

175. Teltschik, *329 Tage*, 339.

176. For his remarks, see "Erklärung von Bundeskanzler Dr. Helmut Kohl am 17. Juli 1990 vor der Bonner Bundespressekonferenz zur Deutschlandpolitik und zu den Ergebnissen seiner Gespräche mit dem Präsidenten der UdSSR, Michail Sergejewitsch Gorbatschow," in *Vereinigung Deutschlands*, 93–97; Genscher, *Erinnerungen*, 839.

177. Note from Scowcroft to Wörner, July 21, 1990, in FOIA 2002-2038-F, BPL.

178. "Schreiben des Bundeskanzlers Kohl an Staatspräsident Mitterrand, Bonn, 17. Juli 1990," document 356, DESE, 1374–76.

179. "Telefongespräch des Bundeskanzlers Kohl mit Präsident Bush, 17. Juli 1990," document 355, DESE, 1371–74; Memcon, the White House, "Telephone Call from Chancellor Helmut Kohl of West Germany," July 17, 1990, 8:48–9:17 a.m. EST, FOIA 99-0393-F, BPL.

180. Kohl, *Erinnerungen 1990–1994*, 179–83.

181. Garthoff, *The Great Transition*, 430.

182. Falkenrath, *Shaping*, 117–19.

183. DCI, NIC 00759/90, July 17, 1990, "Executive Brief: Implications of the Soviet Transfer of Military Equipment from the ATTU Zone to East of the Urals," released by the CIA via FOIA; "Numerical Limits in the CFE Treaty," Falkenrath, *Shaping*, 272, table 3.1.

184. "Schreiben der Ministerpräsidenten Ryshkow an Bundeskanzler Kohl, Moskau, 18. Juli 1990," document 360, DESE, 1400–1401; GDE, 2:426–29; Stent, *Russia and Germany*, 125.

NOTES

185. "Докладная записка Э.А. Шеварднадзе М.С. Горбачеву о представлении проекта советско-германского договора с приложением проекта письма М.С. Горбачева Г. Колю," July 25, 1990, МГ, 545.

186. "Schreiben des Bundeskanzlers Kohl an Ministerpräsident Ryshkow, Bonn, 22. August 1990," document 392, DESE, 1488. For the discussion on internal measures necessitated by unification, including the striking of Article 23 from the Basic Law, see "Rundschreiben des Bundesministers Schäuble an die ständigen Mitglieder des Kabinettausschusses Deutsche Einheit Bonn," document 328, and supporting documents, DESE, 1265–74; "Neufassung der Präambel des Grundgesetzes," document 374B, DESE, 1444–45.

187. Ritter, *Der Preis der deutschen Einheit*, 42–45.

188. "Vorlage des Ministerialdirigenten Stern an den Chef des Bundeskanzleramtes Seiters, Bonn, 31. Juli 1990, Betr.: deutsche Einheit," document 375, DESE, 1446–47; "Vorlage des Regierungsdirektors Nehring an Bundeskanzler Kohl, Bonn, 30. Juli 1990," document 373, DESE, 1423.

189. Naftali, *Bush*, 108.

190. "Notes made by JAB during 9/15/90 mtg. w/FRG Chancellor Kohl in the living room of Kohl's private residence in Ludwigshafen, FRG," folder 5, box 109, 8c monthly files, series 8. See also "Telefongespräch des Bundeskanzlers Kohl mit Präsident Bush, 22. August 1990," document 390, DESE, 1484–86; "Telefongespräch des Bundeskanzlers Kohl mit Präsident Bush, 30. August 1990," document 406, DESE, 1514; "Gespräch des Bundeskanzlers Kohl mit Außenminister Baker, Ludwigshafen, 15. September 1990," document 423, DESE, 1542–44.

191. Douglas Hurd, *Memoirs* (London: Little, Brown, 2003), 384.

192. Horst Teltschik, interview with author, June 13, 2008, phone conversation.

193. Ritter, *Der Preis der deutschen Einheit*, 62.

194. The Soviet Union might simply refuse to turn over its four-power control and keep its troops where they were. Thomas Risse-Kappen, cited in Stephen G. Brooks and William C. Wohlforth, "Economic Constraints and the Turn towards Superpower Cooperation in the 1980s," in *Last Decade of the Cold War: From Conflict Escalation to Conflict Transformation*, ed. Olav Njølstad (London: Frank Cass, 2004), 102.

195. "Schreiben des Präsidenten Delors and Bundeskanzler Kohl, Brüssel, 1. August 1990," document 376, DESE, 1448–49; "Telefongespräch des Bundeskanzlers Kohl mit Präsident Delors, 20. August 1990," document 388, DESE, 1479–81; GDE 2:408–9.

196. Ritter, *Der Preis der deutschen Einheit*, 61.

197. Ritter, *Der Preis der deutschen Einheit*, 30–31; Oskar Lafontaine, *Deutsche Wahrheiten: Die nationale und die soziale Frage* (Hamburg: Hoffmann und Campe Verlag, 1990), 240. On Lafontaine, see also Andreas Rödder, *Deutschland Einig Vaterland* (Munich: Beck, 2009), chapter 4.

198. "Following from Private Secretary, Secretary of State's Call on Chancellor Kohl, 14 May," May 15, 1990, released by the FCO via FOI. This is also the source of Kohl's remarks about costs and sacrifice, cited earlier.

199. "Vorlage des Ministerialdirigenten Hartmann an Bundeskanzler Kohl, Bonn, 3. August 1990, Betr.: Außenpolitischer Regelungsbedarf im Hinblick auf die neue deutschlandpolitische Lage (mögliche gesamtdeutsche Wahlen und Beitritt im Oktober)," document 378, DESE, 1454–56.

200. "Schreiben der Volkskammerpräsidentin Bergmann-Pohl an Bundeskanzler Kohl, Berlin, 25. August 1990," document 397, and supporting document, DESE, 1497.

201. "Gespräch des Bundesministers Genscher mit dem Ministerpräsident de Maizière," document 395, DESE, 1492–94.

202. "Vertrag zwischen der Bundesrepublik Deutschland und der Deutschen Demokratischen Republik über die Herstellung der Einheit Deutschlands—Einigungsvertrag—vom 31.08.1990 (Auszüge)," document 37 in Auswärtiges Amt, *Deutsche Aussenpolitik*, 162–7; Küsters, "Entscheidung für die deutsche Einheit," 212–21.

203. For details on these negotiations, see GDE, 4:567–620. There were also various other issues unresolved, such as one for subsidized food, but the two items described in the text above were the most important ones. Zelikow and Rice, *Germany Unified*, 350.

204. "Vorlage des Ministerialdirektors Teltschik an Bundeskanzler Kohl, Bonn, 27. August 1990," document 398, DESE, 1498–1500.

205. "Gespräch des Ministerialdirektors Teltschik mit dem stellvertretenden Außenminister Kwizinskij, Bonn, 28. August 1990," document 402, DESE, 1505–7.

206. "Zum Vertrag zwischen der Bundesrepublik Deutschland und der UdSSR über die Bedingungen des befristeten Aufenthalts und die Modalitäten des planmäßigen Abzugs der sowjetischen Truppen aus dem Gebiet der Bundesrepublik Deutschland," in Auswärtiges Amt, *Aussenpolitik*, 733–35.

207. "Schreiben des Ministerialdirektors Teltschik an Staatssekretär Sudhoff, Bonn, 30. August 1990," document 407, DESE, 1515; "Vorlage des Vortragenden Legationsrat Dr. Westdickenberg an Ministerialdirektor Teltschik, Bonn, 3. September 1990," document 410, DESE, 1518–20; "Vorlage des Vortragenden Legationsrat Dr. Westdickenberg an Ministerialdirektor Teltschik, Bonn, 20. September 1990," document 425, DESE, 1546–49. Moscow would eventually agree not to carry out the death penalty in Germany. Information on U.S. concerns comes from Robert Hutchings, personal collection.

208. Küsters, "Entscheidung für die deutsche Einheit," 223–24.

209. "Schreiben des Bundesministers Waigel an Bundeskanzler Kohl, Bonn, 6. September 1990," document 413, DESE, 1524–25.

210. "Telefongespräch des Bundeskanzlers Kohl mit Präsident Gorbatschow, 7. September 1990," document 415, DESE, 1527–30; "Телефонный разговор М.С. Горбачева с Г. Колем," September 7, 1990, МГ, 554–59. In the German version, Gorbachev's remarks are as follows: "Es komme ihm vor, als sei er in eine Falle geraten." See also the note that Chernyaev wrote to Gorbachev in preparation for the Monday call: "Докладная записка А.С. Черняева о предстоящем телефонном разговоре с Г. Колем и возможной поездке в Германию 3 октября," September 10, 1990, МГ, 562; analysis of these calls is in Hannes Adomeit, *Imperial Overstretch: Germany in Soviet Policy from Stalin to Gorbachev* (Baden-Baden: Nomos Verlagsgesellschaft, 1998), 539–51.

211. On the impact that such a loss of status can have, see Rogers Brubaker, *Nationalism Reframed: Nationhood and the New National Question in the New Europe* (Cambridge: Cambridge University Press, 1996).

212. Robert Zoellick, interview with author, March 16, 2008, Brussels; Brent Scowcroft, interview with author, September 19, 2008, Washington, DC. See also Vojtech Mastny, "Eastern Europe and the Early Prospects for EC/EU and NATO Membership," in *Europe and the End of the Cold War*, ed. Frédéric Bozo, Marie-Pierre Rey, N. Piers Ludlow, and Leopoldo Nuti (London: Routledge, 2008), 235–45, where he argues that the Poles were in favor early of NATO membership; Jolyon Howorth, "The EU, NATO, and the Origins of CFSP and ESDC," in *Europe and the End of the Cold War*, ed. Frédéric Bozo, Marie-Pierre Rey, N. Piers Ludlow, and Leopoldo Nuti (London: Routledge, 2008), 259–70; Zelikow and Rice, *Germany Unified*, 359–60.

213. "German Unification: Official Level Two Plus Four, Bonn, 22 May," released by the FCO via FOI; Stent, *Russia and Germany*, 139–40.

214. "Vorlage des Vortragenden Legationsrat I Kaestner an Ministerialdirektor Teltschik, Bonn, 7. September 1990," document 416, DESE, 1531; "Vorlage des Ministerialdirektors Teltschik an

Bundeskanzler Kohl, Bonn, 8. September 1990," document 417, DESE, 1532–34; "Vorlage des V.L. I Kaestner an Ministerialdirektor Teltschik, 10. September 1990," document 420, DESE, 1538.

215. "Schreiben des Staatssekretärs Köhler an Bundeskanzler Kohl, Bonn, 9. September 1990," document 418 and document 418A, DESE, 1534–35.

216. Zelikow argues that there was no serious assessment whatsoever of how the money would help Russia; the evidence available to date does indeed suggest scanty analysis. Zelikow and Rice, *Germany Unified*, 326. The British were particularly appalled at this omission; see Percy Cradock, *In Pursuit of British Interests: Reflections on Foreign Policy under Margaret Thatcher and John Major* (London: John Murray, 1997), 118–19.

217. Baker with DeFrank, *The Politics of Diplomacy*, 291.

218. Kohl did not release a transcript of the September 10 phone call, but Gorbachev did: "Из телефонного разговора М.С. Горбачева с Г. Колем," September 10, 1990, МГ, 563–66. Gorbachev also discusses this call in "Из беседы М.С. Горбачева с Г-Д. Геншером," September 12, 1990, МГ, 571. A later German document describes it as well: "Gespräch des Ministerialdirektors Teltschik mit Botschafter Terechow, Bonn, 15. September 1990, Betr.: Kreditanfrage der Sowjetunion über den sowjetischen Botschafter," document 422, DESE, 1541–42. See also Teltschik, *329 Tage*, 362–63.

219. "Die Zwei-plus-Vier Regelung," in *Vereinigung Deutschlands*, 167–73; "Zum Abschluß der Zwei-plus-Vier-Gespräche in Moskau am 12. September 1990: Vertrag über die abschließende Regelung in bezug auf Deutschland mit vereinbarter Protokollnotiz," in Auswärtiges Amt, *Aussenpolitik*, 699–705; GDE, 4:601–2; Genscher, *Erinnerungen*, 870–73; Zelikow and Rice, *Germany Unified*, 355–63. See also the later "Deutsche Note zur Vereinbarung zwischen der Regierung der Bundesrepublik Deutschland und den Regierungen der Französischen Republik, der USA und des Vereinigten Königreichs Großbritannien und Nordirland über die Beziehungen zwischen der Bundesrepublik Deutschland und den Drei Mächten vom 27. September 1990," in Auswärtiges Amt, *Aussenpolitik*, 699–705.

220. "Erklärung der Vier Mächte über die Aussetzung ihrer Vorbehaltsrechte über Berlin und Deutschland als Ganzes in New York vom 1. Oktober 1990," in Auswärtiges Amt, *Aussenpolitik*, 715; on the extention of NATO guarantees, see the paperwork in Wilson Files, NSC, FOIA 2001-1166-F, BPL.

221. "Из беседы М.С. Горбачева с Г-Д. Геншером," September 12, 1990, МГ, 570–73.

222. Hurd, *Memoirs*, 389.

223. The various USSR-FRG bilateral accords were signed in October and November, the last on the anniversary of the collapse of the wall, November 9, 1990; for details, see DESE 1540n8. Shevardnadze began trying to sell the completed 2 + 4 accord to the domestic market right away; see "Выступление Э.А. Шеварднадзе на заседании комитета по международным делам ВС СССР," September 20, 1990, МГ, 575–81; "Постановление Комитета Верховного Совета СССР по международным делам," September 20, 1990, МГ, 582–83. For an insightful discussion of the period immediately after unification, see Klaus Larres, ed., *Germany since Unification: The Domestic and External Consequences* (London: Macmillan, 1998).

224. "Докладная записка А.С. Черняева о предстоящем телефонном разговоре с Г. Колем и возможной поездке в Германию 3 октября," September 10, 1990, МГ, 562.

NOTES TO CONCLUSION

1. W. Szymborska, "Under One Small Star," reprinted in *view with a grain of sand,* trans. Stanislaw Barancak and Clare Cavanaugh (San Diego, CA: Harcourt Brace, 1995); Vladimir Putin, Putin, Vladimir, with Nataliya Gevorkyan, Natalya Timakova, and Andrei Kolesnikov, *First*

Person: An Astonishingly Frank Self-Portrait by Russia's President Putin, trans. Catherine A. Fitzpatrick (New York: Public Affairs, 2000), 69 (translation by the editors).

2. "Из беседы М.С. Горбачева с Г. Колем один на один," November 9, 1990, МГ, 599–609. See also the other paperwork in the same volume from the same visit. Above and beyond the agreements about troop stationing, a larger treaty resulted; see "Vertrag über gute Nachbarschaft, Partnerschaft und Zusammenarbeit zwischen der Bundesrepublik Deutschland und der Union der Sozialistischen Sowjetrepubliken vom 9. November 1990," in Auswärtiges Amt, ed., *Aussenpolitik der Bundesrepublik Deutschland: Dokumente von 1949 bis 1994* (Cologne: Verlag Wissenschaft und Politik, 1995), 738–49.

3. "Vorlage des Ministerialdirektors Teltschik an Bundeskanzler Kohl, Bonn, 25. September 1990," document 427, DESE, 1549–50; "Заявление Верховного Совета СССР," March 4, 1991, "Телефонный разговор М.С. Горбачева с Г. Колем," March 5, 1991, МГ, 637–40. On the deteriorating conditions in the Soviet Union, see the CIA assessment "The Soviet Cauldron," April 25, 1991, released by the CIA via FOIA.

4. On the CFE, see Richard A. Falkenrath, *Shaping Europe's Military Order: The Origins and Consequences of the CFE Treaty* (Cambridge, MA: MIT Press, 1995), xi; see also "Quentin Peel, 'Moscow Report Tells How Thousands of Tanks Avoided CFE Count,'" *Financial Times,* January 10, 1991, reprinted as document 103 in Vojtech Mastny, ed., *The Helsinki Process and the Reintegration of Europe, 1986–1991: Analysis and Documentation* (New York: New York University Press, 1992), 295–96. A fact sheet about the CFE treaty and its signing is available at http://www.state.gov/t/ac/rls/fs/11243.htm. On the CSCE, see the paperwork related to the CSCE meeting in folder 7, box 109, 8c monthly files, series 8, BP; "Gemeinsame Erklärung der 22 Staaten der NATO und der Warschauer Vertragsorganisation in Paris vom 19. November 1990," Auswärtiges Amt, *Aussenpolitik*, 755–57; "Die 'Charta von Paris für ein neues Europa,' vom 21. November 1990, Erklärung des Pariser KSZE-Treffens der Staats- und Regierungschefs," in Auswärtiges Amt, *Aussenpolitik*, 757–71.

5. *Grundgesetz für die Bundesrepublik Deutschland, Textausgabe, Stand: Juni/Juli 1994* (Bonn: Bundeszentrale für politische Bildung, 1994); Gerhard A. Ritter, *Der Preis der deutschen Einheit: Die Wiedervereinigung und die Krise des Sozialstaats* (Munich: Beck, 2006), 81–83; Werner Weidenfeld and Karl-Rudolf Korte, eds., *Handbuch zur deutschen Einheit* (Bonn: Bundeszentrale für politische Bildung, 1996), 349–62. See also Rödder, *Deutschland Einig Vaterland* (Munich: Beck, 2009), chapter 5.

6. Former socialist leaders in eastern Germany were also complaining that they were being persecuted unfairly for what they saw as their service to their state. See "Из беседы М.С. Горбачева с О. Лафонтеном," September 21, 1990, "Докладная записка А.С. Черняева и проект письма Г. Колю," September 24, 1990, МГ, 584–94; "Schreiben des Präsidenten Gorbatschow an Bundeskanzler Kohl, 26. September 1990," DESE 428, 1550–51.

7. Ritter, *Der Preis der deutschen Einheit*, 54–55. For more on the assassination attempt, see Wolfgang Schäuble, *Der Vertrag: Wie ich über die deutsche Einheit verhandelte* (Munich: Knaur, 1991).

8. Vladimir Putin, with Nataliya Gevorkyan, Natalya Timakova, and Andrei Kolesnikov, *First Person: An Astonishingly Frank Self-Portrait by Russia's President Putin*, trans. Catherine A. Fitzpatrick (New York: Public Affairs, 2000), 79; Putin was dismayed that the military support that he was requesting did not come immediately, complaining that it lacked instructions from Moscow; but it did eventually show up. On the issue of Stasi agents inciting violence, see Mark Kramer, "The Collapse of East European Communism and the Repercussions within the Soviet Union (Part 2)," *Journal of Cold War Studies* 6, no. 4 (Fall 2004): 3–64; Anne Worst, *Das Ende des Geheimdienstes* (Berlin: Links, 1991).

9. The exact timing of Mitterrand's decision to support Kohl is a matter of speculation; Frédéric Bozo thinks that it was already in place before the wall came down, whereas I see it evolving in

early 1990. See Frédéric Bozo, *Mitterrand, la fin de la guerre froide et l'unification allemande: De Yalta à Maastricht* (Paris: Odile Jacob, 2005).

10. GDE, 2:431–33, tries to estimate the price of unity at 57.3 billion DMs, but this sum is limited to amounts given to the Soviet Union in 1990–91, which is not sufficient; for a more nuanced discussion of why the "price of unity" depends on what you consider to be the costs, see Rödder, *Deutschland Einig Vaterland*, chapter 5. Evidence that Gorbachev's ideas seemed plausible to leading thinkers elsewhere at the time may be found in Harold James and Marla Stone, eds., *When the Wall Came Down* (New York: Routledge, 1992); see in particular the reference to a 1990 article by John Lewis Gaddis suggesting that Germany should go into both military alliances, 29, and Henry Kissinger's idea that Central Europe should be neutral, 199.

11. Francis Fukuyama, *The End of History and the Last Man* (New York: Penguin Books, 1992), 283.

12. Although I have studied only 1989–90 in detail above, I believe that speculation about its broader significance remains worthwhile. Readers who have made it this far into the fine print will not be surprised to learn that I think we can learn larger lessons from a small number of, or even one, significant event. Those who believe that broad applicability results only from a large number of cases will obviously disagree. I support Edward Ingram, however, when he says that the "historian's single example may be more representative than the political scientist's cluster." As Ingram argues, it is not at all obvious that "a cluster of lightly researched, detached—at best semi-detached—cases, often written up by different scholars, is likely to advance the argument any better" than a thorough analysis of a crucial event. Edward Ingram, "The Wonderland of the Political Scientist," *International Security* 22, no. 1 (Summer 1997): 56. I am grateful to Andrew Moravcsik for drawing my attention to this quotation.

13. "Прощальное письмо М.С. Горбачева Г. Колю," December 25, 1991, МГ, 650–51. The scholar quoted in this paragraph is Mark Kramer, "The Collapse of East European Communism and the Repercussions within the Soviet Union (Part 3)," *Journal of Cold War Studies* 7, no. 1 (Winter 2005): 3–96. For more on this topic, see also Andrei Grachev, *Gorbachev's Gamble: Soviet Foreign Policy and the End of the Cold War* (London: Polity, 2008).

14. Robert M. Gates, *From the Shadows: The Ultimate Insider's Story of Five Presidents and How They Won the Cold War* (New York: Touchstone, 1996), 483. J. D. Bindenagel was the U.S. deputy chief of mission in East Berlin in 1989; J. D. Bindenagel, interview with author, June 28, 2008. Valentin Falin, *Konflikte im Kreml: Zur Vorgeschichte der deutschen Einheit und Auflösung der Sowjetunion* (Munich: Blessing Verlag, 1997), 151. As one article in *Der Spiegel* put it, the 1989 revolution was producing headlines that in normal times, would have occupied "actors and consumers for months or even years," but now disappeared in days, pushed aside by even more spectacular events. See "'Die Macht liegt auf der Straße,'" *Der Spiegel* 50, no. 89, December 11, 1989, 22–26.

15. Ritter, *Der Preis der deutschen Einheit*, 13.

16. Richard H. K. Vietor, *How Countries Compete: Strategy, Structure, and Government in the Global Economy* (Boston: Harvard Business School Press, 2007), 204; Ritter, *Der Preis der deutschen Einheit*, 104–20.

17. Andreas Wirsching, *Abschied vom Provisorium 1982–1990: Geschichte der Bundesrepublik Deutschland* (Stuttgart: Deutsche Verlags-Anstalt, 2006), 679; Ritter, *Der Preis der deutschen Einheit*, 9.

18. Kennan made this remark to the Clinton administration's main Russian expert, Strobe Talbott; it is quoted in Talbott's memoir, *The Russia Hand* (New York: Random House, 2003), 220.

19. James A. Baker, "Russia in NATO?" *Washington Quarterly* (Winter 2002): 95–103.

20. See Talbott's *The Russia Hand* for his (not altogether pleasant) memories from the Paris summit, 246. See also James M. Goldgeier, *Not Whether but When: The US Decision to Enlarge*

NATO (Washington, DC: Brookings, 1999), 108–16; James M. Goldgeier and Derek Chollet, *America between the Wars: From 11/9 to 9/11, the Misunderstood Years between the Fall of the Berlin Wall and the Start of the War on Terror* (New York: Public Affairs, 2008), 124. I am grateful to Ambassador John Kornblum and an expert who wishes to remain anonymous for discussions on this point.

21. George Friedman, "Georgia and the Balance of Power," *New York Review of Books* 55, no. 14 (September 25, 2008): 24; Mark Kramer, "The Myth of a No-NATO-Enlargement Pledge to Russia," *Washington Quarterly* 32, no. 2 (April 2009): 39–61.

22. Ronald D. Asmus, *Opening NATO's Door: How the Alliance Remade Itself for a New Era* (New York: Columbia University Press, 2002), passim; Goldgeier, *Not Whether*, 58–59.

23. I have filed an FOIA request for this document, and I am grateful to Asmus and Kornblum for discussing it and emailing about it. See also Asmus, *Opening NATO's Door*, 307–8n7.

24. Angela Stent, *Russia and Germany Reborn: Unification, the Soviet Collapse, and the New Europe* (Princeton, NJ: Princeton University Press, 1999), 140–41; Philip Zelikow, "NATO Expansion Wasn't Ruled Out," *International Herald Tribune*, August 10, 1995.

25. Putin, with Gevorkyan, Timakova, and Kolesnikov, *First Person*, 81, 169. In making these remarks, Putin said that he was agreeing with an analysis offered by Kissinger. Putin also recalls Kissinger talking about how he (Kissinger) got his start in intelligence, just like Putin (81).

26. Asmus, *Opening NATO's Door*, 4–6; Zbigniew Brzezinski, David Ignatius, and Brent Scowcroft, *America and the World* (New York: Basic Books, 2008), 172; first Medvedev quotation, from speech of November 5, 2008, cited in Sergei L. Loiko, "Russia to Counter U.S. Antimissile System in Eastern Europe," *Los Angeles Times,* November 6, 2008; Mikhail Gorbachev, "Russia Never Wanted a War," *New York Times,* August 20, 2008; Medvedev's idea of new architecture cited in Steven Erlanger, "NATO Duel Centers on Georgia and Ukraine," *New York Times,* December 1, 2008. For more on the 2008 conflict between Russia and Georgia, see Bill Keller, "Cold Friends, Wrapped in Mink and Medals," *New York Times,* August 17, 2008; Charles King, "The Five-Day War: Managing Moscow after the Georgia Crisis," *Foreign Affairs* (November–December 2008). For broader history and context, see Talbott, *The Russia Hand*, 382.

27. "Russia Suspends Arms Control Pact," BBC News, July 14, 2007, online. The quotation from the secretary general is cited in Steven Erlanger, "NATO Chief Defends Engaging with Russia," *New York Times*, December 4, 2008. My assessment here agrees with an earlier insightful investigation by Angela Stent, *Russia and Germany*, 140–41. The literary reference above is to the poem "Homage to a Government" by Philip Larkin, which refers to the British experience with retreat from empire: "Next year we shall be living in a country/That brought it soldiers home for lack of money." Philip Larkin, "Homage to a Government," reprinted in *Collected Poems* (London: Farrar Straus Giroux, 1989).

28. Scowcroft worry noted in chapter 4 above; Robert Hutchings, "The United States, German Unification, and European Integration," in *Europe and the End of the Cold War*, ed. Frédéric Bozo, Marie-Pierre Rey, N. Piers Ludlow, and Leopoldo Nuti (London: Routledge, 2008), 121.

29. Bush quoted in chapter 4 above; Hubert Védrine, *Les mondes de François Mitterrand* (Paris: Fayard, 1996), 443; Goldgeier, *Not Whether*, chapter 2. I am also grateful to Hubert Védrine for an email on this subject, in which he pointed out that he made this comment to highlight the differences between American priorities (NATO) and French priorities (European integration); Védrine emphasized that the two were in no way incompatible.

30. See the discussion of alternative outcomes in Stent, *Russia and Germany*, 145; Stephen Szabo, *The Diplomacy of German Unification* (New York: St. Martin's Press, 1992), 121–22.

31. Discussion of this topic may be found in Robert D. Blackwill, "The Three Rs: Rivalry, Russia, and 'Ran," *National Interest* (January 2008); Stephen F. Cohen, *Soviet Fates and Lost*

Alternatives: From Stalinism to the New Cold War (New York: Columbia University Press, 2009); James M. Goldgeier and Michael McFaul, *Power and Purpose: US Policy toward Russia after the Cold War* (Washington, DC: Brookings, 2003), 13; Stephen Sestanovich, "What Has Moscow Done?" *Foreign Affairs* (November–December 2008); and Dimitri K. Simes, "Losing Russia: The Costs of Renewed Confrontation," *Foreign Affairs* (November–December 2007)."

32. Horst Telschik, interview with author, June 13, 2008, phone conversation.

33. Stephen Kotkin, *Armageddon Averted: The Soviet Collapse, 1970–2000* (New York: Oxford University Press, 2001), 89; Sestanovich, "What Has Moscow Done?"

34. Archie Brown, *Seven Years That Changed the World: Perestroika in Perspective* (New York: Oxford University Press, 2007), 330.

35. See Simes, "Losing Russia"; Stephen F. Cohen, *Failed Crusade: America and the Tragedy of Post-Communist Russia* (New York: W. W. Norton, 2001). Gorbachev is quoted in Baker with DeFrank, *The Politics of Diplomacy*, 529.

36. I have adapted this concept from a passage in Volker Berghahn and Charles Maier, "Modern Europe in American Historical Writing," in *Imagined Histories: American Historians Interpret the Past*, ed. Anthony Molho and Gordon S. Wood (Princeton, NJ: Princeton University Press, 1998), 410: "Europe offers the clearest view of the dialectical conflict . . . between a restless de-territorialization and the claims of the local, the provincial, the national and the regional. Just as Herzen in 1849 claimed that western Europe was the pre-eminent battleground between liberalism and reaction, one might claim that Europe today—eastern as well as western—is the major arena for the contest over territorially based identity."

37. For more on these issues, see Archie Brown, "Perestroika and the End of the Cold War," *Cold War History* 7, no. 1 (February 2007): 1–17; Simes, "Losing Russia." For an insightful discussion on Russians in particular as members of both the elite and the repressed, see Geoffrey Hosking, *Rulers and Victims: The Russians in the Soviet Union* (Cambridge, MA: Harvard University Press, 2006).

38. As cited in the introduction, see Odd Arne Westad, "Bernath Lecture: The New International History of the Cold War: Three (Possible) Paradigms," *Diplomatic History* 24, no. 4 (Fall 2000): 556–57; Adi Ignatius, "A Tsar is Born," *Time*, December 4, 2007, online.

BIBLIOGRAPHY

PRIMARY SOURCES FROM ARCHIVES AND PERSONAL
COLLECTIONS OF PARTICIPANTS
FRANCE

PARIS

Archives Nationales

GERMANY

BERLIN

Bundesarchiv (Federal Archive) and Stiftung-Archiv der Parteien und Massenorganisationen der
   DDR (SAPMO, or former party archive)
Ministerium für Staatssicherheit (MfS), Bundesbeauftragte für die Unterlagen des Staatssicherheits-
   dienstes der ehemaligen Deutschen Demokratischen Republik (BStU, or Stasi Archive)
Robert Havemann-Gesellschaft (RHG, or dissident archive)

BONN/SANKT AUGUSTIN

Konrad Adenauer Stiftung Pressearchiv (KASPA, Konrad Adenauer Foundation Press Archive)

DRESDEN

Sächsisches Hauptstaatsarchiv (Main State Archive of Saxony)

HAMBURG

ARD-NDR Videoarchiv (ARD Video Archive)

KOBLENZ

Bundesarchiv (Federal Archive)

LEIPZIG

Sächsisches Staatsarchiv (State Archive of Saxony)

POLAND

WARSAW

KARTA (Solidarity and opposition materials)

RUSSIA

MOSCOW

Архив Горбачев-Фонда (Gorbachev Foundation Archive)

UNITED KINGDOM

LONDON

Cabinet Office (CO) materials, released under the Freedom of Information law (FOI)
Foreign and Commonwealth Office (FCO) materials, released under the FOI Act

UNITED STATES

CAMBRIDGE, MASSACHUSETTS

Фонд 1989, copy of Russian collection, Government Documents, Harvard University

BIBLIOGRAPHY

COLLEGE STATION, TEXAS
George H. W. Bush Presidential Library (BPL)

PRINCETON, NEW JERSEY
James A. Baker III Papers, Department of Rare Books and Special Collections, Mudd Library, Princeton University (BP)
Robert Hutchings, personal collection
Jack Matlock, personal collection

SIMI VALLEY, CALIFORNIA
Ronald Reagan Presidential Library

WASHINGTON, DC
National Security Archive
CIA materials released under the FOIA
Department of Defense materials released under the FOIA
State Department materials released under the FOIA

PRIMARY SOURCES COLLECTED AND MADE AVAILABLE AT SCHOLARLY CONFERENCES

"Briefing Book for Cold War Endgame." March 29–30, 1996, sponsored by the Woodrow Wilson School and the James A. Baker III Institute for Public Policy. Complied by the National Security Archive.

Cold War International History Project Paris Conference (CWIHPPC). "Europe and the End of the Cold War." June 15–17, 2006, Paris. Organized by the Cold War International History Project in collaboration with other research centers, June 15–17, 2006.

Georgia Conference (GC). "End of the Cold War in Europe, 1989," May 1–3, 1998, Musgrove, Saint Simons Island, Georgia. Organized by the National Security Archive.

Greenstein, Fred I., and William C. Wohlforth, eds. *Cold War Endgame: Report of a Conference.* Center of International Studies Monograph Series No. 10. Princeton, NJ: Center of International Studies, 1997.

Mershon Conference. "US-Soviet Military Relationships at the End of the Cold War, 1988–91." October 15–17, 1999, Mershon Center, Ohio State University.

Miedzeszyn-Warsaw Conference (MC). "Poland 1986–1989: The End of the System." October 20–24, 1999, Miedzeszyn-Warsaw, Poland. Cosponsored by the Institute of Political Studies at the Polish Academy of Sciences and the National Security Archive.

Prague Conference (PC). "The Democratic Revolution in Czechoslovakia," October 14–16, 1999, Prague. Organized by the National Security Archive, the Czechoslovak Documentation Center, and the Institute of Contemporary History, Academy of Sciences of the Czech Republic.

PRIMARY SOURCES, PUBLISHED

Auswärtiges Amt, ed. *Deutsche Aussenpolitik 1990/91: Auf dem Weg zu einer europäischen Friedensordnung eine Dokumentation.* Bonn: Auswärtiges Amt, April 1991.

———, ed. *Aussenpolitik der Bundesrepublik Deutschland: Dokumente von 1949 bis 1994.* Cologne: Verlag Wissenschaft und Politik, 1995.

Bozóki, András, ed. *The Roundtable Talks of 1989: The Genesis of Hungarian Democracy, Analysis and Documents.* Budapest: Central European University Press, 2002.

Cold War International History Project Bulletin. Assembled and distributed by the Cold War International History Project, Washington, DC.

DDR Journal zur November Revolution August bis Dezember 1989, vom Ausreisen bis zum Einreißen der Mauer. A compilation produced by the Western newspaper *taz*, 1990.

Fischer, Benjamin B. *At Cold War's End: US Intelligence on the Soviet Union and Eastern Europe, 1989–1991.* Washington, DC: Central Intelligence Agency, 1999.

BIBLIOGRAPHY

Fischer, Horst, ed. *Schalck-Imperium: Ausgewählte Dokumente*. Bochum, Germany: Brockmeyer, 1993.

Freedman, Lawrence, ed. *Europe Transformed: Documents on the End of the Cold War—Key Treaties, Agreements, Statements, and Speeches*. New York: St. Martin's Press, 1990.

Gesamtdeutsches Institut, Bundesanstalt für gesamtdeutsche Aufgaben. *Analysen, Dokumentationen und Chronik zur Entwicklung in der DDR von September bis Dezember 1989*. Bonn: Bundesanstalt, 1990.

Gorbatschow, Michail S. *Gipfelgespräche: Geheime Protokolle aus meiner Amtszeit*. Berlin: Rowohlt, 1993.

Горбачев, Михаил, Галкин, Александр, и Черняев, Анатолий. *Михаил Горбачев и германский вопрос: Сборник документов 1986–1991*. Moscow: *Весь Мир*, 2006.

Grenville, J.A.S., and Bernard Wasserstein, eds. *The Major International Treaties since 1945: A History and Guide with Texts*. London: Methuen, 1987.

Grundgesetz für die Bundesrepublik Deutschland, Textausgabe, Stand: Oktober 1990. Bonn: Bundeszentrale für politische Bildung, 1990.

Grundgesetz für die Bundesrepublik Deutschland, Textausgabe, Stand: Juni/Juli 1994. Bonn: Bundeszentrale für politische Bildung, 1994.

Haines, Gerald K., and Robert E. Leggett. *CIA's Analysis of Soviet Union, 1947–1991*. Washington, DC: Ross and Perry, 2001.

Hertle, Hans-Hermann. *Der Fall der Mauer: Die unbeabsichtigte Selbstauflösung des SED-Staates*. Opladen: Westdeutscher Verlag, 1996.

Hertle, Hans-Hermann, and Gerd-Rüdiger Stephan, eds. *Das Ende der SED: Die letzten Tage des Zentralkomitees*. Berlin: Links, September 1997.

Jacobsen, Hans-Adolf, ed. *Bonn-Warschau 1945–1991*. Cologne: Verlag Wissenschaft und Politik, 1992.

James, Harold, and Marla Stone, eds. *When the Wall Came Down*. New York: Routledge, 1992.

Jarausch, Konrad H., and Volker Gransow, eds. *Uniting Germany: Documents and Debates, 1944–1993*. Providence, RI: Berghahn Books, 1994.

Kaiser, Karl. *Deutschlands Vereinigung: Die internationalen Aspekte*. Bergisch-Gladbach: Lübbe Verlag, 1991.

Kleßmann, Christoph, and Georg Wagner, eds. *Das gespaltene Land: Leben in Deutschland 1945–1990 Texte und Dokumente zur Sozialgeschichte*. Munich: Beck, 1993.

Küchenmeister, Daniel, and Gerd-Rüdiger Stephan, eds. *Honecker Gorbatschow Vieraugengespräche*. Berlin: Dietz Verlag, 1993.

Küsters, Hanns Jürgen, and Daniel Hoffman, eds. *Dokumente zur Deutschlandpolitik: Deutsche Einheit, Sonderedition aus den Akten des Bundeskanzleramtes 1989/90* (DESE). Munich: R. Oldenbourg Verlag, 1998.

Kowalczuk, Ilko-Sascha, ed. *Freiheit und Öffentlichkeit: Politischer Samisdat in der DDR 1985–1989*. Berlin: Robert-Havemann-Gesellschaft, 2002.

Mastny, Vojtech, ed. *The Helsinki Process and the Reintegration of Europe, 1986–1991: Analysis and Documentation*. New York: New York University Press, 1992.

Mastny, Vojtech, and Malcolm Byrne, eds. *A Cardboard Castle? An Inside History of the Warsaw Pact*. New York: Central European University Press, 2005.

Mitter, Armin, and Stefan Wolle, eds. *Ich liebe euch doch alle! Befehle und Lageberichte des MfS Januar-November 1989*. Berlin: BasisDruck, 1990.

Mitterrand, François. *De l'Allemagne, de la France*. Paris: Editions Odile Jacob, April 1996.

Nakath, Detlef, and Gerd-Rüdiger Stephan, eds. *Countdown zur deutschen Einheit: Eine dokumentierte Geschichte der deutsch-deutschen Beziehungen 1987–1990*. Berlin: Dietz, 1996.

Nakath, Detlef, Gero Neugebauer, and Gerd-Rüdiger Stephan, eds. *"Im Kreml brennt noch Licht" Spitzenkontakte zwischen SED/PDS und KPdSU 1989–1991*. Berlin: Dietz, 1998.

Nathan, Andrew J., Perry Link, and "Zhang Liang," eds. *The Tiananmen Papers: The Chinese Leadership's Decision to Use Force against Their Own People in Their Own Words*. New York: Public Affairs, 2001.

BIBLIOGRAPHY

Noelle-Neumann, Elisabeth, and Renate Köcher, eds. *Allensbacher Jahrbuch der Demoskopie 1984–1992*. Vol. 9. Munich: Saur, 1993.

Schweitzer, C. C., et al., eds. *Politics and Government in the Federal Republic of Germany, Basic Documents*. Leamington Spa, UK: Berg Publishers, 1984.

Stasi-Unterlagen-Gesetz. Munich: C. H. Beck, October 1993.

Stephan, Gerd-Rüdiger, and Daniel Küchenmeister, eds. *"Vorwärts immer, rückwärts nimmer!"* Berlin: Dietz, 1994.

Steury, Donald P. *On the Front Lines of the Cold War: Documents on the Intelligence War in Berlin*. Washington, DC: Central Intelligence Agency History Staff, 1999.

Thaysen, Uwe, ed. *Der Zentrale Runde Tisch: Wortprotokolle und Dokumente* (ZRT-WD). Wiesbaden: Westdeutscher Verlag, 2000.

Die Vereinigung Deutschlands im Jahre 1990: Verträge und Erklärungen. Bonn: Presse- und Informationsamt der Bundesregierung, 1991.

Von Münch, Ingo, ed. *Dokumente des geteilten Deutschland*. 2 vols. Stuttgart: Kröner, 1976.

Von Plato, Alexander. *Die Vereinigung Deutschlands—ein weltpolitisches Machtspiel: Bush, Kohl, Gorbatschow und die geheimen Moskauer Protokolle*. Berlin: Links, 2002. (Note, unlike other books in this category, this one uses lengthy quotations from documents to produce a narrative, rather than reproducing the documents.)

Weber, Hermann, ed. *DDR: Dokumente zur Geschichte der Deutschen Demokratischen Republik*. Munich: dtv, 1986.

Zimmerman, Hartmut. *DDR Handbuch*. Cologne: Verlag Wissenschaft und Politik, 1985.

PRIMARY SOURCES, ONLINE

http://chnm.gmu.edu/1989
http://my.barackobama.com/page/content/berlinvideo
http://rodon.org/other/mgigv/index.htm
http://usa.usembassy.de/etexts/ga6-890531.htm
http://www.2plus4.de
http://www.bmvg.de
http://www.bundesregierung.de
http:// www.chronik-der-mauer.de
http://www.chronik-der-wende.de
http://www.dod.mil/pubs/foi/rdroom.html
http://www.foia.cia.gov/
http://www.gwu.edu/~nsarchiv/
http://www.havemann-gesellschaft.de
http://www.helmut-kohl.de
http://www.margaretthatcher.org
http://www.osce.org/item/15661.html
http://www.state.gov/m/a/ips/
http://www.whitehouse.gov/oa/foia/eop-foia.html

INTERVIEWS, PHONE CONVERSATIONS, AND EMAIL CORRESPONDENCE WITH PARTICIPANTS

Asmus, Ronald D. March 16, 2008, Brussels.
Baker, James A., III. February 11, 2009, Houston.
Bindenagel, J. D. June 28, 2008, phone conversation and email.
Blackwill, Robert. January 9, 2009, phone conversation.
Elbe, Frank. June 10 and 11, 2009, phone conversations.
Chrobog, Jürgen. March 21, 2009, Brussels.
Cooper, Robert. March 20, 2009, Brussels.

Dunkerley, Craig. January 9, 2009, phone conversation.
Falin, Valentin. May 17, 1996, Tostedt, Germany.
Fischer, Joschka. April 17, 2007, Princeton, NJ.
Genscher, Hans-Dietrich. June 2, 2009, Wachtberg-Pech, Germany.
Hurd, Douglas. March 17, 2009, London.
Kiessler, Richard. March 20, 2009, Brussels.
Kornblum, John. April 4, 2008, phone conversation.
Matlock, Jack. April 18, 2007, Princeton, NJ.
Nuland, Victoria. January 9, 2009, phone conversation.
Powell, Charles. March 29, 2009, London.
Powell, Jonathan. October 20, 2008, London.
Ross, Dennis. November 17, 2008, Washington, DC.
Scherbakova, Irina. July 12, 2005, Moscow.
Scowcroft, Brent. September 19, 2008, Washington, DC.
Sicherman, Harvey. December 12, 2008, phone conversation.
Sello, Tom. August 30, 2006, Berlin.
Teltschik, Horst. June 13, 2008, phone conversation.
Védrine, Hubert, June 18, 2009, email.
Vershbow, Alexander. July 15, 2005, Moscow.
Wolf, Markus. June 6, 1996, Berlin.
Zelikow, Philip. July 27, 2008, phone conversation and subsequent emails.
Zoellick, Robert. March 16, 2008, Brussels.
(Scheduled interview with Anatoly Chernyaev in Moscow was canceled due to illness.)

AUTOBIOGRAPHIES, BROADCAST OR PUBLISHED INTERVIEWS, MEMOIRS, AND OTHER ACCOUNTS BY CONTEMPORARIES AND PARTICIPANTS

Ackermann, Eduard. *Mit feinem Gehör: Vierzig Jahre in der Bonner Politik.* Bergisch Gladbach: Lübbe Verlag, 1994.
Asmus, Ronald D. *Opening NATO's Door: How the Alliance Remade Itself for a New Era.* New York: Columbia University Press, 2002.
Baker, James A. "Russia in NATO?" *Washington Quarterly* (Winter 2002): 95–103.
Baker, James A., with Thomas A. DeFrank. *The Politics of Diplomacy: Revolution, War, and Peace, 1989–1992.* New York: G. P. Putnam's Sons, 1995.
Bernhof, Reinhard. *Die Leipziger Protokolle.* Halle: Projekte Verlag, 2004.
Blackwill, Robert. "The Three Rs: Rivalry, Russia, and 'Ran.'" *National Interest* (January 2008): online.
Bohley, Bärbel. "Under Open Skies." *Bulletin of the German Historical Institute* 42 (2008): 27–37.
Boldin, Valery. *Ten Years That Shook the World: The Gorbachev Era as Witnessed by His Chief of Staff.* New York: HarperCollins, 1994.
Brandt, Willy. *My Life in Politics.* New York: Viking, 1991.
———. " . . . *was zusammengehört.*" Bonn: Dietz, 1993.
Brzezinski, Zbigniew. *The Grand Failure: The Birth and Death of Communism in the Twentieth Century.* New York: Charles Scribner's Sons, 1989.
Brzezinski, Zbigniew, David Ignatius, and Brent Scowcroft. *America and the World.* New York: Basic Books, 2008.
Bush, George, and Brent Scowcroft. *A World Transformed.* New York: Knopf, 1998.
Chernyaev, Anatoly. *Die letzten Jahre einer Weltmacht: Der Kreml von innen.* Stuttgart: Deutsche-Verlagsanstalt, 1993.
Chernyaev, Anatoly. "Gorbachev and the Reunification of Germany: Personal Recollections." In *Soviet Foreign Policy, 1971–1991*, ed. Gabriel Gorodetsky. London: Routledge, 1994.

BIBLIOGRAPHY

———. *My Six Years with Gorbachev*. Trans. and ed. Robert English and Elizabeth Tucker. University Park: Pennsylvania State University Press, 2000.

Chiang, Renee, Adi Ignatius, and Bao Pu, eds. *Prisoner of the State: The Secret Journal of Zhao Ziyang*. New York: Simon and Schuster, 2009.

CNN. *Cold War*. Television series, broadcast interviews with participants in events, particularly episode 23.

Cradock, Percy. *In Pursuit of British Interests: Reflections on Foreign Policy under Margaret Thatcher and John Major*. London: John Murray, 1997.

Craig, Gordon. "Die Chequers-Affäre." *Vierteljahrshefte für Zeitgeschichte* 39, no. 4 (October 1991): 611–23.

Drakulic´, Slavenka. *How We Survived Communism and Even Laughed*. New York: Harper Perennial, 1993.

Eppelmann, Rainer, Markus Meckel, and Robert Grünbaum, eds. *Das ganze Deutschland: Reportagen zur Einheit*. Berlin: Aufbau, 2005.

Falin, Valentin. *Politische Erinnerungen*. Munich: Knaur, 1995.

———. *Konflikte im Kreml: Zur Vorgeschichte der deutschen Einheit und Auflösung der Sowjetunion*. Munich: Blessing Verlag, 1997.

Führer, Christian. *Und wir sind dabei gewesen*. Berlin: Ullstein, 2009.

Gates, Robert M. *From the Shadows: The Ultimate Insider's Story of Five Presidents and How They Won the Cold War*. New York: Touchstone, 1996.

Genscher, Hans-Dietrich. *Erinnerungen*. Berlin: Sielder, 1995. Abridged English translation: *Rebuilding a House Divided*. New York: Broadway Books, 1998.

Gorbachev, Mikhail. *Toward a Better World*. London: Hutchinson, 1987.

———. *Memoirs*. New York: Doubleday, 1995.

Gorbachev, Mikhail, Vadim Sagladin, and Anatoli Tschernjajew. *Das Neue Denken*. Munich: Goldmann Verlag, July 1997.

Grachev, Andrei. *Gorbachev's Gamble: Soviet Foreign Policy and the End of the Cold War*. London: Policy, 2008.

Greenspan, Alan. *The Age of Turbulence*. New York: Penguin, 2007.

Havemannn, Robert. *Fragen Antworten Fragen: Aus der Biographie eines deutschen Marxisten*. Berlin: Piper, 1970.

Hensel, Jana. *Zonenkinder*. Hamburg: Rowohlt, 2004.

Hutchings, Robert L. *American Diplomacy and the End of the Cold War: An Insider's Account of US Policy in Europe, 1989–1992*. Washington, DC: Wilson Center, 1997.

Kiessler, Richard, and Frank Elbe. *Ein runder Tisch mit scharfen Ecken: Der diplomatische Weg zur deutschen Einheit*. Baden-Baden: Nomos Verlagsgesellschaft, 1993.

Kissinger, Henry. *Diplomacy*. New York: Simon and Schuster, 1994.

Klein, Hans. *Es begann im Kaukasus: Der entscheidende Schritt in die Einheit Deutschlands*. Berlin: Ullstein, 1991.

Knabe, Hubertus, ed. *Aufbruch in eine andere DDR: Reformer und Oppositionelle zur Zukunft ihres Landes*. Rowohlt: Hamburg, 1989.

Kohl, Helmut. *Erinnerungen 1982–1990*. Munich: Droemer, 2005.

———. *Erinnerungen 1990–1994*. Munich: Droemer, 2007.

Kohl, Helmut, Kai Diekmann, and Ralf Georg Reuth. *Ich wollte Deutschlands Einheit*. Berlin: Ullstein, 1996.

Kowalczuk, Ilko-Sascha, and Tom Sello, eds. *Für ein freies Land mit freien Menschen: Opposition und Widerstand in Biographien und Fotos*. Berlin: Robert-Havemann-Gesellschaft, 2006.

Kotschemassow, Wjatscheslaw. *Meine letzte Mission*. Berlin: Dietz, 1994.

Krenz, Egon. *Wenn Mauern fallen*. Vienna: Neff, 1990.

Kwizinskij, J. A. *Vor dem Sturm: Erinnerungen eines Diplomaten*. Berlin: Siedler, 1993.

Lafontaine, Oskar. *Deutsche Wahrheiten: Die nationale und die soziale Frage*. Hamburg: Hoffmann und Campe Verlag, 1990.

BIBLIOGRAPHY

Leonhard, Wolfgang. *Die Revolution entläßt ihre Kinder*. Cologne: Kiepenheuer and Witsch, 1955.

———. *Spurensuche*. Cologne: Kiepenheuer and Witsch, 1992.

Ligachev, Yegor. *Inside Gorbachev's Kremlin*. New York: Pantheon Books, 1993.

Matlock, Jack F., Jr. *Autopsy on an Empire: The American Ambassador's Account of the Collapse of the Soviet Union*. New York: Random House, 1995.

———. *Reagan and Gorbachev: How the Cold War Ended*. New York: Random House, 2004.

Meckel, Markus. *Selbstbewußt in die deutsche Einheit*. Berlin: Berlin Verlag, 2001.

Mittag, Günter. *Um jeden Preis*. Berlin: Aufbau-Verlag, 1991.

Mitterrand, François. *Ma part de vérité: De la rupture à l'unité*. Paris: Fayard, 1969.

———. *De l'Allemagne, de la France*. Paris: Editions Odile Jacob, 1996.

Modrow, Hans, ed. *Das Große Haus: Insider berichten aus dem ZK der SED*. Berlin: edition ost, 1994.

Neues Forum Leipzig, ed. *Jetzt oder nie—Demokratie! Leipziger Herbst '89*. Leipzig: Forum Verlag, 1989.

Palazchenko, Pavel. *My Years with Gorbachev and Shevardnadze: The Memoir of a Soviet Interpreter*. University Park: Penn State University Press, 1997.

Poppe, Ulrike, et al., eds. *Zwischen Selbstbehauptung und Anpassung*. Berlin: Links, 1995.

Putin, Vladimir, with Nataliya Gevorkyan, Natalya Timakova, and Andrei Kolesnikov. *First Person: An Astonishingly Frank Self-Portrait by Russia's President Putin*. Trans. Catherine A. Fitzpatrick. New York: Public Affairs, 2000.

Reich, Jens. *Abschied von Lebenslügen: Die Intelligenz und die Macht*. Berlin: Rowohlt, 1992.

Rusch, Claudia. *Meine freie deutsche Jugend*. Frankfurt: Fischer, 2003.

Sagladin, Vadim. *Und Jetzt Welt-Innen Politik: Die Außenpolitik der Perestroika*. Rosenheim: Horizonte, 1990.

Schabowski, Günter, and Frank Sieren. *Wir haben fast alles falsch gemacht*. Berlin: Econ, 2009.

Schabowski, Günter, Frank Sieren, and Ludwig Koehne, eds. *Das Politbüro Ende eines Mythos: eine Befragung Günter Schabowskis*. Reinbek bei Hamburg: December 1990.

Schachnasarow, Georg. *Preis der Freiheit: Eine Bilanz von Gorbatschow Berater*. Bonn: Bouvier Verlag, 1996.

Schäuble, Wolfgang. *Der Vertrag: Wie ich über die deutsche Einheit verhandelte*. Munich: Knaur, 1991.

Shevardnadze, Eduard. *The Future Belongs to Freedom*. London: Sinclair-Stevenson, 1991.

Stern, Fritz. *Five Germanys I Have Known*. New York: Farrar, Straus and Giroux, 2006.

Talbott, Strobe. *The Russia Hand*. New York: Random House, 2003.

Teltschik, Horst. *329 Tage: Innenansichten der Einigung*. Berlin: Siedler, 1991.

Tetzner, Reiner. *Leipziger Ring: Aufzeichnungen eines Montagsdemonstranten Oktober 1989 bis 1. Mai 1990*. Frankfurt: Luchterhand, 1990.

Védrine, Hubert. *Les mondes de François Mitterrand*. Paris: Fayard, 1996.

Waigel, Theo, and Manfred Schell, eds. *Tage, die Deutschland und die Welt veränderten*. Munich: edition ferenczy, 1994.

Wolf, Markus. *Die Troika*. Berlin: Aufbau-Verlag, 1989.

———. *Im Eigenen Auftrag*. Munich: Schneekluth, 1991.

———. *Spionagechef im geheimen Krieg: Erinnerungen*. Munich: List, 1997.

Wolf, Markus, and Anne McElvoy. *Man without a Face: The Autobiography of Communism's Greatest Spymaster*. New York: Random House, 1997.

Zelikow, Philip, and Condoleezza Rice. *Germany Unified and Europe Transformed: A Study in Statecraft*. Cambridge, MA: Harvard University Press, 1995.

NEWSPAPERS, RADIO, AND TELEVISION

ABC Primetime Live
Berliner Zeitung
Bild

BIBLIOGRAPHY

Bundestag Report
CBS Evening News
Financial Times
Frankfurter Allgemeine Zeitung
Independent
International Herald Tribune
Los Angeles Times
Le Monde
Der Morgen
Nation
National Public Radio, various news broadcasts
NBC Nightly News
Neues Deutschland
Neue Zeit
Newsweek
New York Times
Правда
Der Spiegel
Süddeutsche Zeitung
Tagesschau
Tagesspiegel
Tagesthemen
taz
Time
Wall Street Journal
Die Zeit

SECONDARY LITERATURE

Abdelal, Rawi. *Capital Rules: The Construction of Global Finance*. Cambridge, MA: Harvard University Press, 2008.

Abteilung Bildung und Forschung, ed. *Wissenschaftliche Reihe des Bundesbeauftragten für die Unterlagen des Staatssicherheitsdienstes der ehemaligen Deutschen Demokratischen Republik*. Vol. 1, *Aktenlage: Die Bedeutung der Unterlagen des Staatssicherheitsdienstes für die Zeitgeschichtsforschung*, ed. Klaus-Dietmar Henke and Roger Engelmann. Berlin: Links Verlag, 1995. Vol. 2, *Akten-Einsicht: Rekonstruktion einer politischen Verfolgung*, ed. Karl Wilhelm Fricke. Berlin: Links Verlag, 1995. Vol. 3, *Inoffizielle Mitarbeiter des Ministeriums für Staaatssicherheit: Richtlinien und Durchführungsbestimmungen*, ed. Helmut Muller-Enbergs. Berlin: Links Verlag, 1996. Vol. 5, *Das Wörterbuch der Staatssicherheit: Definitionen zur "politisch-operativen Arbeit,"* ed. Siegfried Suckut. Berlin: Links Verlag, 1996. Vol. 6, *Sicherungsbereich Literatur: Schriftsteller und Staatssicherheit in der Deutschen Demokratischen Republik*, ed. Joachim Walter. Berlin: Links Verlag, 1996. Vol. 7, *Die Kirchenpolitik von SED und Staatssicherheit*, ed. Clemens Vollnhals. Berlin: Links Verlag, 1996. Vol. 8, *Staatspartei und Staatssicherheit: Zum Verhältnis von SED und MfS*, ed. Siegfried Suckut and Walter Süß. Berlin: Links Verlag, 1997. Vol. 9, *Walter Süß: Staatssicherheit am Ende. Warum es den Mächtigen nicht gelang, 1989 eine Revolution zu verhindern*. Berlin: Links Verlag, 1999.

Adomeit, Hannes. *Imperial Overstretch: Germany in Soviet Policy from Stalin to Gorbachev*. Baden-Baden: Nomos Verlagsgesellschaft, 1998.

Allin, Dana H. *Cold War Illusions: America, Europe, and Soviet Power, 1969–1989*. New York: St. Martin's Press, 1994.

An, Pyeongeok. "Obstructive All the Way? British Policy toward German Unification, 1989–90." *German Politics* 15, no. 1 (March 2006): 111–21.

Anderson, Benedict. *The Spectre of Comparisons*. London: Verso, 1998.

BIBLIOGRAPHY

Anderson, Jeffrey. *German Unification and the Union of Europe*. Cambridge: Cambridge University Press, 1999.

Andrew, Christopher. *The World Was Going Our Way: The KGB and the Battle for the Third World*. New York: Basic Books, 2005.

Andrew, Christopher, and Oleg Gordievsky. *KGB: The Inside Story of Its Foreign Operations from Lenin to Gorbachev*. New York: HarperCollins, 1990.

Andrew, Christopher, and Vasili Mitrokhin. *The Sword and the Shield: The Mitrokhin Archive and the Secret History of the KGB*. New York: Basic Books, 1999.

Antohi, Sorin, and Vladimir Tismaneanu, eds. *Between Past and Future: The Revolutions of 1989 and Their Aftermath*. New York: CEU Press, 2000.

Asmus, Ronald D., J. F. Brown, and Keith Crane. *Soviet Foreign Policy and the Revolutions of 1989 in Eastern Europe*. Santa Monica, CA: RAND, 1991.

Bacevich, Andrew. *The Long War: A New History of US National Security Policy since World War II*. New York: Columbia University Press, 2007.

Bark, Dennis L., and David R. Gress. *A History of West Germany*. 2nd ed. 2 vols. Oxford: Blackwell Publishers, 1993.

Barnett, Michael, and Martha Finnemore. *Rules for the World: International Organizations in Global Politics*. Ithaca, NY: Cornell University Press, 2004.

Barrass, Gordon S. *The Great Cold War*. Stanford, CA: Stanford University Press, 2009.

Bauerkämper, Arnd, and Martin Sabrow, et al., eds. *Doppelte Zeitgeschichte: Deutsch-deutsche Beziehungen 1945–1990*. Bonn: Dietz Verlag, 1998.

Békés, Csaba, and Melinda Kalmár. "The Political Transition in Hungary, 1989–90." *Cold War International History Project Bulletin* 12–13 (Fall–Winter 2001): 73.

Bell, David. *François Mitterrand*. Cambridge, UK: Polity, 2005.

Beissinger, Mark R. *Nationalist Mobilization and the Collapse of the Soviet State*. Cambridge: Cambridge University Press, 2002.

Bennett, Andrew. *Condemned to Repetition? The Rise, Fall, and Reprise of Soviet-Russian Military Intervention, 1973–1996*. Cambridge, MA: MIT Press, 1999.

Bering, Henrik. *Helmut Kohl*. Washington, DC: Regnery, 1999.

Beschloss, Michael R., and Strobe Talbott. *At the Highest Levels: The Inside Story of the Cold War*. Boston: Little, Brown, 1993.

Bessel, Richard, and Ralph Jessen, eds. *Die Grenzen der Diktatur: Staat und Gesellschaft in der DDR*. Göttingen: Vandenhoeck and Ruprecht, 1996.

Bideleux, Robert, and Ian Jeffries. *A History of Eastern Europe: Crisis and Change*. London: Routledge, 1998.

Biermann, Rafael. *Zwischen Kreml und Kanzleramt: Wie Moskau mit der deutschen Einheit rang*. Paderborn: Ferdinand Schöningh, 1997.

Black, J. L. *Russia Faces NATO Expansion*. Lanham, MD: Rowman and Littlefield, 1999.

Boyle, Peter G. *American-Soviet Relations: From the Russian Revolution to the Fall of Communism*. London: Routledge, 1993.

Bozo, Frédéric. *Mitterrand, la fin de la guerre froide et l'unification allemande: De Yalta à Maastricht*. Paris: Odile Jacob, 2005. English translation: *From Yalta to Maastricht: Mitterrand, German Unification, and the End of the Cold War*. London: Berghahn Books, forthcoming.

———. "Mitterrand's France, the End of the Cold War, and German Unification: A Reappraisal." *Cold War History* 7, no. 4 (2007): 455–78.

———. "'Winners' and 'Losers': France, the United States, and the End of the Cold War." *Diplomatic History* (forthcoming).

Bozo, Frédéric, Marie-Pierre Rey, N. Piers Ludlow, and Leopoldo Nuti, eds. *Europe and the End of the Cold War*. London: Routledge, 2008.

Brand Crémieux, Marie-Nöelle. *Les Français face à la réunification allemande, automne 1989– automne 1990*. Paris: L'Harmattan, 2004.

Brands, Hal. *From Berlin to Baghdad: America's Search for Purpose in the Post–Cold War World*. Lexington: University of Kentucky Press, 2008.

Brooks, Stephen G., and William Wohlforth. "Power, Globalization, and the End of the Cold War." *International Security* 25, no. 3 (Winter 2000–2001): 5–53.

———. "From Old Thinking to New Thinking." *International Security* 26, no. 4 (Spring 2002): 93–111.

Brown, Archie. *The Gorbachev Factor*. New York: Oxford University Press, 1997.

———. "Perestroika and the End of the Cold War." *Cold War History* 7, no. 1 (February 2007): 1–17.

———. *Seven Years That Changed the World: Perestroika in Perspective*. New York: Oxford University Press, 2007.

———. "The Change to Engagement in Britain's Cold War Policy: The Origins of the Thatcher-Gorbachev Relationship." *Journal of Cold War Studies* 10, no. 3 (Summer 2008): 3–47.

Brown, J. F. *Surge to Freedom*. Durham, NC: Duke University Press, 1991.

Brubaker, Rogers. *Nationalism Reframed: Nationhood and the New National Question in the New Europe*. Cambridge: Cambridge University Press, 1996.

Bruck, Elke. *François Mitterrands Deutschlandbild: Perzeption und Politik im Spannungsfeld deutschland-, europa-, und sicherheitspolitischen Entscheidungen, 1989–1992*. Frankfurt: Peter Lang, 2003.

Bundy, William. *A Tangled Web: The Making of Foreign Policy in the Nixon Presidency*. New York: Hill and Wang, 1998.

Campbell, John. *Margaret Thatcher*. London: Pimlico, 2004.

Carr, E. H. *What Is History*. New York: Vintage, 1961.

Chakrabarty, Dipesh. *Provincializing Europe: Postcolonial Thought and Historical Difference*. Princeton, NJ: Princeton University Press, 2000.

Childs, David. *The GDR: Moscow's German Ally*. 2nd ed. London: Unwin Hyman, 1988.

Childs, David, and Richard Popplewell. *The Stasi: The East German Intelligence and Security Service*. London: Macmillan, 1996.

Clemens, Clay. *Reluctant Realists: The Christian Democrats and West German Ostpolitik*. Durham, NC: Duke University Press, 1989.

Clemens, Clay, and William E. Paterson, eds. *The Kohl Chancellorship*. London: Frank Cass, 1998.

Cohen, Samy, et al. *Mitterrand et la sortie de la guerre froide*. Paris: Presses Universitaires de France, 1998.

Cohen, Stephen F. *Failed Crusade: America and the Tragedy of Post-Communist Russia*. New York: W. W. Norton, 2001.

———. *Soviet Fates and Lost Alternatives: From Stalinism to the New Cold War*. New York: Columbia University Press, 2009

Collins, Robert M. *Transforming America: Politics and Culture during the Reagan Years*. New York: Columbia University Press, 2007.

Colton, Timothy J. *Yeltsin: A Life*. New York: Basic Books, 2008.

Connelly, Matthew. "Taking off the Cold War Lens: Visions of North-South Conflict during the Algerian War for Independence." *American Historical Review* 105 (June 2000): 739–69.

———. *A Diplomatic Revolution*. Oxford: Oxford University Press, 2002.

Conquest, Robert. *The Great Terror*. New York: Oxford University Press, 1968.

Conze, Eckart. *Die Suche nach Sicherheit: Eine Geschichte der Bundesrepublik Deutschland von 1949 bis in die Gegenwart*. Munich: Siedler Verlag, 2009.

Cooke, Miriam, and Angela Woollacott, eds. *Gendering War Talk*. Princeton, NJ: Princeton University Press, 1993.

Cooper, Robert. *The Breaking of Nations: Order and Chaos in the Twenty-First Century*. London: Atlantic Books, 2003.

Costigliola, Frank. "An 'Arm around the Shoulder': The United States, NATO, and German Reunification, 1989–90." *Central European History* 3, no. 1 (1994): 87–110.

Courtois, Stéphane, et al. *Le livre noir du Communisme: Crimes, terreur, répression*. Paris: Laffont, 1997. Published in English as: *Black Book of Communism*. Cambridge, MA: Harvard University Press, 1999.

Cox, Michael. "Another Transatlantic Split? American and European Narratives and the End of the Cold War." *Cold War History* 7, no. 1 (February 2007): 121–46.

BIBLIOGRAPHY

Craig, Gordon. *Germany, 1866–1945*. Oxford: Oxford University Press, 1978.

Craig, Gordon, and Alexander George. *Force and Statecraft: Diplomatic Problems of Our Time*. New York: Oxford University Press, 1983.

Cronin, James E. *The World the Cold War Made: Order, Chaos, and the Return of History*. New York: Routledge, 1996.

Dale, Gareth. *Popular Protest in East Germany, 1945–1989*. London: Routledge, 2005.

———. *The East German Revolution of 1989*. Manchester: Manchester University Press, 2006.

Dallek, Matthew. *The Right Moment: Ronald Reagan's First Victory and the Decisive Turning Point in American Politics*. New York: Oxford University Press, 2000.

Dalos, György. *Der Vorhang geht auf: Das Ende der Diktaturen in Osteuropa*. Trans. Elsbeth Zylla. Munich: Beck Verlag, 2009.

Daschitschew, Wjatscheslaw. "Die Wechselwirkung der gegenseitigen Beziehungen zwischen der Bundesrepublik Deutschland, der DDR und der Sowjetunion im Zeitraum 1970–1989." *Deutschland Archiv* 12 (December 1993): 1460–88.

Dean, Robert D. "Masculinity as Ideology." *Diplomatic History* 22, no. 1 (Winter 1998): 29–62.

Deckert, Renatus, ed. *Die Nacht, in der die Mauer fiel: Schriftsteller erzählen vom 9. November 1989*. Frankfurt am Main: Suhrkamp, 2009.

De Grazia, Victoria. *Irresistible Empire: America's Advance through Twentieth-Century Europe*. Cambridge, MA: Belknap Press, 2005.

Dennis, Mike. *German Democratic Republic: Politics, Economics, and Society*. London: Pinter, 1988.

DePorte, Anton W. *Europe between the Superpowers: The Enduring Balance*. New Haven, CT: Yale University Press, 1979.

Desch, Michael. "America's Liberal Illiberalism." *International Security* 32, no. 3 (Winter 2007–8): 7–43.

Deutscher Bundestag, 12. Wahlperiode, Enquete-Kommission. *Bericht der Enquete-Kommission "Aufarbeitung von Geschichte und Folgen der SED-Diktatur in Deutschland."* Bonn: Bundestag Drucksache 12/7820, May 31, 1994.

———, ed. *Materialien der Enquete-Kommission "Aufarbeitung von Geschichte und Folgen der SED-Diktatur in Deutschland."* 9 vols. Baden-Baden/Frankfurt a.M.: Nomos Verlag/Suhrkamp Verlag, 1995.

———, 13. Wahlperiode, Enquete-Kommission. *Bericht der Enquete-Kommission "Überwindung der Folgen der SED-Diktaur im Prozeß der deutschen Einheit."* Bonn: Bundestag Drucksache 13/11000, June 10, 1998.

Diedrich, Torsten, et al., eds. *Der Warschauer Pakt: Von der Gründung bis zum Zusammenbruch 1955–1991*. Berlin: Links, 2008.

Dockrill, Saki. *The End of the Cold War Era: The Transformation of the Global Security Order*. London: Hodder Arnold, 2005.

Dülffer, Jost. "Unification in the European Context." *German Historical Institute London Bulletin* 16 (November 1994): 3–17.

Dunbabin, J.P.D. *The Cold War: The Great Powers and Their Allies*. London: Longman, 1994.

Eckart, Karl, and Manfred Wilke, eds. *Berlin*. Berlin: Duncker & Humblot, 1998.

Ehrman, John. *The Eighties: America in the Age of Reagan*. New Haven, CT: Yale University Press, 2005.

Eichengreen, Barry. *The European Economy since 1945: Coordinated Capitalism and Beyond*. Princeton, NJ: Princeton University Press, 2007.

Ellman, Michael, and Vladimir Kontorovich, eds. *The Disintegration of the Soviet Economic System*. New York: Routledge, 1992.

———, eds. *The Destruction of the Soviet Economic System: An Insiders' History*. Armonk, NY: M. E. Sharpe, 1998.

Engel, Jeffrey, ed. *The Fall of the Berlin Wall: The Revolutionary Legacy of 1989*. Oxford: Oxford University Press, 2009.

English, Robert D. *Russia and the Idea of the West: Gorbachev, Intellectuals, and the End of the Cold War*. New York: Columbia University Press, 2000.

BIBLIOGRAPHY

English, Robert D. "Power, Ideas, and New Evidence on the Cold War's End: A Reply to Brooks and Wohlforth." *International Security* 26, no. 4 (Spring 2002): 70–92.

Epstein, Catherine. *The Last Revolutionaries: German Communists and Their Century.* Cambridge, MA: Harvard University Press, 2003.

Evangelista, Matthew. *Unarmed Forces: The Transnational Movement to End the Cold War.* Ithaca, NY: Cornell University Press, 1999.

Falkenrath, Richard A. *Shaping Europe's Military Order: The Origins and Consequences of the CFE Treaty.* Cambridge, MA: MIT Press, 1995.

Fink, Carole, Philipp Gassert, and Detlef Junker, eds. *1968: The World Transformed.* New York: Cambridge University Press, 1998.

Fischer, Beth A. *The Reagan Reversal: Foreign Policy and the End of the Cold War.* Columbia: University of Missouri Press, 1997.

Freeze, Gregory L., ed. *Russia: A History.* Oxford: Oxford University Press, 1997.

Fricke, Karl-Wilhelm. *MfS intern: Macht, Strukturen, Auflösung der DDR-Staatssicherheit. Analyse und Dokumentation.* Cologne: Wissenschaft und Politik, 1991.

Fricke, Karl-Wilhelm. "Ordinäre Abwehr—elitäre Aufklärung? Zur Rolle der Hauptverwaltung A im Ministerium für Staatssicherheit." *Aus Politik und Zeitgeschichte* 50 (December 5, 1997): 17–26.

———. "Wolfs Schuld." *Deutschland Archiv* 4 (July–August 1997): 523–25.

———. "Grundrechtsgarantie und DDR-Grenzregime: Zum Beschluß des Bundesverfassungsgerichts vom 24. Oktober 1996." *Deutschland Archiv* 1 (January–February 1997): 4–6.

Fricke, Karl-Wilhelm, and Bernhard Marquardt. *DDR Staatssicherheit: Das Phänomen des Verrats. Die Zusammenarbeit zwischen MfS und KGB.* Bochum, Germany: Brockmeyer, 1995.

Friedman, George. "Georgia and the Balance of Power." *New York Review of Books* 55, no. 14 (September 25, 2008): 24.

Fukuyama, Francis. "The End of History?" *National Interest* (Summer 1989): online.

———. *The End of History and the Last Man.* New York: Penguin Books, 1992.

Fulbrook, Mary. *A Concise History of Germany.* 2nd ed. Cambridge: Cambridge University Press, 1991.

———. *Anatomy of a Dictatorship: Inside the GDR, 1949–1989.* Oxford: Oxford University Press, 1995.

———, ed. *German History since 1800.* New York: St. Martin's Press, 1997.

———. "Approaches to German Contemporary History since 1945: Politics and Paradigms." *Zeithistorische Forschungen* 1, no. 1 (2004), available at http://www.zeithistorische-forschungen.de.

———. *The People's State: East German Society from Hitler to Honecker.* New Haven, CT: Yale University Press, 2005.

Furet, François. *The Passing of an Illusion: The Idea of Communism in the Twentieth Century.* Chicago: University of Chicago Press, 1999.

Gaddis, John Lewis. *Strategies of Containment: A Critical Appraisal of Postwar American National Security Policy.* Oxford: Oxford University Press, 1982.

———. "History, Theory, and Common Ground." *International Security* 22, no. 1 (Summer 1997): 84.

———. *We Now Know: Rethinking Cold War History.* Oxford: Clarendon Press, 1997.

———. *The Cold War.* New York: Penguin, 2006.

Gardner, Lloyd C. *The Long Road to Baghdad: A History of U.S. Foreign Policy from the 1970s to the Present.* New York: New Press, 2008.

Garthoff, Raymond. *The Great Transition: American-Soviet Relations and the End of the Cold War.* Washington, DC: Brookings Institution Press, 1994.

Garton Ash, Timothy. *We the People.* London: Granta, 1990.

———. *In Europe's Name: Germany and the Divided Continent.* New York: Vintage Books, 1993.

Geisel, Christof. *Auf der Suche nach einem dritten Weg: Das politische Selbstverständnis der DDR-Opposition.* Berlin: Links, October 2005.

George, Alexander L. "The 'Operational Code': A Neglected Approach to the Study of Political Decision-Making." *International Studies Quarterly* 12 (June 1969): 190–222.

BIBLIOGRAPHY

German Marshall Fund, ed. *The Legacy of 1989*. Washington, DC: German Marshall Fund, 2009.

Geschichte der deutschen Einheit (GDE). Vol. 1, *Deutschlandpolitik in Helmut Kohls Kanzlerschaft: Regierugnsstil und Entscheidungen 1982–1989*, Karl-Rudolf Korte; vol. 2, *Das Wagnis der Währungs-, Wirtschafts-, und Sozialunion: Politische Zwänge im Konflikt mit öknomischen Regeln*, Dieter Grosser; vol. 3, *Die Überwindung der Teilung: Der innerdeutsche Prozeß der Vereinigung 1989/90*, Wolfgang Jäger; vol. 4, *Außenpolitik für die deutsche Einheit Die Entscheidungsjahre 1989/90*, Werner Weidenfeld, Peter M. Wagner, and Elke Bruck. Stuttgart: Deutsche Verlags-Anstalt, 1998. Note, these volumes are also listed by author's last name in this bibliography for ease of reference.

Gieseke, Jens. *Der Mielke-Konzern: Die Geschichte der Stasi 1945–1990*. Munich: Deutsche Velags-Anstalt, 2006.

Gildea, Robert. *France since 1945*. Oxford: Oxford University Press, 1996.

Gill, David, and Ulrich Schröter. *Das Ministerium für Staatssicherheit Anatomie des Mielke Imperiums*. Berlin: Rowohlt, 1991.

Gilles, Franz-Otto, and Hans-Hermann Hertle. "Sicherung der Volkswirtschaft." *Deutschland Archiv* 1 (January 1996): 48–57.

Gillingham, John. *European Integration*. Cambridge: Cambridge University Press, 2003.

Glaeßner, Gert-Joachim, and Ian Wallace, eds. *The German Revolution of 1989: Causes and Consequences*. Oxford: Berg, 1992.

Glees, Anthony. *Reinventing Germany: German Political Development since 1945*. Oxford: Berg, 1996.

Goldgeier, James M. *Not Whether but When: The US Decision to Enlarge NATO*. Washington, DC: Brookings, 1999.

Goldgeier, James M., and Derek Chollet. *America between the Wars: From 11/9 to 9/11, the Misunderstood Years between the Fall of the Berlin Wall and the Start of the War on Terror*. New York: Public Affairs, 2008.

Goldgeier, James M., and Michael McFaul. *Power and Purpose: US Policy toward Russia after the Cold War*. Washington, DC: Brookings, 2003.

Görtemaker, Manfred. *Unifying Germany, 1989–1990*. New York: St. Martin's Press, 1994.

Gould-Davis, Nigel. "Rethinking the Role of Ideology in International Politics during the Cold War." *Journal of Cold War Studies* (Winter 1999): 90–109.

Grabner, Jürgen, Christiane Heinze, and Detlef Pollack, eds. *Leipzig im Oktober*. Berlin: Wichern-Verlag, 1990.

Grafe, Roman. "'Niemals Zweifel gehabt' Der Prozeß gegen die Grenztruppen-Führung der DDR." *Deutschland Archiv* 6 (November–December 1996): 862–71.

———. "Die Strafverfolgung von DDR-Grenzschützen und ihren Befehlsgebern: Eine vorläufige Bilanz." *Deutschland Archiv* 3 (May–June 1997): 377–80.

Green, E.H.H. *Thatcher*. London: Hodder Arnold, 2006.

Grosser, Alfred. *Affaires Extérieures: La Politique de la France 1944–1989*. Saint-Amand: Flammarion, 1989.

Grosser, Dieter. *Geschichte der deutschen Einheit*. Vol. 2, *Das Wagnis der Währungs-, Wirtschafts-, und Sozialunion: Politische Zwänge im Konflikt mit öknomischen Regeln*. Stuttgart: Deutsche Verlags-Anstalt, 1998.

Haase-Hindenberg, Gerhard, and Harald Jäger. *Der Mann, der die Mauer öffnete: Warum Oberstleutnant Harald Jäger den Befehl verweigerte und damit Weltgeschichte schrieb*. Munich: Heyne, 2007.

Haber, Stephen H., David M. Kennedy, and Stephen D. Krasner. "Brothers under the Skin: Diplomatic History and International Relations." *International Security* 22, no. 1 (Summer 1997): 34–43.

Hacke, Christian. *Zur Weltmacht verdammt: Die amerikanische Außenpolitik von J.F. Kennedy bis G.W. Bush*. Berlin: Ullsten, 2005.

Haendcke-Hoppe, Maria, and Erika Lieser-Triebnigg, eds. *40 Jahre innerdeutsche Beziehungen*. Berlin: Duncker and Humblot, 1990.

BIBLIOGRAPHY

Haftendorn, Helga. *Coming of Age: German Foreign Policy since 1945*. Trans. Deborah S. Kaiser. Lanham, MD: Rowman and Littlefield, 2006. English translation of *Deutsche Außenpolitik zwischen Selbstbeschränkung und Selbstbehauptung 1945–2000*. Munich: Deutsche Verlags-Anstalt, 2001.

Hanhimäki, Jussi. *The Flawed Architect: Henry Kissinger and American Foreign Policy*. New York: Oxford University Press, 2004.

Hanisch, Günter, et al., eds. *Dona nobis pacem: Fürbitten und Friedensgebete Herbst '89 in Leipzig*. Berlin: Evangelische Verlagsanstalt, 1990.

Hanrieder, Wolfram. *Germany, America, Europe: Forty Years of German Foreign Policy*. New Haven, CT: Yale University Press, 1989.

Harrison, Hope. *Driving the Soviets up the Wall*. Princeton, NJ: Princeton University Press, 2003.

Hart, Gary, and Dimitri K. Simes. "The Road to Moscow." *The National Interest* (May/June 2009): online.

Haslam, Jonathan. *The Soviet Union and the Politics of Nuclear Weapons in Europe, 1969–1987: The Problem of the SS-20*. London: Macmillan, 1989.

Heinen, Armin, and Dietmar Hüser, eds. *Tour de France*. Stuttgart: Franz Steiner Verlag, 2008.

Held, Joseph P., ed. *The Columbia History of Eastern Europe in the Twentieth Century*. New York: Columbia University Press, 1992.

Helwig, Gisela. "Wir wollen raus—Wir bleiben hier." *Deutschland Archiv* 22 (October 1989).

Henke, Klaus-Dietmar, ed. *Wann bricht schon mal ein Staat zusammen! Die Debatte über die Stasi-Akten auf dem 39. Historikertag 1992*. Munich: dtv, June 1993.

———. *Die amerikanische Besetzung Deutschlands*. Munich: Oldenbourg, 1995.

Henrikson, Thomas H. *American Power after the Berlin Wall*. New York: Palgrave Macmillan, 2007.

Herrmann, Richard K., and Richard Ned Lebow, eds. *Ending the Cold War*. New York: Palgrave Macmillan, 2004.

Hertle, Hans-Hermann. "Staatsbankrott: Der ökonomische Untergang des SED-Staates." *Deutschland Archiv* 10 (October 1992): 1019–30.

———. *Chronik des Mauerfalls: Die dramatischen Ereignisse um den 9. November 1989*. Berlin: Links, September 1996.

———. *Der Fall der Mauer: Die unbeabsichtigte Selbstauflösung des SED-Staates*. Opladen: Westdeutscher Verlag, 1996.

———. *When the Wall Came Tumbling Down*. Sender Freies Berlin, 1999. Television documentary.

———. "The Fall of the Wall: The Unintended Self-Dissolution of East Germany's Ruling Regime." *Cold War International History Project Bulletin* 12–13 (Fall–Winter 2001): 131–40.

Heuser, Beatrice. *Transatlantic Relations*. London: RIIA, 1996.

Hirschmann, Albert O. "Exit, Voice, and the Fate of the German Democratic Republic: An Essay in Conceptual History." *World Politics* 45 (January 1993): 173–202.

Hixson, Walter. *The Myth of American Diplomacy: National Identity and US Foreign Policy*. New Haven, CT: Yale University Press, 2008.

Hogan, Michael J. *America in the World: The Historiography of American Foreign Relations since 1941*. New York: Cambridge University Press, 1995.

Holborn, Hajo. *A History of Modern Germany*. 3 vols. Princeton, NJ: Princeton University Press, 1959.

Hosking, Geoffrey. *Rulers and Victims: The Russians in the Soviet Union*. Cambridge, MA: Harvard University Press, 2006.

Howard, Michael. "1989: A Farewell to Arms?" *International Affairs* 65 (Summer 1989): 407–13.

Huelshoff, Michael G., Andrei S. Markovits, and Simon Reich. *From Bundesrepublik to Deutschland: German Politics after Unification*. Ann Arbor: University of Michigan Press, 1993.

Ikenberry, G. John. *After Victory*. Princeton, NJ: Princeton University Press, 2001.

Ikenberry, G. John, and Daniel Deudney. "Who Won the Cold War?" *Foreign Policy* 87 (Summer 1992).

Ingram, Edward. "The Wonderland of the Political Scientist." *International Security* 22, no. 1 (Summer 1997): 56.

BIBLIOGRAPHY

Institut für Marxismus-Leninisums beim ZK der SED, ed. *1949–1989 Vierzig Jahre*. Berlin: Institut für Marxismus-Leninismus, 1989.

Issing, Otmar. *The Birth of the Euro*. New York: Cambridge University Press, 2008.

Jäckel, Eberhard. *Das deutsche Jahrhundert*. Stuttgart: DVA, 1996.

Jäger, Wolfgang. *Geschichte der deutschen Einheit*. Vol. 3, *Die Überwindung der Teilung: Der innerdeutsche Prozeß der Vereinigung 1989/90*. Stuttgart: Deutsche Verlags-Anstalt, 1998.

Jäger, Wolfgang, and Ingeborg Villinger, eds. *Die Intellektuellen und die deutsche Einheit*. Bonn: Rombach, 1997.

James, Harold. *Europe Reborn: A History, 1914–2000*. Harlow, UK: Pearson Longman, 2003.

Janowski, Martin. *Der Tag, der Deutschland veränderte: 9. Oktober 1989*. Leipzig: Evangelische Verlagsanstalt, 2007.

Jarausch, Konrad. *The Rush to German Unity*. New York: Oxford University Press, 1994.

———. *Die Umkehr: Deutsche Wandlungen, 1945–95*. Munich: Deutsche Verlags-Anstalt, 2004.

Jarausch, Konrad, and Martin Sabrow, eds. *Weg in den Untergang: Der innere Zerfall der DDR*. Göttingen: Vandenhoeck und Ruprecht, 1999.

Jervis, Robert L. "Containment Strategies in Perspective." *Journal of Cold War Studies* 8, no. 4 (Fall 2006): 92–97.

Jesse, Eckhard, ed. *Friedliche Revolution und deutsche Einheit: Sächsische Bürgerrechtler ziehen Bilanz*. Berlin: Links, 2006.

Jesse, Eckhard, and Armin Mitter, eds. *Die Gestaltung der deutschen Einheit*. Bonn: Bundeszentrale für politische Bildung, 1992.

Joas, Hans, and Martin Kohli, eds. *Der Zusammenbruch der DDR*. Frankfurt: Suhrkamp, 1993.

Johnson, Chalmers. *Revolutionary Change*. 2nd ed. Stanford, CA: Stanford University Press, 1982.

Jowitt, Ken. *New World Disorder: The Leninist Extinction*. Berkeley: University of California Press, 1992.

Judt, Tony. *Postwar: A History of Europe since 1945*. New York: Penguin, 2005.

Junker, Detlef, ed. *Die USA und Deutschland im Zeitalter des Kalten Krieges 1945–1990: Ein Handbuch*. 2 vols. Stuttgart: Deutsche Verlags-Anstalt, 2001.

Kaelble, Hartmut, Jürgen Kocka, and Hartmut Zwahr, eds. *Sozialgeschichte der DDR*. Stuttgart: Klett-Cotta, 1994.

Kaiser, Robert. *Why Gorbachev Happened*. New York: Simon and Schuster, 1991.

Kehr, Eckart. *Der Primat der Innenpolitik*. Berlin: Gruyter, 1970.

Kempen, Bernhard. *Die deutsch-polnische Grenze nach der Friedensregelung des Zwei-plus-Vier-Vertrages*. Frankfurt: Peter Lang, 1997.

Kemp-Welch, Anthony. *Poland under Communism: A Cold War History*. Cambridge: Cambridge University Press, 2008.

Kennedy, Paul. *The Rise and Fall of the Great Powers*. New York: Random House, 1987.

Kenney, Padraic. *A Carnival of Revolution: Central Europe 1989*. Princeton, NJ: Princeton University Press, 2002.

King, Charles. "The Five-Day War: Managing Moscow after the Georgia Crisis." *Foreign Affairs* (November–December 2008).

Klein, Yvonne. "Obstructive or Promoting? British Views on German Unification, 1989–90." *German Politics* 5, no. 3 (December 1996): 404–31.

Koch, Peter-Ferdinand. *Das Schalck-Imperium lebt: Deutschland wird gekauft*. Munich: Piper, 1992.

Kocka, Jürgen, ed. *Historische DDR-Forschung: Aufsätze und Studien*. Berlin: Akademie, 1993.

Koehler, John O. *Stasi: The Untold Story of the East German Secret Police*. Boulder, CO: Westview Press, 1999.

Kopstein, Jeffrey. *The Politics of Economic Decline in East Germany, 1945–1989*. Chapel Hill: University of North Carolina Press, 1997.

Korte, Karl-Rudolf. *Geschichte der deutschen Einheit*. Vol. 1, *Deutschlandpolitik in Helmut Kohls Kanzlerschaft: Regierungsstil und Entscheidungen 1982–1989*. Stuttgart: Deutsche Verlags-Anstalt, 1998.

BIBLIOGRAPHY

Kotkin, Stephen. *Armageddon Averted: The Soviet Collapse, 1970–2000*. New York: Oxford University Press, 2001.

Kovrig, Bennett. *Of Walls and Bridges*. New York: New York University Press, 1991.

Kowalczuk, Ilko-Sascha. *Endspiel: Die Revolution von 1989 in der DDR*. Munich: Beck, 2009.

Kramer, Mark. "Ideology and the Cold War." *Review of International Studies* 25 (1999): 539–76.

———. "The Collapse of East European Communism and the Repercussions within the Soviet Union (Part 1)." *Journal of Cold War Studies* 5, no. 4 (Fall 2003): 178–256.

———. "The Collapse of East European Communism and the Repercussions within the Soviet Union (Part 2)." *Journal of Cold War Studies* 6, no. 4 (Fall 2004): 3–64.

———. "The Collapse of East European Communism and the Repercussions within the Soviet Union (Part 3)." *Journal of Cold War Studies* 7, no. 1 (Winter 2005): 3–96.

———. "The Myth of a No-NATO-Enlargement Pledge to Russia." *Washington Quarterly* 32, no. 2 (April 2009): 39–61.

Krasner, Stephen. *Sovereignty: Organized Hypocrisy*. Princeton, NJ: Princeton University Press, 1999.

Kraushaar, Tom, ed. *Die Zonenkinder und Wir: Die Geschichte eines Phänomens*. Hamburg: Rowohlt, 2004.

Kuhn, Ekkehard. *Der Tag der Entscheidung: Leipzig, 9. Oktober 1989*. Berlin: Ullstein, 1992.

Kupchan, Charles A., and Peter L. Trubowitz. "Grand Strategy for a Divided America." *Foreign Affairs* 86, no. 4 (July–August 2007).

Küsters, Hanns Jürgen. *Der Integrationsfriede: Viermächte-Verhandlungen über die Friedensregelung mit Deutschland 1945–1990*. Munich: R. Oldenbourg Verlag, 2000.

LaFeber, Walter. *America, Russia, and the Cold War, 1946–2006*. New York: McGraw Hill, 2008.

Larres, Klaus, ed. *Germany since Unification: The Domestic and External Consequences*. London: Macmillan, 1998.

Larres, Klaus, and Torsten Oppelland, eds. *Deutschland und die USA im 20. Jahrhundert: Geschichte der politischen Beziehungen*. Darmstadt: Wissenschaftliche Buchgesellschaft, 1997.

Lauren, Paul Gordon, ed. *Diplomacy: New Approaches in History, Theory, and Policy*. New York: Free Press, 1979.

Lease, Gary. "Religion, the Churches, and the German 'Revolution' of November 1989." *German Politics* 1 (August 1992): 264–73.

Leffler, Melvyn P. *For the Soul of Mankind: The United States, the Soviet Union, and the Cold War*. New York: Hill and Wang, 2007.

Leffler, Melvyn P., and Odd Arne Westad, eds. *The Cambridge History of the Cold War*. 3 vols. Cambridge: Cambridge University Press, forthcoming.

Legro, Jeff. *Rethinking the World: Great Power Strategies and International Order*. Ithaca, NY: Cornell University Press, 2005.

Lettow, Paul. *Ronald Reagan and His Quest to Abolish Nuclear Weapons*. New York: Random House, 2005.

Levy, Jack. "Too Important to Leave to the Other." *International Security* 22, no. 1 (Summer 1997): 22–33.

———. "Explaining Events and Developing Theories: History, Political Science, and the Analysis of International Relations." In *Bridges and Boundaries*, ed. Colin Elman and Miriam Elman. Cambridge, MA: MIT Press, 2001.

Light, Paul. *A Government Ill Executed*. Cambridge, MA: Harvard University Press, 2008.

Links, Christoph, and Hannes Bahrmann. *Wir sind das Volk*. Berlin: Links, 1990.

Links, Christoph, Sybille Nitsche, and Antje Taffelt. *Das wunderbare Jahr der Anarchie*. Berlin: Links, 2004.

Linz, Juan. *The Breakdown of Democratic Regimes*. Baltimore: Johns Hopkins University Press, 1978.

Logevall, Fredrik, and Andrew Preston, eds. *Nixon in the World: American Foreign Relations, 1969–1977*. Oxford: Oxford University Press, 2008.

Löw, Konrad. . . . *bis zum Verrat der Freiheit: Die Gesellschaft der Bundesrepublik und die DDR*. Munich: Langen Müller, 1993.

Lucas, Edward. *The New Cold War: Putin's Russia and the Threat to the West*. New York: Palgrave Macmillan, 2008.

Ludlow, N. Piers, ed. *European Integration and the Cold War*. London: Routledge, 2007.

Lundestad, Geir. *"Empire" by Integration: The United States and European Integration, 1945–1997*. New York: Oxford University Press, 1998.

MacEachin, Douglas J. *CIA Assessments of the Soviet Union: The Records versus the Charges: An Intelligence Monograph*. Washington, DC: Central Intelligence Agency, May 1996.

Mackrakis, Kristie. *Seduced by Secrets: Inside the Stasi's Spy-Tech World*. Cambridge: Cambridge University Press, 2008.

Mählert, Ulrich. *Kleine Geschichte der DDR*. Munich: Beck, 1998.

Maier, Charles, ed. *The Cold War in Europe: Era of a Divided Continent*. 3rd ed. Princeton: Markus Wiener Publishers, 1996.

———. *Dissolution: The Crisis of Communism and the End of East Germany*. Princeton, NJ: Princeton University Press, 1997.

Mandelbaum, Michael. *The Dawn of Peace in Europe*. New York: Twentieth Century Fund, 1996.

Mankoff, Jeffrey. *Russian Foreign Policy: The Return of Great Power Politics*. Lanham, MD: Rowman & Littlefield, 2009.

Marsh, David. *The Euro*. New Haven, CT: Yale University Press, 2009.

Mastny, Vojtech. "Did NATO Win the Cold War? Looking Over the Wall." *Foreign Affairs* (May–June 1999): 176–89.

May, Elaine Tyler. *Homeward Bound: American Families in the Cold War Era*. Rev. ed. New York: Basic Books, 2008.

Mayer, Hartmut. "Review of *Dokumente zur Deutschlandpolitik: Deutsche Einheit*." *International Affairs* 74, no. 4 (October 1998): 952–53.

Maynard, Christopher. *Out of the Shadow: George H. W. Bush and the End of the Cold War*. College Station: Texas A&M Press, 2008.

McAdams, A. James. *Germany Divided: From the Wall to Reunification*. Princeton, NJ: Princeton University Press, 1993.

———. *Judging the Past in Unified Germany*. Cambridge: Cambridge University Press, 2001.

McCarthy, Patrick, ed. *France-Germany, 1983–1993: The Struggle to Cooperate*. Basingstoke, UK: Macmillan, 1993.

McElvoy, Anne. *The Saddled Cow: East Germany's Life and Legacy*. London: Faber and Faber, 1992.

Meissner, Boris. *Die Sowjetunion im Umbruch*. Stuttgart: Deutsche Verlags-Anstalt, 1988.

Merkl, Peter. *German Unification in the European Context*. University Park: Pennsylvania State University Press, 1993.

Mitter, Armin, and Stefan Wolle. *Untergang auf Raten*. Munich: Bertelsmann, 1993.

Moens, Alexander. "American Diplomacy and German Unification." *Survival* 33, no. 6 (November–December 1991): 531–45.

Molho, Anthony, and Gordon S. Wood, eds. *Imagined Histories: American Historians Interpret the Past*. Princeton, NJ: Princeton University Press, 1998.

Moravcsik, Andrew. *The Choice for Europe: Social Purpose and State Power from Messina to Maastricht*. Ithaca, NY: Cornell University Press, 1998.

Moraw, Frank. *Die Parole der "Einheit" und die Sozialdemokratie*. Göttigen: Dietz, 1990.

Naftali, Timothy. *George H.W. Bush*. New York: Times Books, 2007.

Naimark, Norman M. *The Russians in Germany: A History of the Soviet Zone of Occupation, 1945–1949*. Cambridge, MA: Belknap Press, 1995.

———. "Cold War Studies and New Archival Materials on Stalin." *Russian Review* 61, no. 1 (January 2002): 1–15.

Neubert, Erhard. *Geschichte der Opposition in der DDR 1949–1989*. Bonn: Bundeszentrale für politische Bildung, 1997.

Nicholls, Anthony. *The Bonn Republic: West German Democracy, 1945–1990*. New York: Longman, 1997.

Njølstad, Olav, ed. *The Last Decade of the Cold War: From Conflict Escalation to Conflict Transformation.* London: Frank Cass, 2004.

Oberdorfer, Don. *The Turn: From the Cold War to a New Era.* New York: Simon and Schuster, 1991.

Ouimet, Matthew J. *The Rise and Fall of the Brezhnev Doctrine in Soviet Foreign Policy.* Chapel Hill: University of North Carolina Press, 2003.

Paczkowski, Andrej. *The Spring Will Be Ours: Poland and Poles from the Occupation to Freedom.* Trans. Jane Cave. University Park: Pennsylvania State University Press, 2003.

Papenfuß, Dietrich, and Wolfgang Schieder, eds. *Deutsche Umbrüche im 20. Jahrhundert.* Cologne: Böhlau Verlag, 2000.

Patton, David F. *Cold War Politics in Postwar Germany.* London: Macmillan, 1999.

Pfaff, Steven, and Guobin Yang. "Double-Edged Rituals and the Symbolic Resources of Collective Action: Political Commemorations and the Mobilization of Protest in 1989." *Theory and Society* 30, no. 4 (August 2001): 539–89.

Pirker, Theo, M. Rainer Lepsius, Rainer Weinert, and Hans-Hermann Hertle. *Der Plan als Befehl und Fiktion: Wirtschaftsführung in der DDR.* Opladen: Westdeutscher Verlag, 1995.

Podvig, Pavel, ed. *Russian Strategic Nuclear Forces.* Cambridge, MA: MIT Press, 2004.

Pollack, Detlef. *Kirche in der Organisationsgesellschaft: Zum Wandel der gesellschaftlichen Lage der evangelischen Kirchen in der DDR.* Cologne: Kohlhammer, 1994.

Pond, Elizabeth. "A Wall Destroyed." *International Security* 15 (Fall 1990): 35–66.

———. *After the Wall.* New York: Priority Press, 1991.

———. *Beyond the Wall.* Washington, DC: Brookings, 1993.

Potthoff, Heinrich. *Im Schatten der Mauer: Deutschlandpolitik 1961 bis 1990.* Berlin: Ullstein, 1999.

Powaski, Ronald E. *The Cold War: The United States and the Soviet Union, 1917–1991.* New York: Oxford University Press, 1998.

Probst, Lothar. "Zu wenig 'wind of change' im fernen Western." *Deutschland Archiv* (January 1994): 128–30.

Pryce-Jones, David. *The Strange Death of the Soviet Empire.* New York: Metropolitan Books, 1995.

Przybylski, Peter. *Tatort Politbüro.* Vol. 1, *Die Akte Honecker.* Berlin: Rowohlt, April 1991.

———. *Tatort Politbüro.* Vol. 2, *Honecker, Mittag und Schalck-Golodkowski.* Berlin: Rowohlt, 1992.

Pulzer, Peter. *German Politics, 1945–1995.* Oxford: Oxford University Press, 1995.

Rehlinger, Ludwig A. *Freikauf: Die Geschäfte der DDR mit politisch Verfolgten 1963–1989.* Frankfurt: Ullstein, 1991.

Rein, Gerhard, ed. *Die Opposition in der DDR.* Berlin: Wichern-Verlag, 1989.

Rey, Marie-Pierre. "'Europe Is Our Common Home': A Study of Gorbachev's Diplomatic Concept." *Cold War History* 2 (January 2004): 33–65.

Reynolds, David. *One World Divisible: A Global History since 1945.* New York: W. W. Norton, 2000.

———. *Summits: Six Meetings That Shaped the Twentieth Century.* London : Allen Lane, 2007.

Risse-Kappen, Thomas. "The Cold War's Endgame and German Unification." *International Security* 21, no. 4 (Spring 1997).

Ritter, Gerhard A. *Der Preis der deutschen Einheit: Die Wiedervereinigung und die Krise des Sozialstaats.* Munich: Beck, 2006.

———, ed. *1989–1994 Bundesrepublik Deutschland: Sozialpolitik im Zeichen der Vereinigung*, vol. 3, *Geschichte der Sozialpolitik in Deutschland seit 1945.* Baden-Baden: Nomos Verlag, 2007.

Rödder, Andreas. "Zeitgeschichte als Herausforderung: Die deutsche Einheit." *Historische Zeitschrift* 270 (2000): 669–87.

———. "'Breakthrough in the Caucasus'? German Reunification as a Challenge to Contemporary Historiography." *German Historical Institute London Bulletin* 24, no. 2 (November 2002): 7–34.

———. *Die Bundesrepublik Deutschland, 1969–1990.* Munich: Oldenbourg Verlag, 2004.

———. *Deutschland Einig Vaterland.* Munich: Beck, 2009.

BIBLIOGRAPHY

Rosenberg, Tina. *The Haunted Land: Facing Europe's Ghosts after Communism*. New York: Random House, 1995.

Sagan, Scott. *The Limits of Safety: Organizations, Accidents, and Nuclear Weapons*. Princeton, NJ: Princeton University Press, 1993.

Sarotte, Mary Elise. "Elite Intransigence and the End of the Berlin Wall." *German Politics* 2 (August 1993): 270–87.

————. "Under Cover of Boredom: Review Article of Recent Publications on the East German Ministry for State Security, or Stasi." *Intelligence and National Security* 12 (October 1997): 196–210.

————. "Historische Vorläufer der Veränderungen von 1989." In *Deutsche Umbrüche im 20. Jahrhundert*, ed. Dietrich Papenfuß and Wolfgang Schieder. Cologne: Böhlau Verlag, 2000.

————. "Western Europe: Shadow and Substance." In *Strategic Survey*, ed. Sidney Bearman. Oxford: Oxford University Press, 2000.

————. "A Small Town in (East) Germany: The Erfurt Meeting of 1970 and the Dynamics of Cold War Détente." *Diplomatic History* 25, no. 1 (Winter 2001): 85–104.

————. *Dealing with the Devil*. Chapel Hill: University of North Carolina Press, 2001.

————. *German Military Reform and European Security*. Oxford: Oxford University Press, October 2001.

————. *Redefining German Security: Prospects for Bundeswehr Reform*. American Institute for Contemporary German Studies (AICGS) Issues, vol. 25. Joachim Krause and Stephen Szabo, Working Group Cochairs. Washington, DC: AICGS, September 2001.

————. "'Take No Risks: Chinese.'" In *American Détente and German Ostpolitik*, ed. David C. Geyer and Bernd Schaefer. Washington, DC: German Historical Institute, 2004.

————. "Eine Föderalismusdebatte anderer Art." *Internationale Politik* (April 2005): 106–15.

————. "Seeing the Cold War from the Other Side." In *Intelligence and Statecraft: The Use and Limits of Intelligence in International Society*, ed. Peter Jackson and Jennifer Siegel. Westport, CT: Praeger, 2005.

————. "Transatlantic Tension and Threat Perception." *Naval War College Review* 58 (Autumn 2005): 25–38.

————. "The Frailties of Grand Strategies: Comparing Détente and Ostpolitik." In *Nixon in the World: American Foreign Relations, 1969–1977*, ed. Fredrik Logevall and Andrew Preston, 146–65. New York: Oxford University Press, 2008.

————. "The Worst Allies, Except for All the Others: US-European Relations in the Age of George W. Bush." *International Politics* 45, no. 3 (May 2008): 310–24.

————. "Die US-Aussenpolitik und das Ende der deutschen Teilung: Eine Fallstudie zur Demokratisierung?" *Jahrbuch für Historische Kommunismusforschung* (2009): 251–68.

Sassoon, Donald. *One Hundred Years of Socialism: The West European Left in the Twentieth Century*. London: Tauris, 1996.

Schabert, Tilo. *Wie Weltgeschichte gemacht wird: Frankreich und die deutsche Einheit*. Stuttgart: Klett-Cotta, 2002.

Schäfer, Bernd. *Staat und katholische Kirche in der DDR*. Cologne: Böhlau, 1999.

Schlomann, Friedrich. *Die Maulwürfe: Die Stasi-Helfer im Westen sind immer noch unter uns*. Ullstein: Frankfurt, 1994.

Schöllgen, Gregor. *Die Aussenpolitik der Bundesrepublik Deutschland: Von den Anfängen bis zur Gegenwart*. Munich: Beck, 1999.

Scholtyseck, Joachim. *Die Aussenpolitik der DDR*. Munich: R. Oldenbourg Verlag, 2003.

Schönfelder, Jan, and Rainer Erices. *Westbesuch: Die geheime DDR-Reise von Helmut Kohl*. Thuringia: Verlag Dr. Bussert and Stadeler, 2007.

Schröder, Richard. *Die wichtigsten Irrtümer über die deutsche Einheit*. Freiburg: Herder, 2007.

Schroeder, Klaus, ed. *Geschichte und Transformation des SED-Staates: Beiträge und Analysen*. Berlin: Akademie, 1994.

————. *Der SED-Staat: Geschichte und Strukturen der DDR*. Munich: Bayerische Landeszentrale für Politische Bildungsarbeit, 1998.

Schulzinger, Robert. *US Diplomacy since 1900*. New York: Oxford University Press, 2008.

BIBLIOGRAPHY

Schwan, Heribert. *Die Bonner Republik 1949–1998*. Berlin: Propyläen, 2009.

Schwartz, Thomas A. "The Berlin Crisis and the Cold War." *Diplomatic History* 21 (Winter 1997): 139–48.

Sestanovich, Stephen. "What Has Moscow Done?" *Foreign Affairs* (November–December 2008).

Shapiro, Ian. *The Flight from Reality in the Human Sciences*. Princeton, NJ: Princeton University Press, 2005.

Sheehan, James. *German History, 1770–1866*. Oxford: Oxford University Press, 1989.

Shenon, Philip. *The Commission: The Uncensored History of the 9/11 Investigation*. New York: Hachette, 2008.

Simes, Dimitri K. *After the Collapse: Russia Seeks Its Place as a Great Power*. New York: Simon and Schuster, 1999.

———. "Losing Russia: The Costs of Renewed Confrontation." *Foreign Affairs* (November–December 2007): online.

Skinner, Kiron K. *Turning Points in Ending the Cold War*. Stanford, CA: Hoover Institution Press, 2008.

Skocpol, Theda. *States and Social Revolutions: A Comparative Analysis of France, Russia, and China*. Cambridge: Cambridge University Press, 1979.

Smith, Helmut Walser. "Socialism and Nationalism in the East German Revolution." *East European Politics and Society* 5, no. 2 (Spring 1991): 234–46.

Smyser, W. R. *From Yalta to Berlin*. New York: St. Martin's Press, 1999.

Sodaro, Michael J. *Moscow, Germany, and the West from Khrushchev to Gorbachev*. Ithaca, NY: Cornell University Press, 1990.

Soutou, Georges-Henri. *L'alliance incertaine: Les rapports politico-stratégiques franco-allemands, 1954–1996*. Paris: Fayard, 1996.

Spittmann, Ilse. "Eine Übergangsgesellschaft." *Deutschland Archiv* 22 (November 1989).

Staadt, Jochen, Tobias Voigt, und Stefan Wolle. *Operation Fernsehen: Die Stasi und die Medien in Ost und West*. Göttingen: Vandenhoeck and Ruprecht, 2008.

Staritz, Dietrich. *Geschichte der DDR 1949–1989*. Frankfurt: Suhrkamp, 1996.

Stark, Hans. *Helmut Kohl, l'Allemagne et l'Europe: La politique d'intégration européenne de la République fédérale 1982–1998*. Paris: L'Harmattan, 2004.

Stent, Angela. *Russia and Germany Reborn: Unification, the Soviet Collapse, and the New Europe*. Princeton, NJ: Princeton University Press, 1999.

Stokes, Gale. *The Walls Came Tumbling Down*. New York: Oxford University Press, 1993.

Stone, Randall W. *Satellites and Commissars: Strategy and Conflict in the Politics of Soviet-Bloc Trade*. Princeton, NJ: Princeton University Press, 1996.

Stöver, Bernd. *Der Kalte Krieg, 1947–1991: Geschichte eines radikalen Zeitalters*. Munich: Beck, 2007.

Suny, Ronald Grigor. *The Revenge of the Past: Nationalism, Revolution, and the Collapse of the Soviet Union*. Stanford, CA: Stanford University Press, 1993.

Suraska, W. *How the Soviet Union Disappeared: An Essay on the Causes of Dissolution*. Durham, NC: Duke University Press, 1998.

Suri, Jeremi. *Power and Protest*. Cambridge, MA: Harvard University Press, 2003.

———. "The Cold War, Decolonization, and Global Society Awakenings: Historical Intersections." *Cold War History* 6, no. 3 (August 2006): 353–63.

———. *Henry Kissinger and the American Century*. Cambridge, MA: Belknap Press, 2007.

Süß, Walter. "Weltgeschichte in voller Absicht oder aus Versehen?" *Das Parlament* (November 9–16, 1990).

"Symposium: Soviet Archives: Recent Revelations and Cold War Historiography." *Diplomatic History* 21 (Spring 1997): 215–81.

Szabo, Stephen. *The Diplomacy of German Unification*. New York: St. Martin's Press, 1992.

Tannenwald, Nina. "Conference on Understanding the End of the Cold War," *Cold War International History Project Bulletin* 11 (Winter 1998): 277–9.

Taylor, Frederick. *The Berlin Wall*. London: Bloomsbury, 2006.

Taylor, Ronald. *Berlin and Its Culture*. New Haven, CT: Yale University Press, 1997.

Thaysen, Uwe. *Der Runde Tisch, Oder: Wo blieb das Volk? Der Weg der DDR in die Demokratie*. Opland: Westdeutscher Verlag, 1990.

Thomas, Daniel C. *The Helsinki Effect: International Norms, Human Rights, and the Demise of Communism*. Princeton, NJ: Princeton University Press, 2001.

Tickner, J. Ann. *Gender in International Relations: Feminist Perspectives on Achieving Global Security*. New York: Columbia University Press, 1992.

Tilly, Charles. *Contention and Democracy in Europe, 1650–2000*. Cambridge: Cambridge University Press, 2004.

Timmermann, Heiner, ed. *Dikaturen in Europa im 20. Jahrhundert—Der Fall DDR*. Berlin: Duncker and Humblot, 1996.

Torpey, John C. *Intellectuals, Socialism, and Dissent: The East German Opposition and Its Legacy*. Minneapolis: University of Minnesota Press, 1995.

Trachtenberg, Marc. *A Constructed Peace: The Making of the European Settlement, 1945–1963*. Princeton, NJ: Princeton University Press, 1999.

———, ed. *Between Empire and Alliance: America and Europe during the Cold War*. Oxford: Rowman and Littlefield, 2003.

Tucker, Nancy Bernkopf. "China as a Factor in the Collapse of the Soviet Empire." *Political Science Quarterly* 110, no. 4 (Winter 1995–96): 501–19.

Turner, Henry Ashby, Jr. *Germany from Partition to Unification*. 2nd ed. New Haven, CT: Yale University Press, 1992.

Ulam, Adam B. *The Communists: The Story of Power and Lost Illusions, 1948–1991*. New York: Scribner's, 1992.

Vietor, Richard H. K. *How Countries Compete: Strategy, Structure, and Government in the Global Economy*. Boston: Harvard Business School Press, 2007.

Wandycz, Piotr S. *The Price of Freedom*. London: Routledge, 1992.

Webb, Adrian. *Germany since 1945*. London: Longman, 1998.

Weber, Hermann. *Die DDR 1945–1990*. Munich: Oldenbourg Verlag, 1993.

Weidenfeld, Werner, and Karl-Rudolf Korte, eds. *Handbuch zur deutschen Einheit*. Bonn: Bundeszentrale für politische Bildung, 1996.

Weidenfeld, Werner, Peter M. Wagner, and Elke Bruck. *Geschichte der deutschen Einheit*. Vol. 4, *Außenpolitik für die deutsche Einheit Die Entscheidungsjahre 1989/90*. Stuttgart: Deutsche Verlags-Anstalt, 1998.

Weitz, Eric D. *Creating German Communism, 1890–1990: From Popular Protests to Socialist State*. Princeton, NJ: Princeton University Press, 1997.

Wells, Samuel F. *The Helsinki Process and the Future of Europe*. Washington, DC: Wilson Center Press, 1990.

Wendt, Alexander. *Social Theory of International Politics*. Cambridge: Cambridge University Press, 1999.

Wendt, Alexander, and Daniel Friedheim. "Hierarchy under Anarchy: Informal Empire and the East German State." *International Organizations* 49 (Autumn 1995): 689–722.

Westad, Odd Arne. "Bernath Lecture: The New International History of the Cold War: Three (Possible) Paradigms." *Diplomatic History* 24, no. 4 (Fall 2000): 551–65.

———, ed. *Reviewing the Cold War*. London: Routledge, 2000.

———. *The Global Cold War: Third World Interventions and the Making of Our Times*. Cambridge: Cambridge University Press, 2005.

———. "Devices and Desires: On the Uses of Cold War History." *Cold War History* 6, no. 3 (August 2006): 373–76.

White, Stephen, Rita Di Leo, and Ottorino Cappelli, eds. *The Soviet Transition: From Gorbachev to Yeltsin*. London: Frank Cass, 1993.

Winkler, Heinrich August. "Rebuilding of a Nation: The Germans before and after Unification." *Daedelus* 123 (Winter 1994): 107–27.

———. *Der lange Weg nach Westen*. Munich: Beck, 2002.

BIBLIOGRAPHY

Winkler, Henrich August, and Carola Stern, eds. *Wendepunkte deutscher Geschichte 1848–1990*. Frankfurt: Fischer, 1994.

Winter, Peter Jochen. "Wie souverän war die DDR?" *Deutschland Archiv* 2 (March–April 1996): 170–72.

Wirsching, Andreas. *Abschied vom Provisorium 1982–1990: Geschichte der Bundesrepublik Deutschland*. Stuttgart: Deutsche Verlags-Anstalt, 2006.

Wittner, Lawrence S. *Toward Nuclear Abolition: A History of the World Disarmament Movement: 1971 to the Present*. Vol. 3. Stanford, CA: Stanford University Press, 2003.

Wohlforth, William. *The Elusive Balance: Power and Perceptions during the Cold War*. Ithaca, NY: Cornell University Press, 1993.

———, ed. *Witnesses to the End of the Cold War*. Baltimore: Johns Hopkins University Press, 1996.

Wolfrum, Edgar. *Die Mauer: Geschichte einer Teilung*. Munich: Beck, 2009.

Worst, Anne. *Das Ende des Geheimdienstes*. Berlin: Links, 1991.

Young, John W. *The Longman Companion to Cold War and Détente, 1941–1991*. London: Longman, 1993.

———. *Cold War Europe, 1945–1991: A Political History*. 2nd ed. London: Arnold, 1996.

Zatlin, Jonathan R. "Hard Marks and Soft Revolutionaries: The Economics of Entitlement and the Debate about German Monetary Union, November 9, 1989–March 18, 1990." *German Politics and Society* 33 (Fall 1994): 1–28.

———. *The Currency of Socialism: Money and Political Culture in East Germany*. Cambridge: Cambridge University Press, 2007.

Zimmermann, Hartmut. *DDR Handbuch*. 3rd ed. Cologne: Verlag Wissenschaft und Politik, 1985.

Zubok, Vladislav. *A Failed Empire: The Soviet Union in the Cold War from Stalin to Gorbachev*. Chapel Hill: University of North Carolina Press, 2007.

INDEX

Note: entries in bold font indicate references to illustrations.